DATE DUE

GAYLORD   #3522PI   Printed in USA

CRITICAL INSIGHTS

Gwendolyn Brooks

CRITICAL INSIGHTS

Gwendolyn Brooks

116650

Editor
Mildred R. Mickle
Penn State Greater Allegheny

Salem Press, Inc.
Pasadena, California   Hackensack, New Jersey

Cover photo: AP/Wide World Photos

Published by Salem Press

© 2010 by EBSCO Publishing
Editor's text © 2010 by Mildred R. Mickle
"The *Paris Review* Perspective" © 2010 by Jascha Hoffman for *The Paris Review*

∞ The paper used in these volumes conforms to the American National
Standard for Permanence of Paper for Printed Library Materials, Z39.48-1992
(R1997).

Library of Congress Cataloging-in-Publication Data
Gwendolyn Brooks / editor, Mildred R. Mickle.
    p. cm. -- (Critical insights)
Includes bibliographical references and index.
ISBN 978-1-58765-632-3 (alk. paper)
    1. Brooks, Gwendolyn, 1917-2000--Criticism and interpretation. I. Mickle,
Mildred R.
PS3503.R7244Z6594 2010
811'.54--dc22
                                                                2009026437

PRINTED IN CANADA

Contents_____

About This Volume, Mildred R. Mickle   vii

Career, Life, and Influence_____

On Gwendolyn Brooks, Mildred R. Mickle   3
Biography of Gwendolyn Brooks, Charles M. Israel
    and William T. Lawlor   9
The *Paris Review* Perspective, Jascha Hoffman for *The Paris Review*   13

Critical Contexts_____

The Historical and Social Context of Gwendolyn Brooks's Poetry,
    Kathy Rugoff   21
The Critical Reception and Influence of Gwendolyn Brooks,
    Martin Kich   39
Gwendolyn Brooks and the Epic Tradition, Matthew J. Bolton   56
Close Reading as an Approach to Gwendolyn Brooks's
    "The *Chicago Defender* Sends a Man to Little Rock,"
    Robert C. Evans   74

Critical Readings_____

Sweet Bombs, Danielle Chapman   91
The Satisfactions of What's Difficult in Gwendolyn Brooks's
    Poetry, Brooke Kenton Horvath   103
Double Consciousness, Modernism, and Womanist Themes
    in Gwendolyn Brooks's "The Anniad," A. Yemisi Jimoh   116
Heralding the Clear Obscure: Gwendolyn Brooks and Apostrophe,
    Lesley Wheeler   142
Dialectics of Desire: War and the Resistive Voice in
    Gwendolyn Brooks's "Negro Hero" and "Gay Chaps at the Bar,"
    Ann Folwell Stanford   159
"A Material Collapse That Is Construction": History and
    Counter-Memory in Gwendolyn Brooks's *In the Mecca*,
    John Lowney   186

A Prophet Overheard: A Juxtapositional Reading of Gwendolyn
Brooks's "In the Mecca," Sheila Hassell Hughes   210
"My Newish Voice": Rethinking Black Power in
Gwendolyn Brooks's Whirlwind, Raymond Malewitz   254
Signifying *Afrika*: Gwendolyn Brooks's Later Poetry, Annette Debo   277
Reflecting Violence in the Warpland: Gwendolyn Brooks's *Riot*,
Annette Debo   299
Killing John Cabot and Publishing Black: Gwendolyn Brooks's
Riot, James D. Sullivan   317
"The Kindergarten of New Consciousness": Gwendolyn Brooks
and the Social Construction of Childhood, Richard Flynn   342

Resources_____

Chronology of Gwendolyn Brooks's Life   377
Works by Gwendolyn Brooks   380
Bibliography   382

About the Editor   389
About *The Paris Review*   389
Contributors   391
Acknowledgments   394
Index   396

About This Volume

Mildred R. Mickle

The essays in this volume pay tribute to Gwendolyn Brooks's legacy. They explore Brooks's sustained dialectic with American historical events such as World War II and the Civil Rights movement, the cultural complexities of racial segregation, major movements in black letters such as the Black Arts movement, modernist ideas promoting individuality and exploring the feelings associated with loneliness, rejection of the status quo in society, open critique of history and its chroniclers, and revisions of traditional literary forms, such as the epic and the sonnet, as a means to incorporate a neglected black experience and contribution into American history and letters. The essays show how Brooks's quest was at times a lonely one. The poet was often perceived as catering too much to either the white mainstream or the black folk aesthetic, and her agenda to write her own truth as she saw fit is sometimes lost within her subtle intertextual wordplay with black and white literary influences. Still, it is the fine line that Brooks walks between black and white cultural influences that makes her most fascinating to readers.

In addition to biographical information on Brooks provided by Charles M. Israel and William T. Lawlor, this volume contains essays that critique Brooks's poetry from historical, sociopolitical, and cultural contexts; that closely read her poems; and that compare and contrast Brooks's works with those of other authors. Jascha Hoffman's "The *Paris Review* Perspective" provides an overview of the key poems that demonstrate Brooks's range. Kathy Rugoff presents an extended biographical essay on Brooks, interpreting how specific works participate in the Civil Rights movement's fight for equality on local and national levels. Martin Kich examines how scholars have interpreted Brooks's poetry and prose, noting specific themes and historical allusions that inform her work and reporting on how Brooks inspired other blacks to write. Matthew Bolton examines Brooks's revisioning of the epic in "The Anniad" and "Riders to the Blood-Red Wrath," asserting that she melds aspects of the mock epic and the "high-epic mode" to create her own bittersweet portrayal of black life. Robert C. Evans's close reading of "The *Chicago Defender* Sends a Man to Little Rock" discusses how Brooks uses figurative language, rhyme, and meter to represent the heightened racial tension brought about by desegregation.

Danielle Chapman reviews the impact of *The Essential Gwendolyn Brooks*, edited by Elizabeth Alexander, and discusses how the book critiques the oversight of Brooks as a major American author. Brooke Kenton Horvath critiques a poem in Brooks's Pulitzer Prize-winning *Annie Allen* through the lens of modernism and inspires further discussion of how negation in "Do Not Be Afraid of No" ties in with modernism as well as how modernism fits into the larger frame of *Annie Allen*. A. Yemisi Jimoh critiques the historical, literary theoretical, and gender issues raised by "The Anniad." Lesley Wheeler compares and contrasts the progression of lyricism in *Annie Allen* and "The Sermon on the Warpland." Ann Folwell Stanford examines an early martial aesthetic in "Negro Hero" and "Gay Chaps at the Bar," poems about African American soldiers' reception by mainstream America, arguing that Brooks uses these poems to memorialize black soldiers' additional struggles to combat racism despite their sacrifices to protect the United States during World War II.

John Lowney analyzes the realities that Brooks portrays in her poem "In the Mecca" and compares them with the historical events reported when the poem was published in the late 1960s. Sheila Hassell Hughes interprets Brooks's "In the Mecca," arguing that the poem appeals to both white and black audiences because it addresses themes and issues important to both and is designed to represent several perspectives, because the Mecca apartment complex is a microcosm of the larger racial and gender problems plaguing America and American history.

Raymond Malewitz celebrates Brooks's major contributions to the Black Arts movement, and Annette Debo explores how the Black Arts movement's emphasis on Africa influenced Brooks's poetry. In a second essay, Debo examines Brooks's *Riot* and the sympathy the work portrays for the anger blacks felt after Martin Luther King, Jr., was assassinated. Debo argues that this anger and violence did not exist in a vacuum; rather, it was rooted in the many lynchings of blacks that took place from the end of the nineteenth century into the early part of the 1920s. James D. Sullivan also discusses *Riot*, arguing that both the central character in the work, John Cabot, and Brooks's decision to publish her collection of poetry with the black-owned Broadside Press represent Brooks's contribution to the Black Arts movement's struggle for racial equality and positive self-expression. Richard Flynn discusses how Brooks's thematic focus on children celebrates their courage in battling the adult issues of racial discrimination and is yet another means for her to teach the next generation not to repeat the negative cycles of destruction that inform America's past.

The essays in this volume reflect a variety of interpretations of Brooks's poetry. Understandably, they cannot capture all of the richness of Brooks's works, but they mark an excellent start. The authors' interpretations encourage debate, paving the way for further scholarly discussion on Brooks.

CAREER, LIFE, AND INFLUENCE

On Gwendolyn Brooks

Mildred R. Mickle

Gwendolyn Brooks writes in "the children of the poor":

> What shall I give my children? who are poor,
> Who are adjudged the leastwise of the land,
> Who are my sweetest lepers, who demand
> No velvet and no velvety velour
>
> (1-4)

These lines from the second sonnet in a sequence of five in the section titled "The Womanhood" in *Annie Allen* (1949) exemplify a remarkable woman, poet, novelist, and essayist. Gwendolyn Brooks's life and works provide a rich legacy that is difficult to match. She rose from modest roots to become the first African American to win the Pulitzer Prize in poetry and blazed a trail while winning many other honors and distinctions. Her works investigate the major historical landmarks of the twentieth century through the lens of the lives of ordinary people, often ones the American mainstream would dismiss. Brooks's poems challenge us to reexamine what we take for granted. They provoke heated debate and at times comfort us. They reflect an artist who crafted poems of razor-sharp wit and heartbreaking subtlety. And Brooks's words bring to life her most enduring legacy—her unconditional love and respect for black people and their struggles to survive amid adversity.

To understand what Brooks's life and legacy mean, we must refer to Langston Hughes, one of her literary mentors. In his seminal essay "The Negro Artist and the Racial Mountain" (1926), Hughes writes about the struggle black artists have in determining what kinds of art to create and in deciding what kinds of artists to be. He states: "We younger Negro artists who create now intend to express our individual dark-skinned selves without fear or shame" (902). Brooks's life epitomizes Hughes's statement. In her life and her art, she paved the way for twentieth-century black artists to achieve their dreams of producing art that speaks to the black community and that encapsulates the complexities, joys, and pains of black culture.

The twentieth century was a time when black artists made significant headway in several struggles:

1. The struggle to define what black art can be by determining to what degree black artists should assimilate into the American mainstream or speak only to the black community

2. The struggle to determine what the role of the black artist can be, whether as a protester or as an artist who creates only for the self

3. The struggle to establish a place for black art within the larger confines of American art by either adhering to the standards of the mainstream or establishing new standards that would become part of the mainstream

These three issues formed the main debate of the Harlem Renaissance of the 1920s, but they are not exclusive to that time. The debate about what black art and artists are began as early as Phillis Wheatley's *Poems on Various Subjects, Religious and Moral* (1773) and arguably continues in the twenty-first century.

Brooks, born in 1917, grew up to witness, participate in, and affect the debate on the nature of black art. She grew up during the Harlem Renaissance, and in the economic chaos of the 1930s she met Hughes, who advised her to master European art forms. Hughes's advice is interesting, given his call to "express our individual dark-skinned selves without fear or shame." Hughes was vocal about black artists producing art derived from the unique cultural forms exclusive to black culture, and he wrote poems infused with jazz and blues, two of America's truly original art forms. Inherent in Hughes's advice to Brooks is the message that in order to be free to "express the dark-skinned self," the black artist must first embrace, understand, master, and make peace with the traditional art forms sanctioned by the American mainstream. The black artist who has gone through this process can then find his or her own unique, "dark-skinned self." Blackness is a mix of African,

European, and other cultures. It is not monolithic but rather inclusive, and, as such, it comes closer than any other aspect of American culture to manifesting the phenomenon of the melting pot. It is this idea of the melting pot that Brooks's life and legacy represent.

Brooks successfully mastered the traditional European poetic forms of the ballad, the epic, and the sonnet, to name a few. In doing so, she could make peace with them. They had no power over her. As a master, she shaped these forms to do her will. She used sonnets to express the complexity of the love she felt for black people and black culture during a time when mainstream America vilified those subjects. Her use of the epic marks her implicit testament to the heroism displayed by black men and women as they carried out the herculean tasks of eking out a living, loving, and being loved in a racist country that viewed them as unworthy of love. Her ballads sing in celebration of the ordinary lives and loves of black people. Brooks's use of European forms wedded to black subject matter provided a way for mainstream America and black Americans to view black culture and black art, thereby adding to the richness of those forms and creating a uniquely American way of viewing them. In her art "double consciousness," in the sense that W. E. B. Du Bois describes in *The Souls of Black Folk* (1903), is not negative, for there is no war between the European art forms and the African American arts but rather a melding and, more important, a balance and control, however subtly expressed.

Perhaps one of the things that makes her work provocative is that Brooks is so flexible; she cannot, nor should, be classified as just one type of writer. In an interview with B. Denise Hawkins, Brooks relates:

They [readers] need to know that I am interested in Winnie Mandela, not just in Harriet Tubman and Sojourner Truth. They need to know that I am interested in what goes on in the streets, . . . that I started a workshop for some of the hardest youngsters—parts of a group called the Blackstone Rangers, and got to know some of the things that motivated them, and wrote on this subject a poem . . . "The Blackstone Rangers." Critics need to read that. Many critics are not going to read that. They are satisfied with trying to give the public the impression that I'm an "old-fashioned" writer, simplistic and outmoded. . . . I have been changing all along. None of my books is exactly like the other. (Hawkins 275)

What Brooks most likely found frustrating was people dismissing her art based not only on her use of traditional forms such as the sonnet but also on her use of forms such as modernism and jazz. As an artist Brooks worked diligently to use whatever poetic styles she deemed fit to convey her experiences. She witnessed the tragedy of lives wasted to violence and poverty in her South Side Chicago neighborhood and in her many travels throughout the United States and Africa. Whether she was celebrating the bittersweet dignity of the impoverished or immortalizing Emmett Till (a black teenager who was lynched in the American South), the youth in her neighborhood who embraced gang life as a means of survival, or people who do not have to interact with other races, her purpose was to expose readers to different perspectives and encourage critical thinking. Even in one of her most provocative poems, "the mother," she refused to tell readers whether the poem is about abortion. Brooks challenges artists and readers alike to use their imaginations and think critically about poetic form and meaning as well as to expand traditions to include new voices and perspectives.

Brooks is an inspiration for black artists and for all other artists as well. She brought hope to black artists who were struggling to be true to themselves and their art. She showed them how, through hard work and perseverance, she created her own space, and though some before and after the Black Arts movement of the 1960s have argued that she compromised too much, she learned how to make of that compromise her own truth. In the precision of her poetry and prose is a narrative strategy designed to communicate her perspective to diverse audiences. She spoke out against injustices in other countries, such as the system of apartheid in South Africa. She was ever an advocate for children, stressing the importance of education and of teaching children to become productive citizens. And she challenged herself to continue expanding her artistic repertoire. In addition to writing and raising a family, Brooks sponsored writing workshops and gave countless poetry readings at schools and other cultural venues. She was good to people and did not lose sight of the individuals she explored and celebrated in her art. Wherever she went to read or teach, she made time for people.

So what does Brooks "give" to us? In addition to poetry and prose, for those fortunate enough to have met her, she provides stories. I often ask my students how many of them have heard of her, and usually I find that most have not. So, before they read a word of her works, I tell them how I met her. In the 1990s I was a student at the University of North Carolina at Chapel Hill, and Brooks came to the campus to give a talk and a dramatic reading as well as to attend a book signing, among other engagements. I had just bought some of her poetry collections and was waiting in line—I was the penultimate person in line—to get them autographed. Brooks's escort was telling her that it was time for her to go to her next engagement, but she said she would stay to autograph books until the last person's was signed. As each person approached her, she asked his or her name and then personalized her inscription. She made small talk with the people whose books she was signing and showed that she cared about them. As a result of her generosity, she leaves behind untold numbers of people who can testify about how she touched them with her kindness and her wit.

Later that day, Brooks gave a talk and a reading of her poems. In that talk she explained the significance of *Blacks* (1987), an anthology of several of her volumes of poetry and her novel *Maud Martha*. Speaking about her definition of "black," she told the audience that she preferred to refer to herself as "black" rather than Afro-American or African American because "black" is inclusive of all peoples, cultures, and races. It allows all people of African descent spread throughout the world, even the ones who cannot trace their roots precisely to any one African country, tribe, or language, to become a part of a larger extended family. Still, she paid a price for embracing and nurturing that family.

In the 1960s Black Arts movement, Brooks supported black artists and black presses. As one of the few black artists recognized and established in the American mainstream press, she began deliberately to work exclusively with black publishers such as Third World Press, the publisher of *Blacks*. She made the move to write, whether in Black English vernacular or in Standard American English, poems that spoke more directly to a black audience about black experiences. As always, what mattered most to her and her art were the relationships she maintained with people. She spoke to the black community about the black community; however, she did not presume to speak exclusively for black people.

Perhaps this artistic shift alienated Brooks from American mainstream publishers. Perhaps the social and political unrest over desegregation, the Vietnam War, the assassination of Martin Luther King, Jr., the militancy of the Black Power movement, and the women's liberation movement overshadowed Brooks, whose art nevertheless sought to capture this unrest. Brooks, although unfortunately not recognized by the academy as a major American author, was a major force in twentieth-century American letters. Because of her genius, her life and art continue to speak to readers about the vital, life-affirming power that respect for and connection to the black community holds.

Works Cited

Brooks, Gwendolyn. *Annie Allen*. New York: Harper, 1949.

Du Bois, W. E. B. *The Souls of Black Folk*. 1903. New York: Penguin Books, 1996.

Hawkins, B. Denise. "Conversation: Gwendolyn Brooks and B. Denise Hawkins." *The Furious Flowering of African American Poetry*. Ed. Joanne V. Gabbin. Charlottesville: UP of Virginia, 1999. 274-80.

Hughes, Langston. "The Negro Artist and the Racial Mountain." *Call and Response: The Riverside Anthology of the African American Literary Tradition*. Ed. Patricia Liggins Hill. Boston: Houghton Mifflin, 1998. 899-902.

Biography of Gwendolyn Brooks_____

Charles M. Israel and William T. Lawlor

Shortly after Gwendolyn Elizabeth Brooks was born, her family moved to Chicago, where she would live the rest of her life. During the 1930s, Brooks received her associate degree in literature and arts from Wilson Junior College and served as publicity director for the National Association for the Advancement of Colored People (NAACP) Youth Council in Chicago. She married in 1939 and had two children. She and her husband separated in 1969 but were reconciled in 1973.

A major voice in contemporary American poetry, Brooks published her first book of poetry, *A Street in Bronzeville*, in 1945. Here, she introduced the themes that occupied her throughout her life: racism and poverty, life in the American family, the trauma of world war, and the search for dignity and happiness in a society that is often unjust and oppressive.

Brooks's early poetry is characterized by a uniform narrative stance. A sensitive observer tells verse stories about ordinary people, many of whom are ghetto dwellers trapped by social, economic, and racial forces that they can neither control nor understand. Brooks describes the many ways her characters seek security and hope: through religion, through integration of the races, and through careless and profligate living. Pursued to excess, all these attempts to escape fail. Rather than being real solutions, they mask frightful uncertainty and insecurity and actually extend and intensify the cycle of hopelessness.

Taken together, Brooks's poems about ordinary people create a vivid and complex picture of America's poor, with poverty both sign and symbol of racism and injustice. The poor are uneducated (or undereducated), victimized by racism and crime, and trapped by society and their own inadequacies. The poet-narrator's attitude toward them is one of wistful and sometimes ironic sympathy; she herself is a part of the life she describes.

One of Brooks's main contentions at this point in her career was that political and social freedom for African Americans would tear down the walls between the races and offer relief from demeaning poverty and ignorance. It must be added, however, that in the most pessimistic moments in her early poetry, Brooks suggests that it is impossible for African Americans to become free in American society.

Recognition and honors crowned Brooks's early career. She was the first African American to receive the Pulitzer Prize in poetry, and she was appointed poet laureate of Illinois after Carl Sandburg's death.

Beginning in 1968, the direction of Brooks's work changed. In her poetry, essays, and speeches, Brooks launched what she called the "new music." As she explained, "I want to write poetry that will appeal to many, many blacks, not just blacks who go to college but also those who have their customary habitat in taverns and the street. . . . Anything I write is going to issue from a concern with and interest in blackness and its progress." Brooks turned away from the careful portraiture of her early work to pursue a more emotional and personal type of polemic poetry, and she continued to experiment with new poetic forms and new attitudes to express her commitment to the cause of black unity in the United States.

In 1981, Brooks published the collection of poems *To Disembark*, which is composed of alternate versions of several previously published poems. The poems serve as a continuing call for blacks to disengage from all that represents the oppressive life of white America. Brooks suggests in "Riot," as well as in other poems, that this disengagement may require violence and anarchy. The bitter, militant tone of the book caused one critic to label it a "distressing celebration of violence." An important part of the change in Brooks's outlook was a new emphasis on independently publishing African American writers. With her omnibus *Blacks*, a collection of many of her previously published works that was self-published, she established a model.

In 1985, Brooks was appointed poetry consultant for the Library of Congress. In 1987, she became an honorary fellow of the Modern Language Association. She won two Guggenheim Fellowships, and she was made a member of the American Academy of Arts and Letters. She received honorary degrees from more than seventy schools, and in 1994 the National Endowment for the Humanities named her the Jefferson Lecturer for Distinguished Intellectual Achievement in the Humanities. In 1995, President Bill Clinton awarded Brooks the National Medal of Art. She died on December 3, 2000, at the age of eighty-three.

From *Cyclopedia of World Authors, Fourth Revised Edition.* Pasadena, CA: Salem Press, 2004. Copyright © 2004 by Salem Press, Inc.

Bibliography

Bloom, Harold, ed. *Gwendolyn Brooks.* Philadelphia: Chelsea House, 2000. Collection of critical essays includes an informative editor's introduction.

Bolden, B. J. *Urban Rage in Bronzeville: Social Commentary in the Poetry of Gwendolyn Brooks, 1945-1960.* Chicago: Third World Press, 1999. Critical analysis focuses on the impact of Brooks's early poetry. Examines *A Street in Bronzeville, Annie Allen,* and *The Bean Eaters* in clear historical, racial, political, cultural, and aesthetic terms.

"Gwendolyn's Words: A Gift to Us." *Essence* 31, no. 11 (March, 2001): A18. Begins with an account of Brooks's early life and documents the sequence of her compositions. Also covers her professional relationship with Haki R. Madhubuti, who helped publish her works.

Kent, George E. *A Life of Gwendolyn Brooks.* Lexington: University Press of Kentucky, 1990. Biography completed in 1982, just before Kent's death, is based on interviews with Brooks and her friends and family. Integrates discussions of the poetry with a chronicle of her life. Especially valuable is an extensive recounting of the events and speeches at the Second Black Writers' Conference held at Fisk University in 1967, which changed the direction of her poetry.

Melhem, D. H. *Gwendolyn Brooks: Poetry and the Heroic Voice.* Lexington: University Press of Kentucky, 1987. Beginning with a biographical chapter, Melhem employs a generally laudatory tone as she subsequently looks closely at the earlier poetry collections. She surveys the later works within a single chapter and also examines *Maud Martha* and *Bronzeville Boys and Girls.* Melhem's treatment gives attention to both structures and themes. Bibliography of Brooks's works is organized by publisher to show her commitment to black-run presses after the late 1960s.

Miller, R. Baxter, ed. *Black American Poets Between Worlds, 1940-1960.* Knoxville: University of Tennessee Press, 1986. To this collection Harry B. Shaw contributes "Perceptions of Men in the Early Works of Gwendolyn Brooks," which looks at *A Street in Bronzeville*, *Annie Allen*, *Maud Martha*, and *The Bean Eaters* for their largely positive depictions of urban African American men. "'Define . . . the Whirlwind': Gwendolyn Brooks's Epic Sign for a Generation," by Miller, focuses on Brooks's epic achievement in "In the Mecca."

Mootry, Maria K., and Gary Smith, eds. *A Life Distilled: Gwendolyn Brooks, Her Poetry and Fiction*. Urbana: University of Illinois Press, 1987. Collection of essays looks at Brooks's sense of place, her aesthetic, and the militancy that emerged in her "second period." The middle section comprises essays on individual collections, and the book's final two essays examine *Maud Martha*. Selected bibliography lists Brooks's works and surveys critical sources in great detail, including book reviews and dissertations.

Washington, Mary Helen. "An Appreciation: A Writer Who Defined Black Power for Herself." *Los Angeles Times*, December 8, 2000, E1. Discusses the young Brooks who attended the 1967 Fisk University Black Writers' Conference, encountered young black militants led by Amiri Baraka, and was converted. Brooks branded her earlier writing "white writing" and resolved to change.

Wright, Stephen Caldwell, ed. *On Gwendolyn Brooks: Reliant Contemplation*. Ann Arbor: University of Michigan Press, 1996. Judiciously selected collection assembles the most important writings to date about the works of Gwendolyn Brooks in the form of reviews and essays. Three-part organization helpfully separates reviews from essays and later essays from the rest.

the PARIS REVIEW

The *Paris Review* Perspective

Jascha Hoffman for *The Paris Review*

There was never just one Gwendolyn Brooks. To the majority of readers who have encountered her work in anthologies, she remains the stern black poet from Kansas who offered this syncopated rebuke to seven pool players on the South Side of Chicago in 1959:

> We real cool. We
> Left school. We
>
> Lurk late. We
> Strike straight. We
>
> Sing sin. We
> Thin gin. We
>
> Jazz June. We
> Die soon.

That last "We," which never comes, is like a face cut out of a family portrait. But despite its admirable concision, "The Pool Players: Seven at the Golden Shovel" is not among her best poems. It seems melodramatic compared to an early sonnet on black soldiers returning from World War II, whose opening is as restrained as it is wrenching:

> I hold my honey and I store my bread
> In little jars and cabinets of my will.
> I label clearly, and each latch and lid
> I bid, Be firm till I return from hell.

And it is a mere sketch next to the carefully observed portraits of the poor black residents of Chicago in *A Street in Bronzeville*, Brooks's first collection, published in 1945, which evokes the sights and smells of the ghetto with enviable precision:

> But could a dream send up through onion fumes
> Its white and violet, fight with fried potatoes
> And yesterday's garbage ripening in the hall.

The Brooks who rendered the segregated kitchenettes of Chicago with such ferocious attention to technique may not be familiar to those who know her primarily as a prophet of black liberation. By 1967, with the arrival of the Black Arts movement, Brooks had abandoned the strict formalism of her youth for a looser style that she would later describe as "blackness stern and blunt and beautiful,/ organ-rich blackness telling a terrible story." During this period she got *Ebony* magazine to send her to Montgomery, Alabama, to report on conditions there using a genre she called "verse journalism." Her poems took the form of pleas and warnings:

> that we are each other's
> harvest:
> we are each other's
> business:
> we are each other's
> magnitude and bond.

This Brooks was a firebrand, and in her sermons she would urge readers to take spiritual action: "This is the urgency: Live! . . . Conduct your blooming in the noise and whip of the whirlwind."

Later in life, her tone was changeable. By her own admission, she could be "surrealist and cynical" in one line and "garrulous and guttural" in the next. Her work was "vast and secular/ and apt and admirably strange," as she once described a bird outside her window. The only constant was her virtuosity.

None of these versions of Gwendolyn Brooks—the lilting killjoy at the pool hall, the tight-lipped bard of poor black Chicago, the great Afrocentric oracle—is the one I fell in love with when I read the first poem in "the children of the poor," a sequence of sonnets on motherhood in her second book *Annie Allen*, which won the Pulitzer Prize in 1950. Much of *Annie Allen* is so clipped and elliptical that it strains comprehension. But this particular poem demanded to be understood.

The sonnet starts with a direct statement about what it means *not* to be a parent: "People who have no children can be hard." No matter how much danger they face, childless people have only their own lives to lose. Not so for parents:

> . . . through a throttling dark we others hear
> The little lifting helplessness, the queer
> Whimper-whine; whose unridiculous
> Lost softness softly makes a trap for us.
> And makes a curse. And makes a sugar of
> The malocclusions, the inconditions of love.

Each line carries a secret here: The "throttling dark" holds the feeling of waking before dawn to attend to a child in distress. There is a marvelous precision in "little lifting helplessness" and "queer/ Whimper-whine." And that spectacular reclamation of dental jargon—"makes a sugar of/ the malocclusions"—gives fresh expression to the well-worn idea of unconditional love.

From the fictional vignettes of *Annie Allen* I moved on to Brooks's portraits of contemporary figures such as Paul Robeson and, in the following stanzas, Malcolm X:

He had the hawk-man's eyes.
We gasped. We saw the maleness.
The maleness raking out and making guttural the air
and pushing us to walls.

And in a soft and fundamental hour
a sorcery devout and vertical
beguiled the world.

There is something chilling about that "sorcery devout and vertical."
Brooks's poem amounts to an admission that she was ravished by
Malcolm X's rhetorical skill. But she is nonetheless careful to register
her fear of his power to deceive.

The same honest ambivalence can be found in her best political
poems. When taking on a controversial subject, she seldom fell into
polemic. Her commitment was not to ideas or people but ultimately
to the art of poetry. This can be seen in a very short poem in memory of Emmett Till, a teenager from Chicago who was lynched in
Money, Mississippi, in 1955. Brooks titled her little poem "The Last
Quatrain of the Ballad of Emmett Till," cunningly framing it as a fragment of a longer work whose contours are left to the reader's imagination. Then, in sober but irregular meter, she captures the sudden loss of
a son:

Emmett's mother is a pretty-faced thing;
the tint of pulled taffy.
She sits in a red room,
drinking black coffee.
She kisses her killed boy.
And she is sorry.
Chaos in windy grays
through a red prairie.

That last line sweeps out beyond the funeral parlor, beyond the borders of Mississippi, beyond the question of race in postwar America, beyond everything human, to a supremely desolate climax. In her deliberate way, Brooks mourns a loss that is unforgivable. She refuses to fulminate against it. And she makes the occasion into a scene of harsh beauty.

Bibliography

Alexander, Elizabeth, ed. *The Essential Gwendolyn Brooks*. New York: Library of America, 2005.

Bloom, Harold. *Modern Critical Views: Gwendolyn Brooks*. Philadelphia: Chelsea House, 2000.

Brooks, Gwendolyn. *Blacks*. Chicago: Third World, 1987.

_____. *In Montgomery and Other Poems*. Chicago: Third World, 2003.

_____. *Selected Poems*. New York: HarperPerennial, 1999.

CRITICAL
CONTEXTS

The Historical and Social Context
of Gwendolyn Brooks's Poetry_____

Kathy Rugoff

Kathy Rugoff provides an extended biographical essay on Brooks, discussing how some of her works participate in the Civil Rights movement's fight for equality within Chicago as well as within the United States at large. Rugoff reviews Brooks's interactions with Harlem Renaissance writers James Weldon Johnson and Langston Hughes and also examines how Brooks's studies of works by Countee Cullen, T. S. Eliot, E. E. Cummings, and Thomas Hardy, to name a few, inspired her to incorporate in her poetry a variety of literary forms, from the sonnet to modernism. She discusses how Brooks did not shy away from using her poems to denounce intraracial gang violence and interracial violence brought about by racism and how in her later works Brooks brought attention to racial injustices that extended beyond America and into Africa. Rugoff concludes with a call for more scholarship on Brooks's works.   — M.R.M.

Gwendolyn Brooks is one of the most important poets of twentieth-century America. She was a fiercely independent writer who borrowed from both European and African American literary traditions to write poetry that would cut her own path and inspire writers in the twentieth and twenty-first centuries. Her poetry, novel, autobiographies, and short prose works are characterized by an intense awareness of the African American experience, women's roles and feminist perspectives, and literary tradition. Brooks responded to major events during her lifetime, including World War II, the struggle for civil rights, the murders of African American leaders, race riots, and daily life in segregated urban America. Brooks's poetry received numerous prestigious awards and, less formally, has been celebrated by other poets. For example, Haki R. Madhubuti (Don L. Lee), a central figure in the Black Arts movement, wrote in 1972: "Gwendolyn Brooks is the example for us all. . . . she is the continuing storm that walks with the English language as lions walk with Africa" (Brooks, *Report from Part One* 30). From her first book, *A Street in Bronzeville* (1945), to her final publications, Brooks's primary focus was on the lives of African Americans in the context of evolving social, cultural, and political events in the United States. Her portraits are most often based on people from the South Side of Chicago, her home. While it is universally observed that her poetry underwent a transformation in 1967 after she attended the Second Black Writers' Conference at Fisk University, Brooks's work is remarkably consistent in the brilliance of her wit and in her subtle treatment of sound and its impact on sense.

It is the marriage of politics and poetics in Brooks that Elizabeth Alexander—an important twenty-first-century writer and the fourth inaugural poet—admires in her work.[1] In a thought-provoking essay, Alexander maintains that Brooks's *In the Mecca* serves as a model. It reminds her that "none of us lives outside of historical moments" and that Brooks "never feared or shirked what she fervently believed was her responsibility; that sense of responsibility shaped her very aesthetic." Alexander concludes: "Few poets walk with such integrity" (378-79). Brooks's poetry is inextricably grounded in the mid-twentieth-century social and political transformation of the United States and in art's potential to engage with the complexity and variety of experience in African American life. Rita Dove has also responded to Brooks's aesthetic. Like Brooks, but with a focus on earlier events, her collection *Thomas and Beulah* (1986) and other poems include portraits of people in daily life, and *American Smooth* (2004) presents poems in the voices of African American soldiers.

As a writer and teacher, Brooks had a major impact on many writers and scholars. Various anthologies of poems include tributes to her, and she edited and introduced important collections, including *A Broadside Treasury, 1965-1970*, and *Jump Bad: A New Chicago Anthology* (1971).[2] Finally, hundreds of critical discussions have appeared on her work, reflecting various perspectives in literary theory, such as feminism, new historicism, Marxism, and New Criticism, and in various fields, such as African American studies and cultural studies.

Brooks's novel *Maud Martha*, published in 1953, did not receive much attention at the time of its publication, partly because of a general patriarchal bias and partly because it did not meet the various expectations of many black and white readers; it is now recognized as a groundbreaking novel and is noted for its impact on later novelists. *Maud Martha* is a series of thirty-four vignettes illuminating the life of a woman living in Chicago during the Great Depression and the years of World War II. This coming-of-age novel responds to inter- and intraracial, gender, and class divisions. In an important article first published in the early 1980s, Mary Helen Washington argues that early responses to the book were symptomatic of prejudices that suppressed the voice of African American women, causing the silenced anger of the main character to be neither recognized nor understood (54-55). Later critics have commented on the novel's originality and its feminist orientation.[3]

Early in Brooks's career, her models were male writers. She was befriended by Langston Hughes, who praised her work publicly. As a young girl she read *The Weary Blues* (1926), which opened up a world of possibilities; she realized, among other things, that "writing about the ordinary aspects of black life was important" (Brooks, *Report from Part One* 70, 170). This would be the foundation of her poetry. She also wrote bluesy ballads such as her early poems "a song in the front yard," "the ballad of chocolate Mabbie," and "Sadie and Maud" and later ones such as "Priscilla Assails the Sepulchre of Love" and "Steam Song."

By the early 1930s Brooks had read poetry by Countee Cullen, James Weldon Johnson, and other poets anthologized in *Caroling Dusk*, which was edited by Cullen, and in *Negro Poets and Their Poems*, which was edited by Robert Kerlin (Kent 23). Various poets of the Harlem Renaissance wrote sonnets. Brooks also studied well-known poems in the traditional canon that appeared in the *Winged Horse Anthology*, which was edited by Joseph Auslander and Frank

Ernest Hill. Upon the suggestion of James Weldon Johnson, she became acquainted with poems by modernist writers such as T. S. Eliot, Ezra Pound, and E. E. Cummings (Brooks, *Report from Part One* 173).

In 1941, her study of modern poetry and its techniques intensified through the influence of Inez Cunningham Stark when Brooks attended a poetry class held in the South Side Community Art Center led by the well-to-do reader for *Poetry* magazine. Like the early modernists, Brooks paid particular attention to elements of form. The result is "tense, complex, rhythmic verse," Houston A. Baker, Jr., observes, "that contains the metaphysical complexities of John Donne and the word magic of Apollinaire, Eliot, and Pound" (21). Baker concludes that Brooks's poetry "equal[s] the best in the black and white literary traditions" (28).[4] In addition, Gertrude Reif Hughes argues, Brooks transforms some of the tenets of modern poetry as she undermines male white hegemony in poetry that reflects a feminist African American perspective (140-43).

By her late teens, Brooks was contributing to the weekly "Lights and Shadows" column of the *Chicago Defender*, an influential newspaper with a large readership in the African American community. Her first book was published by Harper and Brothers (later Harper & Row), a major New York press, followed by six subsequent books. Although Brooks had a productive relationship with her editors at Harper, her work was subjected to some "requests for revisions," which, as John K. Young points out, "reinforc[ed] the aesthetic and political issues behind white consumption of black texts." In 1969, Brooks began to publish strictly with black presses, including Broadside Press, Third World Press, and her own press, David Company (Young 97, 94). She pointed out in an interview with Young that in the late 1960s Broadside Press's Dudley Randall provided a "platform to young Black poets, people that Macmillan and Harper wouldn't accept" and she "decided to go with a Black publisher and give some assistance to them" (qtd. in Brooks and Hawkins 280).

A Street in Bronzeville exhibits a broad repertoire in tone and structure, from songlike lyrics to sonnets, ballads, and other narrative forms. One critic has observed that the book comprises "a collage of racism, sexism, and classism of America in its illumination of the people who strive to survive Bronzeville" (Bolden 13). Bronzeville from the 1920s into the 1950s, known as the Black Belt, was the heart of the Great Migration from the South, which began in the nineteenth century but increased considerably during the 1920s and 1930s. The community "on Chicago's South Side quickly became a 'Black Metropolis'" and became "the demographic base for Chicago's literary renaissance of Black writers" (Bolden 3).[5]

With a large white audience in mind, Brooks confronts social issues and provides a voice for Chicago's African American underclass in her early poetry. Her particular exploration of black and European literary traditions is disarming. For example, as a poem that engages its reader through lively rhyme and assonance, "the ballad of chocolate Mabbie" addresses the tragedy in a boy's abandonment of a dark-skinned schoolgirl for a girl with lighter skin. Not unlike Emily Dickinson, Brooks, in unidiomatic syntax, in two lines that resist direct paraphrasing, conveys the acute loneliness of the rejected child who learns the cruel lessons of, first, being female and therefore at the mercy of a male's whim and, second, of having dark skin in a society that privileges whiteness. Of this innocent child Brooks concludes: "Mabbie on Mabbie with hush in the heart./ Mabbie on Mabbie to be" (23-24).

"Ballad of Pearl May Lee" is in the voice of a black woman and treats one of the most painful and inflammatory subjects in African American history, the lynching of a black man accused of having sex with a white woman.[6] Brooks deals with the double tragedy of racism regarding the impact of the assumption that white is more desirable than black as well as the impact of the horrendous torture and murder of black men by white men. She places this tragedy in the familiar blues-song figure of the unfaithful lover. Here, it appears that a black woman revels in the consequences of her lover's infidelity in his attention to a white woman:

Then off they took you, off to the jail,
A hundred hooting after.
And you should have heard me at my house,
I cut my lungs with my laughter
(1-4)

This takes a highly ironic turn several stanzas later as a mob drags the man from jail and hangs him from a tree:

And they laughed when they heard you wail.
Laughed,
Laughed.
They laughed when they heard you wail.
(85-88)

Although Pearl May Lee may be a victim of both her lover's racism and that of the murderous whites, Brooks provides her with a powerful voice through synecdoche and metonymic imagery. Pearl May Lee addresses her dead lover: "You paid with your hide and my heart . . ." (98). His body is destroyed and her emotions are damaged. In addition, she addresses him as "Brother," rather than lover (93-94). He is one of many black men who have been caught up in white violence. Finally, Pearl May Lee treats whites like objects, not individuals, reciprocating the treatment blacks have received. The white woman has no name and is described as a "taste of pink and white honey" (99).

Black men treating black women as objects is critiqued, among other things, in "The Sundays of Satin-Legs Smith," a highly satirical third-person portrait of a black man. The man's limitations are a consequence of his secondary status in white America. D. H. Melhem points out that, like Eliot's "The Love Song of J. Alfred Prufrock," Brooks's portrait "deals with an antiheroic vision, but it places the protagonist solidly in his environment" (*Gwendolyn Brooks* 34). While "Prufrock" may be an interior monologue of Prufrock's musings, "The Sundays of

Satin-Legs Smith" is a satirical portrait of a black man who appropriates the trappings of wealthy whites. The poem also conveys an ironic view of the trappings of high art in white culture through visual imagery and prosody.

Smith is a ghetto prince. His closet "is a vault/ Whose glory is not diamond, nor pearls,/ Not silver plate with just enough dull shine./ But wonder-suits in yellow and in wine" (44-47). This zoot-suited man survives by satisfying his appetite for food at Joe's Eats and for sex with an unnamed woman "with the most voluble of veils" (138). One critic notes that in Smith, "the 'choice' of race rebellion is here reduced to consumer preference"; Smith embodies "the displacement of historical consciousness onto the flat surface of the material now" (Mullen 164).

The speaker of the poem—addressing an unidentified "you" and the poet's reading audience (if these distinctions can be made)—draws attention to the details of Smith's world: "alleys, garbage pails," "broken windows" and "foodlessness" (28, 91, 100). Brooks illuminates the contrast between Smith's environment and his showy clothes (which are considered in bad taste by whites) by incorporating meter, diction, and conventional imagery found in traditional poetry. Many lines, for example, use blank verse, and the diction is elevated. For example, the poem opens with Latinate words: "Inamoratas, with an approbation,/ Bestowed his title. Blessed his inclination" (1-2). The heavy rhyme and alliteration may mock Smith, the speaker, and the unidentified "you." In addition, Brooks refers to a garden and includes a catalog of flowers, which is reminiscent of English poets from the Renaissance through the Romantic era. However, "No! He has not a flower to his name" (32). George E. Kent argues that the poet is addressing "a white observer" and that the "speaker's vocabulary and attitudes create sardonic tones of cool condescension and contempt" so that Brooks presents criticism not only of "the hip life" but also "of life and society" (70).

The rarefied society of Eliot may be included. "The Sundays of Satin-Legs Smith" recalls Prufrock in lines such as "Let us proceed. Let us inspect, together/ With his meticulous and serious love" (43-

44), which brings to mind the "let us" figure in Prufrock, and "meticulous" Eliot's "Politic, cautious, and meticulous" (116). Smith, of course, is the inverse of Prufrock; one man is a snappy dresser and loves women, whereas the other is intimidated by women. Between the man in a zoot suit and a man anxious about rolling up his trousers, Brooks may very well find the black man to be, in an important respect, more free.

In an interview concerning literary tradition, Brooks was asked about her sonnets. The sequence of twelve sonnets "Gay Chaps at the Bar," in *A Street in Bronzeville*, presents various experiences of African American soldiers who served during World War II. Speaking metaphorically, suggesting that form is an extension of content, Brooks stated that the poems employ off-rhyme to deal with "an off-rhyme situation" (*Report from Part One* 156). This situation may have been the fact that African American soldiers were treated unequally in the segregated U.S. armed forces and given noncombat and nonleadership positions. Tragically, segregation and lynching continued even after the soldiers returned (Stanford 184). "Gay Chaps at the Bar" is replete with irony and thereby points to the absurdity in the soldiers' treatment. The use of irony is also extensive in the war poetry of some early twentieth-century poets, including Wilfred Owen, Siegfried Sassoon, and Thomas Hardy.

Some of the diction and imagery in Brooks's sequence also has ties to sixteenth- and seventeenth-century British poetry, and the sonnets include few contemporary references and mention no battles or countries; instead, universal themes of war, death, and love emerge. This is an important part of the poet's subliminal message: black soldiers are no different from white soldiers and should not receive separate and unequal treatment. Race relations are dealt with directly in the sonnet "the white troops had their orders but the Negroes looked like men."[7] Brooks considers the absurdity of separating the remains of the dead based on race. She writes in the sestet:

A box for dark men and a box for Other—
Would often find the contents had been scrambled,
Or even switched. Who really gave two figs?
Neither the earth nor heaven ever trembled.
And there was nothing startling in the weather.

(10-14)

By invoking conventional seventeenth-century imagery that alludes to metaphysical and existential certainties, Brooks renders distinctions based on race absurd in two respects: first, straightforwardly, through the analogies in the images and, second, metaphorically, through the enduring quality of these conventional images in the history of poetry. However, Brooks also takes subtle liberties with traditional sonnet structure, particularly through the use of half-rhyme and through the relationship between the rhyme structure and the volta. In addition, as Stacy Carson Hubbard insightfully argues, by appropriating this strictly structured genre to "embody questions of race and gender," Brooks confronts her reader with the "the ideological power of form itself, as well as the subversions which that same power makes possible" (63).

Many of the poems in Brooks's second book, *Annie Allen* (1949), employ traditional forms, which Madhubuti has criticized. He maintains that the poems focus on "poetic style" rather than on African American history or culture, thereby implicitly addressing a white audience; these remarks are followed by his strong praise for her poetry from 1967 forward (Brooks, *Report from Part One* 17). B. J. Bolden, on the other hand, claims that in "*Annie Allen*, Brooks dares to mock poetic conventions and address the ill-treatment of a young naive ghetto girl by infusing her consciousness with the lofty diction and romantic imagery of classical poetry" (89).

The collection, which comprises three parts—"Notes from the Childhood and the Girlhood," "The Anniad," and "The Womanhood"—is the coming-of-age story of Annie, who is confronted by racism and sexism. The first section includes ballads and variations of the sonnet.

"The Anniad" is in seven-line stanzas recalling octava rima and rhyme royal. It echoes the mock-heroic style of eighteenth-century poets, but the tale is realistic and tragic. By ironically using European poetic convention to convey Annie's sad fate, in which the realization of her dream is inverted, Brooks suggests the culpability of white male narratives. In the sonnet sequence in "The Womanhood," Brooks's speaker's words are cast in sonnets to present arguments against the institution of poverty and to highlight the limitations it imposes on African American women and their children.

Several poems in *The Bean Eaters* (1960), Brooks's third collection, deal with the murders of blacks by racist whites, with a focus on women's perspectives. "A Bronzeville Mother Loiters in Mississippi. Meanwhile, a Mississippi Mother Burns Bacon," and "The Last Quatrain of the Ballad of Emmett Till" mourn the death of Emmett Till, who was brutally tortured and murdered and whose body was mutilated beyond recognition in 1955 in Money, Mississippi. The fourteen-year-old boy from the South Side of Chicago was accused of whistling at a white woman. An all-white jury acquitted the men who were charged with his death. Photographs of Till's body appeared in the *Chicago Defender*, as his mother had an open-casket viewing for thousands to witness. This horrific sight helped press forward the urgency of the Civil Rights movement and had no small impact on Brooks. The companion poems diacritically present the problem of treating atrocity within the confines of a literary form.

In a highly symbolic short narrative, the first poem portrays the woman who made the accusations against Till and hints at her second thoughts as she watches her children and her husband, one of the murderers. The glimmerings of the woman's sense of guilt come to light as a bloody redness infuses everything she sees. She also perceives a troubling violence in her husband as he slaps one of his sons after the child threw a jar at his brother. This pairing of brothers symbolically plays out the violence visited upon blacks by their white brothers. In addition, through the pairing of mothers in the title, Brooks points to the injustice in their fates. The final line mentions "the last quatrain," which introduces the poem that follows, "The Last Quatrain of the Ballad of Emmett Till."

This short poem, which describes Till's mother, simmers in under-statement and other forms of irony. The title "The Last Quatrain" suggests earlier quatrains, which in fact are not presented; this intimates the poet's hesitation to attempt to put into an art form unimaginable atrocity. The use of the technical term "quatrain" raises the subject of the relationship between high art and the actual, in this case actual horrendous violence. The particular structure of Brooks's poem, its brevity and inclusion of concrete visual images, places it in the tradition of modern imagist poetry; however, its subject matter and the unstated narrative of events represents a major departure from the art-for-art's-sake orientation of various poems by Ezra Pound, H. D., and other modernist writers. Color imagery—"tint of pulled taffy," "red room," "black coffee," "windy grays," and "red prairie"—instead conveys the dual tragedy of the murder: that it was based on color and that Till's corpse was the manifestation of appalling colors (2, 3, 4, 7, 8).

"The Ballad of Rudolph Reed," although a narrative, also relies heavily on imagery as it pursues white-on-black violence. It begins, "Rudolph Reed was oaken" (1). He is oaken in that he is not deterred by the hostility of his neighbors, even as he is flexible in his ability to improve his circumstances and move into a white neighborhood. After several incidents of vandalism, upon the injury of his daughter Reed retaliates by injuring several whites before he is called "nigger" and murdered. The poem is in traditional ballad form with an *abcb* rhyme scheme. Brooks's tale is an emblem for the actual situation in Chicago during the 1950s. On the edge of Chicago's South Side, the Trumbull Park Housing Projects provided hundreds of desirable apartments for lower-class families. When African Americans began to move in, white resistance and outbreaks of violence endured for months (Bolden 158).

In the Mecca (1968), which also addresses issues of housing, signaled a major shift in Brooks's use of traditional poetic form. The long poem "In the Mecca" comprises 807 lines in 56 stanzas of variable line length; it is followed by the sequence "After Mecca," which includes poems honoring Medgar Evers, and Malcolm X, several dedications for landmarks in Chicago, a short sequence titled "The Blackstone Rangers," and other poems. "The Blackstone Rangers" is named after a gang to which Brooks was introduced and for the members of which she held poetry workshops. She praises this group, the youths and their girlfriends, feared by whites and many blacks; in the second poem in the sequence, "The Leaders," Brooks proclaims, "Their country is a Nation on no map" (10). *In the Mecca*, her final book published by a white press, was written for an African American audience.

Mrs. Sallie Smith, the mother of nine children, is the protagonist of "In the Mecca." She returns home one day from her job as a domestic and discovers one of her children is missing. She searches throughout the apartment building and eventually finds her murdered daughter. As one critic notes, the search for the lost child "reveals the detritus of a failed socioeconomic system, a failed art, a failed religion, and their spawn of isolation and rage. A general want of caritas, Brooks's major theme here, defensively mirrors deficiencies of the white environment and reflects the Black Mecca as a microcosm" (Melhem, *Heroism* 17). The name rings with irony. Built in the last decade of the nineteenth century, the Mecca was a tenement in the South Side that was razed in the course of urban renewal projects during the early 1950s (Melhem, *Gwendolyn Brooks* 158).

The disillusionment and anger conveyed in "In the Mecca" reflects the zeitgeist of the era. Several major events in the United States in the early and mid-1960s drew much public attention and, in some cases, large public outcry: the Vietnam War, the murder of civil rights workers in Mississippi in 1964, the iconic "I Have a Dream" speech of Dr. Martin Luther King, Jr., and the assassinations of President John F. Kennedy and Medgar Evers, a major figure in the NAACP, in 1963 (Melhem, *Gwendolyn Brooks* 156). In addition, in 1966 Stokely Carmichael, the leader of the Student Nonviolent Coordinating Committee (SNCC), issued a call for African Americans to break away from King's nonviolence; Carmichael was a central figure in the Black Power movement and a strong advocate of pan-Africanism. The speeches of Malcolm X and his murder in 1965 had a significant impact in the emergence of these movements. They dismissed the philosophy and actions of the blacks and whites of the Civil Rights movement (Kent 196).

Brooks was in the midst of writing *In the Mecca* when she attended the Second Black Writers' Conference at Fisk University in April 1967. The conference, in which Brooks herself participated, included speeches, poetry readings, and other performances by historians, poets, and other writers; the performance poetry of Amiri Baraka (LeRoi Jones) epitomized the spirit of the gathering, and he would soon be at the epicenter of the Black Arts movement. Brooks later claimed that after hearing Baraka's cry "Up against the wall, white man!" she knew "there is indeed a new black today. . . . And he is understood by *no* white" (*Report from Part One* 85). Brooks would go on to publish strictly with black presses with a black audience in mind and in the spirit of the Black Arts movement. The movement flourished in the 1960s and associated itself with the Black Power movement, which celebrated African Americans and African culture and attacked white racism and seats of power.[8] Brooks's new poetry would retain her predilection for irony and attention to the nuances of language.

The collection *Riot* was published in 1969 by Broadside Press, a black press run by Dudley Randall, a strong Black Arts advocate. The collection includes "Riot" and "The Third Sermon on the Warpland," and was published shortly after the assassination of Martin Luther King, Jr., in 1968 and the subsequent riots that took place in several American cities. "Riot" presents a portrait of a racist white man from an old, wealthy American family that was in the slave trade and in the rum and opium markets. Cabot, an object of derision, is "all white-bluerose below his golden hair" (2). When a group of blacks approach him in the street, he thinks them "sweaty and unpretty" and "not discreet" (11, 15). As he is destroyed in the riot's "smoke and fire" (28), in biting irony Brooks reveals his final words: "'Lord!/ Forgive these nigguhs that know not what they do'" (29-30). The corruption of Christ's words upon his crucifixion, "Father, forgive them; for they know not what they do" (Luke 23:34), bores to the center of white hypocrisy in the treatment of blacks. The reference to the Bible also places the riot within a larger apocalyptic vision.[9]

"The Third Sermon on the Warpland" is informed by a similar vision. The poem is more than one hundred lines long and is told by a narrator and several other voices, including "The Black Philosopher," a child, a passage from a newspaper, "A White Philosopher," whites in general, and members of the Blackstone Rangers. As in other long modernist poems, no transitions link the voices; Brooks thus creates a fractured narrative, and a collage effect emerges. Unlike other poems in this genre, however, the references are primarily to African American culture, and the intended audience is black. The epigraph presents a dictionary definition of "phoenix" that refers to the word's source in Egyptian mythology, and through this reference Brooks implicitly advocates for pan-Africanism.

The poet's association of African American liberty with African identity also arises in "Young Heroes," published in *Family Pictures* (1970). In this collection, Brooks presents portraits of men she admires. One of the young heroes is Keorapetse Kgositsile, a South African poet and activist who lived in Chicago. In humorous but telling lines, Brooks quotes one of his works' titles, "'MY NAME IS AFRIKA!'" and responds, "Well, every fella's a Foreign Country./ This Foreign Country speaks to You," which resonates on many levels (35, 36-37). If "You" is the reader, then Afrika is speaking to the reader; if "You" refers to Kgositsile, then "This Foreign Country" may be the United States. Through the ambiguity Brooks both explicitly and implicitly calls attention to African identity and its relationship to America.[10]

In 1971 Brooks took trips to Nairobi, Kenya, and Dar es Salaam, Tanzania, and later to Accra and Kumasi in Ghana. Although she was greatly inspired by these trips, she faced some disappointment. Annette Debo points out that she was "identified as an 'Afro-American' by Africans and thus situated as an outsider in their country, despite her appearance and heritage"; consequently, while Brooks was "impressed with the African people and their definitive place in the world, she [did] not find the Black unity for which she hoped" (171). Nevertheless, partly in response to her visits to Africa, she addressed apartheid in poems such as "The Near-Johannesburg Boy," "Winnie," and "Song of Winnie." After a thoughtful discussion of the references to Africa in Brooks's poetry, Debo concludes: "In the end Afrika is an expansive signifier—a linguistic tie to African languages, a center of Blackness, an inspiration, and an appellation" (179).

In the poetry of her final years, Brooks continued to call upon her poetic imagination to create portraits of African Americans. These portraits capture moments and movements in American history, particularly African American history. By confronting issues of race, gender, and class, her poems are reflections of the social, political, and artistic worlds of African Americans from the 1930s to the end of the twentieth century. In addition, by borrowing from African American oral and written literary traditions as well as from European literary traditions, Brooks made a remarkable contribution to the history of recent American poetry. It is very likely that in future discussions of twentieth-century American poetry, the work of Gwendolyn Brooks will be given extensive treatment, possibly even more than the work of the seminal poets who captured her imagination as a young woman.

Notes

1. Elizabeth Alexander was the inaugural poet for the forty-fourth president of the United States, Barack Obama. Coincidentally, President Obama's political experience includes work as an activist in Chicago's South Side and as a state senator for Illinois's thirteenth district, which covers the same area of the city.

2. See also *Gwendolyn Brooks and Working Writers* (edited by Jacqueline Imani Bryant), *The Chicago Collective: Poems for and Inspired by Gwendolyn Brooks* (Stephen Caldwell Wright), and *To Gwen with Love: An Anthology Dedicated to Gwendolyn Brooks* (edited by Patricia L. Brown, Don L. Lee, and Francis Ward).

3. These discussions include articles by Barbara Christian and Valerie Frazier.

4. For further consideration of Brooks's literary background, including the poetry of Paul Laurence Dunbar, Melvin B. Tolson, Robert E. Hayden, Emily Dickinson, and Wallace Stevens, see "'Down the Whirlwind of Good Rage': An Introduction to Gwendolyn Brooks" by Maria K. Mootry.

5. For further discussion of Chicago writers, see "'Down the Whirlwind of Good Rage'" by Mootry and *American Voices of the Chicago Renaissance* and "From Chicago Renaissance to Chicago Renaissance: The Poetry of Fenton Johnson" by Lisa Woolley. Woolley supports and problematizes the argument that there were two successive Chicago Renaissances, a white one that included Carl Sandburg, Theodore Dreiser, and Edgar Lee Masters and a black one that included Margaret Walker, Gwendolyn Brooks, and Richard Wright.

6. Lynching in the United States was instituted by slave owners as a means to control slaves through murder and terror. The practice continued long after emancipation and into the mid-twentieth century. In the final decades of the nineteenth century alone, several thousand people, mainly blacks, were lynched in the United States. Although lynchings most often sprung from accusations of murder or robbery, it was "the sexual fears, guilt, and fantasies of white men and sometimes women (and to an almost negligible degree the actions of black men) play[ing] a role in lynching [that] became a central motif in literary representations" (Callahan 465). This motif is borne out in Brooks's treatments of lynching in "Ballad of Pearl May Lee," "A Bronzeville Mother Loiters in Mississippi. Meanwhile, a Mississippi Mother Burns Bacon," and "The Last Quatrain of the Ballad of Emmett Till."

7. In addition, grotesque racism persisted not only among individuals but also within institutions. For example, as Jennifer C. James notes, "the War Department insisted that black blood donations not be given to white soldiers in spite of the American Medical Association's and Red Cross's protestations that theories of 'tainted' black blood had no basis in science" (James 236). See James's discussion of Brooks's sonnet (237).

8. For further discussion of the Second Black Writers' Conference at Fisk University, see George E. Kent's *A Life of Gwendolyn Brooks* (194-202). For further discussion of the poets of the Black Arts movement, see William W. Cook's "The Black Arts Poets."

9. For further discussion of the references in "Riot," see D. H. Melhem's *Gwendolyn Brooks: Poetry and the Heroic Voice* (192-95).

10. In 1971 Brooks compiled *A Broadside Treasury, 1965-1970*, one of the best collections of the works of poets associated with the Black Arts movement. The volume includes poetry by several dozen writers, including Don L. Lee, Walter Bradford, and Keorapetse Kgositsile, all of whom Brooks addresses in "Young Heroes." The collection also includes a large group of poems honoring the slain Malcolm X and a poem by Brooks eulogizing Dr. Martin Luther King, Jr., that appeared in the *Chicago Daily News* the day after his death.

Works Cited

Alexander, Elizabeth. "Meditations on 'Mecca': Gwendolyn Brooks and the Responsibilities of the Black Poet." *By Herself: Women Reclaim Poetry*. Ed. Molly McQuade. St. Paul, MN: Graywolf, 2000. 368-79.

Baker, Houston A., Jr. "The Achievement of Gwendolyn Brooks." *A Life Distilled: Gwendolyn Brooks, Her Poetry and Fiction*. Ed. Maria K. Mootry and Gary Smith. Urbana: University of Illinois Press, 1987. 21-29.

Bolden, B. J. *Urban Rage in Bronzeville: Social Commentary in the Poetry of Gwendolyn Brooks, 1945-1960*. Chicago: Third World Press, 1999.

Brooks, Gwendolyn. *Annie Allen*. New York: Harper, 1949.

_____. *The Bean Eaters*. New York: Harper, 1960.

_____. *Family Pictures*. Highland Park, MI: Broadside Press, 1970.

_____. *In the Mecca*. New York: Harper & Row, 1968.

_____. *Maud Martha*. New York: Harper, 1953.

_____. *Report from Part One*. Detroit, MI: Broadside Press, 1972.

_____. *Riot*. Highland Park, MI: Broadside Press, 1969.

_____. *A Street in Bronzeville*. New York: Harper, 1945.

Brooks, Gwendolyn, comp. *A Broadside Treasury, 1965-1970*. Detroit, MI: Broadside Press, 1972.

Brooks, Gwendolyn, ed. *Jump Bad: A New Chicago Anthology*. Detroit, MI: Broadside Press, 1971.

Brooks, Gwendolyn, and B. Denise Hawkins. "Conversation: Gwendolyn Brooks and B. Denise Hawkins." *The Furious Flowering of African American Poetry*. Ed. Joanne V. Gabbin. Charlottesville: University Press of Virginia, 1999. 274-80.

Brown, Patricia L., Don L. Lee, and Francis Ward, eds. *To Gwen with Love: An Anthology Dedicated to Gwendolyn Brooks*. Chicago: Johnson, 1971.

Bryant, Jacqueline Imani, ed. *Gwendolyn Brooks and Working Writers*. Chicago: Third World Press, 2007.

Callahan, John F. "Lynching." *The Oxford Companion to African American Literature*. Ed. Williams L. Andrews, Francis Smith Foster, and Trudier Harris. New York: Oxford University Press, 1997.

Christian, Barbara. "Nuance and the Novella: A Study of Gwendolyn Brooks's *Maud Martha*." *A Life Distilled: Gwendolyn Brooks, Her Poetry and Fiction*. Ed. Maria K. Mootry and Gary Smith. Urbana: University of Illinois Press, 1987. 239-53.

Cook, William W. "The Black Arts Poets." *The Columbia History of American Poetry*. Ed. Jay Parini and Brett C. Millier. New York: Columbia University Press, 1993. 674-706.

Debo, Annette. "Signifying *Afrika*: Gwendolyn Brooks's Later Poetry." *Callaloo* 29.1 (2006): 168-81.

Eliot, T. S. "The Love Song of J. Alfred Prufrock." *The Complete Poems and Plays*. New York: Harcourt, 1950.

Frazier, Valerie. "Domestic Epic Warfare in *Maud Martha*." *African American Review* 29.1/2 (2005): 133-41.

Hubbard, Stacy Carson. "'A Splintery Box': Race and Gender in the Sonnets of Gwendolyn Brooks." *Genre* 25.1 (1992): 47-64.

Hughes, Gertrude Reif. "Making It Really New: Hilda Doolittle, Gwendolyn Brooks, and the Feminist Potential of Modern Poetry." *Gwendolyn Brooks*. Ed. Harold Bloom. Philadelphia: Chelsea House, 2000. 139-59.

James, Jennifer C. *A Freedom Bought with Blood: African American War Literature from the Civil War to World War II*. Chapel Hill: University of North Carolina Press, 2007.

Kent, George E. *A Life of Gwendolyn Brooks*. Lexington: University Press of Kentucky, 1990.

Melhem, D. H. *Gwendolyn Brooks: Poetry and the Heroic Voice*. Lexington: University Press of Kentucky, 1987.

_____. *Heroism in the New Black Poetry: Introductions and Interviews*. Lexington: UP of Kentucky, 1990.

Mootry, Maria K. "'Down the Whirlwind of Good Rage': An Introduction to Gwendolyn Brooks." *A Life Distilled: Gwendolyn Brooks, Her Poetry and Fiction*. Ed. Maria K. Mootry and Gary Smith. Urbana: University of Illinois Press, 1987. 1-17.

Mullen, Bill V. *Popular Fronts: Chicago and African-American Cultural Politics, 1935-46*. Urbana: University of Illinois Press, 1999.

Stanford, Ann Folwell. "Dialectics of Desire: War and the Resistive Voice in Gwendolyn Brooks's 'Negro Hero' and 'Gay Chaps at the Bar.'" *Gwendolyn Brooks*. Ed. Harold Bloom. Philadelphia: Chelsea House, 2000. 43-56.

Washington, Mary Helen. "Rage and Silence in Gwendolyn Brooks' *Maud Martha*." *Gwendolyn Brooks*. Ed. Harold Bloom. Philadelphia: Chelsea House, 2000. 43-56.

Woolley, Lisa. *American Voices of the Chicago Renaissance*. De Kalb: Northern Illinois University Press, 2000.

_____. "From Chicago Renaissance to Chicago Renaissance: The Poetry of Fenton Johnson." *Langston Hughes Review* 14.1/2 (1996): 36-48.

Wright, Stephen Caldwell. *The Chicago Collective: Poems for and Inspired by Gwendolyn Brooks*. Sanford, FL: Christopher Burghardt, 1990.

Young, John K. *Black Writers, White Publishers: Marketplace Politics in Twentieth-Century African American Literature*. Jackson: University Press of Mississippi, 2006.

The Critical Reception and Influence of Gwendolyn Brooks_____

Martin Kich

Martin Kich examines how scholars have interpreted Brooks's poetry, fiction, and nonfiction essays since the mid-twentieth century, noting specific themes, such as the celebration of black perseverance and faith in attaining equality in America, and historical allusions to racial discrimination. He structures his essay to incorporate what scholars published about Brooks in black-owned and black-focused popular periodicals—such as *Black World*, which prospered because it provided black subscribers with an alternate and more positive perspective on black life than was found in many mainstream American periodicals—and in black-owned and black-focused scholarly journals such as the *College Language Association Journal.* Kich reports on how Brooks's work inspired other black writers to write and publish, and he discusses book-length interpretations of Brooks's works as well as individual essays on specific poems.   — M.R.M.

Gwendolyn Brooks's first collection of poetry, *A Street in Bronzeville*, was published in 1945, when the author was twenty-eight years old. In that decade, few poets of her age, gender, or race could have expected to receive much attention, never mind national attention, for a first book of poetry, but *A Street in Bronzeville* was reviewed very positively in such prestigious periodicals as *The New Yorker*, *The New York Times Book Review*, and *Poetry*. Those reviewers concentrated on Brooks's focus on the black urban experience, on her sometimes startling manipulations of poetic forms, and on the hopefulness and humanity that informed her realistic portraits of a population and milieu often depicted as hopeless and dehumanized. The response to *A Street in Bronzeville* not only launched Brooks's long, productive, and critically appreciated literary career, but it also established the main currents of much of the later criticism of her work.

Brooks's Focal Interest in African American Themes

In a review essay published in *Voices* in 1950, Langston Hughes emphasizes that the personae Brooks assumes in her poetry are vital, upbeat, and current, reflecting her engagement with and understanding of the contemporary African American experience. In "The Black-and-Tan Motif in the Poetry of Gwendolyn Brooks," the first essay on Brooks's work published in a professional journal, Arthur P. Davis emphasizes that the poetic aspects of Brooks's work so outweigh the polemical elements that what emerges is a very nuanced kind of protest poetry; that is, Brooks presents portraits of disillusionment that are so quietly but unequivocally empathetic that the characters' experiences resist being understood as illustrative.

In a two-part profile of Brooks and an appraisal of her stature that appeared in consecutive issues of *Black World* in 1971, George E. Kent emphasizes that one of Brooks's most significant achievements is her ability to adapt to the changing conditions of black urban life from one decade to the next. Although he acknowledges that some of her poems risk triteness in their spare directness, he asserts that the range and depth of her whole body of work make her the most important African American poet of the period between the Harlem Renaissance and the Black Arts movement.

In "The Achievement of Gwendolyn Brooks," published in *Black Scholar* in 1972, Don L. Lee asserts that Brooks has a more powerful sense of herself than any other African American writer of her generation, except perhaps Margaret Walker. He expresses the belief that Brooks's influence as a literary voice for black America is comparable to that of Langston Hughes and Ralph Ellison in the decades between the Great Depression and the Civil Rights movement. Granting that Brooks's work may have begun to seem anachronistic in the volatile political and cultural mix of the mid- to late 1960s, Lee suggests that Brooks's exposure to the work of younger poets reenergized her own work and gave it a fresh relevance.

Much the same perceptions inform Marva Riley Furman's "Gwendolyn Brooks: The 'Unconditioned' Poet," which appeared in the *College Language Association Journal* in 1973. Focusing on *In the Mecca*, *Riot*, and *Family Pictures*, which were published in successive years from 1968 to 1970, Furman emphasizes the reintensification of Brooks's sense of engagement with the African American experience, reflected both in a conspicuous increase in the volume of work she produced and in an equally conspicuous increase in the passion and concentrated effects exhibited in those works.

In two essays published in 1977, "The Poet-Militant and Foreshadowings of a Black Mystique" and "Essences, Unifyings, and Black Militancy," William H. Hansell demonstrates both the continuity and the shifts between the second period of Brooks's career, in which her most expressive poems advocated militant politics, and the third period of her career, begun in the mid-1970s, in which she attempted to move beyond polemic and invest her treatment of the themes from her second period with more subtlety and complexity.

In George E. Kent's "Aesthetic Values in the Poetry of Gwendolyn Brooks" and R. Baxter Miller's "'Does Man Love Art?': The Humanistic Aesthetic of Gwendolyn Brooks," both published in the collection *Black American Literature and Humanism* in 1981, the authors attempt to link the aesthetic values exhibited in Brooks's work with the political, social, and cultural values that were impetus for the creation of the work. Kent's career-long interest in Brooks's work culminates in his posthumously published essay "Gwendolyn Brooks' Poetic Realism," which traces the evolution of her racial consciousness over the course of her career. Published in the same collection as Kent's essay, Addison Gayle, Jr.'s "Gwendolyn Brooks: Poet of the Whirlwind" provides a close analysis of Brooks's use of metaphor to illustrate the significant shift in her work between the late 1960s and the early 1970s. The essay explores linkages between Brooks's metaphors and those of the radicalized generation of poets who emerged during that period.

In *Languages of Liberation: The Social Text in Contemporary*

American Poetry, Walter Kalaidjian discusses Brooks's work at length. Linking her work to that of Robert Bly and Adrienne Rich, Kalaidjian remarks on the ways in which poetry can offer a viable and vital connection between the private and public responses to historical events. In "Reflecting Violence in the Warpland: Gwendolyn Brooks's *Riot*," Annette Debo uses Brooks's poem as a focal point for discussing the efficacy of violence as a method of forcing social change within the African American community as well as the broader American society.

In "'A Material Collapse That Is Construction': History and Counter-Memory in Gwendolyn Brooks's *In the Mecca*," John Lowney considers the history of the building that is the setting for Brooks's collection and identifies the instances in which she provides a distinctly African American view of the events that occurred there, a view of events that is pointedly at odds with the official histories. To provide a context for his discussion of Brooks's book, Lowney identifies other literary works that have focused on the building in some manner and indicates the ways in which those uses of the setting have been similar to or different from Brooks's uses of it.

One of the more unusual slants on Brooks's treatment of racial issues is provided in Marsha Bryant's essay "Gwendolyn Brooks, *Ebony*, and Postwar Race Relations." Granting that the comparison involves very dissimilar subjects, Bryant credibly demonstrates that the poet and the periodical have made parallel attempts to appeal to both black and white audiences.

Poetic Form and Style

In the above-cited review essay, Langston Hughes praises the compression in Brooks's spare style. Almost thirty years later, in "Gwendolyn the Terrible: Propositions on Eleven Poems," Hortense J. Spillers argues that, for all of the attention to Brooks's style and form, as her career has moved from one decade into the next, it has become increasingly difficult to make any sort of generalizations about Brooks's work.

From very early on in Brooks's career, critics have been interested in her choice of forms. In "Bronze by Gold," published in *Poetry*, the poet Stanley Kunitz notes that Brooks's first two volumes demonstrate her interest in exploiting the sonnet. Published more than three decades after Kunitz's essay, Gladys Margaret Williams's "Gwendolyn Brooks's Way with the Sonnet" presents a systematic survey of Brooks's experiments with the form over the course of her long career. A further discussion of Brooks's exploitation of the sonnet form is provided in Heidi Scott's "'Gay Chaps at the Bar': A Close look at Brooks's Sonnets."

In a fairly substantial discussion of Brooks's work included in the collection *The Black Aesthetic*, Dudley Randall explores Brooks's deft manipulations of the ballad, especially in *Annie Allen*. Arthur P. Davis, in a chapter on Brooks in his book *From the Dark Tower*, illustrates Brooks's early reliance on conventional forms even as she manipulated them. In particular, he shows how she adapted tercets and rhyme royal to contemporary urban subjects. With this analysis, he lays the foundation for his main argument that Brooks's later poetry became more openly defiant as she moved increasingly away from conventional forms. Irony gradually gave way to empathy and outrage in her work, he argues. In his essays on *In the Mecca* and *Riot*, William Hansell describes the shift in Brooks's poetry from a focus on the personal to a focus on the communal. In discussing *Riot*, he contends, paradoxically, that the new cultural emphasis on self-identity has become a force—indeed, a weapon—to compel social change not only in African American communities but also, and more critically, in the broader American society.

In "Focus on Form in Gwendolyn Brooks," a short essay published in *Black Books Bulletin* in 1974, Safisha N. Madhubuti identifies the major poetic techniques in *Family Pictures* as repetition, rhythm, image, and contrast. Likewise, in "A Note on the Poetic Technique of

Gwendolyn Brooks," Gloria T. Hull highlights the ways in which Brooks has used alliteration and, irregularly, various kinds of rhyme to accent a distinctive selection of diction for its economy of meaning and tone.

In an essay published in *Obsidian* in 1978, R. Baxter Miller argues that Brooks's career has been marked by her efforts to write an African American epic. Asserting that *Annie Allen* represents a failed attempt to achieve that aim, Miller categorizes the book as an unintentional mock epic, suggesting that its style is too elevated for its subject and themes. Viewing *Maud Martha* as a necessary exercise in characterization and narrative technique, Miller makes the case that *In the Mecca* stands as the largely successful realization of Brooks's ambitions because in this work she achieves a consistently effective and affecting synthesis of subject, voice, and form. In an addendum to this article, Miller suggests that *In the Mecca* provides portraits of historical figures such as Malcolm X and Medgar Evers that move these figures beyond history into the realm of myth.

Countering Miller's dismissal of *Annie Allen* as a failed attempt at writing an epic, Ann Folwell Stanford contends that the book succeeds as an epic treatment of both racial and feminist themes. As the title suggests, Stanford's essay "An Epic with a Difference: Sexual Politics in Gwendolyn Brooks's 'The Anniad'" includes an extended comparison between Brooks's book and Virgil's *Aeneid.*

Yet another take on "The Anniad" is provided by A. Yemisi Jimoh in "Double Consciousness, Modernism, and Womanist Themes in Gwendolyn Brooks's 'The Anniad.'" Double consciousness, Jimoh explains, is the phenomenon in which an African American's identity is bifurcated between his or her own self-conception and a contending awareness of white America's view of African Americans, both individually and communally. Jimoh emphasizes that Brooks's modernist style—in particular, her modernist attitude toward form—enables her to express this double consciousness in singularly powerful ways.

Finally, in "An Oral Interpreter's Approach to the Poetry of Gwendolyn Brooks," the first doctoral dissertation published on Brooks's work, Glenda E. Clyde explores how Brooks subtly synthesizes elements of both the African American oral tradition and textual poetic forms to create a poetry that is truly distinctive.

Studies of Individual Short Poems

Of all of Brooks's poems, "We Real Cool" has probably attracted the most attention from explicators. In an essay published in 1976, Barbara B. Sims attempts to link the economy of the poem with the style of the pool players who are the poem's subject. Gary Smith provides a further analysis of the poem in an essay published in 1985 in *The Explicator.*

In an essay on "The *Chicago Defender* Sends a Man to Little Rock," Sue S. Parks examines Brooks's transformation of historical materials into poetry. Given much of African American literature's emphasis on political consciousness, especially during this period, Parks considers the temptation, articulated by Brooks herself, to let the materials speak for themselves, to invest the materials with at most a very minimal degree of literary embellishment. Although many writers of the period succumbed to this temptation, Parks demonstrates that Brooks's poem and, by extension, her other poems on historical events are marked by a carefully refined technique that allows Brooks to invest her poems with much subtle insight and thematic complexity.

In an essay published in the *College Language Association Journal* in 1980, Larry R. Andrews focuses on the clothes imagery in "The Sundays of Satin-Legs Smith." Andrews observes that the tone of the poem, particularly as it is conveyed through imagery, suggests the paradoxical nature of the focal character, whose flamboyance indicates his self-preoccupation but does not quite conceal his underlying uncertainty. Another lively analysis of the poem, extending Andrews's reading, is provided in Judith P. Saunders's "The Love Song of Satin-Legs Smith: Gwendolyn Brooks Revisits Prufrock's Hell." Karen Jackson

Ford adds still more to the discussion in "The Sonnets of Satin-Legs Smith." In this essay, she also treats other poems featuring the character, such as "Gay Chaps at the Bar" and "the children of the poor." Ford comments as well on the broader use of the sonnet form by contemporary African American poets.

Alan C. Lupack has analyzed Brooks's "piano after war" as a variation on the traditional sonnet. Other short articles for *The Explicator* have included Maria K. Mootry's on "A Bronzeville Mother Loiters in Mississippi. Meanwhile, a Mississippi Mother Burns Bacon," Mark Johnson's on "Gang Girls," and articles by both Ronald R. Janssen and Ron Giles on "A Song in the Front Yard."

Brooks's Interest in Broader Themes

Even while acknowledging that Brooks's poetry constitutes an important contribution to African American literature, critics have insisted, almost from the start of her career, that Brooks's work transcends race and gender to reach toward important truths about the human experience in its broadest sense. In "Gwendolyn Brooks: Poet of the Unheroic," Arthur P. Davis considers the understated irony, humor, and pity in Brooks's approach to her subjects in *A Street in Bronzeville*, *Annie Allen*, and *In the Mecca*, and he compares her approach to that which James Joyce took in composing the character-centered short stories in *Dubliners* (1914). Davis explores the paradox that the experiences of characters so closely identified with a particular urban setting and cultural milieu should at the same time seem so universal.

In "Reckonings," an essay published in *Black World* in 1975, Saundra Towns suggests that, despite the more passionate polemical elements of Brooks's work of the late 1960s and the early 1970s, the poet also attempted to move beyond issues of race to analogous issues of gender and, even more broadly, to a more mythic vision of the archetypal challenges that human beings face.

In "Gwendolyn Brooks's *A Street in Bronzeville* and the Mythologies of the Black Woman," Gary Smith suggests that Brooks's first collection provides a feminist critique of the African American cultural archetypes that emerged out of the Harlem Renaissance. In the essay "Trajectories of Self-Definition: Placing Contemporary Afro-American Women's Fiction," Barbara Christian considers the representations of a distinctively black feminist perspective, first in the novels of Zora Neale Hurston and Brooks and then in the novels of Paule Marshall, Toni Morrison, and Alice Walker.

In *The Wicked Sisters*, Betsy Erkkila examines Brooks's life and work along with the lives and work of Emily Dickinson, Marianne Moore, Elizabeth Bishop, and Adrienne Rich to make the case that the poets' lives and works bear the effects of the conflicts most central to the development of a feminist consciousness. In "A Prophet Overheard: A Juxtapositional Reading of Gwendolyn Brooks's 'In the Mecca,'" Sheila Hassell Hughes focuses on how Brooks's transformative interest in the Black Arts movement was a necessary precondition for her late contributions to the black feminist aesthetic.

The only journal article to date to treat Brooks's writings about and for children is Richard Flynn's "'The Kindergarten of New Consciousness': Gwendolyn Brooks and the Social Construction of Childhood."

Literary Influences on Brooks

In his earlier-cited two-part essay on Brooks in *Black World*, George E. Kent suggests that Brooks was equally influenced by modernist poets such as Ezra Pound and T. S. Eliot and African American poets such as Langston Hughes. In "The Achievement of Gwendolyn Brooks," published in the *College Language Association Journal* in 1972, Houston A. Baker, Jr., makes much the same point about Brooks's influence but suggests that her synthesis of the colloquial elements of the black oral tradition and the more formal elements of canonical literature makes her work most comparable to that of Robert Frost. In his essay in *The Black Aesthetic*, Dudley Randall groups Brooks with Robert Hayden and Melvin Tolson, demonstrating how their work pointedly shows the influence of such modernist poets as Hart Crane and William Butler Yeats as well as Eliot and Pound.

Brooks's Influence on Subsequent Writers

In an article published in *Essence* in 1971, Nikki Giovanni warmly acknowledges the influence of Brooks's work on her own. Suzanne Jahasz also links Brooks and Giovanni in the concluding chapter of her book *Naked and Fiery Forms*, which focuses on the poets' congruent efforts to express the experience of African American women. In an interview conducted by Virginia W. Smith and Brian J. Benson that was published in the *College Language Association Journal* in 1976, the poet Linda Brown Bragg acknowledged the formative influence of Brooks's work on her own.

Two books published by Third World Press are devoted to documenting Brooks's influence on subsequent writers. In *Say That the River Turns: The Impact of Gwendolyn Brooks* (1987), edited by Haki R. Madhubuti, some seventy writers testify to her impact on their work. The most widely known of these writers include Sonia Sanchez and Askia M. Toure. In *Gwendolyn Brooks and Working Writers* (2007), edited by Jacqueline Imani Bryant, seventeen writers provide essays that are part reminiscence and part testimonial. At least one poet, David Ray, has expressed his indebtedness to Brooks in a poem.

Responses to Brooks's Fiction and Autobiographical Works

Although Brooks has always been known primarily as a poet, her novel and her autobiographies have received considerable attention, much of it unstintingly admiring. The title of Coleman Rosenberger's review of *Maud Martha* in the *New York Herald Tribune Book Review* strikes a common note: "A Work of Art and Jeweled Precision." If some reviewers found the novel too loosely structured and impressionistic in style, most praised the poetic qualities of Brooks's prose and the knowing humanity in her depiction of the title character. In her essay "'An Order of Constancy': Notes on Brooks and the Feminine," Hortense J. Spillers argues that the improvisational structure and the impressionistic style of *Maud Martha* are a deliberate strategy to convey the feminist themes of the novel—specifically, the corollary between the protagonist's indefatigable imagination and the idea of women's liberation.

In "'Taming All That Anger Down': Rage and Silence in Gwendolyn Brooks's *Maud Martha*," Mary Helen Washington explores the sometimes very intuitive evidence that Brooks's novel presents a feminist polemic against sexism. In striking contrast, in their essay "Vision in Gwendolyn Brooks's *Maud Martha*," Patricia H. Lattin and Vernon E. Lattin argue that the novel takes a comic approach to the everyday things of life and that the protagonist's capacity to perceive the positive aspects of even the most discouraging experiences mitigates any sense that the narration is primarily a polemic against racism. Indeed, these authors see *Maud Martha* as presenting a pointed alternative to, if not a direct response to, Richard Wright's *Native Son* (1940).

In "Nuance and the Novella: A Study of Gwendolyn Brooks's *Maud Martha*," Barbara Christian argues that the novel deserves not just much more attention than it has received but much closer textual analysis—which Christian then attempts to provide. After describing the novel as a series of vignettes and showing how the style of the vignette shapes the novel's themes, Christian attempts to demonstrate that any dismissal of the novel as somewhat thematically simplistic is the result of a failure to appreciate the thematic nuances in the novelist's attention to the small details of her protagonist's experience.

Treating *Report from Part One* as postmodern autobiography, Saundra Towns argues that its direct presentation of the biographer's usual materials—interviews, letters, and personal notes—permits a more direct insight into the workings of Brooks's literary imagination and its intimate connection to the poet's social, political, and racial awareness.

A Survey of Book-Length Studies of Brooks's Work

Following the standard format of the volumes in the Twayne United States Authors Series, Harry B. Shaw combines an extended biographical profile of Brooks with an overview of her literary career and the critical responses to her work. Organizing his chapters around the major social themes in Brooks's poetry, Shaw centers his analysis on the transformative effects of political and cultural radicalism on Brooks's conceptions of the functions and possibilities of poetry.

The definitive Brooks biography remains George E. Kent's *A Life of Gwendolyn Brooks*, published in 1990. A more recent biography is Christine M. Hill's *Gwendolyn Brooks: "Poetry Is Life Distilled,"* published in 2005. Martha E. Rhynes's *Gwendolyn Brooks: Poet from Chicago* (2003) is a biography aimed at younger readers (sixth grade and older). Sixteen interviews with Brooks have been collected in the 2003 volume *Conversations with Gwendolyn Brooks*, edited by Gloria Wade Gayles.

Monograph studies have included D. H. Melhem's *Gwendolyn Brooks: Poetry and the Heroic Voice* (1987), which, like Shaw's volume, combines biographical and critical elements and is organized chronologically, and B. J. Bolden's *Urban Rage in Bronzeville: Social Commentary in the Poetry of Gwendolyn Brooks, 1945-1960*, which focuses on the poetry of Brooks's early period and combines literary criticism with social history.

The collections of essays on Brooks's work include *A Life Distilled: Gwendolyn Brooks, Her Poetry and Fiction* (1987), edited by Maria K. Mootry and Gary Smith, in which the essays are divided into three sections—general assessments, analyses of individual poems, and essays on *Maud Martha*. *On Gwendolyn Brooks: Reliant Contemplation* (1996), edited by Stephen Caldwell Wright, includes several reviews of each of Brooks's collections and a selection of more broadly focused essays. Several volumes edited by Harold Bloom have also examined Brooks's work, in the series Bloom's Modern Critical Views (2000), Bloom's Major Poets (2003), and Bloom's Biocritiques (2005). The volume in the Major Poets series includes close analyses of a fairly large number of individual poems.

Works Cited

Andrews, Larry R. "Ambivalent Clothes Imagery in Gwendolyn Brooks's 'The Sundays of Satin-Legs Smith.'" *College Language Association Journal* 24 (Dec. 1980): 150-63.

Baker, Houston A., Jr. "The Achievement of Gwendolyn Brooks." *College Language Association Journal* 16 (Fall 1972): 23-31.

Bloom, Harold, ed. *Gwendolyn Brooks.* Bloom's Biocritiques. Philadelphia: Chelsea House, 2005.

_____. *Gwendolyn Brooks.* Bloom's Modern Critical Views. Philadelphia: Chelsea House, 2000.

_____. *Gwendolyn Brooks: Comprehensive Research and Study Guide.* Bloom's Major Poets. Philadelphia: Chelsea House, 2003.

Bolden, B. J. *Urban Rage in Bronzeville: Social Commentary in the Poetry of Gwendolyn Brooks, 1945-1960.* Chicago: Third World Press, 1999.

Bryant, Jacqueline Imani, ed. *Gwendolyn Brooks and Working Writers.* Chicago: Third World Press, 2007.

_____. *Gwendolyn Brooks' "Maud Martha": A Critical Collection.* Chicago: Third World Press, 2002.

Bryant, Marsha. "Gwendolyn Brooks, *Ebony*, and Postwar Race Relations." *American Literature* 79 (Mar. 2007): 113-41.

Burr, Zofia. *Of Women, Poetry, and Power: Strategies of Address in Dickinson, Miles, Brooks, Lorde, and Angelou.* Urbana: U of Illinois P, 2002.

Callahan, John F. "'Essentially an Essential African': Gwendolyn Brooks and the Awakening to Audience." *North Dakota Quarterly* 55.4 (1987): 59-73.

Christian, Barbara. "Nuance and the Novella: A Study of Gwendolyn Brooks's *Maud Martha.*" *Black Feminist Criticism: Perspectives on Black Women Writers.* Ed. Barbara Christian. New York: Pergamon, 1985. 127-41.

_____. "Trajectories of Self-Definition: Placing Contemporary Afro-American Women's Fiction." *Conjuring: Black Women, Fiction, and Literary Tradition.* Ed. Marjorie Pryse and Hortense J. Spillers. Bloomington: Indiana UP, 1985. 233-48.

Clyde, Glenda E. "An Oral Interpreter's Approach to the Poetry of Gwendolyn Brooks." Ph.D. dissertation, Southern Illinois University-Carbondale, 1966.

Davis, Arthur P. "The Black-and-Tan Motif in the Poetry of Gwendolyn Brooks." *College Language Association Journal* 6 (Dec. 1962): 90-97.
_____. "Gwendolyn Brooks." *From the Dark Tower*. Washington, DC: Howard UP, 1974. 185-93.
_____. "Gwendolyn Brooks: Poet of the Unheroic." *College Language Association Journal* 7 (Dec. 1963): 114-25.
Dawson, Emma W. "Vanishing Point: The Rejected Black Woman in the Poetry of Gwendolyn Brooks." *Obsidian II* 4.1 (1989): 1-11.
Debo, Annette. "Reflecting Violence in the Warpland: Gwendolyn Brooks's *Riot*." *African American Review* 39 (Summer 2005): 143-52.
Erkkila, Betsy. *The Wicked Sisters: Women Poets, Literary History, and Discord*. New York: Oxford UP, 1992.
Flynn, Richard. "'The Kindergarten of New Consciousness': Gwendolyn Brooks and the Social Construction of Childhood." *African American Review* 34 (Fall 2000): 483-99.
Ford, Karen Jackson. "The Sonnets of Satin-Legs Smith." *Contemporary Literature* 48 (Fall 2007): 345-73.
Furman, Marva Riley. "Gwendolyn Brooks: The 'Unconditioned' Poet." *College Language Association Journal* 17.1 (1973): 1-10.
Gayle, Addison, Jr. "Gwendolyn Brooks: Poet of the Whirlwind." *Black Women Writers, 1950-1980: A Critical Evaluation*. Ed. Mari Evans. New York: Doubleday, 1984. 79-87.
Gayles, Gloria Wade, ed. *Conversations with Gwendolyn Brooks*. Jackson: UP of Mississippi, 2003.
Gery, John. "Subversive Parody in the Early Poems of Gwendolyn Brooks." *South Central Review: The Journal of the South Central Modern Language Association* 16.1 (1999): 44-56.
Giles, Ron. "Brooks' 'A Song in the Front Yard.'" *The Explicator* 57 (Spring 1999): 169-71.
Giovanni, Nikki. "For Gwen Brooks." *Essence* Apr. 1971: 26.
Hansell, William H. "Essences, Unifyings, and Black Militancy: Major Themes in Gwendolyn Brooks's *Family Pictures* and *Reckonings*." *Black American Literature Forum* 11 (1977): 63-66.
_____. "Gwendolyn Brooks' *In the Mecca*: A Rebirth into Blackness." *Negro American Literature Forum* 8 (Summer 1974): 199-217.
_____. "The Poet-Militant and Foreshadowings of a Black Mystique: Poems in the Second Period of Gwendolyn Brooks." *Concerning Poetry* 10 (1977): 37-45.
_____. "The Role of Violence in Recent Poems of Gwendolyn Brooks." *Studies in Black Literature* 5 (Summer 1974): 21-27.
Harris, Victoria F. "The Voice of Gwendolyn Brooks." *Interpretations: Studies in Language and Literature* 11 (1979): 56-66.
Hill, Christine M. *Gwendolyn Brooks: "Poetry Is Life Distilled."* Berkeley Heights, NJ: Enslow, 2005.
Horvath, Brooke Kenton. "The Satisfactions of What's Difficult in Gwendolyn Brooks's Poetry." *American Literature* 62 (Dec. 1990): 606-16.

Hudson, Clenora F. "Racial Themes in the Poetry of Gwendolyn Brooks." *College Language Association Journal* 17 (1973): 16-20.

Hughes, Gertrude R. "Making It *Really* New: Hilda Doolittle, Gwendolyn Brooks, and the Feminist Potential of Modern Poetry." *American Quarterly* 42.3 (1990): 375-401.

Hughes, Langston. "Name, Race, and Gift in Common." *Voices* 140 (Winter 1950): 54-56.

Hughes, Sheila Hassell. "A Prophet Overheard: A Juxtapositional Reading of Gwendolyn Brooks's 'In the Mecca.'" *African American Review* 38 (Summer 2004): 257-80.

Hull, Gloria T. "A Note on the Poetic Technique of Gwendolyn Brooks." *College Language Association Journal* 19 (Dec. 1975): 280-85.

Janssen, Ronald R. "Brooks' 'A Song in the Front Yard.'" *The Explicator* 43 (Spring 1985): 43.

Jimoh, A. Yemisi. "Double Consciousness, Modernism, and Womanist Themes in Gwendolyn Brooks's 'The Anniad.'" *MELUS* 23 (Fall 1998): 167-86.

Johnson, Mark. "Brooks' 'Gang Girls.'" *The Explicator* 61 (Summer 2003): 229-31.

Juhasz, Suzanne. *Naked and Fiery Forms: Modern American Poetry by Women—A New Tradition*. New York: Harper, 1976.

Kalaidjian, Walter. *Languages of Liberation: The Social Text in Contemporary American Poetry*. New York: Columbia UP, 1989.

Kent, George E. "Aesthetic Values in the Poetry of Gwendolyn Brooks." *Black American Literature and Humanism*. Ed. R. Baxter Miller. Lexington: UP of Kentucky, 1981. 75-94.

_____. "Gwendolyn Brooks' Poetic Realism: A Developmental Survey." *Black Women Writers, 1950-1980: A Critical Evaluation*. Ed. Mari Evans. New York: Doubleday, 1984. 88-105.

_____. *A Life of Gwendolyn Brooks*. Lexington: UP of Kentucky, 1990.

_____. "The Poetry of Gwendolyn Brooks, Part 1." *Black World* 20 (Sep. 1971): 30-43.

_____. "The Poetry of Gwendolyn Brooks, Part 2." *Black World* 20 (Oct. 1971): 36-48.

Kunitz, Stanley. "Bronze by Gold." *Poetry* 76 (15 Apr. 1950): 52-56.

Lattin, Patricia H., and Vernon E. Lattin. "Vision in Gwendolyn Brooks's *Maud Martha*." *Critique* 25 (1984): 180-88.

Lee, Don L. "The Achievement of Gwendolyn Brooks." *Black Scholar* 3 (Summer 1972): 32-41.

Lindberg, Kathryne V. "Whose Canon? Gwendolyn Brooks: Founder at the Center of the 'Margins.'" *Gendered Modernisms: American Women Poets and Their Readers*. Ed. Margaret Dickie and Thomas Travisano. Philadelphia: U of Pennsylvania P, 1996. 283-311.

Lowney, John. "'A Material Collapse That Is Construction': History and Counter-Memory in Gwendolyn Brooks' *In the Mecca*." *MELUS* 23 (Fall 1998): 3-20.

Lupack, Alan C. "Brooks' 'Piano after War.'" *The Explicator* 36 (Summer 1978): 2-3.

Madhubuti, Haki R., ed. *Say That the River Turns: The Impact of Gwendolyn Brooks*. Chicago: Third World Press, 1987.

Madhubuti, Safisha N. "Focus on Form in Gwendolyn Brooks." *Black Books Bulletin* 2.1 (1974): 25-27.

Marsh, Carole. *Gwendolyn Brooks: Chicago's Celebrated Poet*. Peachtree City, GA: Gallopade International, 2002.

Melhem, D. H. *Gwendolyn Brooks: Poetry and the Heroic Voice*. Lexington: UP of Kentucky, 1987.

Miller, R. Baxter. "'Define . . . the Whirlwind': In the Mecca—Urban Setting, Shifting Narrator, and Redemptive Vision." *Obsidian* 4.1 (1978): 19-31.

_____. "'Does Man Love Art?': The Humanistic Aesthetic of Gwendolyn Brooks." *Black American Literature and Humanism*. Ed. R. Baxter Miller. Lexington: UP of Kentucky, 1981. 95-112.

_____. *Langston Hughes and Gwendolyn Brooks: A Reference Guide*. Boston: G. K. Hall, 1978.

Mootry, Maria K. "A Bronzeville Mother Loiters in Mississippi. Meanwhile, a Mississippi Mother Burns Bacon." *The Explicator* 42 (Summer 1984): 51-52.

Mootry, Maria K., and Gary Smith, eds. *A Life Distilled: Gwendolyn Brooks, Her Poetry and Fiction*. Urbana: U of Illinois P, 1987.

Parks, Sue S. "A Study in Tension: Gwendolyn Brooks's 'The *Chicago Defender* Sends a Man to Little Rock.'" *Black American Literature Forum* 11.1 (1977): 32-34.

Randall, Dudley. "The Black Aesthetic in the Thirties, Forties, and Fifties." *The Black Aesthetic*. Ed. Addison Gayle, Jr. New York: Anchor, 1972. 212-21.

Ray, David. "For Gwendolyn Brooks." *MELUS* 29 (Fall/Winter 2004): 353.

Rhynes, Martha E. *Gwendolyn Brooks: Poet from Chicago*. Greensboro, NC: Morgan Reynolds, 2003.

Rosenberger, Coleman. "A Work of Art and Jeweled Precision." *New York Herald Tribune Book Review* 18 Oct. 1954: 4.

Saunders, Judith P. "The Love Song of Satin-Legs Smith: Gwendolyn Brooks Revisits Prufrock's Hell." *Papers on Language and Literature* 36 (Winter 2000): 3-18.

Scott, Heidi. "'Gay Chaps at the Bar': A Close Look at Brooks' Sonnets." *The Explicator* 66 (Fall 2007): 37-42.

Shaw, Harry B. *Gwendolyn Brooks*. Boston: Twayne, 1980.

_____. *Social Themes in the Poetry of Gwendolyn Brooks*. Urbana: U of Illinois P, 1972.

Sims, Barbara B. "'We Real Cool.'" *The Explicator* 34 (1976): item 58.

Smith, Gary. "Gwendolyn Brooks's *A Street in Bronzeville* and the Mythologies of the Black Woman." *MELUS* 10 (1983): 33-46.

_____. "'We Real Cool.'" *The Explicator* 43 (Winter 1985): 49-50.

Smith, Virginia W., and Brian J. Benson. "An Interview with Linda Brown Bragg." *College Language Association Journal* 20 (1976): 75-87.

Spillers, Hortense. "Gwendolyn the Terrible: Propositions on Eleven Poems." *Shakespeare's Sisters: Feminist Essays on Women Poets*. Ed. Sandra M. Gilbert and Susan Gubar. Bloomington: Indiana UP, 1979. 233-44.

_____. "'An Order of Constancy': Notes on Brooks and the Feminine." *Centennial Review* 29 (1985): 223-48.

Stanford, Ann Folwell. "An Epic with a Difference: Sexual Politics in Gwendolyn Brooks's 'The Anniad.'" *American Literature* 67 (June 1995): 283-301.

Taylor, Henry. "Gwendolyn Brooks: An Essential Sanity." *Kenyon Review* 13 (Fall 1991): 115-31.

Towns, Saundra. "Black Autobiography and the Dilemma of Western Artistic Tradition." *Black Books Bulletin* 2.1 (1974): 17-23.

_____. "Reckonings." *Black World* 25.2 (1975): 51-52.

Washington, Mary Helen. "'Taming All That Anger Down': Rage and Silence in Gwendolyn Brooks's *Maud Martha*." *Massachusetts Review* 24.2 (1983): 453-66.

Williams, Gladys Margaret. "Gwendolyn Brooks's Way with the Sonnet." *College Language Association Journal* 26 (1982): 215-40.

Wright, Stephen Caldwell, ed. *On Gwendolyn Brooks: Reliant Contemplation*. Ann Arbor: U of Michigan P, 1996.

Gwendolyn Brooks and the Epic Tradition _____

Matthew J. Bolton

Matthew Bolton analyzes Brooks's two epics "The Anniad" and "Riders to the Blood-Red Wrath." Both poems comment on Brooks's own epic quest to conquer standard European forms and use them to critique the notion of belles lettres. Bolton briefly outlines the innovations that John Milton and Alexander Pope brought to the epic and the mock epic, respectively. He discusses how Brooks was inspired by Pope and compares Annie, the protagonist of "The Anniad," to T. S. Eliot's timid, repressed J. Alfred Prufrock. Although Prufrock does not appear in an epic poem, what makes both him and Annie epically tragic is that they allow their fears to dominate them and prevent them from loving themselves or anyone else. In "The Anniad" Brooks takes elements of the mock and the "true" epic and makes of them her own expression. The poem rests in the liminal space between mock and "true," and its internal juxtapositions illustrate Brooks's own artistic tensions. "Riders to the Blood-Red Wrath," in contrast, is in the "high-epic mode" in its celebration of the tragedy and sacrifice of blacks who persevere in the face of adversity. Bolton notes that "Riders" may have some ties to *Beowulf*, but Brooks's poem is more suited to the themes and epic questions about redemption that Virgil and Milton treat.   — M.R.M.

A reader who first encounters Gwendolyn Brooks's work in a poetry anthology may draw some overly hasty conclusions about the natures of her subject matter and her verse forms. Having read several of Brooks's most frequently anthologized short poems, such as "We Real Cool," "The Bean Eaters," or "A Sunset in the City," he or she may be ready to characterize Brooks as a poet who uses colloquial language and a simplicity of diction and rhyme to craft portraits of poor or working-class African American city dwellers. This is not a bad working definition; in fact, it is one that many critics and editors echo. The afterword to the 1999 Perennial Classics edition of Brooks's 1963 *Selected Poems*, for example, outlines the poet's abiding preoccupations:

> Her major themes and concerns have remained remarkably consistent: the details of day-to-day existence; the lives of 'ordinary' people; the nature and consequences of racial and ethnic identity, and of prejudice; black pride and solidarity; family strengths and weaknesses; women's lives and loves; and the particulars of motherhood. (129)

For a road map through Brooks's poetry, one could do much worse. But there is a danger in following such a map too closely, just as there is a danger in limiting oneself to the poems included in an anthology or a volume of selected poetry: in both cases, the reader adopts a theory first and then looks for evidence to support that theory. The editorial process of choosing "representative" poetry is bound up with the impulse to define and categorize the poet. Definition informs selection, while selection informs definition. The lens narrows and narrows, and suddenly a poet who published twenty volumes of verse is defined by "We Real Cool":

> We real cool. We
> Left school. We
>
> Lurk late. We
> Strike straight. We . . .
> (1-4)

The question is not whether "We Real Cool" is a good poem—it is— but whether this and a handful of other short, colloquial, frequently anthologized poems adequately represent the scope and depth of Gwendolyn Brooks's accomplishment.

A good way to broaden one's understanding of any given author is to read him or her in a different context from the one in which that au-

thor is usually encountered. The idea is not to replace one pat definition with another but rather to see the author as working in multiple
traditions and multiple contexts. In the case of Brooks, what happens
to the anthologist's representation of the poet when we identify a
strain in her work that is not bound up with "day-to-day existence" and
"the lives of 'ordinary' people"? How does reading Brooks in the epic
tradition challenge and inform our understanding of her poetry's significance and import? Studying Brooks's appropriation of epic and
mock-epic themes and conventions prompts the reader to locate elements of Brooks's work that do not fit readily into her own place and
time. She uses epic conventions to both comic and dramatic effect,
redeploying them to underscore either the paucity or the richness of
her characters' lives. In some cases, a single stanza finds Brooks
modulating between a mocking and a serious tone, between tongue-in-
cheek and heart-on-the-sleeve. Comparing the mock-epic "The Anniad"
with the high-epic "Riders to the Blood-Red Wrath"—and comparing both to the sources on which they draw—shows Brooks exploiting a full range of effects that the epic tradition offered her. Brooks's
investment in this literary tradition suggests that it is a mistake to
think of her work as being limited to the concerns and modes of expression of her own milieu; rather, Brooks explores her own place
and time, in part, by exploring the literary tradition that she has inherited.

"The Anniad" announces its epic character through its title. If
Homer's *Iliad* is the story of Ilium, or Troy, and Virgil's *Aeneid* is the
story of Aeneas, a Trojan prince who would father the Roman people,
then Brooks's "Anniad" must be the story of someone named Annie.
The long poem originally appeared in the 1949 collection *Annie Allen*,
which garnered Brooks a Pulitzer Prize in 1950 and which is reprinted
in its entirety in Brooks's 1987 collection *Blacks*. The reader who first
encounters the poem in this context readily identifies the Annie to
which its title refers. The other poems in the collection detail the contrast between Annie's humble upbringing and her "proud" mind ("the

ballad of late Annie" 12). Arguing with her mother over chores, for example, in "the ballad of late Annie," the girl thinks: "Men there were and men there be/ But never men so many/ Chief enough to marry me" ("the ballad of late Annie" 9-11). As its title suggests, the poem is a ballad. Its iambic feet, alternating rhyme scheme (*abab*), and alternating lines of four and three feet are drawn directly from the ballad tradition and cast Annie's exchange with her mother into the dramatic, narrative form of such early English works as "Barbara Allen"—a character with whom Annie shares a surname—and "The Twae Corbies." Other poems in the collection, such as "the sonnet-ballad," are written in the form of the Shakespearean sonnet (consisting of three quatrains followed by a couplet). Annie's life story is therefore caught up in the story of English poetry, bodied forth in a series of poems that engage with the literary tradition and that partake of canonical forms and themes. The explicitly referential nature of the poems in *Annie Allen* helps to contextualize the longest poem in the collection; by the time the reader gets to "The Anniad," he or she understands that the history of this girl from Chicago is being explored through a series of literary forms. Ballad, sonnet, and now epic are being reshaped around her.

The first stanza of "The Anniad" further places it in the epic tradition by announcing the poet's theme. Homer and Virgil begin their epics in this mode, declaring the subject matter they will address and then invoking the muse to aid them in their song. The *Iliad* begins with a reference to the wrath of Achilles; the *Odyssey*, to the wanderings of that "man of twists and turns,/ driven time and again off course" (1.1-2). Virgil begins the *Aeneid* with "*Armo virumque cano . . .*," or "Arms and the man, I sing . . ." (1). Brooks likewise outlines the theme that her brief epic will address:

Think of sweet and chocolate,
Left to folly or to fate,
Whom the higher gods forgot
Whom the lower gods berate;
Physical and underfed
Fancying on the featherbed
What was never and is not.

(1-7)

If the title announces that this poem will be an epic, the first line and stanza gradually subvert this expectation. For the epic takes its materials from war: the wrath of Achilles is an epic subject, the journey of Odysseus is an epic subject—but "sweet and chocolate" is not. Nor does the setting of the poem lend itself to an epic treatment. The *Iliad* begins midway through the Trojan War, while the *Odyssey* and the *Aeneid* begin after Troy has fallen. Brooks's poem, on the other hand, opens with a girl daydreaming on a featherbed. The poet is playing with the gap between epic form and the mundane details of everyday life. Sound informs sense here, for the singsong exact rhymes and the short, ballad-length lines create a comic rather than a heroic mood. This contrast between epic form and comic content moves "The Anniad" into a tradition that is far more recent than that of Homer and Virgil: the tradition of the mock epic.

To understand the mock epic, one must have some familiarity with what is arguably the greatest epic in the English language: *Paradise Lost* (1667). In his preface to the poem, John Milton explains his position on rhyme:

The measure is English heroic verse without rhyme, as that of Homer in Greek and of Virgil in Latin; rhyme being no necessary adjunct or true ornament of poem or good verse, in longer works especially, but the invention of a barbarous race. (6)

Homer and Virgil did not write in rhyme, Milton argues, and neither should a poet working in the English language. Instead, Milton composes his epic in blank verse: unrhymed ten-syllable lines of iambs. The pattern is familiar, of course, to readers of Shakespeare and the other Elizabethan and Jacobean playwrights. But Milton brings to the form a remarkable flexibility, composing complex sentences that spill across several of these ten-syllable lines. This enjambment allows him to create a tension between the end of the line and the end of a particular idea; he can follow a regular meter without being contained by it. Here, for example, Milton, following the classical tradition of invoking the muse, calls on the Holy Spirit to aid him in his song:

> And chiefly thou, O Spirit, that doest prefer
> Before all temples th' upright heart and pure,
> Instruct me, for thou know'st; thou from the first
> Wast present, and with mighty wings outspread
> Dove-like sat'st brooding on the vast abyss
> And mad'st it pregnant: what in me is dark
> Illumine, what is low raise and support;
> That to the highth of this great argument
> I may assert Eternal Providence,
> And justify the ways of God to men.
>
> (1.17-26)

This is a long and complex sentence that comes to a full stop twice: at "know'st" and "pregnant," words that fall midway through two lines. There is a tremendous power, grandeur, and solemnity in the unfurling of this Miltonic line.

Some two generations after Milton, Alexander Pope would respond to the epic tradition in a very different fashion. In *The Rape of the Lock* (1712), Pope casts a trivial event in the elevated language and conventions of the epic. A young woman named Belinda goes to a party at Hampton Court, where an admirer snips off a lock of her hair as a keepsake. The poem is based on an actual event, and in fact Pope was commissioned to write the comic piece to end a feud between the families of the two young people involved. He begins the poem by stating his theme: "What dire offence from amorous causes springs,/ What mighty contests rise from trivial things,/ I sing . . ." (1.1-3). The conventional invocation is instantly recognizable: the reader understands that Pope is aligning himself with Homer, Virgil, and Milton. Yet the effect is entirely silly, for the rhymes of "springs," "things," and "sing" jangle off each other with a sprightliness that establishes the light theme of the poem. Consider this climactic speech in which Belinda mourns her stolen lock of hair:

> For ever cursed be this detested day,
> Which snatched my best, my favorite curl away!
> Happy! Ah ten times happy had I been,
> If Hampton Court these eyes had never seen!
> (4.147-50)

The speech is comic rather than tragic, for the situation does not justify Belinda's reaction. She may have cause to be upset, but that cause is not of epic proportions. Pope's end-stopped lines and exact rhymes add to the mirth, for the silliness of the verse further undercuts Belinda's and her narrator's epic vision of the situation. The mock epic couches trivial matter in epic form, and the gap between the two is a source of comedy.

Brooks's "The Anniad" therefore opens in the tradition of Pope and his Age of Enlightenment contemporaries, such as Jonathan Swift, rather than in the tradition of Milton. Like Pope, Brooks uses the conventions of the epic to comic effect, matching high form to trivial matter. Here, for example, the epic narrator describes Annie's longing for a suitor:

Watching for the paladin
Which no woman ever had,
Paradisiacal and sad
With a dimple in his chin

(22-25)

The line about the imagined paladin having "a dimple in his chin" is at once touching and humorous, for it highlights how naive and superficial Annie's vision of a Prince Charming really is. The lofty word "paradisiacal" prepares the reader for an equally lofty conclusion, but instead we get this minutely specific physical attribute. This is a girl's, rather than a woman's, daydream of love. The line may echo a similar juxtaposition of high sentiment and highly specific physical attributes in T. S. Eliot's "The Love Song of J. Alfred Prufrock." Prufrock muses,

And indeed there will be time
To wonder, "Do I dare? And, "Do I dare?"
Time to turn back and descend the stair,
With a bald spot in the middle of my hair—

(43-46)

Annie, like Prufrock, dwells on her appearance. Gazing into her mirror, she is "emotionally aware/ Of [her] black and boisterous hair" (33-34) and of the "unembroidered brown" of her skin (31). This intense self-consciousness is the concern of a modern man or woman, not of an epic hero such as an Achilles or an Odysseus. When Odysseus makes a public appearance, his patron goddess ensures that he will look his best. In this scene, he has just spent seven years marooned on an island, twenty days sailing on a raft, and three days and nights swimming at sea. He has crawled ashore and spent the night sleeping under an olive bush. Yet when he wakes up and meets the Princess Nausicaa,

Zeus's daughter Athena made him taller to all eyes,
His build more massive now, and down from his brows
She ran his curls like thick hyacinth clusters
Full of blooms.

(6.253-56)

Belinda, Annie, and even Prufrock might envy Odysseus his "curls like thick hyacinth clusters." The epic hero never looks into a mirror and frets about his hair or his skin, but his appearance will be godlike when the occasion requires it. Modern readers and characters are marked by a self-consciousness that is absent from the epic hero.

Yet it would be a mistake to read "The Anniad" as a wholly comic work. While Brooks begins the poem in the mode of the mock epic, she modulates into a progressively more serious tone as her heroine's relationship with her paladin develops. Whereas earlier in the poem Brooks qualifies the "paradisiacal" vision of a suitor with the silly requirement that he have a dimple, she now alternates between high idealism and low realism to a quite different effect. Annie has met her suitor, who now

Leaves the heaven she put him in
For the path his pocket chooses;
Leads her to a lowly room.

Which she makes a chapel of.
Where she genuflects to love.

(61-65)

High gives way to low, as an actual man takes the place that had been held by an imaginary Prince Charming. Flesh-and-blood men have to pay bills and live within their means, so Annie's suitor spirits her away not to some castle but to "a lowly room" that he can afford. Here, then, is a familiar mock-epic pattern of mundane considerations making their way into an elevated form. Yet in the next stanza, Brooks reverses the pattern. Annie makes "a chapel of" the lowly room, elevating it again to the paradisiacal realm that she had once imagined. Full of love, she transforms the humble place as surely as Athena transformed the haggard Odysseus.

Brooks's poem moves further into the domain of the true epic rather than the mock epic when Annie's lover is enlisted to fight in World War II. The draft comes in the form of a "Doomer . . . prophesying hecatombs" (78-79). *Hecatomb* is Greek for "a hundred oxen" and denotes a massive sacrifice. Millions of men will be sacrificed in the war, and millions of others will survive but be psychologically scarred. The Doomer "spits upon" and "denigrates" Annie's little paradise, sending her lover to the front,

> Where he makes the rifles cough,
> Stutter. Where the reveille
> Is staccato majesty.
> Then to marches. Then to know
> The hunched hells across the sea.
>
> (87-91)

Annie's lover returns from the war, but he is not the same man who went off to fight. The experience of battle has changed him. He "twitches: for for long/ Life was little as a sand/ Little as an inch of song" (106-8). Perhaps he is shell-shocked; the reference to twitching would be consistent with some of the symptoms of post-traumatic stress disorder. Brooks's narrator notes that civilian life "baffles" him and that the soldier, having taken off his helmet and his power, "wants his power back again" (124, 130). Whatever the nature of the veteran's emotional damage, it manifests itself in an aversion to his former life with Annie: "Not that woman! (Not that room!/ Not that dusted demi-gloom!)/ Nothing limpid, nothing meek" (141-43). Hardened by war, Annie's lover comes back from the front looking for an entirely different kind of lover. He gets "a sleek slit-eyed gypsy moan" from a "mad bacchanalian lass" (149, 153). The war has ground love out of him, and only lust is left to take its place.

A poem that opened in the mock-epic mode of Pope has moved steadily toward the high-epic mode of Milton's *Paradise Lost*. In fact, Brooks's poem shares the Miltonic theme: Annie dreamed of a paradise and made that paradise a reality but then lost it to war and war's aftermath. One might identify her with several different characters in Milton's epic. She is the loving God who creates a Heaven for the angels and a Paradise for men and women, only to be betrayed by both. Like Milton's Satan, Annie's lover trades Heaven for Hell; wanting his power back, he might agree with Satan that it is "better to reign in hell, than serve in heav'n" (1.263). If Satan is physically transformed from beautiful angel to hideous devil, Annie's lover is emotionally transformed. His time in "the hunched hells" of the trenches has ruined him, and he cannot return to the heaven from which he has fallen (91). Yet Annie is also a banished Eve, cast out of the garden of paradise. Here, she wanders through a spiritual wilderness that might be the land east of Eden:

> Perfumes fly before the gust,
> Colors shrivel in the dust,
> And the petal velvet shies,
> When the desert terrifies
>
> (231-34)

If at the start of the poem Brooks's short lines and exact rhyme scheme created a mood of comic lightness, now they create one of stark emptiness. Annie is in desolation. Her hell or her place of exile, like Milton's, fuses biblical and classical sources; as she tries to make a new life for herself, she is haunted by "hyacinthine devils" and "pucks and cupids" (172, 174). By poem's end, Annie's lover has left his mistress, yet he has not returned to her. She can regain her paradise only in her own mind, and the poem closes with Annie "Kissing in her kitchen-ette/ The minuets of memory" (299-300).

The gradual evolution of Annie as a heroine and of "The Anniad" as a poem blurs the line between comedy and tragedy, mock epic and true epic, and ordinary and extraordinary lives. In this respect, Brooks engages with some of the same contradictions that the classical and neo-classical epic poets faced. Homer's *Odyssey*, for example, begins with a scene of the gods meeting in counsel on Olympus. Yet toward the epic's end, Odysseus, disguised as a beggar, enters a boxing match with an actual beggar over the prize of a sausage. The epic runs the gamut, there-fore, from the highest to the lowest of subjects. Pope, on the other hand, may write in a wholly comic mode, but the impetus for his poem came from two families taking great offense at the incident that he describes. His stated purpose in writing the poem is to recast an event that these feuding families were taking quite seriously into the mode of comedy. The epic and the mock epic alike therefore represent a full range of life.

Over the course of Brooks's poem, the gap between the materials of Annie's life and the conventions of the epic steadily closes, until by its end the girl from Chicago does, in fact, qualify as an epic heroine. Af-ter all, "The Anniad" dwells on the two themes that have animated all of the great epics: love and war. If Homer's *Iliad* follows the Greeks to the battlefields of Troy, Brooks's poem stays behind to measure the toll war takes on the women whose men are taken from them. The war it-self is described in just a few short lines, because Annie does not actu-ally visit the trenches, yet it has a devastating effect on Annie's life. It would be better for Annie, perhaps, were she able to dwell forever in the light, comic mode of the mock epic. When she was a girl dreaming of a lover with a dimple in his chin, the conventions of the epic hung loosely about Annie, as if she were a child wearing an adult's suit of clothes. But the war makes her grow into these conventions. The epic, which seems at first far removed from modern life, turns out to be a lit-erary mode that is entirely appropriate for expressing Annie's story of love, war, and a lost paradise.

If in "The Anniad" Brooks modulates between mock epic and high epic, the poem "Riders to the Blood-Red Wrath" finds her writing entirely in the latter mode. In this poem, first published in 1963, Brooks draws on epic conventions to retell the story of the African diaspora, American slavery, and emancipation. Her brief epic ends with a vision of herself as one of the titular riders—a reference to the freedom riders, activists in the Civil Rights movement who traveled to the South to challenge the Jim Crow segregation laws—who are ushering in the next stage of the African American experience. Writing in an epic mode allows Brooks to create a language that can adequately portray the sweep and momentum of these historical events. Yet despite its epic theme, "Riders to the Blood-Red Wrath" does not explicitly invoke the conventions of the classical epic, as does "The Anniad." Rather, Brooks channels the language of the first English epic, the Anglo-Saxon *Beowulf*, while assuming the Virgilian or Miltonic role of the epic poet who writes not of a single hero but of an entire race.

While Brooks does not begin her poem with an invocation of the muse or a statement of her theme, as would a Greek or Roman poet, the force of the poem's first stanza nevertheless announces its epic character:

> My proper prudence toward his proper probe
> Astonished their ancestral seemliness.
> It was a not-nice risk, a wrought risk, was
> An indelicate risk, they thought. And an excess.
>
> (1-4)

The relentless alliteration and assonance of these lines is familiar to readers of *Beowulf*, for Brooks draws on the Anglo-Saxon poet's fondness for repeating consonant and vowel sounds. In the first line, for example, four words begin with a "pruh-" sound, while the second line hisses with "a" and "s" sounds. Compare Brooks's use of alliteration to that of the *Beowulf* poet, in Seamus Heaney's translation:

> Then as dawn brightened and the day broke
> Grendel's powers of destruction were plain:
> Their wassail was over, they wept to heaven
> And mourned under morning
>
> (126-29)

Brooks composes the poem in iambic pentameter, the line of the *Beowulf* poet and of so much English verse, and, like the Anglo-Saxon poet, she tends to construct lines that have a natural break or pause in the middle. When she wishes, however, she expands the line to as many as a dozen syllables or contracts it to as few as five (and, in fact, one line consists of the single word "I"). By appropriating all of these features of Anglo-Saxon poetry, Brooks musters a primal and warrior-like voice. The hard-lined and muscular form verse of the Anglo-Saxon epic lends itself well to Brooks's heroic subject.

Yet Brooks does not limit herself to Anglo-Saxon diction, mixing in Latinate words that would be more at home in *Paradise Lost* than in *Beowulf*. The captain and crew of a slave ship, for example, are "Half fainting from their love affair with fetors/ That pledged a haughty allegiance for all time" (63-64). The alliterative "f" in the first line and the assonant "allegiance" and "all" in the second are characteristic of Anglo-Saxon poetry, but many of the words themselves, such as "fetors" and "allegiance," are Latinate. Brooks is not interested in creating ersatz Old English verse; rather, her language in this poem is an act of cultural and linguistic synthesis. She evokes the grandeur of an African culture whose language she cannot speak by drawing on the heritage of the language she does speak. Epic language re-creates an epic past:

I remember kings
A blossoming palace. Silver. Ivory . . .
I remember my right to roughly run and roar,
My right to raid the sun, consult the moon,
Nod to my princesses or split them open,
To flay my lions, eat blood with a spoon.
You never saw such running and such roaring!

(45-53)

The "I" of the poem speaks not of personal memories but of cultural and historical ones. This is the memory of a whole people rather than that of a single person, and the elevated language of the poem reflects the lost paradise of an African homeland. The alliteration and regular iambs of the *Beowulf* poet act as a sort of cultural placeholder; it is a heroic English line that conjures up a heroic African lineage.

The language of "Riders" may owe something to the Anglo-Saxon *Beowulf*, but in its scope and its purpose the poem has a distinctly Virgilian or Miltonic character. Virgil's *Aeneid* and Milton's *Paradise Lost* are both epics that concern themselves less with the story of a single hero than with that of a whole people. This shift from the individual to the communal may have something to do with Virgil's and Milton's relationships to the epic tradition that they inherited. Scholars sometimes make a distinction between primary epics, such as the works of Homer and the *Beowulf* poet, and secondary ones, such as the *Aeneid* and *Paradise Lost*. The former are written by poets who undertook their work at the end of a long oral tradition. Homer, like the blind bard who sings in book eight of his *Odyssey*, was the product of an oral storytelling culture. The *Iliad* and the *Odyssey* codify and set down in written form stories, modes of expression, and conventions that had first been developed through generations of recitations and sung performances. Virgil and Milton, on the other hand, knew the epic as a literary form. Their epics are secondary, therefore, in that they draw not on an oral culture but on a written one. Virgil modeled the *Aeneid* on the two epics of Homer, while Milton modeled *Paradise Lost* on the works of both Homer and Virgil as well as the Bible. Working at a distance from the Homeric Greek culture that produced the epic, both Virgil and Milton were in a position to appropriate and redeploy the conventions of the genre in new ways and to new purposes. Each used the epic genre as the machinery by which to tell a story that has a greater mythic, historic, and metaphysical sweep than do the Homeric epics. Virgil's epic is a nationalistic one, telling the story not only of Aeneas but also of all of Roman history. Aeneas is a hero of a different order than Achilles or Odysseus: he is charged with leading the scattered Trojans, whom Virgil posits as the ancestors of the Romans, to a new land where they will forge for themselves a new identity.

If Virgil appropriated the epic for nationalistic purposes, Milton did so for religious ones. He writes to "justify the ways of God to men" (1.23), fusing classical form with Christian subject matter. While both the *Aeneid* and *Paradise Lost* tell the histories of a people, they are as concerned with the future as they are with the past. Both epics are characterized by a prophetic tone that is essentially absent from Homer. Where Aeneas's struggles foretell the future greatness of the Roman state and people, Satan's and Adam and Eve's falls from grace anticipate Christ's eventual sacrifice to atone for their fall. The epic may chronicle a mythic past, but ultimately it does so in order to direct the reader's attention toward the present and the future.

Brooks likewise appropriates epic form as a means of telling the story of a people, from a tragic past to a triumphant future. After moving through the stages of the African American experience, from the African diaspora through the present day, she adopts a prophetic tone that looks ahead to the future of the Civil Rights movement and of America:

Democracy and Christianity
Recommence with me.

And I ride ride I ride on to the end—
Where glowers my continuing Calvary.
(81-84)

Like Virgil and Milton before her, Brooks uses the elevated language and symbology of the epic tradition to speak not only of the heroic past but also of a heroic and predestined future. If the legacy of slavery and segregation is America's original sin, then the freedom riders are the nation's saviors, riding to their own Mount of Calvary. Their heroic task is to restore the democratic and Christian principles that slavery betrayed. The outcome is far from guaranteed and can be brought about only with great sacrifice, for her epic heroes must ride into "the blood-red wrath" of the segregated American South. In a pair of closing lines that may owe something to the end of Tennyson's "Ulysses" ("To strive, to seek, to find, and not to yield"; 70), Brooks catalogs her heroes' coming struggle: "To flail, to flourish, to wither or to win./ We lurch, distribute, we extend, begin" (89-90).

Gwendolyn Brooks is at once a poet of her own time and one of the ages. In "The Anniad," "Riders to the Blood-Red Wrath," and several other seminal poems, she appropriates epic forms in order to give voice to her epic themes. Whether her subject is the devastating aftermath of war or the heroic struggle of civil rights activists, the poet recognizes that the right to live an ordinary life can sometimes be won only through an epic struggle.

Works Cited

Beowulf. Trans. Seamus Heaney. New York: Farrar, Straus and Giroux, 2000.
Brooks, Gwendolyn. "The Anniad." *Blacks.* Chicago: David, 1987.
_____. "the ballad of late Annie." *Blacks.* Chicago: David, 1987.

_____. "Riders to the Blood-Red Wrath." *Selected Poems*. 1963. New York: HarperCollins (Perennial Classics), 1999.

Eliot, T. S. "The Love Song of J. Alfred Prufrock." *The Complete Poems and Plays*. New York: Harcourt, Brace & World, 1962.

Homer. *The Iliad*. Trans. Robert Fagles. New York: Penguin Books, 1996.

_____. *The Odyssey*. Trans. Robert Fagles. New York: Penguin Books, 1996.

Milton, John. *Paradise Lost: A Norton Critical Edition*. New York: Norton, 1975.

Pope, Alexander. *The Rape of the Lock*. New York: Vintage, 2007.

Tennyson, Alfred, Lord. "Ulysses." *Alfred, Lord Tennyson: Selected Poems*. New York: Gramercy, 2007.

Virgil. *The Aeneid*. Trans. Rolfe Humphries. New York: Charles Scribner's Sons, 1951.

Close Reading as an Approach to Gwendolyn Brooks's "The *Chicago Defender* Sends a Man to Little Rock"_____

Robert C. Evans

Robert C. Evans argues the merits of revisiting the practice of "close reading" poems. He discusses the question of whether formalism is the best way to interpret poetry, concluding that so far no one has made a definitive case against formalism and that it is an effective tool for beginning literary analysis. Evans spends the bulk of the essay performing a close reading of "The *Chicago Defender* Sends a Man to Little Rock." He argues that Brooks's deliberate use of rhyme, meter, and figurative language conveys the psychological ambivalence whites had toward the integration of schools and toward a black journalist's right to record the reality of the radical change introduced by desegregation.   — M.R.M.

"In the current critical climate," wrote the eminent literary analyst Heather Dubrow not too long ago, "many scholars are far more comfortable detailing their sexual histories in print than confessing to an interest in literary form" (59). Obviously Dubrow was exaggerating for comic effect, but her joke does convey some sense of the distance we have traveled since the mid-twentieth century, when "formalism," with its close attention to the nitty-gritty artistic details of literature, was the dominant critical approach. In the decades since then, many influential critics have tended to discuss literary texts in terms of anything *but* their effectiveness as well-crafted works of art. Race, class, gender, psychology, politics, ecology, evolution, and a wide variety of "historical" and "cultural" issues have been emphasized, often at the expense of detailed studies of literary texts as skillfully designed, intensely beautiful, and emotionally compelling pieces of writing. "Beauty," indeed, has often been a highly suspect term, and in fact Dubrow does not exaggerate when she mentions the "virulence" that formalism "often evokes" in those who oppose

---

it (59). Fortunately, however, in recent years the tide has begun to turn (or at least to flow in more than one direction), and more and more critics have begun to confess that what interests them most in a work of literature is not so much "what" a work means as "how" it means. This is not, it should be emphasized, a return to formalism per se; instead, it is simply a renewed interest in "close reading" as a practical technique for coming to grips with the precise details of texts and with the intimate, line-by-line, word-by-word experience of understanding texts. Close reading need not entail all the specific doctrines associated with formalism (such as the "intentional" or "affective" fallacies); instead, close reading is a technique that can be used profitably in conjunction with a wide variety of theoretical assumptions, as a major recent anthology edited by Frank Lentricchia and Andrew DuBois has made abundantly clear.

Helen Vendler, in a highly stimulating essay titled "Reading a Poem," begins by vigorously defending the formalists (which is not, I should stress, part of my own present purpose), but then she soon turns her attention to the matter of close reading itself. Noting that many of the early formalists were themselves poets and novelists, she suggests that the technique of close reading should more properly be called "'a writer's reading'—the study that another writer would give to what had been attempted, and accomplished, on the page" (129). Vendler then proceeds to examine very closely a particular poem by Robert Lowell, paying detailed attention not only to its form and techniques but also to its various historical and literary contexts, only to conclude that

such a poem is simply more interesting than a single-layered poem. And of course I've said nothing about many other things, such as the construction of stanzas, or the management of space, or the binding of words to each other. One can't simply abstract statements of ideas or themes from such a poem and represent it faithfully; that is why those writer-critics of the New Criticism wanted readers to notice tonality, and originality of strategy, and whimsicality, and mood, and syntactic punctuation, and the redefinition of genre, and the poetry of the idea, and a multitude of other triumphs. (135)

Vendler has always been a careful close reader, and so perhaps a better indication of the recent change in critical climate can be seen in the publication of one of the latest books by Terry Eagleton, an enormously influential critic and theorist who has often been perceived as hostile to traditional approaches to literary study. In his 2007 book *How to Read a Poem*, however, Eagleton explicitly advocates and defends close reading (2), which he associates with "attending to language in all its material density." It is not, Eagleton writes, as if the language of a literary work "is a kind of disposable cellophane in which the ideas come ready-wrapped. On the contrary, the language of a poem is *constitutive* of its ideas" (2). In other words, form cannot be divorced from content; technique cannot be separated from meaning. These are ideas with which any old New Critic would definitely have agreed, but it is reassuring to hear them expressed by Eagleton, who then spends much of the rest of his book showing how to read poems closely by attending to such matters as tone, mood, pitch, intensity, pace, texture, syntax, grammar, punctuation, ambiguity, rhyme, rhythm, meter, and imagery (102-42)—all the old warhorses of traditional close reading.

It would be easy enough to continue to cite examples of the recently renewed interest in close reading among a wide variety of literary critics, but by now the point is clear. What, however, does any of this have to do with the poetry of Gwendolyn Brooks? Quite a lot, as it turns out, especially to anyone who is interested in the ways that Brooks's technique and artistry shape the meaning of her poems and contribute to their effectiveness. Brooks, by one of those strange accidents of history, began to receive widespread critical attention precisely during the decades in which formalism as a theory, along with close reading as a practice, was in decline, and so her poems have sometimes more often been examined for their paraphrasable "meanings" than for the nitty-gritty details of their art. That Brooks was a woman, an African American, and a political leftist writing during an era of great political and social turmoil also contributed to a tendency to read her works in terms of their content rather than their form. Yet it is in the detailed texture of a work that its fullest meaning lies. This is a proposition I wish to support by paying close attention to one of the most obviously "social" and "political" of Brooks's poems—her long, sixty-line lyric titled "The *Chicago Defender* Sends a Man to Little Rock" (Brooks 330-32).

In this poem, which explicitly refers to events from the fall of 1957, Brooks describes the responses of a reporter dispatched from the *Chicago Defender,* a prominent black Chicago newspaper, to report on the city of Little Rock, Arkansas, which was then the center of national attention because of efforts by numerous local whites to prevent the racial integration of the local public schools through violence and intimidation. Brooks's poem begins by describing Little Rock and its citizens as completely unremarkable; the poem depicts people engaged in the normal, ordinary concerns of day-to-day living. Nothing about the town or its inhabitants strikes the reporter as exceptional—and this, of course, is the point. The fact that such a town, with such a populace, is capable of the kinds of violence, prejudice, and racial hatred described as the poem draws to a close helps give the poem its heavy sense of grim and sardonic irony.

Perhaps the best way to approach this, or any, poem by means of a truly close reading would be to move through it line by line, word by word, and sound by sound. However, since such a method might seem *too* close (and too lengthy) in the present context, a useful alternative might be to read the poem by looking at the various devices it employs, such as structure, sound, diction, tone, and imagery. Brooks deals in this work with highly topical and controversial matters, but the poem will continue to survive as a *poem*—as a work of art—because of Brooks's skill and craft as a writer.

I

Brooks's craft is immediately evident in the first two lines of the poem: "In Little Rock, the people bear/ Babes, and comb and part their

hair." With one exception, these lines (like the rest of the entire opening stanza) are perfectly "regular" in meter. Each line of the opening
four-line stanza, except for one, consists of eight syllables, and, except
for that one variation, all four of the opening lines consist of four iambic
feet, in which one unaccented syllable is immediately followed by an
accented syllable. The basic rhythm of the opening stanza, then, is something like the following: "ta-DUM, ta-DUM, ta-DUM, ta-DUM."[1] Only
at the very beginning of the second line is there any substantial variation
from this pattern: the monosyllabic opening word—"Babes"—gets full
metrical stress, as if to emphasize its importance, and the second line consists of seven syllables rather than the expected eight. For the most part,
though, the opening stanza seems highly predictable, both in rhyme and
in rhythm. Everything seems routine; nothing, with the exception of the
opening of the second line, seems out of the ordinary. The almost perfectly regular cadence of the lines matches the humdrum, but closely observed, details of the ordinary daily life the stanza so effectively depicts.
Clearly Brooks wants to create in these opening lines, and in most of the
first half of the poem, an impression of nothing unexpected going on.

This impression of predictable regularity is reinforced by the opening stanza's rhyme scheme, which has little variation. The poem's first
thirteen lines stress only four different rhyme sounds, apportioned as
follows: *aaa* (lines 1-3); *bb|bb* (4-7); *ccc* (8-10); and *ddd* (11-13). By
placing rhymes in adjacent lines rather than alternating them (e.g.,
abab, *cdcd*) as might have been expected from the practice of many
previous poets, Brooks reinforces the sense of monotony she seems determined to create in these opening stanzas.[2] Later the rhyme scheme,
rhythms, line lengths, diction, and even the meanings of the poem will
become much more difficult to anticipate or interpret, but in the first
several stanzas, especially, Brooks varies little from the patterns established in the opening lines: mostly iambic meter; mostly eight syllables
to a line; and a heavy emphasis on repetition, as in the three references
to "Sunday" in lines 9, 10, and 12, or the repeated phrase "In Little
Rock" at the beginnings of the first and third stanzas.

Still, Brooks keeps both the rhymes and the rhythms from seeming *too* predictable through a heavy use of enjambment (i.e., lack of punctuation at the ends of lines), so that the first four stanzas flow smoothly and easily. This very sense of smoothness, moreover, helps contribute to the opening effect of calm, colloquial, everyday simplicity. Life in Little Rock, like the form of the poem itself, seems ordered but relaxed, routine but not rigid.

Having established a sense of regularity and predictability in the rhythms and rhymes of the first four stanzas, Brooks thereby achieves all the more emphasis and impact when these patterns are disrupted, beginning in the fifth stanza. The first two lines of that stanza are much briefer and more abrupt than anything that has come before; they consist of merely three and four syllables, respectively, and suddenly, in these lines, the perspective shifts from the people of Little Rock themselves to the explicit first-person perspective of the journalist, the "man" from the *Defender*, who, it turns out, has been speaking and reporting all along. A sense of regularity briefly returns in the last three lines of the fifth stanza, but rhyme, rhythm, and stanza lengths all become far more erratic and unpredictable in the sixth, seventh, and eighth stanzas, and the imagery, phrasing, and meaning of the lines (especially, as I will demonstrate later, in stanza seven) become far more difficult to interpret.

The sudden sense of unpredictability can be seen in the varying numbers of syllables in the lines of each of these middle stanzas. In stanza six, the syllable count for each line is as follows: 10, 18, 7, 13, 15, 14, 6. In stanza seven, the number of syllables per line is equally erratic: 13, 8, 7, 6, 3, 9, 11, 10, 9, 10. Likewise, the syllable count per line is just as variable in stanza eight: 6, 16, 14, 10, 13. Only with stanza nine does a real sense of syllabic regularity return: 10, 10, 10, 10, 8, 9, 8. In the same way, the rhyme schemes used in the sixth, seventh, and eighth stanzas vary much more than the rhyme schemes used in the opening and closing groups of stanzas. The pattern of rhymes in stanza six is as follows: *ghhijkjj*. In stanza seven, the pattern is just as unpredictable: *lmmnnopqrp*. The same is true of the pattern of rhymes in stanza eight: *stuvu*. These rhyme schemes are a far cry from the regularity of the first stanza (*aaabb*) or the third and fourth (*ccc, ddd*). Further, the rhyme patterns of the sixth, seventh, and eighth stanzas also vary greatly from the regularity that resumes in stanza nine (*wwxxyyy*) and the couplets that dominate the final stanzas of the poem. Clearly, then, in stanzas six, seven, and eight, Brooks achieves an effect of formal disruption and irregularity—an effect she almost certainly chose to create.

II

Just as striking as the irregularity of line lengths and rhyme schemes in these middle stanzas is the way the imagery and phrasing become more obscure, especially in stanza seven, where the language becomes quite abstract and difficult to interpret. Before trying to wrestle with the diction of the seventh stanza, however, it seems worth discussing the kind of diction that precedes and follows it.

Nothing in the imagery or phrasing of the first five stanzas seems especially hard to understand. The first stanza is perfectly lucid and seems intended to suggest the regular concerns and activities of normal daily life. Only in retrospect does the phrasing of the opening stanza seem especially ironic, especially when that stanza is read in connection with stanza eleven (lines 51-57). The same people who carefully "comb and part their hair" in the first stanza are the people who threaten and attack little black girls with "bows and barrettes in the curls" in line 56. The people who constructively "put repair/ To roof and latch" in lines 3-4 are the same people who later act so destructively in the eleventh stanza. Furthermore, the same kind of people who, as the poem opens, pay such careful attention to nurturing "multiferns" (4) are the very sort of people who form a destructive, metaphorical "scythe/ Of men harassing brownish girls" in stanza eleven (54-55). Indeed, Brooks structures the first and final sections of the poem so that the relations between them are full of numerous iro- nies, especially involving religious imagery and phrasing. Thus the third and fourth stanzas (8-13) describe the behavior of the white citi- zens of Little Rock both during and after Sunday church services. Dur- ing their time in church, the citizens seem devoted Christians, although there is a hint of unattractive pride and pretentiousness in the reference to "Sunday pomp and polishing" (10). Likewise, when they return home from church, the citizens seem models of bourgeois respectabil- ity as they "soften Sunday afternoons/ With lemon tea and Lorna Doones" (12-13). The reporter even mentions the citizens' devotion to the joyful if somewhat superficial aspects of celebrating Christ's birth with "Christmas tree and trifle" (17).

All this religious imagery and phrasing, however, seems highly ironic by the time one reaches the end of the poem, which describes white citizens behaving in anything but a true Christian spirit. In stanza eleven, they are depicted "hurling spittle, rock,/ Garbage and fruit" (51-52), and the journalist reports having seen a "coiling storm a-writhe" on the faces of the beautiful "bright madonnas" of the town (54), who behave in ways that stunningly contrast with the most common conno- tations of the word, which is normally associated with the Virgin Mary, the mother of Jesus. The fact that these white mothers are full of such unmaternal wrath toward children of a different race is just one of the many ironies of the final portion of the poem, while the fact that people who normally sip tea while munching on Lorna Doones are later capa- ble of hurling stones and garbage at aspiring students is an ironic con- tradiction of some of the deepest of middle-class values. Ironically, the supposedly polite, well-mannered, and well-behaved bourgeois citi- zens of Little Rock turn into violent thugs when their privileges and settled way of life seem threatened.

The greatest irony, of course, is that the same people who take joy in celebrating the birth of Jesus behave like the very mob that demanded the death of Christ—an irony strongly implied by the poem's very last line, which sardonically concludes, "The loveliest lynchee was our

Lord" (60). Everything about this line is ironic. The loaded adjective "loveliest" seems full of sarcasm, since it calls attention to the ugly execution of a man who beautifully embodied the spirit of love or charity. Likewise, the unusual word "lynchee," which appears nowhere in the *Oxford English Dictionary*, suggests a fate so specific, and yet so unfortunately common, that a special term has to be invented to describe it (the simple word "victim," for instance, would not have had the same effect; "lynchee" is powerfully specific in alluding directly to one of the most notorious and heinous of all the crimes committed against African Americans). Similarly ironic is the plain word "our," since this word implies the common Christianity supposedly shared both by the mob, the reporter, and the objects of the mob's hatred. The word "our" thus ironically helps highlight the very divisions it ostensibly denies. Finally, the word "Lord" is an especially appropriate final piece of irony, since the members of the mob who consider themselves representatives of just order and proper authority violate both the spirit and the law of the very God they claim to worship. The final word of the poem links the 1957 events in Little Rock to biblical events that occurred nearly two thousand years earlier.

Who are these people who ultimately prove capable of such violence? They are people who, in addition to thinking of themselves as good, middle-class Christians, are capable of enjoying not only baseball but also classical music imported from Europe, as the sixth stanza makes clear. Their range of interests thus seems commendably broad: "baseball" is literally juxtaposed with "Barcarolle," a kind of music most notably associated with a famously slow-paced and highly sentimental song of love from Jacques Offenbach's *Tales of Hoffmann* (Melhem 111). Brooks thus uses precise imagery and phrasing to evoke the kinds of pleasant summer-evening activities that might, did, and do occur anywhere in America, but even as she does so she uses language that can seem, in retrospect, tinged with ominous foreshadowing. The description of the "uniformed figures raw and implacable/ And not intellectual" (20-21) most obviously describes the baseball players, but for anyone with knowledge of events in Little Rock in the fall of 1957, such language cannot help but also suggest the behavior of the Arkansas National Guard troops whom the state governor ordered to support the efforts of the segregationists. Likewise, the reference to baseball players "clawing the suffering dust" (22) adds to this undercurrent of implied violence, as does even the reference to Beethoven's music, which is sometimes "brutal" (24). The sixth stanza thus creates an atmosphere of calm, enjoyable relaxation that also implicitly foreshadows the violence that is to come.

The sixth stanza thereby demonstrates how Brooks, in addition to deploying the already discussed techniques of rhyme, rhythm, irony, structural foreshadowing, and verbal echoes (as in the refrain repeated in lines 1, 8, 19, and 37), also complicates the local texture of her specific phrasing. Much the same effect is evident, for instance, when she refers in line 7 to the "small concerns" of Little Rock's citizens, where the adjective "small" can suggest the meanings "normal" or "routine" while also subtly foreshadowing the pettiness and meanness the citizens display at the very end of the work.

As these examples suggest, important aspects of Brooks's poem— or indeed of nearly any skillful work of literature—lie not only in what is explicit but also in what is merely suggested or implied, or, indeed, left unsaid altogether. Thus, in this poem, Brooks never makes it obvious, until the very end of the work, that the people she is describing are almost certainly and entirely white. The people who go about their household chores, who attend church, relax with tea, celebrate Christmas, attend baseball games, and listen to open-air concerts are white people. Blacks are silently excluded from much of the poem's attention, just as they are excluded from much of society's concern, until the very end of the work. Church services, Christmas celebrations, baseball games, and public concerts are all part of a reiterated pattern in the poem in which people come together to share their lives; however, all of these activities shut off or shunt out a large part of the community. Ironically, it is only in the final confrontation that the two parts of the community actually come together. It is only in the closing stanzas that the whites form a group in which blacks are literally central, but the chief purpose of this group is exclusion, not inclusion. The implied pattern that helps structure so much of the poem—a pattern that involves whites coming together for common purposes—finds its ironic fulfillment as the poem violently ends.

III

Similarly ironic is the way the final stanzas, with their heavy stress on such violence and hatred, contrast with the strong emphasis on affection and tenderness in stanza seven. That stanza, as I have already mentioned, is especially perplexing. Now, however—having examined the stanzas that precede and follow it—we may be in a better position to come to grips with the seventh stanza itself. That section begins quite clearly (and promisingly): "There is love, too, in Little Rock. Soft women softly/ Opening themselves in kindness . . ." (lines 27-28). These lines manage to be both tender and erotic; they imply a kind of love that is both genuinely affectionate and genuinely sexual. From this point forward, however, the phrasing becomes much more difficult to comprehend, and, indeed, the phrasing of stanza seven makes this stanza perhaps the most obscure and most challenging section of the poem, the section that most obviously resists straightforward close reading. In what senses, for instance, are these women "pitying one's blindness" (29)? Who is the "one" mentioned here, and in what sense is this person blind? Is the blindness literal or metaphorical, and, if the latter, metaphorical in what sense? The next line, "Awaiting one's pleasure," seems clear enough, but what are we to make of all the color imagery that begins to flood the stanza in lines 31-34? What, exactly, is the "anguished rose at the root" in line 32? (Are the connotations sexual, or are they somehow religious?) What, exactly, are "old semi-discomfitures," and in what sense can they be "wash[ed] away" (33)? How, precisely, do the affectionate women "re-teach purple and unsullen blue" (34)? What are "wispy soils"? In what senses do they "go" (35)? What is their relation to the rest of the stanza or to the poem as a whole? And, finally, what does it mean, precisely, to say, apparently concerning these women, that "uncertain/ Half-havings have they clarified to sures" (35-36)? Presumably these lines refer to some kind of affectionate or erotic fulfillment, but the meaning of these lines, like the meaning of most of stanza seven (and, to a lesser extent, of stanza eight) seems far more obscure than the meaning of the rest of the poem.

Confronted with such obscurity, a reader has at least three choices: ignore the puzzles provoked, confidently solve them, or simply and honestly confess his or her puzzlement.[3] Of these options, I feel compelled to choose the third, although I wish to offer a few tentative suggestions. First, stanza seven seems deliberately and intentionally obscure. Certainly Brooks demonstrates her ability to write with graphic and even brutal plainness elsewhere in the poem. She seems to want, in stanza seven, to create a sense of mystery, beauty, and evocative profundity, perhaps because the subject is love. Second, stanza seven seems the most intentionally "modernist" section of the poem; it most obviously sounds like the sort of poetry that was in fashion during the 1920s. Indeed, some of the self-conscious alliteration, odd syntax, and whimsical wordplay could easily have come from Wallace Stevens, particularly in such a line as "Half-havings have they clarified to sures" (36), which is beautifully musical and suggestive even if its exact meaning is not entirely clear. Finally, the very strange and hazy beauty of stanza seven seems designed to highlight, by contrast, the revolting ugliness that comes later, as the poem concludes. The tone, imagery, and diction of stanza seven contrast strikingly with all those same aspects of stanza eleven, and establishing that sort of contrast, I would suggest, is perhaps the main function of the seventh stanza. It creates an impression of beautiful, ineffable loveliness and lovingness, an impression that is then violently undercut by the poem's grim, sardonic conclusion.

In any case, by the time we reach the ninth stanza, the obscurity that characterizes stanzas seven and eight has disappeared. The reporter from the *Chicago Defender* has apparently tried to phone some residents of Little Rock for interviews and has either been refused or given equivocations (37-38), but by the ninth stanza he has reached some conclusions nonetheless. Indeed, stanza nine gains much of its impact because the anonymous journalist has thus far been acting mainly as an objective reporter; with a brief exception in the fifth stanza, he has so far refrained from personal comment. Stanza nine is so important, then, because it marks an obvious transition to a more personal voice and a more personal perspective. In fact, the reporter even seems to admit openly that he came to Little Rock prepared to hate its citizens (42), only to discover that the real story is not that those citizens are bizarre monsters but, in fact, that "'They are like people everywhere'" (48). This is not the "news" he had expected to find (46), but it is the sad and, in retrospect, unsurprising and depressing truth. Stanza nine gains much of its power because of its very plainspoken honesty, and Brooks emphasizes the effect of directness and simplicity by punctuating the endings of so many lines. She uses periods at the ends of five of the stanza's eight lines—a striking contrast to the heavy use of enjambment earlier in the poem. It is as if the journalist is stunned by his discovery of the ordinariness of the citizens of Little Rock and can register this discovery only in short, abrupt, almost telegraphic sentences. Each sentence thereby gains added impact for the reader as well, and, in some ways, the ninth stanza is a welcome return to plainness after all the obscurities of stanzas seven and eight. Those earlier stanzas, however, help contribute to the effectiveness of stanza nine by providing such strong contrasts to it.

With this poem, as with so many of her others, Brooks has created a carefully designed and highly complex work of art—a work in which practically every detail of rhyme, rhythm, sound, imagery, diction, tone, stanzaic structure, and point of view matters, is meaningful, and contributes to the power of the poem as a whole. She has written, in other words, the sort of work that clearly lends itself to the sort of close reading that the best literary texts encourage, require, and inevitably reward. Fashions in critical theory may come and go, and particular theorists may rise and fall, but interest in the precise details of literary texts seems likely to remain permanent, at least among those who care about works of literature as works of art.

Notes

1. For a sensitive discussion of many aspects of the rhythms (as well as the binary structures) of this poem, see Sue S. Park's article "A Study in Tension." The poem is touched on only briefly in the Bloom's Biocritiques volume edited by Harold Bloom; it is not discussed in Bloom's edited volume in the Modern Critical Views series. Stephen Caldwell Wright's edited volume on Brooks contains no index, but passing references to the poem can be found on the following pages in that work: 20, 24, 33, 36, 76, 77, 87, 98, and 102.

2. The rhyme scheme and some other formal aspects of the poem are discussed by D. H. Melhem (108-14).

3. Park tends to avoid discussing the meaning of stanza seven at any great length, as does Carol F. Bender. Melhem does discuss it (111-13), but I must confess that much of her discussion strikes me as highly speculative and unconvincing.

Works Cited

Bender, Carol F. "'The *Chicago Defender* Sends a Man to Little Rock.'" *Master-plots II: Poetry Series Supplement*. Vol. 7. Ed. John Wilson and Philip K. Jason. Pasadena, CA: Salem, 1998. 2731-33.

Bloom, Harold, ed. *Gwendolyn Brooks*. Bloom's Biocritiques. Philadelphia: Chelsea House, 2005.

_____, ed. *Gwendolyn Brooks*. Bloom's Modern Critical Views. Philadelphia: Chelsea House, 2000.

Brooks, Gwendolyn. *The World of Gwendolyn Brooks*. New York: Harper & Row, 1971.

Dubrow, Heather. "Guess Who's Coming to Dinner: Reinterpreting Formalism and the Country House Poem." *Modern Language Quarterly* 61.1 (2000): 59-77.

Eagleton, Terry. *How to Read a Poem*. Malden, MA: Blackwell, 2007.

Lentricchia, Frank, and Andrew DuBois, eds. *Close Reading: The Reader*. Durham, NC: Duke University Press, 2003.

Melhem, D. H. *Gwendolyn Brooks: Poetry and the Heroic Voice*. Lexington: University Press of Kentucky, 1987.

Park, Sue S. "A Study in Tension: Gwendolyn Brooks's 'The *Chicago Defender* Sends a Man to Little Rock.'" *Black American Literature Forum* 11.1 (1977): 32-34.

Vendler, Helen. "Reading a Poem." *Field Work: Sites in Literary and Cultural Studies*. Ed. Marjorie Garber, Paul B. Franklin, and Rebecca L. Walkowitz. New York: Routledge, 1996. 128-36.

Wright, Stephen Caldwell, ed. *On Gwendolyn Brooks: Reliant Contemplation*. Ann Arbor: University of Michigan Press, 1996.

CRITICAL READINGS

Sweet Bombs

> Danielle Chapman investigates *The Essential Gwendolyn Brooks*, a posthumous collection of Brooks's poetry, and raises questions as to why Brooks is not as appealing to the American literary canon as are other poets. Brooks's early poems are objective and show the influence of T. S. Eliot's major modernist poems, Chapman writes, comparing Eliot's repressed and shy Prufrock to Brooks's ridiculously dressed and pathetic ladies' man, Satin-Legs Smith. She analyzes "The Anniad," "The Children of the Poor," and "Gay Chaps at the Bar" and notes that by the time Brooks reached middle age, Eliot's solitariness was no longer helping her engage readers, and so she discarded it. The poems in *The Bean Eaters* are far more emotional in their tone. As time progressed, Brooks became more involved in the Black Arts movement aesthetic, and her poems engaged the reader with more open, direct, and sustained pathos.   — M.R.M.

The Essential Gwendolyn Brooks. Ed. by Elizabeth Alexander. Library of America. $20.00.

What's better, love or respect? Most poets would probably prefer a combination of the two—that is, worship—by friends, family, the public, and all people in all generations to come. Yet when we consider some of the most respected poets in recent memory—Eliot, Larkin, Lowell, Plath—we come across people who seem to have squandered whatever affection came their way in their lifetimes. Maybe it takes a ruthless, calculating egoist to transform pain into product. Or maybe all the attention that the neophyte clamors for feels suffocating to the full-grown artist. After all, love is a reciprocal relation: the poet who garners it must love those who love her back, and that requires the sort of compromise that can be lethal to art. So what do we do with a poet who was generous to her community, faithful to her family, and loved by everyone; who, only six years after her death, has libraries, schools, parks, institutes, conferences, scholarships, and prizes too numerous to list named after her; who is called "Mama" by the young writers whom she supported? How do we account for, and do justice to, her talent?

The answer of anthologists thus far, which the Library of America has endorsed with this vividly-colored, classy, but *tiny* volume of Gwendolyn Brooks's poems, introduced and edited by Elizabeth Alexander, has been to respectfully—but not very enthusiastically—canonize her. This might not seem like such a shabby fate if Brooks hadn't dreamed of taking her place among the Greats since she was a preteen; if this book didn't succeed *Blacks*, the starkly-titled, barely-edited tome of Brooks's complete works put out by Third World Press in 1987; and if it didn't come at a time when Robert Lowell (born in 1917, the same year as she) has just been charioted into immortality with a twelve-hundred-page doorstop of collected poems from FSG and a ticker-tape parade of critical articles. Reading through *The Essential Gwendolyn Brooks*, one finds poems that are often as formally impressive as Lowell's, while usually more directly relevant to the issues of the time, and generally more nutritive to one's humanity. They are not, however, nearly as personally revealing, which may account for why they haven't gotten the serious attention they deserve.

Despite coming of age with the Confessionals, and despite the politics she espoused later in life (which helped to set the stage for today's identity poetry), Brooks's own body of work is staunchly impersonal. This is her primary aesthetic tenet, and it is, I think, what has kept much of her work from being understood—partly because it places her under the influence of Eliot (whose prejudices have made him anathema to many of Brooks's fans), and partly because it forces us to reckon with her as a serious, and therefore problematic, artist rather than revelling in a love-fest or giving her the token nod that political correctness bestows on "historical black writers."

It's not so hard to imagine the witch's brew that Eliot's ruined cities, his haunted melodies drifting down from windows, and his nerve-damaged, impotent Europhiles might have stirred up in the imagination of a lonely, bookish Chicago South Sider like Brooks. A shy girl, without the "brass" or "sass" of others in the neighborhood, she preferred holing up in her room and practicing pentameter to going to dance parties. She kept meticulous notebooks in which she laid out incredibly determined writing goals and composed verses that showed an obsessive formal sense. In Eliot, Brooks would have found the pure, selfish stuff of poetry, the thoughts and music of the interior life removed from other people, suspended from one's obligations to family, friends, community.

In "kitchenette building" Brooks responds to Eliot's prophetic melancholia with both envy and reproach. The poem seems to practically lift its opening lines—"We are things of dry hours and the involuntary plan,/ Grayed in and gray"—from *The Waste Land*, but these ruminations are quickly crowded out by the clamor of everyday life on the South Side:

> We wonder. But not well! Not for a minute!
> Since Number Five is out of the bathroom now,
> We think of lukewarm water, hope to get in it.

Brooks felt the world with a consuming emotional intensity and, like most poets, she resented the world of practical concerns, which she shows to be exacerbated by poverty. Eliot's robust pathos and unapologetic despair probably felt particularly seductive to a young woman who had always been told by her mother, the strict but loving Keziah, that she would grow up to be "the *lady* Paul Laurence Dunbar," and who likely already felt the heavy mantle of Responsibility To The Race coming down on her shoulders. Yet there's a note of proud and playful sanity in the rhymed ending of "kitchenette building," which acknowledges the silliness of getting too carried away with one's poeticism. One senses that Eliot's trances irritated Brooks even as they enamored her, ripening the antagonism.

And she *was* antagonistic. Stubbornness, one might say, was the defining feature of her temperament, and it was no ordinary stubbornness, but a staunch Baptist brand inherited from her mother. While she possessed stylistic nerve, which can be seen in the flourishes of tone and diction, the neologisms, the inversions—the "dim dears," "livingest chits," and "chocolate companions had she"—that add flair to the poems, Brooks wasn't really willing to take on all that much. Her poetic foundation was narrower—and more home-grown—than Eliot's. In addition to Dunbar and Langston Hughes, the two iconic black writers of the time, she'd absorbed the popular poetry of folk music and the Blues: the hard-stopped, end-rhymed rhythms of hymns and the darkly humorous melodrama of ballads, meant to be bawled or belted rather than sung. It was an insistently American poetry: poetry of passion and bad luck, sustained poverty, and the common-sense religion and gallows humor that remedy it.

As a foundation for her own work, this meant that Brooks could *handle* suffering and sin (particularly that of an American shade) in a way that the neurasthenic Eliot couldn't: though she saw her characters' faults clearly, she was able to laugh at them, even to delight in them, whereas Eliot could only respond to human imperfection with despair. Brooks's was not a spiritual but a practical morality: it concerned itself with people rather than theory or heightened states of consciousness. While this meant that she didn't often attain the prophetic brilliance of Eliot's best poems, it also meant that she was able to portray the vibrancy and comedy of life, qualities which she surely found lacking in much of his work.

It's a particular Eliot—the lolling, amused Eliot who feasts on swollen images and revels in all that is vividly corrupt, the Eliot of "The Love Song of J. Alfred Prufrock," "Portrait of a Lady," and parts of *The Waste Land*—that Brooks responded to most. In "The Sundays of Satin-Legs Smith" she invents the ultimate anti-Prufrock. The poem takes us through a day in the life of a flagrant peacock of a hustler, a man who dresses in "wonder-suits in yellow and in wine,/ Sarcastic green and zebra-striped cobalt. . . . Ballooning pants that taper off to ends/Scheduled to choke precisely." Though in places the mock-allusions to Eliot can feel heavy ("Let us proceed. Let us inspect, together . . . the innards of this closet"), this meditation shows Brooks taking the sort of license that no pious imitator would dare:

> His lady alters as to leg and eye,
> Thickness and height, such minor points as these,
> From Sunday to Sunday. But no matter what
> Her name or body positively she's
> In Queen Lace stockings with ambitious heels
> That strain to kiss the calves, and vivid shoes
> Frontless and backless, Chinese fingernails,
> Earrings, three layers of lipstick, intense hat
> Dripping with the most voluble of veils.
> Her affable extremes are like sweet bombs
> About him, whom no middle grace or good
> Could gratify.

The impersonal, conversational purity that Brooks attained in lines like these is unmatched by anyone in her generation; the only poet who does this as well is Eliot. And in some ways she surpasses him, for, in her pure delight in Satin-Legs, she enables the character to come alive and exist independently of her own interests, her pathos, herself. This was something that Eliot—for all his talk of escaping his personality—could never completely do.

Some people will complain that it's useless to compare these two poets without analyzing the imbalance of power, literary and otherwise, that existed between them. Yet nothing that has come after Brooks in the way of criticism—and Multicultural theory in particular—seems adequate to describe the confidence and acuity with which she renders the lives of her black characters, from the "old oaken waiter" in "*I Love Those Little Booths at Benvenuti's*" who amusedly endures a group of silly white patrons who come to the South Side to observe "tropical truths/ About this—dusky folk, so clamourous!" to the lady in "at the hairdresser's" (not included in the LOA book) who says:

> Gimme an upsweep, Minnie,
> With humpteen baby curls.
> Bout time I got some glamour.
> I'll show them girls.

Brooks felt no need to explain, justify, or translate her characters' attitudes. This blitheness was criticized from opposite viewpoints: white critics often condescended to the poems' "charming depiction of Negro life" or criticized them for being "too specialized" and therefore "not universal." Meanwhile, some black critics found Brooks too passive in light of the injustices that surrounded her. But time has proven that the poems are no double-decker bus tour of the ghetto: if her Bronzevillians were just specimens in a curiosity shop, they would have shriveled up by now, but they still arrest us with their individual demands to be seen and heard.

Annie Allen (1949) christened Brooks as "the first Negro to win the Pulitzer," a title which would haunt her the rest of her life. It also doomed her, at the dawn of Confessionalism, to be called a Modernist. This conclusion was based mostly on the centerpiece poem "The Anniad," which, as Henry Taylor has observed, is a "technical tour de force: 301 lines in forty-three seven-line stanzas, employing thirty different rhyme schemes, a compelling meter (trochaic tetrameter catalectic) and a diction that is elaborate, dense, and compressed." The poem is a grand dirge of doomed love, alternately swooning with feeling and gnarling itself into encoded language-bits. The naïve Annie goes through many moods of ecstasy and devastation, and the poem, despite several incomprehensible moments, eventually propels itself toward a beautifully sober ending, which strips Annie of all romantic notions and leaves her alone, "Kissing in her kitchenette/ the minuets of memory."

It's a stunning display, and it shows how much Brooks had internalized the Modernist dictums of allusion and compression. Yet Brooks admitted that this poem was autobiographical, and indeed it (as well as "Notes from the Childhood and the Girlhood," which precedes it) is full of self-enamored trifles. Strangely, it's here, where we feel Brooks straining hardest for Modernist credentials, that she is at her most unpleasantly personal. To her credit, she responded more genuinely to the singular influence of Eliot than to the Modernist movement as a whole.

While "The Anniad" is the most obvious manifestation of Brooks's ambition, in many ways it is less mature and less distinctive (both in style and in subject matter) than her earlier work. You get the sense that the world-wise (and wise-assed) teenager who had inwardly rebuked Eliot's excesses had been overcome by lust for those same excesses. But "The Anniad" was more of an expiation of Brooks's Modernist pretensions than a declaration of them. By this time Brooks had two small children at home, and the kitchenette felt smaller than ever: under such pressure it wouldn't be long before the old practical morality kicked in.

"People with no children can be hard/ Attain a mail of ice and insolence," she writes in a breakthrough of directness in "The Children of the Poor," the sonnet series at the end of *Annie Allen*. "And shall I prime my children, pray, to pray?" she asks, taking no pains to disguise her skepticism. In another poem she gives aggressive advice for dealing with prejudice: "First fight. Then fiddle." Like her early sonnet sequence "Gay Chaps at the Bar," these sonnets become too abstract in parts, yet one has to admire the vanquishing clarity, the fierce pragmatism, that grounds them all. Most important, maybe, is the way they set the stage for Cousin Vit, the irrepressible subject of the last sonnet in this series, who breaks through all the Modernist grey matter like a specter who's heard it's time for Mardi Gras:

Carried her unprotesting out the door.
Kicked back the casket-stand. But it can't hold her,
That stuff and satin aiming to enfold her,
The lid's contrition nor the bolts before.
Oh oh. Too much. Too much. Even now, surmise,
She rises in the sunshine. There she goes,
Back to the bars she knew and the repose
In love rooms and the things in people's eyes.
Too vital and too squeaking. Must emerge.
Even now she does the snake-hips with a hiss,
Slops the bad wine across her shantung, talks
Of pregnancy, guitars and bridgework, walks
In parks or alleys, comes haply on the verge
Of happiness, haply hysterics. Is.

Once again we have Brooks's imagination at its purest, with its wryly comic details and its effortless blend of conversational clarity and sonic precision—evoking Eliot, even as she joyously scandalizes him.

There's a certain point at which Eliot stops being an influence one can respond to and dematerializes into a vapor one breathes. I'm in awe of the brilliantly complex, disembodied voice of his late poems, yet I'm often vexed by the feeling that they aren't entirely real, or even entirely human. Apparently his deliberate eradication of personality had worked; he'd hollowed out his own particular quirks and pains and made room for the breath of God. "The more perfect the artist, the more completely separate in him will be the man who suffers and the mind which creates," Eliot wrote. Perhaps, but what about the artist whose sufferings are inflicted rather than savored? What about the violence that can't be compartmentalized, that assaults you every time you look out the window?

By middle age Brooks was not only a wife and mother but a pillar of the community—one which was in deep pain and immediate strife. If Eliot's exalted melancholy had seemed attractive to her as an adolescent, by now it was utterly impractical, even decadent. *The Bean Eaters*, which many white critics of the time called "too social," is full of defiant, bitter poems portraying despicably arrogant, racist white people. Often the rage results in flat characters who commit their misdeeds in the grim monotone of pulp fiction. However, in these poems more than in any others, Brooks gets at the corrosive evil of racism and the particular suffering that it creates. The stand-out here is "The Lovers of the Poor," a lambasting depiction of "The Ladies from the Ladies' Betterment League," whom we follow into a South Side housing project where their half-hearted hopes of doing good collapse under their horror at the scene:

> But it's all so bad! and entirely too much for them.
> The stench; the urine, cabbage, and dead beans,
> Dead porridges of assorted dusty grains,
> The old smoke, *heavy* diapers, and, they're told,
> something called chitterlings.
> . . . .
> Nothing is sturdy, nothing is majestic,
> There is no quiet drama, no rubbed glaze, no
> Unkillable infirmity of such
> A tasteful turn as lately they have left,
> Glencoe, Lake Forest, and to which their cars
> Must presently restore them. When they're done
> With dullards and distortions of this fistic
> Patience of the poor and put-upon.

These ladies may be stereotypes, yet the speaker imagines their prejudice with the sort of faceted specificity that can only come from deep and varied personal experience (indeed Brooks had encountered such women from many angles: as a maid on the North Side, as an eager student of poetry, and later as the "pet" of Chicago literary society). It doesn't matter whether a "universal" truth about rich, white women is revealed here; what the poem conveys in its irreducible lines is the impossibility—perhaps even the amorality—of an impersonal aesthetic in circumstances as offensive as those in which Brooks found herself in America in 1960. The despair of racial injustice has eaten into the language of this poem, which scathes the reader with its electrifying combination of intelligence and sarcasm.

In 1967 Brooks attended the Black Writers' Conference at Fisk University in Nashville, an event which marked the ascendance of the Black Arts movement. While Brooks felt herself "coldly respected" by the young, hip crowd, it was clear that Amiri Baraka—and his incendiary politics—was the main attraction, and the way forward. From then on, much of what Brooks wrote would be influenced by her revelation at Fisk, her ensuing embrace of a more radical black consciousness, and—not least—an artistic rivalry with Baraka and his followers. Her ironic view of the world and her formal leanings would be deep-sixed as she attempted a full overhaul of her style, which she now self-consciously felt to be "too white."

There's a smattering of work from this period that starkly and powerfully symbolizes the violence that Brooks was wreaking on her own poetry in order to make it match her newfound purposes. "The Second Sermon on the Warpland" blends revolutionary conviction with prophetic intensity into lines of pure apocalyptic fury, hissing on the page like the yanked-out fuses of a hard-wired poetic temperament:

> The time
> cracks into furious flower. Lifts its face
> all unashamed. And sways in wicked grace.

There are also many occasional poems, such as her tributes to Medgar Evers and Malcolm X, that offer startling snapshots of American history. However, there is much schlocky debris scattered around the scorching insights of Brooks's late work as well, often within the same poems.

The most striking difference from the early work is not the politics, but how simultaneously personal and public Brooks's work became. She was writing poems that were meant to be heard, felt, and loved *immediately*. Often it feels as if the self—that vain, pandering child-star that lives inside every poet, whom Brooks admirably repressed for most of her career—has risen up with a vengeance, demanding to be heard and adored. Too often these poems are padded with the applause-ready line; too often they wallow in sentimentality; too often they sound like Keziah's daughter—a woman who'd once called herself "impossibly prim"—basking in the admiration of cats cooler than she. To hear a poet as temperamentally prone to rigor and precision as Brooks adopting the hip languor used by Haki Madhubuti and Sonia Sanchez screams mid-life crisis.

In human terms, Brooks's sudden abandon, her ability to love her community and to fight for it, feels like a triumph. No one should begrudge her the affection and popularity she enjoyed late in life, and no one should dismiss the effect of her activism on real-life events. Yet there was a trade-off: Brooks abandoned her discipline in order to be beloved and successful; as a result, very little of that love or success found its way into her own distinctive idiom. One can't help but rue the portraits of fiery clarity that Brooks might have created if she'd expressed her newly radicalized beliefs in the clear, conversational form that she'd spent her whole life mastering.

Alexander leaves out the long late poem "In the Mecca," supposedly for the sake of length, though she has written in her book *The Black Interior* that she was disturbed by the poem's bleak view of the poet as an ineffectual agent for social change. "In the Mecca" is missed here, as it shows that Brooks's ambition to write great poetry was still intact in 1968, even if it was thwarted by her newfound desire to be immediately relevant. What's more befuddling is that "In the Mecca" has been left out to make room for selections from *Beckonings* (1975), *The Near-Johannesburg Boy* (1986), *Children Coming Home* (1991), and *In Montgomery and Other Poems* (2003). These cutesy, maudlin poems, about which Brooks herself felt deeply ambivalent, often read more like postcards from Grandma than the last dispatches of a great poet as she approached death.

The inclusion of Brooks's latest poems here is emblematic of the double bind that her work finds itself in now that she has died. On one hand, she's so loved in her community that editors can't perform the critical culling of her work that is necessary for the longevity of any poet's reputation. (*Blacks*, for instance, included her novel *Maud Martha*, which provides an unflattering backdrop to the poems.) On the other hand, this single tribute by the LOA—coming in the midst of the critical silence that has followed her death—is a reminder that Brooks is in the process of being shelved away, if not forgotten. By granting her "fair representation" but no fanfare and no debate, the literary establishment is quietly consigning her to the realm of "minor poetry."

A book like *The Essential Gwendolyn Brooks* can't make the statement that needs to be made: Gwendolyn Brooks is as important to twentieth-century American poetry as Robert Lowell. While Lowell met the times—and rebelled against Eliot—with the spectacle of his mad, egomaniacal charm, Brooks hunkered down and used Eliot's tradition of impersonality to portray the troubles and the joys of survival in black America. Her best poems offer a curative, not only to the narcissistic gloom that we've inherited from the Confessionals, but to Eliot's overaestheticized visions of social life. That Brooks's purposes were so different from Eliot's only strengthens the connection. It shows the vitality of true poetic inspiration, how it can cut across time, temperament, race, and even the motives of its own practitioners.

From *Poetry* 189, no. 1 (October 2006): 54-64. Copyright © 2006 by Danielle Chapman. Reprinted by permission of Danielle Chapman.

The Satisfactions of What's Difficult in Gwendolyn Brooks's Poetry_____

Brooke Kenton Horvath

Brooke Kenton Horvath provides a brief look at modernism before moving into a discussion of the delicate balance between Brooks's use of modernism and her larger objective to present racial issues in "Do Not Be Afraid of No," a poem in *Annie Allen*. Horvath argues that the "No" in the title and developed in the body of the poem represents a collective black refusal to act out or be a stereotype or to accept the status quo. It is a strong affirmation of freedom.— M.R.M.

Gwendolyn Brooks has been both praised and condemned for her often mandarin style. Thus David Littlejohn, writing in 1966, could acknowledge her craft—"she exercises, customarily," he wrote, "a greater degree of artistic control than any other American Negro writer"—but not, finally, the results of that craftsmanship. "In many of her early poems," Littlejohn felt,

> Mrs. Brooks appears only to pretend to talk of things and of people; her real love is words. The inlay work of words, the *precieux* sonics, the lapidary insets of jeweled images (like those of Gerard Manley Hopkins) can, in excess, squeeze out life and impact altogether, and all but give the lie to the passions professed in the verbs.[1]

For other critics, the real bone of contention has been the fact that, despite her efforts to forge a black aesthetic, Brooks has practiced a poetics indebted as much to T. S. Eliot as to Langston Hughes (though brought to bear on black subject matter). This white style/black content debate can be heard clearly in Houston A. Baker's *Singers of Daybreak*: "Mrs. Brooks," says Baker, "writes tense, complex, rhythmic verse that contains the metaphysical complexities of John Donne and the word magic of Apollinaire, Pound, and Eliot." Yet this style is em-

ployed "to explicate the condition of the black American trapped behind a veil that separates him from the white world. What one seems to
have is 'white' style and 'black' content—two warring ideals in one
dark body."[2]

Both of these issues are complex. Behind the former—the emotional effectiveness of the poet's meticulous "inlay work of words"—
lies in part the vexed question of modernism, which under the aegis of
T. S. Eliot has been responsible, according to Christopher Clausen, for
"the decline in the American poetic audience" and "the disappearance
of poetry as a major cultural force."[3] Behind the latter—the problem
of a "proper" aesthetic for a poet wrestling with an artistic double
consciousness—stands the still-troubled assessment of, say, Phillis
Wheatley and Paul Laurence Dunbar as well as more recent poets as diverse as Melvin Tolson and the Armageddon school of the Sixties.[4] In
the pages that follow, I would like to add to this discussion of the ap-
propriateness of Brooks's "tense, complex" early style as it relates to
black concerns and, more centrally here, as it does or does not justify
itself at its most elliptical *apart* from racial considerations. I intend to
do this by examining in some detail one poem notable initially for its
opacity: "'Do Not Be Afraid of No,'" which constitutes section nine of
the "Notes from the Childhood and the Girlhood" sequence in *Annie
Allen*, Brooks's Pulitzer Prize-winning collection of 1949.[5]

A succinct example of Brooks's complexity at its most revealing/
concealing, "'Do Not Be Afraid of No'" has received little close attention. Those critics who have commented upon the poem do so only
briefly and with the intention of explaining its problematic place
within the larger work of which it is a part. Thus, Charles Israel suggests that the poem reveals some of the "moral and ethical lessons
of Annie's youth"; D. H. Melhem offers two paragraphs arguing that
the poem constitutes "Annie's motto," her refusal "to emulate her
mother's submission"; and Harry B. Shaw reads the poem as equating
"the high life with death" and admonishing Annie not to choose prosti-
tution as the only alternative to "the death of no life," a reading that

finds parallels between "'Do Not Be Afraid of No'" and other poems such as "Gang Girls" and "Big Bessie Throws Her Son into the Street."[6] If none of these readings confronts fully the interpretive difficulties introduced by the poem's appearance as part of *Annie Allen*— for instance, determining who is offering Annie this advice (the answer will affect one's assessment of the wisdom of that advice and its impact upon Annie) or establishing the connection between the advice offered in the poem's opening lines and the remainder of the poem (for surely the response to this initial advice cannot be credited to even the most precocious young girl, as the poet's use of the third-person pronoun indicates)—this is not the greatest cause for disappointment.[7] Rather, what one feels most is the lack of any extended analysis of the poem that would account not only for its "meaning" but also for the poet's stylistic choices and for the relation of both message and style to Brooks's concerns as a black female poet. I suggest that such a close reading reveals a style not merely justified by the poem's content but essential if readers are to *experience* (rather than simply be told) the truth the poem embodies.

"'Do Not Be Afraid of No'" begins straightforwardly enough by reiterating the advice of its title in two lines enclosed by quotation marks and concluded by a colon, which suggests that what follows will be a gloss upon this advice, the development of an argument in support of this thesis.

> "Do not be afraid of no,
> Who has so far so very far to go"

"Do not be afraid [to say] no" seems simple advice; indeed, now that "just say no" has become the lamest sort of response to social problems, Brooks's opening lines may seem not so much simple as simpleminded (they will prove to be neither). But certain problems arise even here: Who is speaking and to whom? Are these lines something the poet has been told or read (hence the quotation marks)? One can of course fall back upon the response that these lines are spoken by someone to Annie (although I don't find this wholly clarifying for reasons such as those sketched above), but here I am suggesting that for "Annie" one might—for the duration of the poem—substitute "any young (black) girl" or, more generally, "anyone"—and here it is useful to recall George Kent's observation that in *Annie Allen* one advantage of the poetic form is to "move experiences immediately into symbols broader than the person serving as subject."[8] But further, to whom or what does the "who" of line two refer: to "no," its grammatical antecedent (in which case, why "who" instead of "which"?), or to the addressee—Annie aside, the choices would seem to be the poem's readers, self-reflexively the poet, or some unknown third party—who has "so far so very far to go"? And "to go" where? In life? One can be no more precise than that for now. These questions, however, are only mildly vexing because one presumes they will be answered (they won't be) in language similarly direct (it won't be but will tend toward greater confusion before somewhat clarifying itself). Stanza two acknowledges that saying "no" is never easy:

> New caution to occur
> To one whose inner scream set her to cede, for
> softer lapping and smooth fur!

As noted above, the opening lines appear in quotation marks possibly to suggest they contain received wisdom the perspicacity of which the poet intends to ponder. For one thing, she knows that saying "yes" means reaching agreement, solving a problem, accepting a plan, a truth, a life mate: "yes" is at least superficially positive, resolves that often unsettling uncertainty and probable antagonism "no" involves; "no" leaves one in suspense, in suspension, dissatisfied, perhaps closed off from comforts and companions. To say "no" to something is not, after all, necessarily to say "yes" to something else.

But through stanza two (and beyond), what exactly is at issue remains terribly amorphous. The reader, aware of who has written the poem and the historical circumstances surrounding its composition, might conclude that Brooks has something racial to denounce but is couching that denunciation in self-protectively cryptic language. But what? Is the poem an example of what Gary Smith has labelled Brooks's "remarkably consistent" identification of "white racism and its pervasive socioeconomic effects" on the black community?[9] If so, how so? Or perhaps the poem is not primarily racial but speaks of some political, economic, or ideological crisis on the international scene? Or perhaps this is a prototypical instance of confessional poetry that speaks of larger concerns only as they impinge upon the private psyche?

If Clara Claiborne Park is correct in reading *Annie Allen* as "a varied and inventive sequence of poems evoking a poor black woman's progress from exquisite illusion to the recognition of a harder yet more satisfying reality," and if one recalls Brooks's early poetic successes (encouraged by a mother who "intended her to be 'the *lady* Paul Laurence Dunbar'") within the white world of poetry and subsequent break in the late Sixties with that world in favor of poetry intent on speaking to African Americans of their concerns and in their language, then the poem might well be read as offering an elliptical rejection of poetic success in white literary terms (as either the black T. S. Eliot or the "lady" Paul Laurence Dunbar).[10] Such a reading is possible, but without seeking extratextual aid one cannot say "yes" to any of these possibilities—and so the poem is already teaching the reader the wisdom of the provisional "no."

At any rate, the advice of stanza one is a "new caution" to one predisposed to saying "yes," a new word of warning whose wisdom has occurred to the poet. The "she" of line four may refer to Everywoman, but the advice is pertinent to anyone—that is, to all of us—whose heart cries out to accede, to surrender by conceding and so avoid unpleasantness and secure comfort, that "softer lapping and smooth fur!" This last phrase is a wonderfully odd and unexpected evocation of pseudo-desiderata that, in conjunction with "set her to cede" (which recalls the cliché "gone to seed"), suggests that "yes" buys the reader something that leaves her less than human. And here one recalls John Updike's remark that "a person who has what he wants"—or thinks he has—"ceases to be a person," is "just an animal with clothes on," as Brooks's images of lapping and fur imply.[11] But perhaps at this point the poem now seems more feminist than racial, the combination of the feminine pronoun and the sensual, vaguely sexual imagery suggesting that women ought not sell out by acquiescing to marriage or a subordinate position in a relationship—although this is, obviously, as conjectural as those racial/political/autobiographical concerns hypothesized earlier. Whatever surrender is to be avoided, the exclamation point registers the poet's shock that such capitulation could even be considered for the tawdry prizes it would win one.

Stanzas three and four analyze and thereby judge the kind of person who could so easily acquiesce as well as the shortsightedness of such a maneuver:

> Whose esoteric need
> Was merely to avoid the nettle, to not-bleed.

> Stupid, like a street
> That beats into a dead end and dies there, with nothing left
> to reprimand or meet.

Such an individual's need is "esoteric," not in the sense of being understandable only to a few (the poet has implicitly—through her avoidance of greater specificity—acknowledged the universality of the desire to avoid pain and to seek pleasure) but in the sense of being "difficult to understand," of being "not publicly disclosed."[12] To seek merely to "not-bleed," to sell one's birthright for a mess of ease, *is* finally difficult to fathom and rarely the reason offered publicly to explain one's ceding. For instance, to return (for illustrative purposes only) to the possibility of the poem offering us a feminist commentary upon marriage: a bride's "I do" does not normally confess to a desire "merely to avoid the nettle" but rather professes acceptance of a noble calling, honorable commitments.

However, as the reader moves into stanza four, "yes" becomes more than demeaning; it is also "stupid": a dead end where one dies. The "no" that typically may seem pure denial now becomes by contrast the means of opening one to possibility, of keeping one in motion and alive in a world where, yes, there still exists the chance of severe censure but also of further experiences to encounter, to undergo (for the experience "no" makes possible never loses here its sense of trial). And beyond the multiple apposite senses of "meet," one may also recall that "repri-mand" derives from *reprimere*, "to repress": in death those fears "yes" repressed will indeed be at an end. In the context of the poem, "yes" be-comes a denial of life, "no" implicitly its affirmation. Brooks is here advocating an invigorating sort of denial not unlike that "No! in thun-der" Melville spoke of and which Leslie Fiedler has argued underlies all first-rate literature.[13] For now, the redefinition of "yes" and "no" these lines are effecting is perhaps best suggested by reference to Mel-ville's famous letter to Hawthorne in which he observes that "All men who say *yes*, lie; and all men who say *no*,—why, they are in the happy condition of judicious, unincumbered travellers in Europe; they cross the frontiers into Eternity with nothing but a carpetbag—that is to say Ego. Whereas those *yes*-gentry, they travel with heaps of baggage, and damn them! they will never get through the Custom House."[14] But again, if the reader is unwilling to assent to these remarks, she is learn-ing Brooks's lesson.

Stanzas five and six elaborate and complicate the yea-sayer's in-creasingly dismal situation through images and syntax themselves in-creasingly elaborate and complex.

And like a candle fixed
Against dismay and countershine of mixed

Wild moon and sun. And like
A flying furniture, or bird with lattice wing; or gaunt thing, a-stammer
down nightmare neon peopled with condor, hawk, and shrike.

These lines are difficult to negotiate in part because the key to under-standing Brooks's symbolic candle is buried—like the implications of "yes," whose consequences now seem a nightmare deferred—midway through a grammatical fragment (the poem's third so far, each hinting at the level of sentence structure at the incompleteness of the yes-man or yes-woman, at his or her inability to entertain a complete thought on what consent signifies). The key is "wild" and is underscored by the "flying furniture" of line twelve: in the face of present reality, "yes" is no more than a candle in the wild winds of dismay that will send one's (domestic) ease flying like tables and chairs in a tornado.

Stanza six's imagery is apocalyptic ("countershine of mixed // Wild moon and sun"), Bosch-like ("A flying furniture, or bird with lattice wing," this last a hopeless image of impossible flight), and violent with the predatory horror of nightmarish phantasm. At this point in the poem, the reader has been sucked deep into the maelstrom of the once-benign "yes." The language has reached fever pitch with its invoca-tion of a neon-lit landscape "peopled" by condor, hawk, and shrike (also known, tellingly, as the butcherbird) across which "stammers" a "gaunt *thing*"—perhaps the yes-victim, perhaps her assassin.

So that the point will not be lost, the poet recapitulates bluntly in stanza seven. Earlier, such a direct, unambiguous assertion could have passed as so much lame rhetoric, but now it strides forth as stark sum-mation:

To say yes is to die
A lot or a little. The dead wear capably their wry

Enameled emblems. They smell.
But that and that they do not altogether yell is all that we know well.

The reader has heard before—in the final line of stanza two—the exasperated sarcasm that reappears with "a little." This modifier is neither a crumb thrown to one's desire for mitigation nor a means of toning down the poem's rhetorical frenzy. Rather, it implies that yes-people have but a small transition to make from nominal living to quiet, smelly death, a condition they wear "capably," their headstones no doubt bearing affirmative "enameled" (protective possibly, but probably merely decorative) "emblems."

The case against "yes" complete, the poem moves explicitly into its advocacy of "no":

It is brave to be involved,
To be not fearful to be unresolved.

Her new wish was to smile
When answers took no airships, walked a while.

Nay-saying, as observed before, is not to be perceived as resolution, as a negative means (otherwise similar to "yes") of closing the books. It is instead a way of bravely remaining "involved" while vitally "unresolved." "No" engenders life and keeps that life in conceivably uncomfortable but nonetheless healthy motion. Although the specific concerns being addressed remain undefined even at poem's end, its final lines suggest that those answers to which allegiance may one day be pledged *will* come, but they must be worked for and may be some time in arriving (they walk; they do not fly). This hope, this promise of resolution has, one notices, been present throughout the poem. In line two, for instance, the reader realizes that "so very far" was actually not a feeble attempt to intensify the initial "so far"; rather, "so far" was qualifying "so very far" in the sense of "at the moment." Thus the sense of line two is not primarily that "no" has "very very far to go" but that, although it does have a long way to go, every day, every line, will find "no" closer to its goal. And after all, the poem is written in rhyming couplets manifesting consonance (a correspondence of sound implying agreement, harmony, accord), although line lengths and rhythm vary wildly, postponing for varying lengths of time that consonance (a consonance most readily apparent in those most regular couplets devoted to the virtues of "no"). Here, then, at the level of sound, rhythm, and structure, the poem bodies forth its message that agreement will come (though necessarily delayed) but must not be sought prematurely or expected as a matter of (strict metrical) course.

The poem's final images are clear and positive, sparkling with hope, cheer, courage, and newness (just as they introduce a new tone into the poem). They also highlight what should be obvious by now: "no" is safer than "yes," just as walking is (whatever airlines may say) safer than flying (with the walking nay-sayer contrasted with the dead yea-sayer and dead-end streets where motion comes to an end, while the airships, associated with the yea-sayer's wish for trouble-free rapid transit, recall the flying furniture of the poem's horrific sixth stanza).

The complexity of "'Do Not Be Afraid of No'" is, then, aesthetically justified because the poem teaches at every level of itself the need to remain actively engaged (as one must be involved with it) yet wary of reaching closure (as one must be when confronted by a poem that refuses too quickly to relinquish its meaning). No image easily elicits the reader's consent, which must anyway await one's understanding of each part in relation to the whole, just as one must assess any extra-textual consent in relation to its effect on one's life as a whole. Similarly, the poem's terribly precise vagueness is likewise justified insofar as it leaves the poem open to speak to anyone confronted by any situation where a preemptive assent seems the path of least resistance (a message as intensely relevant for blacks in 1949 as it ever was before or after this date). Just as does Brooks's famous sonnet "First fight. Then fiddle," "'Do Not Be Afraid of No'" places stylistic resistance at the center of her message concerning the need for resistance at the social/political level. And if "'Do Not Be Afraid of No'" is still worlds away from the directness of, say, "We Real Cool," Brooks might be seen in this early poem to be considering already that stylistic maneuver Park discovers in the much later "In the Mecca" (1968), wherein the critic finds Brooks "los[ing] faith in the kind of music she had loved and was so well qualified to sing" but which "blacks now found unusable."[15]

At the poem's end, as I have noted, whatever it was—social issue, personal concern, aesthetic challenge—that planted the seed of the poem in Brooks's mind ("set her to cede") remains as indefinite as it was when we began. We can ask, Does she wish to urge "no" upon blacks too willing to accept token adjustments of the status quo? Or does she desire to tell women not to surrender their dreams too easily? Or to tell readers not to dismiss her work too quickly? Does she wish to say "no" to a poetic style already proving itself unsatisfactory? All would be provocative messages—and Brooks allows us to entertain each of them—but I see no special textual support for any of them.

"'Do Not Be Afraid of No'" works hard at keeping the reader involved with it by making her feel she has not yet fully gotten into it, leaving open a multiplicity of interpretive possibilities by neither sanctioning nor precluding any of them. And if this assessment is accurate, the poem reveals as well the wisdom of Brooks's strategy as the vehicle for black (social/political) content, for she knows, as do we all, that America will, alas, always provide situations demanding rejection but tempting us to acquiesce either because we grow exhausted and resigned or because the carrot on the stick is lusciously attractive. And beyond the circumference of these concerns, and to return to Melville by way of Fiedler, Brooks knows the aesthetic correctness of the "no! in thunder," a denial not circumscribed completely by events of the moment any more than "'Do Not Be Afraid of No'" is delimited by its appearance originally as part of *Annie Allen*. As the engaged, topical poetry of the early Nikki Giovanni or of Don L. Lee (Haki Madhubuti) suggests, the easy "no"—to racism, poverty, whatever—can make finally for limited art.[16] Alternatively, "'Do Not Be Afraid of No'"— which might now be seen working metapoetically—offers instead a timeless "no," a "no" applicable in any circumstance that tempts anyone with the desire to acquiesce. Thus, Brooks offers a poem that is both timely and timeless, which is, after all, one definition of a classic.

Indeed, logically, no ready consent to the poem's message is possible even after lengthy explication, for to say "yes" to "'Do Not Be Afraid of No'" is to imply one has possibly misread it. On the other hand, to say "no" to the poem is, willy-nilly, to act upon the poem's advice, hence to concur with the wisdom of that advice, suggesting once again that the lesson has been lost upon one. In this logical conundrum the reader is left, nettled by interpretive possibilities no gloss can smooth but that serve to keep the game and so the poem alive. The poem's difficulties are, in this sense, both its content and its style, which is as it should be, for such are the ends, and the satisfactions, of Gwendolyn Brooks's craft.

Notes

1. *Black on White: A Critical Survey of Writing by American Negroes* (1966; rpt. New York: Viking-Compass, 1969), pp. 89, 90.

2. *Singers of Daybreak: Studies in Black American Literature* (Washington: Howard Univ. Press, 1974), p. 43.

3. "The Decline of Anglo-American Poetry," *Virginia Quarterly*, 54 (1978), 74.

4. Other issues are equally at stake, issues extending beyond poetry proper and suggested by remarks such as Littlejohn's contention that Brooks is "far more a poet than a Negro," p. 89, and Dan Jaffe's observation that "the label 'black poetry' cheapens the achievement of Gwendolyn Brooks" ("Gwendolyn Brooks: An Appreciation

from the White Suburbs," in *The Black American Writer*, ed. C. W. E. Bigsby [DeLand: Everett/Edwards, 1969], II, 92). On Brooks's poetics and her desire to produce work espousing a black aesthetic, see Norris B. Clark, "Gwendolyn Brooks and a Black Aesthetic," in *A Life Distilled: Gwendolyn Brooks, Her Poetry and Fiction*, ed. Maria K. Mootry and Gary Smith (Urbana: Univ. of Illinois Press, 1987), pp. 81-99; and Clara Claiborne Park, "First Fight, Then Fiddle," *The Nation*, 26 September 1987, pp. 308-12. For Brooks's comments on this matter, see Martha H. Brown and Marilyn Zorn, "GLR Interview: Gwendolyn Brooks," *Great Lakes Review*, 6, No. 1 (1979), 48-55.

5. *Annie Allen* (New York: Harper, 1949), pp. 12-13.

6. Charles Israel, "Gwendolyn Brooks," in *American Poets Since World War II, Part 1: A-K* (*Dictionary of Literary Biography, Vol. 5*), ed. Donald J. Greiner (Detroit: Gale, 1980), p, 101; D. H. Melhem, *Gwendolyn Brooks: Poetry and the Heroic Voice* (Lexington: Univ. Press of Kentucky, 1987), p. 60; and Harry B. Shaw, *Gwendolyn Brooks* (Boston: Twayne, 1980), pp. 71-72, 108-09.

7. As a "note" on Annie's childhood and girlhood, "'Do Not Be Afraid of No'" is not alone in hearing a puzzling relation to the sequence and to the hook as a whole: cf. "'Pygmies Are Pygmies Still, Though Percht on Alps,'" *Annie Allen*, p. 14.

8. "Gwendolyn Brooks' Poetic Realism: A Developmental Survey," in *Black Women Writers (1950-1980): A Crucial Evaluation*, ed. Mari Evans (New York: Doubleday, 1984), p. 92. Kent's observation is echoed elsewhere: see Blyden Jackson and Louis D. Rubin, Jr., *Black Poetry in America* (Baton Rouge: Louisiana State Univ. Press, 1974), pp. 81-85; Jackson and Rubin argue, with particular reference to *Annie Allen*, that Brooks's method is constantly to subordinate matters of sex or race to universal insights.

9. "Gwendolyn Brooks's *A Street in Bronzeville*, the Harlem Renaissance and the Mythologies of Black Women," *MELUS*, 10, No. 3 (1983), 45.

10. Park, "Fight First, Then Fiddle," p. 308.

11. "One Big Interview," in *Picked-Up Pieces* (Greenwich, Conn.: Fawcett, 1975), p. 485.

12. *American Heritage Dictionary*, New College Ed., 1979.

13. On the reasons why both "yes" and the easy "no" make for poor art, see Leslie Fiedler, "No! In Thunder," in *No! In Thunder* (Boston: Beacon, 1960), pp. 1-18.

14. Letter to Nathaniel Hawthorne, 16 (?) April 1851, in *The Portable Melville*, ed. Jay Leyda (New York: Viking, 1952), p. 428.

15. "Fight First, Then Fiddle," pp. 311, 310.

16. This assessment is admittedly a matter of personal taste. Brooks herself is clearly—and particularly after 1967—not averse to writing just such poetry, as *In the Mecca* and critical favorites such as "We Real Cool" indicate. Again, I would direct the interested reader to Park, Clark, and Brown and Zorn.

Double Consciousness, Modernism, and Womanist Themes in Gwendolyn Brooks's "The Anniad"

A. Yemisi Jimoh

A. Yemisi Jimoh explains briefly the interplay of literary theory, history, and psychology in Brooks's epic poem. Jimoh investigates ties to Emily Dickinson and the mock-epic and heroic choices Brooks makes for "The Anniad." In addition, Jimoh reviews W. E. B. Du Bois's history and names psychological and philosophical writers who may have influenced Du Bois. She addresses how Du Bois's definition of "double consciousness" distinguishes itself from William James's and Hegel's definitions. She uses Houston A. Baker's definition of black modernism as a "deformation of mastery" and a "mastery of form" to conclude that Brooks's "The Anniad" accomplishes only the "mastery of form." In the final section, Jimoh discusses the feminist angle of "The Anniad." At the poem's heart are Annie Allen, the protagonist, and her relationship with her black male lover, "tan man." She concludes that both Annie and "tan man" are tragic because both are at war with themselves; both try to assimilate to a worldview that negates their right to romance, or true love for each other, and to self-affirmation.   — M.R.M.

Double consciousness in African American literature is the phenomenon whereby a text simultaneously responds to two conflicting definitions of African American identity: a prevailing and debilitating European American definition as well as a more self-determined African American definition. This literary definition of double consciousness parallels Du Bois's description of psycho-philosophical double consciousness in *The Souls of Black Folk*. In Gwendolyn Brooks's "The Anniad" such double consciousness is perceptible in her poem's many subtle yet searing lines which reveal a prevailing astigmatism concerning race as well as gender in the United States. Gwendolyn

Brooks's Janus-like poem—with its simultaneous focus on both gender and race—depicts some of the effects that an emerging media culture has had on standards of beauty among African American women, who often present a contrast to the definitions of beauty that are pervasive in the United States. Through this poet's use of double consciousness in "The Anniad," readers perceive that Brooks is acutely aware of the urban, black Chicago that shapes her aesthetic as well as the prevailing culture in the United States that could shape her success as a poet.

While my discussion does not contribute to the notion (nor do I insist on such regularity) that Brooks's content is incompatible with her form, I do find that the combined impetus of this poet's response to a segregated 1940s black Chicago as well as a segregated artistic and publishing milieu in the United States contributes to a tenuously poised, yet successfully meshed, content and form in "The Anniad." Both the content and the form strain against being silenced, in this poetic struggle against double consciousness. The form strains to contain the content which it must convey, as Brooks often subtly voices her sexual, gender, and racial topics in oblique images, allusions, and equivocal sexual word play that veil the plenitude that is barely contained in the margins of her form—the mock-epic.

Specific instances of Brooks's slant or indirect poetics include veiled allusions to writers whose artistry she appreciates, yet, who—at the time—were not regarded favorably or had lost value in the dominant cultural setting. Brooks opens "The Anniad" with a poet's nod to Paul Laurence Dunbar[1] and his novel *The Sport of the Gods* when she refers to Annie as a young girl "Whom the higher gods forgot,/ Whom the lower gods berate." Other agnatic poetic echoes in "The Anniad" include lines from Langston Hughes and Countee Cullen, especially Brooks's apt image of black women in relation to their hair: "Then emotionally aware/ Of the black and boisterous hair,/ Taming all that anger down." Hughes presents a similar idea concerning black hair in his 1947 poem "Trumpet Player": "Has his head of vibrant hair/ Tamed down" (Hughes 338). This image also occurs in Cullen's 1925 poem "Heritage": "Crowned with dark rebellious hair" (Cullen 247). In all three poets the idea of black people's hair collects images of "rebellion," and in the later poems by Hughes and Brooks this sense of revolt is "tamed." In both male poets, however, the emotional *angst* about hair that angers Annie does not exist for Hughes's trumpet player and Cullen's Jesus. These poets, in fact bring positive connotations to their references to hair, connotations which are not present for Brooks's Annie. This character's negative perception of hair, however, along with other gender-limiting issues are subtly critiqued in this poem.

In terms of her poetic style as well as in her uses of irony as a means through which she presents resistance to traditional gender roles, Brooks suggests enatic[2] poetic echoes of Emily Dickinson's technique. Dickinson's poetic includes images of the secreted or concealed female poet, transformations of traditional form, punctuation, and line rhythms, and her depiction of male-female relations in—often ironic— divine or royal terms. This last stylistic quality is particularly apparent in lines from "The Anniad" such as "No dominion is defied" (100) as well as in Brooks's use of words and phrases such as diadem, sovereign, godhead, celestial, devotee, "nun of crimson ruses" (101) and other terms which recall Dickinson's uses of noble and heaven-focused language in her poems: "None suspect me of the crown,/ For I wear the 'Thorns' til *Sunset*—/ Then—My diadem put on" (704-05); or "And now we roam in Sovereign Woods" (369); as well as "Title divine—is mine! . . ./ Royal—all but the Crown!" (487). Also, in terms of technique, Brooks illustrates Annie's sovereignty over a dissipated tan man in Dickinsonian fashion with unusual uses of uppercase letters in "Slide a bone beneath Her head,/ Kiss Her eyes so rash and red."[3] Finally, Dickinson's intriguing funeral poem, "I felt a funeral, in my Brain" (128), seems to resonate in the section of "The Anniad" in which Brooks presents tan man's funeral: "In the indignant dark there ride/ Roughnesses and spiny things . . ./ Cyclone concentration reels./ Harried sods dilate, divide,/ Suck her sorrowfully inside" (109).

Brooks suggests that Annie—while at tan man's funeral—feels a burial in her brain, her own mental or psychic live burial—which, of course, is quite different from the metaphysical mood that Dickinson establishes in her poem.

Brooks's style and form in this poem indicate her ability to conform to dominant ideas about art—ideas which she illustrates with concepts, experiences, and critiques that resonate from the poem as a marginalized black female voice in tense relations with the dominant culture. Gloria Hull in "A Note on the Poetic Technique of Gwendolyn Brooks" characterizes this poet's style in the following terms: "quaint and unusual diction," "imperative tone," "verbal economy," "slyly satirical humor," "quaint colloquial tone" (281-84). In "The Anniad," then, this poet's Janus-like and double conscious responses to artistic hegemony add to her themes of race and gender, and this results in her artistic rendering of Gloria Wade-Gayles's term "triple jeopardy" (218), which refers to the race, gender, and artistic restrictions that African American women writers encounter. Brooks's double-looking themes of race and gender in "The Anniad" portray a black woman's unsuccessful quest to make an image of herself that she can position comfortably within her world—a world which seeks to delimit her in both gendered and racial ways.

Brooks's setting is a post World War II America, in which the war contributes to Annie Allen's defeat, but the effect of the war on Annie's life is not the major, or at least not the only, theme of the poem. Brooks as a "Double-conscious sister in the veil" (Harper ix) expresses her major theme—the injurious effects of the cultural hegemony of the dominant society in the United States on marginal groups such as black people and women—beneath a safe tale which speaks of the effects of the havoc inflicted on the women to whom the World War II soldiers returned. In this poem Brooks employs images of devastation that depict Annie Allen's debilitating inability to achieve self-consciousness as a black woman—neither through art nor through domesticity as she perceives it. Brooks's own "mastery of form" and her elusive critiques and comments on it, as well as the events in the poem which show Annie Allen in constant contradiction with herself (because she is immersed in external definitions of gender roles and beauty), demonstrate the alienation of double consciousness in "The Anniad."

Houston Baker in *Modernism and the Harlem Renaissance* formulates the concepts "mastery of form" and "deformation of mastery." He designates "mastery of form" as a means through which black people established for themselves a literary voice. This voice, however, revises the socially produced minstrel distortions of black people and transforms them into art, a "Promethean cultural appropriation" in Baker's terms (33). For him mastery's signal text is Booker T. Washington's *Up From Slavery*. In addition to "mastery of form" Baker further defines a "specifically Afro-American" discursive practice in the literary modernism of black writers in the United States with his correspondent concept—the "deformation of mastery" (xiv). Deformation unmasks the minstrel and reveals the folk—that is, the "territory within their own vale/veil." That territory is claimed boldly. Thus, Baker's deformation describes the process by which black writers claim and assert their own modern literary voice (50-51). In Baker's formulation of deformation, Du Bois's definition of double consciousness in *The Souls of Black Folk* exemplifies Baker's strategy. Baker asserts that he does not view these terms in a determined opposition, yet "[a]ny instance of mastery of form is always suggestive of its correspondent and vice-versa" (99).

In "The Anniad" Brooks not only masters the dominant modernism she also employs mastery of form as she wears modernity's ventriloquist's mask—the 1940s mask of similarity that informs her "strateg[y] of attraction" (29). These strategies respond to the dominant culture's requirements that a black poet's voice must prove its worthiness by imitating an established modernist dominant model of art instead of demonstrating an established jim crow minstrel difference—which artistically conceals its coded subversion while ironically displaying its distorted difference. This modernist mastery of form—the ventriloquist's mask—is evident in Brooks's poetic technique and in her content. After, for instance, all of Annie's plots to gain love fail her, she turns to education and poetry: "Twists to Plato, Aeschylus,/ Seneca and Mimnermus,/ Pliny, Dionysius . . ." (106). Before, however, Brooks actually lists the subjects of Annie's classical education, the poet employs mastery of form and demonstrates her own depth of knowledge and positions herself within classical culture when she alludes to Plato in connection with Annie's crude imitation of paladins and their debauched parroting of her idealized notions of love while she is a prostitute (106). These men and this life for Annie are "copies of all her bright/ Copies." This sort of "mastery" is required of Brooks in order for her to draw to her poetry the attention of the dominant culture.

Mastery, indeed, not only is true of Brooks's poetic strategies but also is true in her portrayal of Annie. In "The Anniad" Brooks depicts Annie's educational and literary success as "Pirouettes to pleasant shrill/ Appoggiatura with a skill" (106). Annie here performs a properly refined dance in response to the comforting appreciation that her writing receives; she, apparently, does not have to jump jim crow if she renders a precise pirouette. Claudia Tate refers to this strategy as "literary hair-straightening" (*Black Women* 45). Additionally, Annie's music/ poetry only ornaments the dominant cultural practices; there is not a place at the center of the dominant culture for Annie's talent, not even for her poetry that replicates dominant strategies. Indeed many of the African American poetic cultural qualities in "The Anniad" are so cryptic that a number of the possibly culture-specific lines in this poem suggest many plausible readings—which might easily distract readers away from the subtle, yet serious social critique imbedded in this poem. When, for instance, Brooks describes tan man's other women as "bad honey," (104) the poet reaps the benefits of the African American vernacular meaning of "bad"—which evokes connotations of the righteous outlaw whose rebellion has value from the perspective of the oppressed; thus, her or his outlaw or "bad" behavior is good. Hortense Spillers notes that in the vernacular "bad" has "appropriated its antonym" (229). This African American meaning for the word "bad" combines with its general English meaning and creates the possibility for plural implications in this poem. The same plurality exists in Brooks's uses of the word "passing" (104). Again, the African American vernacular meaning for "passing" adds both ironic and plural meanings to the lines in "The Anniad" in which Brooks uses it: "Minus passing-magistrate,/ Minus passing-lofty light,/ Minus passing-stars for night" (104). Here Brooks suggests the concept of passing as the act of presenting oneself as a member of the dominant group by denying or ignoring one's connections to an oppressed group; she also suggests the general meaning of passing as a momentary encounter—just passing through.[4] For Brooks's Annie, it seems, innocence is lost. She no longer has in her life "passing"—either false or brief—(male) authority, artistic inspiration, and defining media images of beauty. These lines exemplify Brooks's coded vernacular in "The Anniad." As a poet she "conceal[s] and disguise[s]," yet respects her indigenous voice. Baker's deformation of mastery, then, is not present in "The Anniad," because of the muted black voice in this poem (Baker, *Modernism* 51).

W. E. B. Du Bois—Baker's noteworthy strategist of deformation—defines a basis for aspects of Brooks's poetic technique in his description of double consciousness. His use of this term seems most firmly based in Hegel's German idealism, which Du Bois revises and re-inscribes and by which means he explains the American paradox of some of the enslaved, the formerly enslaved, and their descendants in the United States. Du Bois raises the issue of a particularly African American consciousness and he situates the notion of this consciousness within the psycho-philosophical intellectual knowledge with which he was familiar: "One ever feels his two-ness—an American, a Negro: two souls, two thoughts, two unreconciled strivings; two warring ideals in one dark body, whose dogged strength alone keeps it from being torn asunder" (8-9).

According to Dickson Bruce, the concept of a double soul or consciousness is found not only in Du Bois but also in literary texts such as

Emerson's 1843 "The Transcendentalist," Goethe's *Faust*, Whittier's "Among the Hills," and George Eliot's "The Lifted Veil" (300). Bruce's discussion of Du Bois and double consciousness emphasizes the influence of Du Bois's Harvard professor William James. This influence, however, seems less viable than the effects of strong Hegelian inspiration acting in concert with a rapidly industrializing and fragmentary modern society—which produced a heightened sense of alienation in people—as well as with Du Bois's sense of the disjointed and disconnected antebellum lives of black people in the United States.

In William James's *The Principles of Psychology*, his descriptions of "double or alternating personality" include a spontaneous onset of memory lapses during which time the person engages in behavior which s/he attributes to an alternate personality of which no one else is familiar—including the original personality of the individual who is experiencing double consciousness (379). James's diagnosis of alternating personality, though, has become the standard way to discuss Du Bois's concept. James states that secondary personalities "are *always* abnormal and result from the splitting of what ought to be a single complete self into two parts, of which one lurks in the background whilst the other appears on the surface as the only self the man or woman has" (227). This schizoid effect of alternate personality does not correspond with Du Bois's double consciousness. In *W. E. B. Du Bois: Biography of a Race*, David Levering Lewis also questions "to what extent, if at all, the insights of James's *Principles of Psychology* were the source of Du Bois's own special insights into what he would describe as the double nature of African-American psyche" (96). Lewis, however, continues to discuss Du Bois's concept as if it were a Jamesian schizophrenic secondary consciousness lurking in the background. Lewis refers to double consciousness as "psychic subordination" that has the potential to become an asset when it no longer is an African American image of self "reflected from a white surface" (281). This reading of Du Bois's double consciousness has persisted over time and resulted in a number of counter-statements such as those in

Gerald Early's collection of essays *Lure and Loathing: Essays on Race, Identity, and the Ambivalence of Assimilation.*

Arnold Rampersad in his 1976 autobiography *The Art and Imagination of W. E. B. Du Bois* presents another perspective on Du Bois's reconceptualization of double consciousness. Rampersad discusses the distinctly parallel qualities of the "two warring ideals" that exist in an "American *world*" (8 [emphasis added]) that "Yields . . . [African Americans] no true self-consciousness." For Rampersad, *Souls* "affirms . . . [Du Bois's] faith in the strength of the African soul, against which that other powerful soul implanted by the white world wages constant war" (88). Gerald Early also recognizes the solidity of both poles of Du Bois's "two souls" and the error in too closely associating Du Bois's concept with James's. Early points out that with Du Boisian double consciousness people "consciously [know] the temptations of both" sides of their two souls, and they know "that both exist" (xxi). Du Bois was a student of and clearly influenced by William James, yet Du Bois also was a student at the University of Berlin when a major "Hegelian revival" took place (Adell 12).

In her book *Double-Consciousness/Double Bind*, Sandra Adell examines Du Boisian double consciousness as a Hegelian "consciousness containing a contradiction within itself" (18). Her position is that the major influence on Du Bois's concept are two forms of double consciousness described in Hegel's *Phenomenology of Spirit*. Hegel's philosophy of the formation of consciousness posits a self-consciousness that arises from a dialectic (within a triadic process) by which one becomes aware that one is separate from and differs from an/other. As a result of the tension and the reciprocal influence resulting from the interaction between each consciousness, both move beyond mere recognition of an other to a more developed consciousness than they previously had. Hegelian consciousness, then, is not developed *ex nihilo*. This process necessarily makes the initial formation of self-consciousness double, and any growth in consciousness, then, proceeds through the Hegelian triadic process. When, however, an other ("a being") does not provide a reciprocal acknowledgment of otherness—as in the master-slave relationship—the process of developing self-consciousness is impeded; thus, it actually is double consciousness, according to Adell, that Du Bois describes as being denied to black people—because for Hegel "consciousness, if it exists at all, is always double consciousness" (19).

A second form of Hegelian double consciousness that one can draw from Du Bois's term is the self-contradictory or in Hegelian terms the "unhappy consciousness." One way that this self division occurs is that an individual never receives any external acknowledgment of his or her selfhood, which Hegel's absolute idealism requires—the knowledge that one is not a cipher in the larger world. In the case of an "unhappy consciousness," an individual forms a compensating internal or self division, instead of establishing selfhood in tension with an other/different self. Internal division results in a "false self" as well as a "true self." This true self is identified with perfection while the false self is a distortion created out of one's lack of contrast with an external other (Copleston 185). It is on this point that I will make my final comments on the operations of double consciousness.

Jamesian readings of Du Bois's double consciousness often result in comments such as the following made by sociologist C. Eric Lincoln in his essay "The Du Boisian Dubiety and the American Dilemma: Two Levels of Lure and Loathing"; for him, double consciousness "implies self hatred." Because of ambiguous assertions in Du Bois's description of double consciousness, his term has produced this assessment in literary analyses as well as by other scholars. Lincoln says, however, that "people do not ordinarily hate themselves. . . . Self-loathing is a counter function to survival and to the will to survive." Hatred of one's group, according to Lincoln, "originates outside the group and is learned" (198). Yet, when one indeed reads closely Du Bois's description of double consciousness with Hegelian concepts in mind, this process of selfhood—that Du Bois posits—consists in two internal conflicting definitions of consciousness, a false or debilitating consciousness and a self-determined true consciousness—thus, Hegel's unhappy consciousness. Du Bois's description also suggests the lack of reciprocal acknowledgment of selfhood that precedes an unhappy consciousness. Du Bois is not specific, however, on the issue of which side of the two souls engages in "always looking at one's self through the eyes of others." I must conclude that it is in the false consciousness that this perception exists; this is a consciousness derived from an "American world" in which we find distorted images of black people that allow this world to refuse to acknowledge another self when it is in a black body.

My position on Du Boisian double consciousness is based in the evidence of Du Bois's Hegelian background and in the comments that precede his brief discussion of double consciousness. These comments refer, favorably, I believe, to folk beliefs that connect black people to root/spirit-knowledge or Du Bois's African American version of the absolute: "seventh son" of the seventh son—a folk reference to a person who is born lucky or with spiritual insight; being born with a "veil" (the membrane of the birth sac covering one's face)—also a folk sign of deep spiritual insight; and being "*gifted* with second sight" (8; emphasis added).[5]

Readers of "The Anniad" need not agree with Hegel's absolute idealism in order to understand Du Bois's appropriation of it and Brooks's execution of it in her poem. One also need not conclude, as Thomas Holt does, that African Americans "should celebrate" double consciousness as the "source of 'second-sight,'" nor need one agree that it is self hate. Clearly, though, Du Boisian double consciousness is the type of doubled awareness of self, the double consciousness, with which Brooks shapes the poetic techniques in "The Anniad."[6]

In form Brooks's "The Anniad" reflects her discovery of the literary Modernism of the United States. Her first exposure to the mainstream writers that shaped her era came from James Weldon Johnson who, after reading some poems a youthful Brooks sent him, suggested she "study carefully the works of the best modern poets—not to imitate them, but to help cultivate the highest possible standard of self-criticism" (qtd. in Mootry and Smith 166-67). Consequently, Brooks expanded her reading in Dunbar, Hughes, Dickinson, Milton, Shakespeare, Donne, and Spenser with Frost, Eliot, Cummings and Pound. Years later, in 1941, Brooks's poetry was influenced by Inez Stark, who had been a reader for the important national magazine *Poetry*. Stark encouraged Brooks's Modernism; her criticism influenced Brooks to strip her poetry to the bare essentials: "be careful not to list the obvious things. . . . Use them only to illustrate boredom and inanity." She further advised Brooks to cultivate a highly compressed style in which words merely suggest meanings or images and in which time and place are disrupted. Commenting on one of Brooks's poems, Stark says, "[d]ig at this until you have us see all the skeleton and no fat" (qtd. in Mootry and Smith 167). Such contracted, and seemingly impervious, poetry, lacking deictic aspects, results in Brooks's perfecting the style that shaped her own poetic practice. Many of these qualities—except imperviousness— persist in her poetry today. Still, "The Anniad" is far less perplexing than Eliot's landmark modernist poem *The Waste Land*.

Of additional interest, in terms of compression in "The Anniad," is the compression of form in this poem. Appearing to take seriously Eliot's advice concerning a poet's relationship to the past as defined in "Tradition and the Individual Talent," Brooks recalls the epic form in order to serve her modern poetic ends, and she depicts her times, not necessarily her unique self in this poem. Also, in light of the traditional function of an epic as a long verse narrative that in some way helps to shape a society or to form a nation, Brooks's choice of the epic form is fitting; the traditional breadth of such a poem, however, would fatigue the appreciation of many of this poet's contemporaries as well as today's readers of poetry. Thus, Brooks compresses her mock-epic into forty-three septets of terse, allusive, and compressed poetry. Perhaps, though, Brooks's use of language in "The Anniad" goes a bit beyond Eliot's concept of being immersed in the traditions and literature of the past. The language in this poem is often archaic and Latinate—though perhaps a reflection of the high reaching language of the epic tradition. Such language, however, is more reminiscent of the English Renaissance than the American modernism of Williams, Moore, and Stevens—which emphasized the use of colloquial language—or of international modernism which occasionally disrupted a colloquial voice with words or phrases from Provençal, Latin, or Greek—as in the case of Eliot and Pound.

In "The Anniad" Brooks uses archaic English phrases such as "doughty meanings die" (103), "helmets final doff" (103), and "bejeweled diadem" (102) as well as Latinate and French words such as "paradisiacal" (105) and "bijouterie" (106). It is in such language that Brooks conveys her satire in this mock-epic. Clearly, though, the poet's use of what seems to be over-reaching erudition in "The Anniad" evinces her "mastery of form." Baker states that mastery of form is a literary strategy associated with Harlem Renaissance writers' (Brooks's direct literary ancestors) expression of Modernism. Baker defines this strategy as a mocking minstrel perfection of European American literary models. Through mastery of form, African American writers create a space for their own voices. This space, simultaneously critiques European American models and speaks for itself (*Poetics* 15-24). For Brooks—at the time a young, black, female poet—mastery of form in "The Anniad" is satirical, thus a critique.[7] She presents a dazzling display of formal technique, which was required by the dominant society; in light, however, of Annie's defeat at the end of the poem, Brooks indicates that this dazzling art is false, gilded. This technique does not nurture Annie's aesthetic. To this end, in an interview with Hull and Gallagher, Brooks comments that *Annie Allen* is a book in which she did not "always have the best motives. I wanted to prove that I could write well" (32).

Brooks, further, demonstrates both epic tradition as well as the allusiveness of modernist poetry in her title, which plays on both Homer's and Virgil's titles.[8] Just as Virgil gives his Latin epic *The Aeneid* a Greek title, thereby situating his Latin poem within the epic tradition of his predecessor from the dominant culture—the Greek Homer—Brooks's title accomplishes the same end by recalling seminal Greek and Latin poetic texts from the ancient Western tradition which shapes the dominant culture in the United States. Brooks further writes her poem into the branch of ancient Greek and Latin tradition that exists in the United States when she employs Virgilian purposes in her modernist poem. Brooks demonstrates the poetic seriousness, beauty, and complexity of a culture that has limited currency in the contemporary cultural milieu.

Another important aspect of an epic poem is its hero or central character. Again, in this instance Brooks's modernity updates, but does not mock, her central character. In fact, Annie Allen, the central figure in "The Anniad," is characteristic of what Arthur Davis identifies as the "unheroic" in the writing of Gwendolyn Brooks. Likewise, Claudia Tate finds that such characters not only appear in Brooks's work but also represent a particular type of character that is present in the texts of other African American women writers: Pecola in Morrison's *The Bluest Eye*, Eva in Gayl Jones's *Eva's Man*, and Beau Willie in Shange's *For Colored Girls*, for example (xxiv). Unheroic characters, suggests Tate, are worthy subjects in the writing of black women because they exemplify the unjustly defeated in whose fall others can locate and avoid qualities that are likely to bring similar defeat on them (xxiv). It is perhaps the unheroic in Brooks's Annie Allen that prompts D. H. Melhem's perceptive assertion that "The Anniad" "is a mock heroic, more compassionate than critical or satirical" (62).

Again, if "The Anniad" is in any way satirical, that satire is conveyed through Brooks's mocking use of high reaching language and is not directed toward the poet's central character. When, for instance, Brooks refers to Annie's "lofty light," she uses this language in order to demonstrate the sharp contrast between Annie's real life circumstances, and her confused perceptions (104). Annie, then, is the object of an empathetic critique (not satire) because she accepts, without question, the very social ideas that destroy her. Thus, Brooks has chosen the words of this poem so that they resonate a plenitude of ideas associated with her motifs of idealized notions of love, the myth of

Americanism, and narrow concepts of beauty as well as other delimiting notions of the female. This poem illustrates the failure of these notions in the lives of Annie and tan man.

In "The Anniad" Brooks, clearly, satirizes the society that produces Annie. To that end, Brooks uses the language in her poem as well as Annie's dainty attitude as metaphors that signal artifice; both are gaudy ornaments covering the beauty and simplicity of the objects on which they have been placed: Annie and Brooks's poem. Brooks levels a subtle yet biting criticism at such ornamentation and at a society that encourages such artifice in its art and for its women. Language in this poem—when viewed as a satirical device—is purposely overdone to provide a mocking contrast in a poem written—during the post-war boom era in the United States—about a woman who is "physical and underfed" (99) and whose environment is described with oxymoronic contrasts such as "Pretty *tatters* blue and red,/ Buxom berries *beyond rot*" (99; emphasis added). Additionally, the demure and dainty role Annie accepts at the beginning of the poem is exposed at the end as a farce, when Annie has become "tweaked and twenty-four" and her "soft aesthetic is looted lean" (108). Annie, however, is not the object of Brooks's mocking; it is the ornament that is mocked because of its devastating effects.

The modernist, skeletal structure of "The Anniad" and its epic form confirm Brooks's immersion in the prevailing culture that sets poetic standards. Brooks recalls the epic tradition through her use of brisk lines, repetitions, and an episodic or imagistic structure instead of a smoothly connecting narrative. These aspects of the poem evoke the qualities of oral transmission even though "The Anniad" is a literary epic. Also, as in other epics, this work begins *in medias res*, has magical forces that aid the central character, has a serious tone and exalted diction, as well as battles and boasts. Yet, according to Melhem, Brooks forges a precise equilibrium when she encounters the challenging contrast that exists between "strict compression" of modernist poetry and the capacious qualities of the epic tradition (Melhem 63).

Brooks's themes in combination with her modernist diction, allusiveness, and lack of deictic aspects in "The Anniad" make it a double-voiced modernist poem. On the whole, then, Brooks combines modernist poetics, epic tradition, as well as black and womanist themes in "The Anniad."

Brooks also probes gender relations, which often are reinforced in the dominant media as well as in social discourse; and she critiques the prescriptive nature of those relations. One of the major gendered themes in "The Anniad" is black women—represented by Annie Allen—who are trapped in the beauty and gender role fictions of the dominant society in the United States. Mary Helen Washington defines this motif as the "intimidation of color," which she finds is a consistent issue in many African American women writers' works (xiv). Brooks also depicts Annie as unheroic, which in this instance, is this poet's transformation of epic heroism. Brooks critically employs both the unheroic as well as the "intimidation of color" in ways that exemplify her covert poetic move toward establishing a black female consciousness that is constructed as more self-defined than double. Through Brooks's themes in "The Anniad," she demonstrates that a black woman's belief in the dominant beauty and gender role fictions will cause her to suffer immensely—more than the typical white woman—because the image of womanhood and physical beauty that is projected by the dominant culture is unreal and almost unattainable (without tremendous physical alterations) for most black women. Brooks enjoins her readers to

> Think of thaumaturgic lass
> Looking in her looking glass
> At the unembroidered brown;
> Printing bastard roses there;
> Then emotionally aware
> Of the black and boisterous hair,
> Taming all that anger down.
> (100)

In this stanza Annie prepares herself to meet with "tan man." The blush she uses on her clear brown skin is an obvious aberration since her cheeks in no way lack color. Thus, the black—not blond—and "boisterous"—not straight—hair becomes an obvious symbol of her pretense as well as a symbol of the falsity of the prevailing beauty fictions. Despite the "bastard roses"[9] (100) Annie prints on her cheeks and the "taming" (100) to which she subjects her hair, she is still notably different from the fictitious image she emulates. Annie's misdirected conjuration is contrasted in this poem by the magic worked from the root or from within by the other women that tan man chooses.

Some of tan man's choices in women are dangerous; they will be the death of him. Unlike Annie, though, these other women are vibrant and alive within themselves. Perhaps more than anything else, tan man rejects the weak, spiritless, feigned attitude that Annie adopts. Yet there is no doubt that he also doesn't value her chocolate skin-color. Tan man's post-war women are "gold," "maple," and an indeterminate (probably Filipino) "gypsy." These women not only are lighter shades of brown than Annie but also are in possession of their own voices as well as their own methods of conjuration. The woman with the gold skin is a "shriek." She voices strongly stated opinions, and enchants tan man so that he is blind to her imperfections: "Hissing gauzes in her gaze,/ Coiling oil upon her ways." His "maple banshee" also is associated with spirit-work or preternatural knowledge, which she conveys through the sweet wailing of her powerful voice. Tan man, ostensibly, ignores her message or is oblivious to its importance. The final woman among tan man's "violent vinaigrettes" or "bad honey[s]" is his "gypsy moan." Her voice may not be articulated as clearly as the voices of the other women; her eyes may not be as open to the spirit-world as the eyes of the other women, or perhaps her eyes are shaped differently; but she still is associated with other-worldly—gypsy—knowledge and a voice of her own—instead of a received voice that she takes from an external source (104). These women speak for themselves; they are saucy flavoring, that enliven Annie's nearly wasted tan man.

Annie, nevertheless, undercuts her own worth in her relationship with tan man. "Sweet and chocolate" Annie is uncomfortable with the demure and coy attitude she believes society prescribes for women, but she decides to adopt this attitude anyway. Realistically, though, Annie is not an "icy jewel" (105) for tan man's "bejeweled diadem" (8). She is a woman who can "remark his feathers off" (108), but she feels compelled to tame herself, in the same way she tames the tumult of her hair. To complement her adopted attitude, Annie fantasizes about a man who is as unreal as the woman into which she attempts to make herself. She hopes tan man will be her paladin. Such a role for him or, in fact, any man is unrealistic. Yet Annie's romantic perceptions of the world do not allow her to see tan man in the context of the society in which they live. Through her narrator Brooks demonstrates that for Annie and tan man the myth of the United States that is perpetuated in the dominant society is as fictitious for them as Annie's idealized notions of love are for her.

In the opening stanzas of "The Anniad," Brooks employs oblique allusions that point to post-war patriotism as part of the myth of Americanism: freedom, democracy, opportunity. This myth is juxtaposed against Annie's idealized notions of love and is depicted as equally fantasy-laden. Brooks opens her second stanza with a double-focused line that points to Annie's illusions about romance in the first stanza and at the same time moves readers forward to the illusory splendor of a segregated United States: "What is ever and is not." Brooks uses oxymoronic contrasts of beauty and decay to describe Annie and to describe her relationship to the beacon of democracy in which she lives: "Pretty tatters blue and red." This image suggests a ragged flag in which Annie is wrapped or a dress in similar disrepair. The next two lines of "The Anniad" continue to develop this image. The fruited plains are dried-up and spoiled: "Buxom berries beyond rot." The blue skies are cloudy and the bright stars are not at their fullest brilliance. All of the patriotic images which refer to the United States as well as patriotic songs such as "America the Beautiful" are "Fairy-sweet of old guitars/ Littering the little head": old music[10] altered by pleasing illusions of change (99).

Tan man's relation to the promises of the United States is similarly exposed as false. Brooks depicts the war as "Surrealist and cynical," a nightmare of grotesque slaughter which—among black people—results in realistic disbelief in the sincerity of the promises that things will improve after the war (102). As a soldier, tan man's American dream of freedom is crushed. After the war, for example, the disappointment tan man experiences upon his return home causes him to see himself and Annie differently: "With his helmet's final doff/ Soldier lifts his power off" (103). Tan man can no longer live the fantasy of freedom and democracy, for which he fought in the war; and he can no longer pretend he can live according to the received concept of reality (the American Dream) in the United States either. This knowledge leads tan man not only into rejecting Annie but also into debasing himself. The patriotic fiction is a ruin for Annie and for tan man. Tan man does not find truly viable options to the false promises of the United States, so he is destroyed. And Annie does not abandon her equally destructive adherence to gender role and beauty fictions which obliterate her mind.

Brooks suffuses this poem with themes such as gender role and beauty fictions, Washington's "intimidation of color," Hull and her co-editors' spiritual activities of "root working, conjure, and midwifery," and Walker's woman as suppressed artist. This poet's elemental concern with gender-focused imagery that scholars now find collected around images of women, particularly black women's portrayal of black females in literature, illustrates her use of womanist social and literary concerns in "The Anniad." Hence, three motifs—black self-definition, the constrained artist, and womanist concerns—concatenate in this poem to allow readers a glimpse of what Gloria Wade-Gayles terms "the narrow space of race and the dark enclosure of sex" (21).

Brooks's "The Anniad" is the tale of Annie Allen, a plain brown "sweet and chocolate" woman with a plain name who lives in a fantasy world of "cinema mirage" (104) in which her desires over-reach reality. Her world is dream-like, a world of "fancying on the featherbed." Annie rests her head/thoughts on insubstantial dreams instead of the thoughts that Brooks will evoke in readers—thoughts for which she requests inspiration in her invocation of the muse.[11] Annie is described as a woman "Whom the higher gods forgot,/ Whom the lower gods berate" (99). Brooks begins her poem by informing readers that this "chocolate" woman is forgotten by whites ("higher gods") because she is a black woman and, because of her dark skin, is berated by ("lower gods") blacks.[12] This color motif in "The Anniad" indicates that the poem reflects both interracial and intraracial "exile rhythms," or the "desire for at-homeness in the universe of . . . [one's] native land" (Kent 84). Equally important is Brooks's subtle suggestion that Annie consciously and against her own disposition acquiesces in a socially imposed female silencing. Annie shows, for example, "gilt humility" (100) after losing her virginity to tan man. She pretends to swoon and feigns being overwhelmed by tan man's sexual prowess, so instead of expressing the "hot theopathy" (100) she feels during their encounter, she displays a "dusted demi-gloom," which is apparently consistent with the attitude that "respectable" women have toward sex.

Later, however, tan man returns from the war dismayed to find that he is still just another black man in the United States. He must now face "this white and greater chess" (103) of racism. Such a situation "baffles tan man" (103). He didn't expect to continue his overseas war games (fighting for freedom) when he returned. The benefits of being a World War II veteran, he learns, will not give him an equal position in society; he decides that "woman fits for recompense" (104). As for Annie Allen, tan man says, "Not that woman! (Not that room!/ Not that dusted demi-gloom!)" (104). So the respectable Annie who, when tan man went to war had retreated to a ". . . lowly room./ Which she makes a chapel of./ Where she genuflects to love" (101) is rejected by a newly aware and bitter "tan man." He chooses "Nothing limpid, nothing meek./ But a gorgeous and gold shriek," a "maple banshee," and a "sleek slit-eyed gypsy moan" (21-22). Clearly tan man is self destructive; he, thus, prefers each "random bacchanalian lass/ That his random passion has" (104) to Annie's feigned ornaments of coyness. Annie's "... paladin/ Which no woman ever had,/ Paradisiacal and sad" (99) is an example of her idealized and unreal concept of male and female gender roles. She, however, does get tan man, whom she loves and perhaps feels fortunate to have, but she loses him after his return from the war leaves him infirm and disillusioned.

Now that Annie's "set excess" (101) or unreal expectations have come tumbling down, Brooks shows that over time—through all of the seasons—and without tan man Annie attempts to adjust her perceptions—even though she desires palliation from tan man. Each season brings Annie a different disposition as well as varied insights into her situation. And perhaps each season also represents a different type of man. Annie's emotions in winter are frozen "icy jewels"; she experiences emotional stasis as she "Seeks for solaces in snow"—perhaps assuages tan man's rejection of her by taking a white lover. Brooks also seems to suggest that Annie's sadness, "Half-blue shadows," is not alleviated by the money that this lover provides: "blue and silver rime." His gestures, in fact, are cold and only freeze her emotions to a harder "crust."[13] Conversely, spring for Annie is pastoral, sprite-filled, and airy: "fluting spring," "Bubbles apple-green," "Pucks and cupids." In this more light-hearted season of her disposition Annie "Seeks for solaces in green," or consolation in younger men. Annie's "Hyacinthine devils"—in their association with conjure—parallel tan man's "Hissing" and "coiling" woman, his "banshee," as well as his "gypsy moan." When, however, summer arrives Annie has become more careful in her selection process, so she "Runs to summer gourmet fare." She finds that her love environment becomes "inert," and "summer hoots at solitaire." Autumn, however, seems to suit her most because "All gone papery and brown"; here Brooks indicates the thinness of Annie's character through her image of the papery, brown leaves. And Brooks's line "[a]ll's a falling falling down" evokes Annie's depressed emotional condition. Brooks may also suggest in this stanza that when Annie visits the park she is there among other lonely women on "respectable walks" (104-05). With this in mind and in her depressed mood, Annie desperately cries out for love from anyone saying, "'I am bedecked with love!'/ 'I am philanthropist!'/ 'Take such rubies as ye list.'" When Annie fails to get adoration from the preceding actions, she attempts to "find kisses pressed in books." Books and brief fame are, however, a "thin Hurrah" (106). So Annie wraps her fantasies around her children until a "Preshrunk and droll prodigal" tan man (107) returns. This time when a seriously dissipated tan man leaves, it is through death. Brooks depicts this last disappointment in romantic love as the catalyst that pushes Annie further into her dream world which "Suck[s] her sorrowfully inside" (109). Annie does not survive psychologically; this is the case even though, after tan man returns—and before his death—she has acquired enough self-respect to advise him that he has little to offer her because his age—"rust"—and infirmity—"cough"—can "scarcely re-launch/ That is dolesome and is dying"; this refers to tan man himself as well as their relationship (108). Nevertheless, after tan man is gone, Annie thinks back and remembers that she was no competition in the battles with his mistresses for his love. She realizes that even now the telephone's ring "hoists her stomach to the air," while surely his mistress "Who is starch or [the one] who is stone/ Washes coffee-cup and hair,/ Sweeps, determines what to wear" to tan man's funeral. Unable to bear her life after her fantasy fails, Annie retreats into liquor and the "minutes of memory" (109).

From the apartment and neighborhood bar of one conjure woman whose "culprit magics fade" (107), Gwendolyn Brooks in "The Anniad" deftly examines the insidious nature of prescribed beauty standards, the destruction racial prejudice engenders, and the emptiness in the "Pirouettes to pleasant shrill" (106) of constrained women artists who write against the grain of the dominant culture. Brooks's poem is a subtle critique presented through the poetry of indirection that results from a diminishing of double consciousness among black people who are beginning to reject the internalized negative definitions of themselves that evolve from the mainstream culture in the United States. As an African American, female poet in the 1940s, for Brooks to write a modernist mock-epic poem that ostensibly addresses the issue of postwar disappointment in love was clearly more acceptable than a direct comment on intraracial as well as interracial discrimination or on the cultural hegemony of the dominant society in the United States. Despite her constraints, Brooks's multiple themes emerge through the palimpsest of "The Anniad." In this poem Brooks examines and critiques the hegemony of the dominant society, and at the same time she critiques women's facile acceptance of mainstream notions about beauty and gender-roles. Brooks also validates the experiences of African American women who find themselves overwhelmed by these fictions, yet she subtly suggests that they abandon them.

From *MELUS* 23, no. 3 (Fall 1998): 167-186. Copyright © 1998 by *MELUS*. Reprinted by permission of *MELUS*.

Notes

1. See Mootry and Smith. Brooks's mother Keziah admired Dunbar's poetry and wanted her daughter to become the "Lady Dunbar" (8).
2. Ellison responds to Irving Howe's "Black Boys and Native Sons" in a series of essays titled "The World and the Jug" and "A Rejoinder," both reprinted under the first title in *Shadow and Act*. Ellison, in "The World and the Jug," explains his literary heritage as consisting in literary "relatives"—Langston Hughes and Richard Wright—and literary ancestors—Ernest Hemingway, T. S. Eliot, etc. (139-140). I make a similar distinction between Brooks and the Harlem Renaissance writers, Hughes and Cullen, and Brooks and Emily Dickinson.
3. See Emily Dickinson's #306 for a poem on a similar topic; another interesting note in terms of Brooks's use of uppercase and lowercase letters is her consistent lack of specific uses of Annie's name in this poem and her use of lowercase letters in reference to tan man. Both practices seem to inscribe in this poem the relative position each character holds in relation to the dominant society in the United States.
4. See a similar discussion in Stanford (301n).
5. Paul Gilroy in his book *The Black Atlantic* also positions Du Bois's double consciousness within the context of his experiences at the University of Berlin and in the

context of German idealism. Gilroy, in response to Cornel West's observations on double consciousness in West's *The American Evasion of Philosophy*, also focuses on Du Bois's references to profound vision. I, however, in contrast to Gilroy, locate Du Bois's references to sight in *The Souls* within an African American cultural construct which has shaped and is shaped by Du Bois's revision of Hegel.

6. On double consciousness in Brooks see also Norris B. Clark (87) and Houston Baker (21, 28), both in Mootry and Smith.

7. See George Kent's discussion of high-reaching language in African American texts. For Kent such language allows the poet to demonstrate a high level of intellectual and creative virtuosity based in European-American poetic traditions. Such poetic overreaching is an expression of "exile rhythms," or poetic expressions of "a people experiencing resistance to their desire for at-homeness in the universe of their native land, and seeking firm establishment of it [at-homeness]" (84).

8. Brooks says that she had in mind Homer's *Iliad*—see Spillers "Gwendolyn the Terrible" (226); see Tate's "Anger so Flat: Gwendolyn Brooks's *Annie Allen*." Tate discusses Brooks's title in relation to Homer; see also Stanford's "An Epic with a Difference." She discusses Brooks's title as an echo of Virgil's *Aeneid*.

9. Stanford associates Annie's makeup with artistry and beauty, instead of misdirected conjure as I do. This critic also associates Annie's "bastard roses" with an inappropriate romantic context to which Annie has no access (283) instead of the inappropriate beauty context that I discuss in this paper. (Of course, Annie's media exposure illustrates that she has had as much access as any other 1940s woman had to such fictions. Perhaps, though, she had fewer opportunities to act them out); see also Tate's "Anger So Flat." Tate reads "bastard roses" as a figure for "ill conceived daydreams." Tate also reads Annie's "boisterous hair" as a figure of the flattened "vitality of . . . Annie's internal life," yet she does not address the related issue of beauty fictions (148).

10. This may be a veiled allusion to integrated big band music, which reshaped earlier blues/jazz and was often referred to as "sweet."

11. See Stanford for a different reading of Annie and the featherbed (289). On the muses I am thinking of possible echoes of Homer's invocation in the *Odyssey* which begins with an apostrophe, requesting that the muse inspire the poet with the *story* of the brilliant Odysseus and in the Iliad which begins with an apostrophe to the muse, requesting that she inspire him with the *song* of Achilles' anger; also in Virgil's *Aeneid*, the poet *sings* of war and men at war. Interestingly, Brooks does not request a story, song, or music from her muse. She requests thought, which at the time was rarely acknowledged as something which black people possessed.

12. See Davis's "The Black-and-Tan Motif in the Poetry of Gwendolyn Brooks."

13. Spillers also suggests that Brooks hints that Annie has a white lover in the "Anniad" (231).

Works Cited

Adell, Sandra. *Double-Consciousness/Double Bind: Theoretical Issues in Twentieth-Century Black Literature*. Urbana: U of Illinois P, 1994.

Baker, Houston A., Jr. *Afro-American Poetics: Revisions of Harlem and the Black Aesthetic*. Madison: U of Wisconsin P, 1988.

_____. *Modernism and the Harlem Renaissance*. Chicago: U of Chicago P, 1987.

Brooks, Gwendolyn. *Blacks*. Chicago: The David Company, 1987.

Copleston, Frederick. *A History of Philosophy*. Vol. 7. London: Search P, 1963.

Cullen, Countee. "Heritage." *Harlem Renaissance Reader*. Ed. David Levering Lewis. New York: Viking, 1994. PS153.N5 p. 67.

Davis, Arthur. "The Black-and-Tan Motif in the Poetry of Gwendolyn Brooks." *CLAJ* 6 (1962): 90-97.

Early, Gerald. *Lure and Loathing: Essays on Race, Identity, and the Ambivalence of Assimilation*. New York: Allen Lane-Penguin, 1993.

Eliot, T. S. *Selected Prose of T. S. Eliot*. Ed. Frank Kermode. New York: Harcourt, 1975.

Ellison, Ralph. *Shadow and Act*. 1953. New York: Random House, 1964.

Gilroy, Paul. *The Black Atlantic: Modernity and Double Consciousness*. Cambridge: Harvard, 1993.

Harper, Michael. "Madimba: Gwendolyn Brooks." *A Life Distilled: Gwendolyn Brooks, Her Poetry and Fiction*. Eds. Maria K. Mootry and Gary Smith. Urbana: U of Illinois P, 1987.

Holt, Thomas C. "The Political Uses of Alienation: W. E. B. Du Bois on Politics, Race, and Culture, 1903-1940." *American Quarterly* 42 (1990): 301-23.

Hughes, Langston. "Trumpet Player." *The Collected Poems of Langston Hughes*. Ed. Arnold Rampersad and David Roessel. New York: Knopf, 1994.

Hull, Gloria T. "A Note on the Poetic Technique of Gwendolyn Brooks." *CLAJ* 19 (1975): 280-85.

Hull, Gloria T., and Posey Gallagher. "Update on *Part One*: An Interview with Gwendolyn Brooks." *CLAJ* 21 (1977): 19-40.

Hull, Gloria T., Patricia Bell Scott, and Barbara Smith, eds. *All the Women Are White, All the Blacks Are Men, But Some of Us Are Brave: Black Women's Studies*. Old Westbury, NY: Feminist P, 1982.

James, William. *The Principles of Psychology*. Vol. 6. New York: Dover, 1890.

Kent, George. "Aesthetic Value in the Poetry of Gwendolyn Brooks." *Black American Literature and Humanism*. Ed. Baxter R. Miller. Lexington: UP of Kentucky, 1981.

Melhem, D. H. *Gwendolyn Brooks: Poetry and the Heroic Voice*. Lexington: UP of Kentucky, 1987.

Mootry, Maria K., and Gary Smith, eds. *A Life Distilled: Gwendolyn Brooks, Her Poetry and Fiction*. Urbana: U of Illinois P, 1987.

Spillers, Hortense. "Gwendolyn the Terrible: Propositions on Eleven Poems." *A Life Distilled: Gwendolyn Brooks, Her Poetry and Fiction*. Ed. Maria Mootry and Gary Smith. Urbana: U of Illinois P, 1987. 223-35.

Stanford, Ann Folwell. "An Epic with a Difference: Sexual Politics in Gwendolyn Brooks's 'The Anniad.'" *American Literature* 67 (1995): 283-301.

Tate, Claudia. "Anger So Flat: Gwendolyn Brooks's *Annie Allen.*" *A Life Distilled: Gwendolyn Brooks, Her Poetry and Fiction.* Eds. Maria Mootry and Gary Smith. Urbana: U of Illinois P, 1987. 140-52.

———, ed. *Black Women Writers at Work.* New York: Continuum, 1983.

Wade-Gayles, Gloria. *No Crystal Stair: Visions of Race and Sex in Black Women's Fiction.* New York: Pilgrim, 1984.

Walker, Alice. *In Search of Our Mothers' Gardens: Womanist Prose.* San Diego: Harcourt, 1979.

Washington, Mary Helen, ed. *Black-Eyed Susans: Classic Stories by and About Black Women.* Garden City, NY: Anchor, 1975.

Heralding the Clear Obscure:
Gwendolyn Brooks and Apostrophe_____

Lesley Wheeler

Lesley Wheeler discusses how Brooks's use of apostrophe in her lyric voice shows her consistent, logical, and progressive search for language that addresses the truth of black lives and experiences. In the process of writing lyrically and using apostrophe to draw the reader even closer into the world of the poem, Brooks does justice to her own experiences as an artist. Wheeler focuses her discussion on Brooks's artistic development, from her use of a modernist and objective tone in *Annie Allen* to her tonal shift toward revolutionary rhetoric in "The Sermon on the Warpland."   — M.R.M.

... Now the address must be to blacks; that shrieking into the steady and organized deafness of the white ear was frivolous—perilously innocent; was 'no count.' There were things to be said to black brothers and sisters and these things—annunciatory, curative, and inspiriting—were to be said forthwith, without frill, and without fear of the white presence.

—Gwendolyn Brooks, *A Capsule Course in Black Poetry Writing* (4)

As Brooks herself insists, the question of audience is of vital concern in her poetry, and not only after her famous change of heart at the 1967 Fisk University Black Writers' Conference. From *A Street in Bronzeville* through the more deliberately instrumental work of her maturity, Brooks's poetry enacts a tension between the lyric convention of isolate interiority and the poem's status as public speech. Brooks extends her lyric voice to animate and address an absent other, characterized variously in different poems and at different stages of her career. She utilizes many speakers, from the experienced mother of *Annie Allen* to the enigmatic proselytizers of her later "sermons," but whether she announces as a leader, cures as a mother, or inspirits as a preacher, her poetic mode is defined by apostrophe. She uses that most

lyric of devices to undermine one of the most pervasive, though argu-
able, assumptions about the post-Romantic lyric: its removal from politics. Brooks forces her version of the lyric to become a public forum,
to sustain the marks of and even participate in political struggle. However, from her earliest volumes onward but especially in her "Sermons
on the Warpland," which purport to advise from a position of authority
in the explicit context of race riots, her imperatives perplex as much as
illuminate.

In "Apostrophe, Animation, and Abortion," Barbara Johnson begins discussing Brooks in relation to the figure of apostrophe, which
she defines as "the direct address of an absent, dead, or inanimate being
by a first person speaker," specifically in terms of one of Brooks's early
and most famous poems, "the mother" (185). The "mother" of this
piece addresses aborted children; Johnson reads this situation as a reversal of the "primal apostrophe" that informs the entire history of the
lyric, a demand addressed to a mother by an infant, "which assures life
even as it inaugurates alienation" (198). Johnson notes that the Brooks
poem exists "*because* a child does not" (195), reminding us of the competition for some women writers between poetry and motherhood.
"The attempt to achieve a full elaboration of any other discursive position than that of a child" in poetry, psychoanalysis, or politics, is
fraught with difficulties, but, Johnson theorizes, might have enormous
impact in all three arenas (199).

In fact, Gwendolyn Brooks's lyrics often wield apostrophes; specifically, they most frequently apostrophize children or adults who, child-
like, need care, advice, or motivation. Brooks repeatedly writes as a
mother, addressing her readers as children in imperatives that reach out
of the private world of the lyric long before she asserts this expansion
as a political goal of her poetry. Although Brooks has been criticized
for apparently abandoning her compelling depictions of women's lives
in her early poetry, this rhetorical innovation remains as important (and
perhaps as feminist) as Johnson suggests. Brooks creates a powerful
kind of mother, a public actor, fusing her speech with that of a preacher

or prophet, articulating an unusually authoritative, distinctly female voice.

Further, Brooks's invocations are not apostrophes in the usual sense of a speaker's deflection of address away from her readers. A poetic opening like "Stand off, daughter of the dusk" (*Blacks* 137) surpasses overheard imperative; it also names, brings into being, her intended readers. In fact, in a 1949 review, J. Saunders Redding chastises Brooks for this same poem, which, he argues, excludes white audiences by its overly "special and particularized" subject (6). While the apostrophes Brooks employs inevitably circle backward to constitute her identity as a poet, mother, and/or minister, she primarily intends to influence her real audience. Thomas M. Greene writes that apostrophe, an address to the absent, constitutes one half of an invocation, which also includes "a summons to appear or make its influence felt in the invoker's experience" (495). Jonathan Culler, likewise, asserts that "to apostrophize is to will" (139). Through so vividly imagining and animating her readers, Brooks gradually constructs a poetic that demands active, collaborative audiences: in her work the binary of private and public which has so deeply shaped the lyric poem begins to dissolve.

Brooks's critics increasingly argue for such continuity in her work. Gwendolyn Brooks's own autobiographies, tellingly entitled *Report from Part One* and *Report from Part Two*, divide her career into two sections, a sort of Before and After separated by the Black Arts Movement. Some interviews with and essays on Gwendolyn Brooks duplicate this division, recounting her transformative experience at Fisk University, followed by her work with the Chicago teenage gang the Blackstone Rangers; although William H. Hansell locates three periods in her oeuvre, his essay and other important pieces by George Kent (1987) and Houston Baker emphasize the 1960s as a crucial hinge for Brooks. She encountered in that conference and, more crucially, in her mentorship of young poets a new kind of energy and pride in Black identity to which Brooks attributes a change in both her life and her writing. In the narrative usually told by anthology headnotes (see, for instance, *The Norton Anthology of Modern Poetry* or *The Harper American Literature*), Brooks moved from poetry in a mix of traditional forms (some European, some African-American) to work in open forms, from an integrationist philosophy to Black nationalism, from lyrics written for private reading to an oral orientation, drastically reconceiving her audience and intentions. Critics often quote the manifesto from the Appendix to the first *Report*:

> My aim, in my next future, is to write poems that will somehow successfully "call" (see Imamu Baraka's "SOS") all black people: black people in taverns, black people in alleys, black people in gutters, schools, offices, factories, prisons, the consulate; I wish to reach black people in pulpits, black people in mines, on farms, on thrones; *not* always to "teach"—I shall wish often to entertain, to illumine. My newish voice will not be an imitation of the contemporary young black voice, which I so admire, but an extending adaption of today's G. B. voice. (183)

Here Brooks seems on the one hand to announce a new orientation: she wishes that her writing might unify a black community. On the other hand, even within this proclamation, she signals the continuity between phases of her work: her "newish," not "new," voice will be an "extending adaption" of her current poetry, extending its dependence on apostrophe, adapting that address to a newly configured readership.

Brooks radically marked her commitment to this change in focal audience by cutting her tie to Harper and Row and, after 1971, only publishing at black presses. Some of Brooks's critics ally themselves with one Brooks or the other, arguing either that her early work transcends race or betrays her blackness, that her late work either fails aesthetically or finally breaks through its bondage to white forms. The most partisan are often poetic inheritors. Don L. Lee (Haki Madhubuti) naturally favors her post-1967 efforts, while Rita Dove and Marilyn Nelson Waniek lament the detrimental influence of the Black aesthetic on

Brooks's later work. Yet, to draw too dramatic a contrast between the early and later works is to misread them; as Brooks herself insists, although the world around her has changed, "I just continue to write about what confronts me" (*Report from Part One* 151). In an interview with Claudia Tate, Brooks points out the political nature of many of her early poems, arguing that "in 1945 I was saying what many of the young folks said in the sixties" (42). D. H. Melhem asserts, in fact, that "no facile demarcations exist" in Brooks's canon (2), supporting recent work by Kathryne V. Lindberg and Betsy Erkkila. Although she carefully explicates certain transformations in Brooks's work, Erkkila argues that "the simple opposition between early Euro-American and politically incorrect Brooks and later African-American and politically correct Brooks breaks down in any careful reading of her work" (201). Not only are there continuities in her rhetorical poses and her imagery, but in perpetually revising herself Brooks frequently alludes to and incorporates her earlier language in the later poetry.

One of these subtle shifts in Brooks's use of the lyric is that the maternal rhetorical position Brooks so frequently occupies in her early volumes becomes fused with the more public, sermonic voice that resonates throughout her later poetry. From *Annie Allen* to the "Sermons on the Warpland," however, the voice of the mother and its metaphoric extension into the voice of the minister enables her to investigate whether, or to what extent, the lyric has a social function. Her use of apostrophe, finally, takes the tradition of enclosed lyrics from which she emerges—especially the confine-conscious lyrics of previous American women poets, from Emily Dickinson onward—and stretches it, exploiting the lyric's public possibilities. Intriguingly, the poems that manifest this struggle have also been labeled her most "mandarin," suggesting, as Brooke Kenton Horvath notes, a link between stylistic and political resistance (213, 221).

* * *

With *Annie Allen*, her second book of poetry, Gwendolyn Brooks was the first African American to win the Pulitzer Prize (1950); yet, as Claudia Tate observes, it receives less critical attention than many of Brooks's other works (140). It seems less hopeful than *A Street in Bronzeville*, less determinedly political than *The Bean Eaters*, and may be the least accessible of Brooks's poetry, dense with word-play and formal experiment; Don L. Lee later singles it out as Brooks's work most obviously focused on "poetic style," and therefore at a white audience (84). More specifically, he laments "an overabundance of the special appeal to the world-runners" (86); Lee accurately notes the racial converse of Redding's remark that certain poems, by their manner of address, construct a readership that excludes him.

While this collection, a series detailing the life of its title character, plies a more cryptic style than other early Brooks, in the last third of this book Brooks makes an important move toward increased accessibility. She explicitly identifies the voice of the poet with the voice of the mother, in this case a mother of imperiled and lost progeny. *Annie Allen*, in fact, narrates this move toward the mature, mother's voice, a voice (in her poetic world) of leadership and authority. The volume consists of three sections, "Notes from the Childhood and the Girlhood," "The Anniad" and its appendix, and "The Womanhood." The first section shows the literal narrowness of Annie's life as well as the cramping of her will and imagination by her mother; the discipline of form demonstrated by Brooks duplicates the discipline of meek and obedient femininity imposed on Annie. "The Anniad" offers the mock-epic of Annie's failed marriage. In "The Womanhood" Brooks "writes beyond the ending" of heterosexual romance and announces the need for a new direction, which perhaps Brooks only fully finds twenty years later.[1]

All of the work from the first phase of Brooks's career speaks in uneasy dialogue with Anglo-American poetic tradition; *Annie Allen* grapples with some of its most powerful exemplars. "Notes from the Childhood and the Girlhood" consists mainly of light lyrics, especially in ballad stanzas, to set up Annie's expectations for a happy ending through marriage. Brooks writes none of these poems in the second person, except for the last piece in the sequence, "my own sweet good," Annie's quoted address to her future lover. "The Anniad" bows to the epic as it encompasses both a World War and the war between Annie and her husband, or Annie's fantasies and reality; "Appendix to the Anniad" searches further and ends up with "the sonnet-ballad," a love-lament, to tell the story of the failed marriage. In both of these subsections, body and appendix, Brooks addresses the reader: "The Anniad" begins, "Think of sweet and chocolate" (*Blacks* 99) and ends with parallel imperatives including "Think of tweaked and twenty-four" (109). Many of the sonnets and ballads in the last third of the book, "The Womanhood," direct love not at husbands or lovers but at children, and the whole volume ends on the seriousness of blank verse, addressing a deaf tradition personified as a group of resistant white men and finally asserting Annie's alienation from it and its forms. The collection continuously searches among the Anglo-American traditions of poetic expression for a form that will both hold what Annie's life has been, and direct her in her maturity. Her conclusion is that there are no "timely godmothers to guide us," that she can expect no admittance to any estate, but that she must innovate her own way forward.

Apostrophe offers a crucial tool for such pathfinding, especially in the prescient final poem of this volume. Untitled, it apostrophizes, in a form suggesting blank verse, "Men of careful turns, haters of forks in the road," demanding that they "Admit me to our mutual estate" (139). This voice, distinctly not maternal, does employ the second-person address and imperatives often associated with that pose. Brooks, as a poet, only barely still in the persona of Annie Allen, knocks on the doors of the Anglo-American tradition, demanding to be admitted to its "high" company. She genders her alienation first, comparing her previous relationship to this tradition to a woman loving but fearing a husband who seems alternately brutal and indifferent. Next, Brooks notes the racial component of her ostracization, as these men who hate change respond that "prejudice is native" and "ineradicable," but that she should be satisfied with their new "politeness" (140). Brooks refers not only to a black woman's relationship to "civilization" but to her place in the literary world, as she makes clear by the use of the resonant word "line" to describe her confinement within other people's assessment of her worth: "For the line is there./ And has a meaning . . . the line is/ Long and electric" (140). Here Brooks herself calls her use of Anglo-American forms a bondage in politeness; the line, the unit of poetry, itself represents a kind of electric fence.

Annie rejects such enclosure, and Brooks seems to repudiate the limited conception of the brief, expressive, well-wrought lyric she has inherited. She moves from first person singular to a plural "we," and suddenly seems to turn to a new audience: "Rise./ Let us combine. There are no magics or elves/ Or timely godmothers to guide us. We are lost, must/ Wizard a track through our own screaming weed" (140). The ending of "men of careful turns" so clearly expresses the necessity of innovation that one might expect Brooks's next volume to strike out in an entirely new direction, past the fence and through weedy unmapped land, with its newly defined army. As Henry Taylor asserts, "If there are sharp divisions in Brooks's career, one of them comes at this point" (266). However, Brooks spoke her subversions obliquely enough through forms familiarly safe enough to a white audience that apparently her disgust was not visible, or at least not threatening. Brooks's next work in poetry, *The Bean Eaters*, does make some movement in a new direction, and her novel was certainly meant to reach a larger audience. *Annie Allen*'s apostrophic gestures support Brooks's own implication that her 1967 "change" is not so utter as it may at first seem.

In "and shall I prime my children, pray, to pray," from *Annie Allen*, Brooks also experiments with the voice of the minister or the spiritual guide, in an imperative mode of address which strongly resembles the tone of her advising mothers. Brooks fully realizes this mode in her "Sermons on the Warpland." Erkkila notes how "Brooks addresses the black community as a kind of female preacher, a role that would have been denied to her in the more traditional structures of the black church" (220). Like the mother, the preacher stands taller than her less-powerful listeners and dispenses guidance. Although this hortatory voice grows out of Brooks's maternal pose, it reaches more widely, acknowledging the public role poetry can exercise, the multiplicity of potential readers, the world context and not only the intimate indoor spaces in which poetry is often composed and read. Sermons are primarily oral and public. Despite Brooks's consequent widening of the lyric's introspective space, however, on the level of language these poems remain private, even enclosed, and intensely literary.

Brooks published two "Sermons on the Warpland" at the end of *In the Mecca*, and one in her next book of poetry, *Riot* (1969). Brooks needs to work her way into this powerful voice in stages, always apparently ambivalent; in the first sermon she encloses her preaching in quotation marks, in the second she pronounces without mediation, and in the third she steps back from sermonizing directly, although her attitudes about the rioting she depicts remain implicit. Within the series, the title accumulates many different resonances. First, as R. Baxter Miller notes, Brooks alludes to the Sermon on the Mount (150). Her alternate geography also suggests the "warped land" or even the "Waste Land" of a racist and riot-torn America; it refers, especially in the first poem, to the "war planned" by black nationalists against white America, and even a "warplane," a carrier for this militant message.[2]

The first "sermon" is the shortest, and Brooks sets off its homily in quotation marks, distinctly marking its voice as not her own. Brooks may be engineering this distance partly to avoid, with characteristic reticence, the presumption of divine inspiration. However, the "Single Sermon" is delivered by a chorus of "several strengths," suggesting that the poet functions as a medium through which many people speak; the sermon then becomes a people addressing itself, minimizing Brooks's literary authority. This poem emphasizes mediation through this chorus and through the quotation marks, but such intercession occurs implicitly in all of Brooks's sermons: while the mother speaks for herself, the preacher always serves as a conduit for higher forces. Brooks's shift to a mediating sermonic voice suggests her new role as spokesperson, if an ambivalent one, in the Black Arts Movement.

"The Sermon on the Warpland" avoids traditional poetic form, instead organizing itself around the imperative and inspiring rhetoric of the pulpit. "Prepare to meet/ (sisters, brothers) the brash and terrible weather," the poem demands; "Build now your Church" (*Blacks* 451-52). Although the sentence structures are vocative, however, the poem also contains a metaphoric and intensely alliterative, randomly rhyming language that counteracts its apparent purposes. The sound-play pleases the ear, but some phrases do not possess any clearly assignable meaning. The second "Sermon on the Warpland" amplifies this effect by giving orders that make no immediate sense. Brooks does not tell her flock to march, to pray, to fight; she demands that they read, think, and interact with her language so that they themselves bear responsibility for interpreting her imperatives. The goal her sermon states, the "health" that will be achieved, involves "the heralding of the clear obscure" (451): this oxymoron declares the rightful place of the difficult, or even the irrational, in any poetry, including the poetry of the pulpit (and, here, of the oracle).

Lyric brevity and compression, figured in images of enclosure, perform a positive function in the first poem. The future, the sermon declares, germinates in "doublepod," containing "seeds for the coming hell and health together" (451). Progress becomes organic, the word "hell" breaking out of its pod, swelling or maturing into "health," the full-grown flower. This blossoming out of stasis requires the building of a new church, "never with brick nor Corten nor with granite," but "with lithe love" (452). Again, Brooks invokes paradox as her ideal; this building will resemble a Church, will shelter and enclose, but it will exist as an imaginative, not a physical, structure. Its cement will correspond to the bonds between people.

In "The Second Sermon on the Warpland," slightly longer and written in four numbered parts, Brooks addresses her community directly. Her imperatives are metaphorical: "Live!/ and have your blooming in the noise of the whirlwind" (*Blacks* 453); "Define and/ medicate the whirlwind" (455); "Conduct your blooming in the noise and whip of the whirlwind" (456). The most difficult series of directives occurs in the second section of this quartet:

> Salve salvage in the spin.
> Endorse the splendor splashes;
> stylize the flawed utility;
> prop a malign or failing light—
> but know the whirlwind is our commonwealth.
>
> (454)

Brooks may be here assuming a public pose, meaning to inspire, but this is no populist poetry; this passage sounds less like oratory and more like an excerpt from an avant-garde literary journal. Her diction again mimics growth, and blooming as "salve" is repeated more largely in "salvage," echoing the movement from "hell" to "health." As Brooks continues to argue, there exists no "easy" way to "straddle the whirlwind" that is the chaotic world of 1968; apparently a collo-quial voice won't do it any better than the "sweetest sonnet" (454). She orders each reader to do his or her own "defining," rather than provid-ing clear directives herself.

In the fourth and last section of the "Second Sermon," Brooks resur-rects the speaker of "Big Bessie throws her son into the street" (400) at the end of *Selected Poems*. In the earlier piece, Big Bessie produces large but relatively lucid orders: "Be precise," "Hunt out your own or make your own alone," "Go down the street" (400). Her inclusion rein-forces the connection between these two kinds of voices, the maternal and the preacherly. In the "Second Sermon,"

Big Bessie's feet hurt like nobody's business,
but she stands—bigly—under the unruly scrutiny, stands
   in the wild weed.

In the wild weed
she is a citizen,
and is a moment of highest quality; admirable.

                                            (Blacks 456)

Erkkila argues that Brooks "represent[s] herself in the figure of Big Bessie who moves out of the house" into a public sphere (221); certainly the presence of a strong maternal figure here emphasizes the continuity between all of Brooks's rhetorical positions. The "wild weed" imagery comprises another thread that binds Brooks's work back to *A Street in Bronzeville*: from "a song in the front yard" to "men of careful turns" to this "whirlwind"/"wild weed" scenery, uncultivated land means free and uncharted space where black women can define their own identities. Elsewhere, Brooks speaks affectionately of dandelions, flowers that can grow and delight the eye where nothing else will (*Blacks* 144). Her summons to "live and go out" (455) demands abandoning enclosures and prim front yards, a recapitulation of her decision back at the end of *Annie Allen* to "wizard a track through our own screaming weed."

"The Third Sermon on the Warpland" continues revisiting Brooks's earlier poetry, but eliminates Bessie and abandons its confident, if obscure, imperatives. This poem, reacting to the 1968 street disturbances in Chicago after Dr. Martin Luther King, Jr.'s assassination (Kent 236), instead includes different black male voices: "The Black Philosopher," twelve-year-old "Yancey," the Blackstone Rangers. Erkkila argues that, from *In the Mecca* on, Brooks becomes gradually silenced by the male-identified Black power movement, citing Brooks's decreased poetic production and increased address to and emphasis on black masculinity in her poetry (218-19). While Brooks does not cease to speak through apostrophe, this poem does enact a relative stifling of the mother and of Brooks's own authority to guide African-American response to racism.

In the middle of the theft and violence and sirens, a maternal figure surfaces, this time apparently a casualty rather than a tired but strong "citizen."

> A woman is dead.
>
> Motherwoman.
>
> She lies among the boxes
>
> (that held the haughty hat[s], the Polish sausages)
>
> in newish, thorough, firm virginity
>
> as rich as fudge is if you've had five pieces.
>
> Not again shall she
>
> partake of steak
>
> on Christmas mornings, nor of nighttime
>
> chicken and wine at Val Gray Ward's
>
> nor say
>
> of Mr. Beetley, Exit Jones, Junk Smith
>
> nor neat New-baby Williams (man-to-many)
>
> "He treat me right."
>
> That was a gut gal.
>
> (*Blacks* 476)

This virgin mother resembles Pepita of "In the Mecca," who dies sacrificially (Erkkila 218), yielding up her body and voice to "the war planned." Brooks honors her with a scrap of elegy in the middle of this poem full of angry men. The "Third Sermon" does not represent the death of maternal power or the sermonic voice in Brooks, but it does register the tension between the importance of women's voices and the loyalty to Black Power that threatens Brooks's later poetry.

Kent characterizes this poem as utilizing "the ordinary speech, loose rhythms, and communal reference points that could communicate to a mass audience" (*A Life* 237). The third sermon seems far more likely than the others to achieve Brooks's stated goal of appealing to a wider audience, as the above passage demonstrates. Even here, however, as Kent notes, Brooks can quickly "leave directness for the metaphorical"; he feels "that in such passages she is in territory that some of the younger writers, with their freer use of street language, would handle more effectively. Thus Gwendolyn's old style invaded the new one she was attempting to create" (237). I see these sermons not as failures to communicate at the level Brooks professed to be targeting, but as continuations of her aesthetic of complexity and deliberate indirection.

One of the interesting places where Brooks's old poetry "invades" the new is the allusion to "Gay Chaps at the Bar" in the "Third Sermon." The labeled jars and cabinets in which "my dreams, my work" are internally preserved become, in the later poem, the larder of the "keeper":

> The Black Philosopher says
> "Our chains are in the keep of the keeper
> in a labeled cabinet
> on the second shelf by the cookies,
> the sonatas, the arabesques . . .
> There's a rattle, sometimes.
> You do not hear it who mind only
> cookies and crunch them . . ."
>   (472)

The constraining chains, themselves enclosures, are concealed in another enclosed space, something like the back of the mind of the dominant white culture. The chains share their space with sweets like sonnets/ sonatas, "snacks" that distract their enjoyers from the ominous rattling of irons. The black soldier in Brooks's early sequence about World War II deposits his peacetime aspirations himself, although the war certainly constrains his options, but Brooks's black philosopher has no ability to unlock these containers, except through violence. Both, however, address an audience that does not properly understand the direness of the situation. Brooks models "Gay Chaps" on soldiers' letters to the uncomprehending women back home; this latter speech might be directed to those resisting or disapproving of the explosive anger of Chicago rioters, implicitly including Brooks herself. In this last "Sermon," Brooks gives far more direct voice to opinions she seems to disagree with than to her own ideas.

Brooks's most recent work abandons her early conception of the lyric, conceiving it negatively as a fixed, boxed in, static, dead form. She intends to write occasional poetry, speaking to immediate needs with specific purposes. Similarly, the distinction between public and private upon which the lyric often rests—itself private and claiming timelessness, in contrast to public and historical forms like the epic, the novel, and drama—finally collapses for Brooks. Although her poems continue to depend structurally on apostrophe, linking the latest productions with so many of the earliest, the directives emerge more plainly: the suggestively titled *Beckonings* (1975), for example, illustrates this through the inspirational pieces "A Black Wedding Song" and "Boys. Black. *a preachment.*" As the voices of the mother and the preacher fuse, public and private worlds and their separate discourses become indistinguishable.

From *Callaloo* 24, no. 1 (Winter 2001): 227-235. Copyright © 2001 by Charles H. Rowell. Reprinted with permission of The Johns Hopkins University Press.

Notes

1. See Rachel Blau DuPlessis' *Writing Beyond the Ending: Narrative Strategies of Twentieth Century Women Writers*, which does not analyze *Annie Allen* although its thesis illuminates that collection admirably.

2. For some of my observations and ideas about the three "Sermon(s) on the Warpland," especially the word "Warpland," I am indebted not only to Miller's essay but to the discussions in John Shoptaw's graduate seminar on contemporary poetry in the fall of 1992 at Princeton University.

Works Cited

Baker, Houston. "From 'The Florescence of Nationalism in the 1960s and 1970s.'" *On Gwendolyn Brooks: Reliant Contemplation*. Ed. Stephen Caldwell Wright. Ann Arbor: University of Michigan Press, 1996. 116-23.

Brooks, Gwendolyn. *Beckonings*. Detroit: Broadside, 1975.

——————. *Blacks*. Chicago: Third World, 1987.

——————. *A Capsule Course in Black Poetry Writing*. Detroit: Broadside, 1975.

——————. Interview. *Black Women Writers at Work*. Ed. Claudia Tate. New York: Continuum, 1983. 39-48.

——————. *Report from Part One*. Detroit: Broadside, 1972.

——————. *Report from Part Two*. Chicago: Third World, 1996.

Culler, Jonathan. *The Pursuit of Signs: Semiotics, Literature, Deconstruction*. Ithaca: Cornell University Press, 1971.

Dove, Rita, and Marilyn Nelson Waniek. "A Black Rainbow: Modern Afro-American Poetry." *Poetry After Modernism*. Ed. Robert McDowell. Brownsville, Oregon: Story Line Press, 1991. 217-75.

DuPlessis, Rachel Blau. *Writing Beyond the Ending: Narrative Strategies of Twentieth Century Women Writers*. Bloomington: Indiana University Press, 1985.

Ellman, Richard, and Robert O'Clair, ed. *The Norton Anthology of Modern Poetry*. Second Edition. New York: Norton, 1988.

Erkkila, Betsy. *The Wicked Sisters: Women Poets, Literary History and Discord*. New York: Oxford University Press, 1992.

Greene, Thomas A. "Poetry as Invocation." *New Literary History* 24.3 (1993): 495-517.

Hansell, William H. "The Poet-Militant and Foreshadowings of a Black Mystique: Poems in the Second Period of Gwendolyn Brooks." *A Life Distilled: Gwendolyn Brooks, Her Poetry and Fiction*. Ed. Maria K. Mootry and Gary Smith. Chicago: University of Illinois Press, 1987. 30-46.

Horvath, Brooke Kenton. "The Satisfactions of What's Difficult in Gwendolyn Brooks's Poetry." *On Gwendolyn Brooks: Reliant Contemplation*. Ed. Stephen Caldwell Wright. Ann Arbor: University of Michigan Press, 1996. 213-23.

Johnson, Barbara. "Apostrophe, Animation, Abortion." *A World of Difference*. Baltimore: Johns Hopkins University Press, 1987. 184-222.

Kent, George E. "Aesthetic Values in the Poetry of Gwendolyn Brooks." *A Life Distilled: Gwendolyn Brooks, Her Poetry and Fiction.* Ed. Maria K. Mootry and Gary Smith. Chicago: University of Illinois Press, 1987. 30-46.

_____. *A Life of Gwendolyn Brooks.* Lexington: University Press of Kentucky, 1990.

Lee, Don L. "Gwendolyn Brooks: Beyond the Wordmaker—The Making of an African Poet." *On Gwendolyn Brooks: Reliant Contemplation.* Ed. Stephen Caldwell Wright. Ann Arbor: University of Michigan Press, 1996. 81-96.

Lindberg, Kathryne V. "Whose Canon? Gwendolyn Brooks: Founder at the Center of the 'Margins.'" *Gendered Modernisms: American Women Poets and Their Readers.* Ed. Margaret Dickie and Thomas Travisano. Philadelphia: University of Pennsylvania Press, 1996.

McQuade, Donald, ed. *The Harper American Literature*, Vol. 2. Second Edition. New York: HarperCollins, 1993.

Melhem, D. H. *Gwendolyn Brooks: Poetry and the Heroic Voice.* Lexington: University Press of Kentucky, 1987.

Miller, R. Baxter. "'Define . . . the Whirlwind': Gwendolyn Brooks's Epic Sign for a Generation." *On Gwendolyn Brooks: Reliant Contemplation.* Ed. Stephen Caldwell Wright. Ann Arbor: University of Michigan Press, 1996. 146-60.

Redding, J. Saunders. "Cellini-Like Lyrics." *On Gwendolyn Brooks: Reliant Contemplation.* Ed. Stephen Caldwell Wright. Ann Arbor: University of Michigan Press, 1996. 6-7.

Taylor, Henry. "Gwendolyn Brooks: An Essential Sanity." *On Gwendolyn Brooks: Reliant Contemplation.* Ed. Stephen Caldwell Wright. Ann Arbor: University of Michigan Press, 1996. 254-75.

Dialectics of Desire:
War and the Resistive Voice in Gwendolyn Brooks's "Negro Hero" and "Gay Chaps at the Bar" _____
Ann Folwell Stanford

Ann Folwell Stanford examines an early martial aesthetic in Brooks's two poems about African American soldiers' reception by mainstream America. Brooks uses these poems to discuss the tense racial climate following World War II. On one hand are the black soldiers who return home expecting to be rewarded for their service but instead find increased discrimination from whites. On the other hand are the black soldiers who must deal with post-traumatic stress disorders that they developed during their tours of duty. Stanford notes how Brooks's two poems present yet another aspect of W. E. B. Du Bois's double consciousness, for the soldiers must reevaluate and reconcile with the struggle between serving in the military and fighting clearly defined European enemies and living as veterans and having to fight overt and covert racism in America. This is an epic struggle that Brooks maintains to expand the concept of "heroism." Stanford discusses Brooks's narrative strategy of employing the sonnet form to critique the deplorable lack of acceptance of black soldiers and to elevate their struggles to gain recognition as her own way to memorialize black soldiers' contributions to continued American liberty.   — M.R.M.

Brooks, Black Soldiers, and World War II

The early poems of Gwendolyn Brooks's *A Street in Bronzeville* are remarkable for many reasons, not the least of which is the powerfully resonant voice of those poems devoted to the experience of black soldiers in World War II. The dramatic monologue "Negro Hero" and a twelve-sonnet sequence "Gay Chaps at the Bar" are both written from the point of view and in the voices of soldiers in the midst of battle.

These poems are especially interesting in their multivoiced interrogation of racial politics in America. In these poems, Brooks reconstructs "The Enemy" not as foreigners holding howitzers, but as fellow Americans with white skin. "Negro Hero" and "Gay Chaps at the Bar" address in varying ways the tenuous and contradictory situation of black soldiers in a white man's army. However, they do so by making the direct link between war and racism, thus narrowing the gap between military (foreign) and racial (American) struggle, between soldiers and civilians.[1]

This is not a war poetry that elevates the courage or sacrifice of soldiers, or focuses on physical injury, or sentimentalizes love and looks back longingly on women and children at home—or even a poetry that protests war *qua* war. Brooks's war poems express a profound perplexity and a muted anger, neither denouncing war nor valorizing those who fight in it. War becomes the trope for the equally injurious institutionalized racism at home. In this poetry, Brooks displaces both the site and meaning of war, and in her hands it becomes a civil struggle, one fought on the terrain of white racism.

Given that war poetry up to the 1940s (especially poems from the front) had been written primarily by male writers and had been accorded value on the basis of an authority of experience not available to women, Brooks's apparent first-person accounts and meditations about war represent something of an anomaly in women's poetry. Pointing out that Brooks's method in these poems "is not a poetic celebration of women's reading," Susan Schweik argues that it is, instead, "a free, creative masking, violating completely all the home-front taboos against literary impersonation of soldiers" ("'A Word'" 157). Political theorist Jean Bethke Elshtain explains why this kind of writing was a literary taboo: "Because women are *exterior* to war, men *interior*, men have long been the great war-story tellers, legitimated in that role because they have 'been there' or because they have greater entrée into what it 'must be like'" (212). Brooks, however, adopts the personae and voices of male soldiers with remarkable ease. Moreover, she rewrites "war" as a complex tissue of meaning and signification; the battlefield exists simultaneously on foreign fronts, in the trenches, on Chicago streets, and even at home.

Further, Brooks's war poetry contradicts Paul Fussell's statement that women haven't written many good war poems: ". . . bereaved women are, next to the permanently wounded, the main victims in war, their dead men having been removed beyond suffering. Yet the elegies are written by men, the poems registering a love of soldiers are written by men, and it is not women who seem to be the custodians of the subtlest sort of antiwar irony" (*The Great War* 213). Brooks's project in this early collection, however, was not to write elegies for male soldiers. Instead, she appropriated the voices of soldiers in order to extend and develop the possibilities inherent in the web of associations "war" suggests. In so doing, Brooks indeed creates "the subtlest sort of antiwar irony" that Fussell cannot seem to find in women's poetry. For Brooks, it is a revisionary gesture, one in which war becomes the means to explore not just the story of war, but other stories as well. Alicia Ostriker explains that women poets have used myth (and, I would add, masks) as a means to change the "old stories . . . so that they can no longer stand as foundations of collective male fantasy or as the pillars sustaining phallocentric 'high' culture. Instead, they are corrections . . . in some cases . . . instructions for survival" (215).

While Susan Schweik states that one of Brooks's major aims for *Bronzeville* was to "write the Black soldier into war poetry," I think there is more to it. Schweik goes on to argue that Brooks intended "to recognize the fact of [the Black soldier's] existence at the Second War's 'fronts,' and most importantly to force her readers to notice the terms of Black men's exclusion from both heroic and ironic modern mythologies of warfare" ("'A Word'" 158). Although this seems to be a part of Brooks's project, something far more subversive is going on in this poetry. By writing in male voices, by revising "the old stories," Brooks resituates herself, moving from the peripheral "woman's" place of observing war, to the center of the action. In so doing she both decenters the traditional male voice and reinscribes war with her multileveled meanings, resisting and refuting the traditional notion of women's exteriority to war. The poet's female and marginalized voice then, by cross-dressing in soldier's garb, gains a more central position from which to speak.

Unlike much male war poetry, Brooks's poetry deals more with psychological injury and pain than with bodily injury. Her war poems bear little resemblance to a poem like Wilfred Owen's "Mental Cases," describing badly shell-shocked World War I soldiers for whom "night comes blood black;/ [and] Dawn breaks open like a wound that bleeds afresh" (169). Neither do Brooks's soldiers resemble Randall Jarrell's World War II soldier who "woke to black flak and the nightmare fighters," and who reports with a remarkable economy of detail the horrible disposal of his body: "when I died they washed me out of the turret with a hose" (144). Brooks's war poems do not resemble the morale-boosting "patriotic drivel" Fussell attributes to World War II poems by MacLeish, Sandburg, and Millay, among others (*Wartime* 175). Instead, Brooks's war poetry demonstrates the sustained fracturing of the psyche that war (in all its multiple meanings) causes.[2]

It is the utter perplexity, the sense of having been duped, with which the soldiers in Brooks's poetry must deal. These are poems of journey, the open-ended journey toward a "truth" or truths the soldiers must face in order to be healed of war's (and by extension, racism's) psychic injuring. These and many of Brooks's poems begin with the assumption that the social, cultural, political, and religious rhetoric on which American life is based is an essentially blinding, numbing force. It is this blinding force with which (especially) black men and women in racist America must struggle, must "unbandage" their eyes.[3] Within the poems, speakers oscillate between belief (or faith) and disbelief (or repudiation) in the patriotic/religious (and blinding) discourse that attempts to render injustice invisible. The process of coming to terms with the truth of American religio-political rhetoric is a heroic one, and the "site" of bodily wounding becomes the "sight" which has been blinded or blurred by racism. The poems invert the healing process: Instead of covering wounds, Brooks's poems insist that wounds be uncovered, that the horrible be acknowledged, and that the light of truth be allowed to apply its painful, but ultimately healing, powers. While Brooks's poems remake the enemy and resituate the locus of war, they also demand that the real battles be fought both within the hearts and minds of individual soldiers and on the ground of social and cultural struggle.

It is important to remember that these poems were written at a time when real black men were fighting in real wars, and were enduring conditions of racism even as they served their country. Black dissent was rife during World War II and centered on denial of combat roles and exclusion from many jobs, especially leadership positions. One observer writes that "perhaps the sorriest chapter in the story of the war . . . is the treatment accorded Negroes in . . . a war ostensibly fought against a racist ideology [where] we ourselves have practiced the same ideology" (Foner 133). Indeed, black soldiers were acutely aware that they were not Americans but *black* Americans:

When they were often turned away while trying to contribute blood to the Red Cross Program, when America, "the last bulwark of democracy," was planning separate air-raid shelters for Blacks and whites in Washington, D.C., when lynchings continued unabated during the war, when race riots broke out against Black GIs trying to use the same facilities as their white counterparts, it was only natural that Blacks should feel that they were involved in two simultaneous wars—one against Hitler in Germany and the other against the Hitlers in the United States. This attitude was embodied in the "Double V" concept among Blacks during the war—that the war must end in two victories, one against Hitler, one against American racism. (Mullen 54)

Brooks's "Negro Hero" and "Gay Chaps at the Bar" scrutinize this "Double V" concept. Brooks links the war poems to the material conditions of military combat while she simultaneously establishes the war on home ground as well. While the poems treat the human experiences of alienation, bravery, and honor that are peculiar to war, they also give form and shape to the less visible, but no less dangerous, war that black men and women living in a predominantly white racist culture knew intimately in the forties.

Deconstructing Heroism

"Negro Hero," the first poem in *A Street in Bronzeville* to deal directly with war, was written "to suggest Dorie Miller," a black soldier who, as messman, was confined to the galley of his ship as a cook, but broke through the color line to save his ship from attack. In this dramatic monologue, the speaker meditates on his rash act of defiance.[4] The poem's tone is by turns reflective and mutedly angry, as the speaker recounts his emergence from the "underground" of his galley. It was an action that violated the strict rules of segregation maintained aboard ship, but one that allowed the speaker to save himself and his shipmates as he seized a machine gun and shot down attacking Japanese airplanes:

> I had to kick their law into their teeth in order to save them.
> However I have heard that sometimes you have to deal
> Devilishly with drowning men in order to swim them to shore.
> Or they will haul themselves and you to the trash and the fish
>   beneath.
> (When I think of this, I do not worry about a few
> Chipped teeth.)
>
> (*Blacks* 48)

Two wars occur simultaneously: one with the Japanese and one on board ship. And it is the latter war with which the speaker is all too familiar, and which poses the greater threat.

The speaker knows the risks he ran in shifting, momentarily, the balance of power on board ship. For four stanzas, he asserts the necessity, the thrill, and the good will behind his actions. He knows, however, that had he not given "glory," had he not "put gold on their name," he would have paid dearly and "there would have been spikes in the afterward hands." Fully aware that the risk was grave, he also knows that "it was hardly The Enemy my fight was against/ But them." And here the speaker approaches one of the primary points of the poem: Enemy ground exists not across the ocean, not in the Japanese airplanes, but persists whenever he is in the presence of American whites. As with "war," the notion of heroism undergoes redefinition and revision in Brooks's hands, as she layers it with multiple associations. Most important in this poem is the speaker's own heroic (but halting) struggle toward understanding the racial dynamic that underwrites the response of the white community to his "heroism."

The hero, who is "a gem," who has his "pictures in the Caucasian dailies/ as well as the Negro weeklies," understands, though, that his act was complicated by his own mixed motives. In lines that diminish the glory of masculine aggression (war is not "manly" but "boyish"), the speaker ruminates further about the reasons for his actions, concluding that he "was rolled on wheels of [his] boy itch to get at the gun" and that his "first swallow of the liquor of battle bleeding black air dying and demon noise/ Made [him] wild." But it was more than that, he says: "I loved. And a man will guard when he loves./ Their white-gowned democracy was my fair lady."[5] The speaker of "Negro Hero" finds himself in an absurd position, wanting to believe in a "white-gowned democracy" that has "her" foot on his neck and a "knife lying cold" up her sleeve. Although he is pulled toward the public dream of democracy, the central question of the poem erodes his attempt to maintain faith:

> Still—am I good enough to die for them, is my blood bright
>   enough to be spilled . . . ?
> Am I clean enough to kill for them, do they wish me to kill
> For them or is my place while death licks his lips and strides
>   to them In the galley still?

(49)[6]

While the speaker tries to answer the initial questions affirmatively, his language (a war of words itself) undermines his attempts to believe in the good will of his white compatriots. The number of qualifiers in the text ("However," "But," "Of course," "Still") suggests that the speaker is trying to convince himself about a truth that remains evanescent.

These questions are not about the speaker's ontological worth; they are, instead, attempts to see as clearly as possible his own status in the eyes of the white soldiers. Moreover, his questions are not so wistful and self-doubting as they may first appear. They represent, rather, the beginning of an intense critique of white racism. The questions point to the very structure of enclosure upon which a racist system depends to maintain itself, and the speaker's restriction to the galley epitomizes this structure.[7] When he thinks of the possibility of "spikes in the afterward hands," he quickly interdicts the thought: "But let us speak only of my success." However, the "possible horror" that whites might prefer "their law in all its sick dignity" to "their lives" becomes *probable*, a likelihood the speaker himself deduces as he considers the various possibilities. At play in the text also is the dynamic of desire and revulsion: I want to believe in democracy/ I can't possibly believe in democracy. It is a dynamic that will be continued and augmented in "Gay Chaps at the Bar."

"Negro Hero," however, does not stop with racial enclosure, but instead (to borrow from Ralph Ellison) "changes the joke and slips the yoke." The text becomes a fence or frame for a petulant and dangerous white man's voice, hedging in and entrapping the only "white" lines in the poem ("In a southern city a white man said . . ."). Strictly rhymed and metrically regular, these lines aggregately provide an answer to the speaker's central question of the status of his heroism. The white man's words are:

> Indeed, I'd rather be dead;
> Indeed, I'd rather be shot in the head
> Or ridden to waste on the back of a flood
> Than saved by the drop of a black man's blood.
>
> (49)

The almost sing-song, mostly iambic tetrameter lines sound much like a school child's playground song even as the words themselves simultaneously speak the skewed logic and horror of white racism. In addition, the lilting quality illustrates how ingrained and traditional such an attitude is, how thoughtlessly, reverberatingly present it is. The sing-song rhyme sounds unsettlingly similar to the familiar racist jingle "Eeny, meeny, miney, mo. . . ."

It is, perhaps, the property of a jingle to make itself especially accessible to memory. These two rhymes are simple, silly, and dangerous. Both employ a double voice: childish playfulness and malicious hatred. But instead of fighting, tolerating, forgiving, or laughing at this double voice (which historically has been a voice of power), the text upsets the power balance by surrounding the white man's voice with the speaker's more mature, more searching, more logical, and certainly more heroic discourse. The ramifications of the speaker's (and indeed any speaker's or poet's) need to silence or interdict an oppressive voice before being able to create and/or discover his or her own are obvious. However, the etiological tradition in black literature—the quest for origins and the making of a self in a place that denies selfhood—makes this silencing an especially important factor in understanding the hero's quest in the poem. The speaker is, in effect, facing the racism embedded within his own discourse, perhaps internalized, and unmaking the "heroism" imposed upon him by the white community to remake it in a truer, more real context of self-knowledge. It is this making of a self—or, more appropriate to the poet's task, making of a voice—that is first figured in "Negro Hero" and continues, in different form, in "Gay Chaps at the Bar."

The speaker concludes by restating the poem's central issues:

> Even if I had to kick their law into their teeth in order to do that
>   [heroic deed] for them.
> And I am feeling well and settled in myself because I believe it
>   was a good job,
> Despite this possible horror: that they might prefer the
>   Preservation of their law in all its sick dignity and their knives
> To the continuation of their creed
> And their lives.
>
> (50)

Thus, the real heroism does not reside in the action that was performed as the speaker's "blood was/ Boiling about in my head and straining and howling and singing me on," or in the "wheels of my boy itch to get at the gun," but in his resistance of white racism and his refusal to accept entirely his status as a hero. He is no blind fool, but he *could* have been. The truly heroic gesture is the move toward an unbandaging of his eyes, and a concurrent articulation of his sense of truth. The speaker ends the poem with a clear look at his actions, at the risks behind them, and (most painful of all) at the persisting horror of white racism.

Shifting Ground: War as Racism

Like "Negro Hero," Brooks's sonnet sequence "Gay Chaps at the Bar" foregrounds war only to undo and remake it. These sonnets, even more than "Negro Hero," represent the halting progress toward truth-seeing and knowing, toward dismantling a rhetoric of lies. They too insist on multiple signification—that war is "both/and." It is both a military war and a racial war. Read not so much as stanzas in a long poem, but as separate poems retaining their separate integrity, these sonnets form a polyphony of voices, perspectives, and methods of new seeing.

The primary mode of voicing in each sonnet is dialectic. Each sonnet articulates a desire (I want to be a functioning person, to know who I am; I want my dreams to wait until after the war ["hell"]; I want to believe in democracy and civil religion); and an oppositional reality, a pull toward the truth (war and racism erase my identity; my dreams may not survive the war; white democracy is an unfaithful lover, and civil religion a blinding, numbing force). Like "Negro Hero," whose speaker wants to love democracy, but cannot avoid seeing it for what it is, the sonnets also resist the impulse to believe in the desire at the expense of the reality.

In all twelve sonnets, the situation of the black soldier on the front is very like that of the black (male and female) civilian at home. The poems deal with loss of language and identity in the face of a hostile "other" ("gay chaps at the bar," "still do I keep my look, my identity"); the silencing of dreams and an ensuing artistic hunger ("my dreams, my works must wait till after hell"); the inability to protect a loved one ("looking"); the ways old ghosts (old histories) invade and control the present ("piano after war," "mentors"); death's power to annihilate racial differences ("the white troops had their orders but the Negroes looked like men"); the dissolution of belief in a patriotic god ("firstly inclined to take what it is told"); the revolutionary impulse that challenges traditional religious dependence ("'God works in a mysterious way'"); the need for love and the fear of losing it ("love note I: surely," "love note II: flags"); and the emergence of a deepening consciousness of the absurdity of war—and, by extension, racism ("the progress").

Not a neatly tied package, Brooks's sonnet sequence covers a variety of topics in a range of voices that bridges the structural (but not ontological) difference between war and racism. However, the sonnets do more than simply posit a relationship between war and racism; they represent a collective consciousness that gropes toward a critical and reflective stance—one that in fractured ways approaches a "truth."[8] And the sonnets are, finally, prophetic warnings: They look back at the devastation of war, and forward toward a time of revolution and rebellion that was to come in the sixties.

Brooks began "Gay Chaps" (*gay* here meaning 'outwardly cheerful'), when she received a letter from her friend and colleague William Couch,[9] who included the title phrase as he described the soldiers he had seen and known on the front in World War II. Brooks writes that, when she realized "there [were] other things to say about what [was] going on at the front . . . [, she wrote] more poems, some of them based on the stuff of letters that [she] was getting from several soldiers" (*Report* 156). The result was the sequence of twelve sonnets spoken in the voices of black soldiers in combat. The epigraph to the first poem of the sequence (the title poem) quotes Couch's letter directly:

> . . . and guys I knew in the States, young officers, return from the front crying and trembling. Gay chaps at the bar in Los Angeles, Chicago, New York. . . .
>
> —Lieutenant William Couch in the South Pacific (*Blacks* 64)

Contrasting extreme battle fatigue ("crying and trembling") with joviality and bravado ("gay chaps"), the epigraph perhaps stands as a before-and-after portrait of the black soldiers: "Gay" before the war, they are now "crying and trembling." Another reading, however, signals strategies Brooks will use in the sequence (and has used in other poems). What if the soldiers are both gay *and* devastated? What if "gay" signifies false bravado as the presenting feature of these returning soldiers, but hardly the whole picture? Indeed, the soldier's gaiety serves to mask the anguishing effects of war. What the surface of the poem reveals, the epigraph suggests, will rarely exhaust the poem's possibilities. In fact the poems, like the "gay chaps" sitting at the bar, contain and mask other, more painful, realities.

Deconstructing Racism

The first sonnet, "gay chaps at the bar," with its oppositional epigraph ("gay chaps" versus "trembling and crying" men), structures a dialectic between knowing and not knowing, between before and after. The difference in behavior and understanding before the war and now, during the war, is as vast as the difference between being a "gay chap" and one who is "crying and trembling." The war (military and racial) radically alters the men's relation to the world, dismantling familiar language and ways of knowing. The octave describes the ease with which the pre-wartime soldiers "knew how to order":

> . . . Just the dash
> Necessary. The length of gaiety in good taste.
> Whether the raillery should be slightly iced
> And given green, or served up hot and lush.
>
> (*Blacks* 64)

These men know how to posture, how to function with ease and grace in the world of whites (they "knew white speech") as well as the world of romance and women (they knew "beautifully how to give to women/ The summer spread, the tropics, of [their] love"). Not unlike the contest (and injury) of military conflict, this kind of posturing and sexual conquest constitutes another form of struggle or warfare. Although the next several lines undercut the ease with which the men flaunt their maleness, it is in these lines that Brooks establishes the power nexus of war, racism, and sexism.[10]

The soldiers ("we") knew the "necessary" dash and raillery, knew "good taste," "when to persist, or hold a hunger off." Having adapted and adopted acceptable cultural patterns, including masking their blackness just enough to practice "white speech," they are well-versed in survival. Their "knowing," however, has been contingent on the response of the white male or (presumably) black female "other." The soldiers know how to survive by posturing and speaking "white" lan-

guage and through sexual conquest—and if either of these fail, the soldiers have failed. These soldiers perhaps know themselves as well as
the speaker of "Negro Hero," but in order to function within the constraints of racism (and sexual conquest), they have had to dissociate
from themselves an appropriate other self or persona, therefore eroding
access to what self-knowledge they may have.[11] Now that they are in a
declared war, the soldiers' language and epistemology fail them, much
as the acquired behavior of a "good Negro" would fail him or her during
declared domestic wars—race riots, lynchings, and violent enforcement
of segregation. As long as the war is *sub rosa* (as much racist/sexist ideology and its ensuing oppressive systems are), undeclared and masked,
these men can function, although tenuously. Brooks's rhyme scheme
underscores this tenuousness. While the abba/abba structure of the octave rhymes loosely—"dash"/"lush," "taste"/"iced," "women"/"omen,"
"love"/"off"—even the loose rhyme falls apart in the sestet. It employs
slant or non-rhymes ("islands," "hour," "stout," "brought," "talents,"
"air") to signal a kind of dissolution or at least disjuncture of language.

The sestet, leading out of the octave, turns from the black soldiers'
use of "necessary" language (survival—both literally and with one's
identity intact) to the radical *failure* of language and acquired knowledge in the "chat with death" that war occasions:

> But nothing ever taught us to be islands.
> And smart, athletic language for this hour
> Was not in the curriculum. No stout
> Lesson showed how to chat with death. We brought
> No brass fortissimo, among our talents,
> To holler down the lions in this air.
>
> (64)

The absence of power in language becomes a metaphor for the powerlessness of the soldiers in battle. Nothing has prepared them for being thrust into the "air" of war wherein bravado and cool are lost (and

language is literally obliterated in the roar of airplanes flying over-head).[12] But not only is this the "air" of foreign war, it is also an atmo-sphere typical of black women's and men's lived experience in a racist culture which refuses to "see" (or hear) them as human beings, drowning out all but its own sounds, maintaining the illusion of centrality by defin-ing them as "other." The poem enacts a deconstruction of identity in the face of such constricting circumstances. It is as if the poet asks, When one is invisible, unheard; when one's language and sense of self are obliterated by a more powerful and silencing entity (airplanes/racism), what is left? In both war and racism, the self is deconstructed (though not *destroyed*), language falls apart, and what is left is a harrowing poverty of history and culture that constitutes the many aspects of a self.

Another sonnet examines unmaking, but this time it is the unmaking of racist ideology. In the seventh sonnet, "the white troops had their or-ders but the Negroes looked like men," the speaker's focus shifts from his black comrades to the white soldiers who "had supposed their for-mula was fixed," who "had obeyed instructions to devise/ A type of cold, a type of hooded gaze," but who could not follow instructions to separate white and black corpses for burial. It would seem that rigid adherence to the restrictions of racism fall apart in the face of death, much as the lan-guage of the black soldiers in the first sonnet fails them in the "chat with death." Similar to the black soldier's stylized posing in the first sonnet, these white soldiers have their own pose to maintain. The two poems link the black and white soldiers both textually and thematically, posit-ing a sameness while suggesting that the deconstruction of these poses can occur only in the extreme circumstances of battle (read *revolution*). Here, the white troops realize "these Negroes looked like men," and

> Besides, it taxed
> Time and the temper to remember those
> Congenital iniquities that cause
> Disfavor of the darkness.
>
> (70)

Once again, the act of seeing is a potentially healing one—this time, however, for the *bearers* of racism. Here, the white troops see that the "Negroes looked like men"; they realize that the effort of maintaining racism is costly, and they are at least temporarily freed from the "cold . . . hooded gaze" that blinds them to the humanity of their black compatriots.

But the poem also mocks the white soldiers and the racist system in which they are captive. Those who "boxed/ Their feelings properly," and expected a correlative boxing of the "dark men" in one coffin and the white men in another, "would often find the contents had been scrambled./ Or even switched." However, the sonnet itself does some switching. By making the white soldiers "Other" (with deliberate capitalization), this poem, like "Negro Hero," shifts the balance of power. Instead of defining blacks as "other" in relation to a central white presence, the sonnet reverses the terms of hegemony, dislodging the center of white authority. The *white* soldiers' bodies are now "Other," defined against the bodies of "dark men." It is a good joke, and one that becomes even more amusing when linked with the wry conclusion: "Neither the earth nor heaven ever trembled./ And there was nothing startling in the weather" (70).

"The white troops had their orders but the Negroes looked like men" inverts the pathetic fallacy and reveals both the absurdity and the contingency of racism: When racism works to the benefit of the racist, fine; when it is an inconvenience, let it go. With the crush of war and death upon both black and white soldiers, "who really gave two figs?" Racism constrains and taxes both the bearer and the receiver of its consequences.[13]

In other sonnets, Brooks continues her scrutiny of racism. Moving from a focus on white or black soldiers, the third sonnet, "my dreams, my works, must wait till after hell," employs domestic imagery to describe the deferral of dreams that both war and racism entail. The poem is especially interesting for its introduction of images usually relegated to a traditionally female realm, which is not necessarily a *naturally* female realm. The poem takes symbols that are markers of gender and exploits them to their fullest potential in what is a subversive relocation of "dreams" and "works." With a tone evocative of a mother speaking about unruly children she has recently left behind, the sonnet begins:

> I hold my honey and I store my bread
> In little jars and cabinets of my will.
> I label clearly, and each latch and lid
> I bid, Be firm till I return from hell.
>
> (66)

Direct and simple, the lines bespeak intentionality and purpose; their very regular iambic pentameter and soft caesuras sound almost prim. In fact, these lines seem as though they were meant to be sung, lightly and sweetly.

The dreams and works are "honey" and "bread"—sweet (or embellished) and elemental. The speaker sorts, labels, and encloses his dreams, an efficient and effective method of putting one's life on hold for the duration of a siege time. For Brooks, however, this is a variation on the theme of enclosure. As I have observed in footnote 7, enclosure for Brooks is usually a negative, constricting force. But here it sounds almost protective, much like the warm and enclosing arms of a parent intentionally keeping a vulnerable child safe from harm. It is interesting that this intentionality seems to have been lost on critics. Clenora Hudson, for example, argues that ". . . one finds no indications of anger, unrest or any of the seeds of discontent so prominent in the young Blacks. Here we have a sense of helplessness, an attitude which suggests no control of one's life, or destiny. The ability to negotiate with life in all its responsibilities is beyond reach" (19).

Within these four lines, however, many voices do battle for a hearing—the efficient, the prim, the protective, the angry, and the resigned—all of which are intentional and strategic. Even the "hell" in line four is eclipsed (and could easily be elided in a quick reading) by the internal slant rhyme of "firm" and "return." But this line subtly introduces an anger and resignation that will characterize the rest of the poem. The protective storing of dreams begins to look similar to the boxing of dead bodies in "the white troops had their orders but the Negroes looked like men."

The fifth line of "my dreams, my works" abruptly breaks the songlike rhythm: "I am very hungry. I am incomplete." Sundering the line, the heavy caesura functions as a sigh or even a moan. The lighter, though determined, opening lines of the sonnet give way to an exhaustion that results from the constant effort of keeping all these dreams and works on hold. In this poem, hunger becomes the controlling image, as language has been in the first sonnet, and body in the second ("still do I keep my look"). These sonnets resist a transcendence of the body, and instead insist that deferred dreams cause a pain as real as the gnaw and claw of hunger. War takes a remarkable toll, but this toll is not limited to the predictable cost of physical injury and life. Equally intense on the battlefield of World War II or in racial battlefields closer to home, a significant effect of war is psychic exhaustion and incompleteness (read *powerlessness*).[14] The raw and exhausted voice of the fifth line links, as it were, the "hell" of war to the "hell" of racism.

It is not difficult, then, to imagine hearing the next four lines (again, spoken simply) in an urban ghetto:

> I am very hungry. I am incomplete.
> And none can tell when I may dine again.
> No man can give me any word but Wait,
> The puny light. I keep eyes pointed in. . . .
>
> (66)[15]

"Wait" is one of the most common interdictions to a rhetoric of revolution and social justice, and was heard frequently in the United States during the years leading up to and during the struggle for civil rights. In Brooks's hands, "Wait" stands in metonymic relation to artistic, spiritual, and psychological starvation.[16] Brooks also employs the metaphor of "puny light" to describe the effect of "Wait." The speaker's only defense is to look within, to keep to himself (not unlike the strategies of those bounded by a society that sees them as "other" and therefore inferior). Here, however, although the eyes point inward, they are *not* blindfolded and do *not* evade the truth. The speaker knows honey and bread must be protected and stored away, that his creative and productive efforts must be put on hold. But these self-protective gestures carry with them a grave risk: the possibility of losing appreciation for and sensitivity to the very things that have been locked away in storage. The speaker hopes that, with what legs and heart are left him, as he "remember[s] to go home," his "taste will not have turned insensitive/ To honey and bread old purity could love." After the battle, the poem asks (with some fear), what will be left of those deferred dreams?

In addition, the use of bread and honey as an image for "dreams" links those artistic endeavors inextricably to the body: The creative urge is as basic and important as food to the body. These images are homey and simple, elements traditionally associated not with the bravery or agony of soldiers in battle, but with women at home. The attribution of female imagery to the male speaker causes a slippage of gender roles that simultaneously opens up and bridges the gap between "male experience" and "female experience," again linking the horror of war to the horror of racism at home (where, presumably, women wait for their fighting men to return). Further, while this domestic metaphor signals a gendered feminine presence in the work, it also wrests "dreams" from the domain of the male soldiers and resituates them in a female realm. Honey is sweet, bread is elemental. The dreams "old purity could love" include both subsistence and beauty, and here Brooks flags those dreams and works as her own (or, if not simply hers, many women's).

Anatomies of Belief: Seeing and Blindness

In Brooks's sonnets, the larger "war" functions not only as a trope for racism, but as the crucible within which her speakers grope toward an unveiling of sight—the stripping away of those elements that bandage the eyes, occluding unpleasant realities. For Brooks, those who continue the slow progress toward clear sight are the real soldiers, the real heroes.

While all of the sonnets in some way contain a dialectic of seeing and blindness, those placed later in the sequence do so more obviously. The eighth sonnet, "firstly inclined to take what it is told," very directly (and sarcastically) describes the kind of comforting faith that blinds "frail" youth. An anatomy of belief, the sonnet begins much like a hymn or psalm:

> Thee sacrosanct, Thee sweet, Thee crystalline,
> With the full jewel wile of mighty light—
> With the narcotic milk of peace for men
> Who find Thy beautiful center and relate
> Thy round command. . . .
>
> (71)

The smoothness of the mostly iambic pentameter lines halts abruptly with the trochaic beat of *center,* which jars the meter and, in so doing, actually decenters the creed-like rhythm of the faith affirmation. Further, while the religious imagery is unmistakable, its sincerity is undermined by the words *wile* and *narcotic.* The "mighty light" beguiles, and "peace" is a lulling, numbing chimera, recalling Marx's dictum that religion functions as an "opiate of the people." Civil religion (and, with it, belief in a white god) was (and, in many cases, continues to be) one of the mainstays of American racist systems.

The focus in this poem is less on the loss of belief than on the anatomy of belief, of what belief consists and what motivates the desire for faith in the "beautiful center." The process of dissecting and understanding that which has held one in thrall is the beginning of liberation. Foucault, for example, observes that the *why* and *what* of domination ("what they seek, what is their overall strategy") is not nearly so important as "how things work at the level of ongoing subjugation, at the level of those continuous and uninterrupted processes which subject our bodies, govern our gestures, dictate our behaviors" (97). Brooks's sonnet represents the beginning of that analytic process. Here the speaker sees his youth (both in terms of chronology and maturity, presumably), frailness, fear, and dependence as those things predisposing him to a blind faith ("Firstly inclined to take what it is told/ Firstly inclined to lean").

The text of "firstly inclined" incisively analyzes the effects of cultural imperialism and domination. When a people are repeatedly and in various ways "told" they are dependent, they are more inclined to believe or internalize that telling. This poem marks the first step in the practice of reflection that precedes resistance and revolutionary action. The placing of a poem like this in a group of sonnets about soldiers and war makes inevitable the connection between struggle, injury, and the "narcotic milk of peace." War moves from global to personal struggle in this sonnet. But, because personal, it is also political. The poem meditates on the effects of domination, establishing the first step in the process of seeing more clearly.

As a companion to "firstly inclined," the ninth sonnet, "'God works in a mysterious way," extends the reflective gesture to include a repudiation of former belief. While the speaker of "firstly inclined" says, "I had been ready to believe," the speaker of "God works," answers, *But now* the youthful eye cuts down its/ Own dainty veiling" (emphasis added). Action must follow critical reflection, for if it does not, "the youthful eye . . . submits to winds," and the consequence of not cutting down *the* obfuscating veil is a continuing diminution of power—personal and political:

And many an eye that all its age had drawn its
Beam from a Book endures the impudence
Of modern glare that never heard of tact
. . . it merely can direct
Chancing feet across dissembling clods.

(72)

Unveiling the eye is a matter of survival. The disillusion caused by
war, or war's wounding, becomes the catalyst for the soldier/speaker's
awakening and subsequent healing (from blindness into sight).

The musing tone in the sonnet's octave is abruptly interdicted by the
stern, almost dictatorial, tone of the sestet:

Out from Thy shadows, from Thy pleasant meadows,
Quickly, in undiluted light. Be glad, whose
Mansions are bright, to right Thy children's air.

(72)

Strident? Militant? Uppity? Here the speaker's rather daring reversal
of roles enables him to issue an outright command to the God who, in
the previous sonnet, the youth had found "delicately lovely to adore."
This speaker firmly and summarily rejects the "puny light" that "Wait"
brings (in "my dreams, my works"), insisting that the light must be
"undiluted," and clear.[17] Seeing, in this case, is absolutely fundamental
and prior to believing.

But not only does the speaker demand clear light, he also calls on the
sovereign to "be glad . . . to right Thy children's air." Do not simply do
this, but be *happy* to do so, the poem insists. The children's "air" recalls
the air of the first sonnet, in which the soldier cannot holler down the
lions. The air of racism, of war, is no longer tolerable to the speaker.
"Mortify our wolves," the poem commands. If you (God) don't (cant,
won't) do something to quiet the raging hunger within, the speaker
warns, then "we assume a sovereignty ourselves." This is clearly a bat-

tle cry, a challenge to that "narcotic milk of peace" the previous sonnet describes. By using a voice that opposes the god of "narcotic peace" (and patriotism with racism as its subtext), the poem reverses the terms of the divine hierarchy, insisting that resistive and restorative action must grow out of belief, and if it does not, that belief is a blinding and destructive one.

The final sonnet, "the progress," closes the sequence with an ominous note of despair. Even after all the unbandagings, even after the halting progress toward truths,

> Still we applaud the President's voice and face.
> Still we remark on patriotism, sing,
> Salute the flag, thrill heavily, rejoice
> For death of men who too saluted, sang.
>
> (75)

However, the sonnet's sestet offers a warning. Even though we do these things, the speaker says, no one on the outside can really see the full picture of what we see, and hear, and know ("we keep eyes pointed in," says the speaker of the third sonnet).

> But inward grows a soberness, an awe,
> A fear, a deepening hollow through the cold.
> For even if we come out standing up
> How shall we smile, congratulate. . . .
>
> (75)

The process of unveiling has not stopped. In fact, as the title of the poem suggests, it is in progress. Now the soldiers are left, not with the problem of hollering down the "lions in the air," as they were in "gay chaps," but, despite knowing what they now do, they must continue to maintain their cover.

How indeed, the rather Prufrockian speaker asks, can he possibly continue the charade of obeisance and patriotism, given what he now knows? The poem does not answer the question, but rather concludes with an image. Unlike Prufrock's unfortunate sense of himself drowning in human voices, the speaker of this sonnet is alert to and hears the sound of "iron feet again." While this sound may be simply the never ending round of racial and military struggle, it also works as a muted threat: This time the iron feet will step not to the beat of white commands, but toward resistance and perhaps revolution. The war will continue even after armistice. The unmasking of lies has enabled the speaker(s) to be ready for the possibility of another, closer war.

From *African American Review* 26, no. 2 (Summer 1992): 197-211. Copyright © 1992 by Ann Folwell Stanford. Reprinted by permission of Ann Folwell Stanford.

Notes

1. In "Writing War Poetry Like a Woman," Susan Schweik points out that during World War II the distinctions between male and female (and soldier/civilian) were not so pronounced as they had been in WWI. "Public discussions of war and literature in the United States dwell[ed] frequently on the new conjunctions between civilians and soldiers, front and home front, and men and women, focusing on their shared morale or effort as well as on their common deprivation and vulnerability" (534). Schweik here puts her finger on a phenomenon that probably fueled Brooks's conflation of war with racial and sexual politics.

2. And yet the poems remain grounded in the body and physicality. None of the war poems (or any of Brooks's *Bronzeville* poems) exhibit the tendency Laura Doyle has pointed out in Toomer, Joyce, and other modernist writers, who "remystify the mother and the body as a source of ambivalent transcendence." Doyle adds that writers like Toni Morrison and Virginia Woolf, on the other hand, do not "reject pessimistically whatever revitalization a return to physical groundedness might offer" (4).

3. The image of unbandaging sight occurs in many of Brooks's poems. In *Bronzeville*'s war poems, she writes of cutting the eye's veiling ("firstly inclined to take what it is told"). In "the funeral," people wait for a "dear blindfold" to mute and dull their grief, preferring the blindfold to the raw (but real) feelings clear sight would bring them. Later, in *Annie Allen* ("the children of the poor"), Brooks writes of "Holding the bandage ready for [the children's] eyes" so that they may "sew up belief."

4. Miller, born in 1919 near Waco, Texas, was a Navy steward and the first black to be awarded the Navy Cross for Bravery on December 7, 1941, for "unusual heroism in action." The Department of Navy Office of Information writes that, "while serving

aboard the USS West Virginia which was docked at Pearl Harbor, Miller performed heroically when the vessel was attacked by Japanese aircraft. Miller first assisted his mortally wounded captain to cover and then manned a machine gun, which he was not accustomed to operate, and successfully destroyed two of the attacking aircraft. Miller was awarded the Navy Cross for Bravery by Admiral Nimitz" (Greene 202). Interestingly, Miller was only promoted to Mess Attendant First Class. In 1943, he was a member of the crew of 700 men who were killed when a Japanese submarine torpedoed and sank the aircraft carrier USS Liscomb Bay (Greene 202).

5. In an image that recalls Richard Wright's figure of white philanthropy in *Native Son*, the blind Mrs. Dalton in her white dress, lady democracy belongs to white men and is duplicitous—virginal and murderous, by turns. To blacks, Brooks suggests, she is untouchable and dangerous.

6. Throughout this and many of Brooks's poems I am reminded of Paulo Freire's analysis of oppressive relationships where "dehumanization . . . marks not only those whose humanity has been stolen, but also (though in a different way) those who have stolen it" (28).

7. The figure of enclosure is important in much of Brooks's early poetry. It appears at the beginning of both *A Street in Bronzeville* and her second collection, *Annie Allen*. *Bronzeville*'s first poem, "the old-marrieds," opens with the same kind of qualifying language as "Negro Hero" and describes enclosure in the first line: "But in the *crowding darkness* not a word did they say" (19; emphasis added). Similarly, the first of the *Annie Allen* poems is entitled "birth in a narrow room" and describes the beginning of Annie's life as she is born from the enclosure of the womb into another "narrow" enclosed space (83). So, too, the hero is confined to the narrow space of the galley.

8. Maria Mootry describes "Gay Chaps" as a collage, "with a modernist aesthetic of indeterminacy, fragmentation, multi-locused meaning, and difficulty of interpretation. . . . In [collage] the paradox between the true and the false induces equivocal resonances that involve the metamorphosis of one reality into another. The result is a message—indirect, witty, and shocking—fit to convey the complexities of the modern world" (81).

9. William Couch was a fellow member of the Chicago South Side poetry workshop where Brooks and other writers studied with wealthy socialite Inez Cunningham Stark during the early 1940s.

10. Space constraints make it impossible to explore the relation of sexual struggle to war in these sonnets, but several of them (particularly "love note I," "piano after war," "mentors," and "love note II") inscribe sexual struggle within their texts.

11. Here I think Brooks anticipates Ellison's *Invisible Man* (1952), whose main character adopts multiple personae in the frustrating attempt to discover who he is. Obviously not all of Brooks's characters are so limited in self-knowledge, the speaker of "Negro Hero" providing a notable example. Satin-Legs Smith and, later, Annie Allen will struggle with self-definition and are both ultimately shaped by constructions based on race and gender.

12. The roaring airplanes overhead recall, again, Wright's *Native Son* (1940), in which Bigger Thomas hears and sees an airplane flying and announces that he would like to be a pilot, while knowing he can never do so in the circumscribed racist environment of the United States.

13. In no way am I suggesting that the effects of racism are as devastating to the oppressor as to the oppressed. Indeed, if that were so, racism would not exist. I am, however, asserting that racism injures, in differing ways, both oppressor and oppressed. Alice Walker adumbrates this theme in *The Third Life of Grange Copeland*, in which a white woman's distaste for blacks outweighs her survival instinct and she refuses Grange's help, thereby drowning in icy water (146-52).

14. However, for Brooks, war does not always mean powerlessness to its participants. In *Annie Allen*, the "man of tan" has his first taste of power (and I think it is safe to say that Brooks uses this notion ironically) in Europe as a soldier and cannot cope with the constraints of racism and his perceived loss of "manhood" once he gets home.

15. "I hold," "I store," "I label," and "I bid" convey an intentionality not unlike that of many black slaves who deliberately hid signs of their intelligence and creativity from their white masters in order to survive. "I keep eyes pointed in" suggests an evasiveness that, again, is a survival strategy.

16. This poem recalls Langston Hughes's many poems in "Montage of a Dream Deferred," but especially "Dream Boogie:" "Good morning daddy!/ Ain't you heard/ The boogie-woogie rumble/ Of a dream deferred?" (89).

17. The image of light is not a static one for Brooks. In "firstly inclined to take what it is told," it is "mighty light" that blinds and beguiles. Light can both blind and illuminate, and Brooks plays with its countervailing properties.

Works Cited

Brooks, Gwendolyn. *Blacks*. Chicago: David, 1987.

_____. *Report from Part One*. Detroit: Broadside, 1972.

Doyle, Laura. "Crossing Boundaries, Mothers' Bodies: Joyce, Toomer, and Morrison." MLA Convention. New Orleans, 28 Dec. 1988.

Elshtain, Jean Bethke. *Women and War*. New York: Basic, 1987.

Foner, Jack D. *Blacks and the Military in American History*. New York: Praeger, 1974.

Foucault, Michel. *Power/Knowledge: Selected Interviews and Other Writings 1972-1977*. Ed. Colin Gordon. Trans. Colin Gordon et al. New York: Pantheon, 1980.

Freire, Paulo. *Pedagogy of the Oppressed*. Trans. Myra Bergman Ramos. New York: Seabury-Continuum, 1968.

Fussell, Paul. *The Great War in Modern Memory*. New York: Oxford UP, 1975.

_____. *Wartime: Understanding and Behavior in the Second World War*. New York: Oxford UP, 1989.

Greene, Robert Ewell. *Black Defenders of America, 1775-1973: A Reference and Pictorial History*. Chicago: Johnson, 1974.

Hudson, Clenora F. "Racial Themes in the Poetry of Gwendolyn Brooks." *CLA Journal* 17 (1973): 16-20.

Hughes, Langston. "Dream Boogie." *The Langston Hughes Reader.* New York: Braziller, 1958. 89.

Jarrell, Randall. "Death of a Ball Turret Gunner." *The Complete Poems.* New York: Farrar, 1969.144.

Mootry, Maria K. "'The Step of Iron Feet': Creative Practice in the War Sonnets of Melvin B. Tolson and Gwendolyn Brooks." *Obsidian* II 2.3 (1987): 69-87.

Mullen, Robert W. *Blacks in America's Wars: The Shift in Attitudes from the Revolutionary War to Vietnam.* New York: Monad, 1973.

Ostriker, Alicia Suskin. *Stealing the Language: The Emergence of Women's Poetry in America.* Boston: Beacon, 1985.

Owen, Wilfred. "Mental Cases." *Wilfred Owen: The Complete Poems and Fragments.* Ed. Jon Stallworthy. New York: Norton, 1984.169.

Schweik, Susan. "'A Word No Man Can Say for Us': American Women Writers and the Second World War." Diss. Yale U, 1984.

_____. "Writing War Poetry Like a Woman." *Critical Inquiry* 13 (1987): 532-56.

Walker, Alice. *The Third Life of Grange Copeland.*1970. New York: Harvest-Harcourt, 1977.

Wright, Richard. *Native Son.* 1940. New York: Perennial-Harper, 1966.

"A Material Collapse That Is Construction":
History and Counter-Memory in
Gwendolyn Brooks's *In the Mecca*_____

John Lowney

John Lowney provides a historical and cultural investigation of Brooks's depiction of the Mecca apartment complex. Lowney discusses the popular-culture representations and conceptions of the complex from magazines such as *Life* and *Harper's*. Historically, the Mecca housed affluent whites, but it fell into ruin after the Great Depression, and whites gradually vacated the complex. It became a residence for blacks, an ironic representation of the kind of affluence to which blacks could aspire in some parts of the North. Brooks revises history with her poem about life in "Chicago's most celebrated slum." Lowney gives further insight by noting Brooks's own personal ties to the Mecca, which she incorporates into the poem. The bulk of the essay is devoted to analysis of what the residents of Brooks's poem represent. — M.R.M.

From the Chicago Loop, where sunlight off the lakefront strikes the shining towers, State Street runs straight south, wide, busy with streetcars and heavy trucks. Quickly the buildings get shabby—little stores selling auto parts, a junkyard crammed with rusting wreckage. The city is harsh: concrete streets, brick building walls, black steel viaducts. Beyond 22nd Street the faces of the people are black. This is the South Side Negro section. Here the street is quieter, the sun is hazy and dirty and pale . . .

—John Bartlow Martin, "The Strangest Place in Chicago"

So begins a 1950 journey in *Harper's* magazine to "one of the most remarkable Negro slum exhibits in the world" (87), the Mecca Building on Chicago's South Side. This journey from shining towers to shabby tenements, where even the sun is dirty, follows what was becoming a familiar rhetorical path for describing deteriorating urban neighborhoods, the racialized discourse of urban decline. Perhaps no other building symbolized post-World War II urban decline more starkly than the Mecca Building. Built by the D. H. Burnham Company in 1891, the Mecca was at first celebrated as a boldly innovative architectural prototype for luxury apartment living. With its atrium courtyards, its skylights and ornamental iron grillwork, its elaborate fountains and flower gardens, the Mecca was a major tourist attraction during the Columbian Exposition. Beginning with the movement of Chicago's wealthy to the North Side at the turn of the century, however, and culminating with the economic devastation wrought by the Great Depression, the Mecca gradually became an overcrowded tenement. By 1950, the Mecca Building had become notorious not because of its architectural magnificence, but because of the poverty of its remaining inhabitants.[1] It was demolished in 1952 so that its final owner, the Illinois Institute of Technology (I.I.T.), could expand its new campus, designed by the renowned Modernist architect Ludwig Mies van der Rohe.

Before the Mecca Building was obliterated, it had become the subject of national media attention as a monumental example of urban decline, an example depicted in racialized rhetoric that foreshadows the discourse of urban decline in the 1960s. It also became the subject of an important collection of poems that begins with an epigraph from Martin's "The Strangest Place in Chicago," but contests the dominant discourse of urban decline, Gwendolyn Brooks's *In the Mecca*. The title poem of this collection reconstructs the vanished city of the Mecca in a dialogical narrative of counter-memory that questions official historical accounts of the building. Rather than presenting a presumably disinterested "statistical report" on urban poverty, Brooks was interested in writing about the Mecca with "a certain detachment, but only as a means of reaching substance with some incisiveness." She aimed in her long poem to "present a large variety of personalities against a mosaic of daily affairs, recognizing that even the *grimmest* of these is likely to have a streak or two streaks of sun."[2] Brooks's representation of the Mecca resembles neither the utopian space its designers had envisioned nor the dystopian place its commemorators disparaged. Instead, "In the Mecca" interrogates the dystopian discourse of urban decline so often invoked to characterize postwar African American life; as such, it is an "incisive" intervention into the construction of African American historical memory.

Robert Beauregard documents in *Voices of Decline: The Postwar Fate of US Cities* how the 1950s discourse of urban decline was becoming more racialized. The postwar years saw an increased migration of rural blacks to northern cities. Chicago continued to be a "mecca" for Southern blacks, but, as in other urban centers, the lack of housing and jobs for unskilled workers resulted in greater crowding in inner-city neighborhoods.[3] The demolition of deteriorating buildings and neighborhoods for redevelopment projects did not result in adequate new housing for the urban poor; slums instead grew larger and more concentrated with the absorption of people displaced by demolition, while dehumanizing large public housing projects themselves became slums. With the movement of white families to the suburbs, and with the decrease in the flow of immigrants to cities, urban poverty was increasingly seen as a "Negro" problem: the slum problem had become a ghetto problem. By the 1960s, Beauregard writes, the discourse of urban decline was defined by

> . . . a single theme that unified its various fragments and turned urban decline into a society-wide problem. The theme was race, the problem was the concentration, misery, and rebellion of Negroes in central cities, and the reaction was one of fear and eventually panic. Commentators could no longer avoid racial prejudice and institutional discrimination. (169)

It is this apocalyptic mood of social crisis through which Brooks depicts the Mecca.

In the Mecca consists of two sections: the long narrative title poem, which was planned and drafted in the 1950s but not completed until

1968; and a second section of more topical poems written in the later 1960s entitled "After Mecca." Dedicated to "the memory of Langston Hughes; and to James Baldwin, Amiri Baraka, and Mike Alexandroff, educators extraordinaire," this volume is extremely important in Brooks's development as a writer, as it registers her growing commitment to a more politically engaged, cultural nationalist position in the Chicago black community.[4] This stance is most evident in "After Mecca," which includes such uncompromising poems on African American urban life as "Boy Breaking Glass," who "has not Congress, lobster, love, luau,/ the Regency Room, the Statue of Liberty" (439), and "The Blackstone Rangers," whose "country is a Nation on no map" (447). "After Mecca" also includes poems celebrating African American cultural heroism such as "Medgar Evers," "Malcolm X," and "The Wall," written for and read at the dedication of the Wall of Respect, a mural commemorating African American history painted on a South Side slum building.

"In the Mecca" likewise appeals to the mood of urban crisis experienced most acutely by inner-city Blacks in the late 1960s, but evoked also by critics of modernist urban planning.[5] Brooks's empathetic participant/observer's narrative stance in representing the Mecca world contrasts sharply with the more detached mass media representations that had commemorated the building's decline before it was razed. Her poem is a narrative of counter-memory that employs the formal and rhetorical strategies that George Lipsitz cogently defines in "History, Myth, and Counter-Memory: Narrative and Desire in Popular Novels." According to Lipsitz,

> . . . counter-memory forces revision of existing histories by supplying new perspectives about the past. . . . Counter-memory focuses on localized experiences with oppression, using them to reframe and refocus dominant narratives purporting to represent universal experience. (213)

With its emphasis on the local, the immediate, and the personal, with the multiple discordant stories that redefine the collective memory of the Mecca, Brooks foregrounds orally transmitted forms of remembering that are often erased from dominant historical narratives. More specifically, her polyvocal reconstruction of the Mecca counters reductively racist sociological narratives of urban decline.

The racialization of the discourse of urban decline can be seen as early as 1950 in national mass media representations of the Mecca. A *Life* magazine photographic essay on the building's last days exemplifies how such discourse is not only racialized but also often more blatantly racist in its representations of urban black life. The initial photo, which Brooks submitted to her publisher as the jacket cover for her book (but was denied permission to use by *Life*), depicts a solitary child dwarfed by the immensity of the building's courtyard, empty except for refuse littering the floor. The explanatory paragraph below all but attributes the decline of the building to the arrival of black tenants:

> It was a mecca for Chicago's rising rich until the South Side became less stylish. By 1912 the first Negro tenants had moved in. The building's noisy jazz activities gave a name to the *Mecca Flat Blues* and the apartment steadily trumpeted its way downhill. I.I.T. bought it in 1941 but could not wreck it until the 700 occupants could find homes in Chicago's crowded Negro area. Since September I.I.T. has collected no rent from the 51 remaining tenants and hopes to have them all moved out by year's end. (133)

This brief historical narrative of the Mecca's transformation from "Chicago's showiest apartment" to its "most celebrated slum building" suggests an almost inevitable decline that follows the "first Negro tenants." The one-sentence explanation of the years between 1912 and 1941 implies a causal relationship between black noise—"the building's noisy jazz activities"—and urban decline. With the arrival of black tenants, the "apartment" becomes a synecdoche for its "noisy" inhabitants, as it "trumpeted its way downhill." Rather than a response to urban poverty, the blues are instrumentally related to a "steady" process of decline, a stubbornly slow process, however, that stands in the way of progress. The subsequent photographs in the article include several portraits of elderly residents, who themselves stand in the way of I.I.T.'s plans for urban renewal (or urban removal, from their perspective). But most of the photographs concentrate on the building itself, highlighting the contrast of faded elegance and current chaos, which is most evident in the second image of the article, a gracefully arched entrance above the sign, "This Building to be Vacated and Wrecked." In the subsequent images the human presence of the building's tenants can be seen only through the signs of its disrepair: an interior of an apartment with a bullet-damaged window, the result of "a random shot fired by hoodlums" (136); or a stairway with decorative railings and paintless, graffiti-covered walls, the "handiwork of swarms of children who have overrun Mecca in recent years" (134).

Such dehumanizing language to characterize the children of the Mecca is even more evident in the *Harper's* article by John Bartlow Martin, "The Strangest Place in Chicago." Outside the building, Martin writes in his initial description, "An old man pulls a handcart filled with junk across an empty lot. From a deep hole tunneled under the sidewalk emerges the head of a little Negro boy, playing. The sidewalk is cracked and broken" (87). The inside of the building is equally decrepit, and its inhabitants are likewise conveyed in degrading terms, whether they be children or adults. The visitor is assaulted by a "powerful odor . . . a smell compounded of urine and stale cooking and of age" (87). Even the atrium skylights are obscured by dirt and darkness: they let in only "the kind of unreal light found underseas" (87). The only recognizable human activity inside this gloomy, musty setting is a janitor patching broken tile. Otherwise, all that can be heard are:

. . . the sound of distant human voices—women talking, a baby squalling, children screaming, men muttering, no words distinguishable. Spittle splats flatly on the tile floor, falling from a great height, spat by a man or a woman standing on an upper balcony. All day long people stand at the balconies . . . gazing out at other people facing them across the well in silence, gazing down at the floor far below, spitting, small human figures in a vast place. . . . (87)

Whereas the *Life* article foregrounds the contrast of solitary Mecca residents with their squalid surroundings, in "The Strangest Place in Chicago" any human presence is at first subsumed within the building's overall atmosphere of decay. From the impressionistic literary journalist's perspective, the spectacular squalor of the Mecca speaks only through the signs of its physical degradation. The initial voices of its residents are presented as indecipherable utterances whose significance can be gauged only in relation to the "vast" emptiness of the Mecca. With "no words distinguishable," these voices are a muted version of *Life*'s "noisy jazz."

When the residents' voices are eventually distinguished from each other in "The Strangest Place in Chicago," they are done so in terms that accentuate their degradation: a child crying "Mummy, Mummy"; the "high mad cackling laughter of an old man"; a woman yelling at a child who is urinating from a third floor balcony (88-89). The article goes on to profile individual Mecca residents in more depth, and their stories variously follow a common plot of hopeful migration to Chicago from the South, disappointment over limited employment and housing opportunities, and despair during the Depression, which left them stranded in a building scheduled for demolition since its purchase by I.I.T. in 1941. Martin situates the Mecca residents within a historical narrative of considerable sociological detail, but their individual stories of hardship are muted by the alarming din with which he frames the story. On the one hand there are undisciplined children, shouting, crying, running madly, armed with improvised weapons, throwing garbage at each other; on the other hand there are elderly people, trapped, resigned, silent, or unintelligible. The story concludes with an especially pathetic example of unintelligibility: an old woman in a rocking chair, muttering loudly, but her "words are not intelligible, it is just a human voice, muttering, and it is impossible to tell whether in anger or in joy, it is only sound" (97).

Brooks's poetic representation of the Mecca reads as if she is responding directly to Martin's conclusion, "it is *just* a human voice . . . it is *only* sound." Her poem suggests that such unintelligibility is a failure of the listener rather than the speaker. Brooks had gained first-hand knowledge of life in the Mecca as a young woman in the 1930s while working there for four months as a sales assistant to a spiritual adviser, who, she explains,

> had a fantastic practice; lucrative. He had us bottling medicine as well as answering letters. Not real medicine, but love charms and stuff like that he called it, and delivered it through the building; that was my introduction to the Mecca building. (*Interview* 162)[6]

Brooks's recollections of this experience haunted her for years: "In the Mecca" was first drafted as a novel and was subsequently redrafted many times before it was published in its current form.[7] The result of this delayed completion and publication was a retrospective poem of greater political resonance. Like Martin's story, "In the Mecca" shows how a utopian architectural space has become a dystopian site; however, Brooks's poem foregrounds how even the most idealistic plans of modernist urban design cannot be dissociated from the contradictions inherent in a racist society. While the digressive, discordant narrative form of "In the Mecca" ironically contrasts with the building's monumental design, Brooks is ultimately less concerned with the architectural history of the Mecca than with the stories of those who live there. Unlike the Mecca residents of Martin's story, Brooks's characters are sharply individuated *and* connected with each other.

"In the Mecca" revolves around the story of a domestic worker's quest for her lost (and, as we ultimately find out, abducted and murdered) child, but through this story the poem portrays the everyday struggles of Mecca inhabitants in an array of voices and styles. These voices mix colloquial urban diction with more formal African American traditions of oratory, sermon, and proverb. Brooks's poem is, paradoxically, both elevated and intimate in its localized mode of address. The narrator's stance combines the synoptic, lofty vision of the epic poet with the more provisional, vernacular voice of the oral storyteller. This narrative stance corresponds with the dialogic interplay of speech acts that convey the social complexity of the Mecca world. Moreover, there is no linguistic hierarchy of speech acts that organizes the narrative; as Gayl Jones writes: "In Brooks's poetry there is no such hierarchy because any kind of language may occupy any space; indeed, different languages may almost occupy the same space" (195). Unlike the journalistic representations of the Mecca, Brooks does not sharply differentiate the "distinguishable" utterance from the "indistinguishable," whether from positions of moral or scientific (sociological) authority. She instead foregrounds how each character—as well as the narrator—is constructed by conflicting discourses.

The opening page of "In the Mecca," a single sentence situated apart from the rest of the narrative, demonstrates how Brooks's mixed mode of address is paradoxically inviting and disorienting at the same time: "Now the way of the Mecca was on this wise" (406). This sentence sounds authoritative, even prophetic, with the allusive resonance of the holy place of Islam underscoring the narrator's ironic stance toward the Chicago Mecca. The location and temporality of the narrator are unspecified, however, while this speech act points to a specific site with its indeterminate deictic indicators. "Now" could refer to the narrator's present, thus suggesting a retrospective assessment of the Mecca's past, or it could refer to the time indicated by the past tense verb form, "was." "Now" could also serve the narrative purpose of drawing attention to the importance of the story that follows, whether it be a command, request, or warning addressed directly to the audience or a term suggesting a transition in an ongoing narrative. The initial effect is one of questioning temporality, the "now" of the present and the "now" of the remembered past, but also of questioning how narratives represent the past. "Now" draws attention to the urgency of the moment, yet suggests a continuity between the narrated past and the narrator's present.

The rest of the first sentence likewise raises unsettling questions about the locality of the opening statement, especially about the narrator's position in relation to the social world she is representing. The "way of the Mecca" could imply purpose, direction, a course of action, or it could imply more mundanely, more naturalistically, the condition, and physical locale, of the Mecca as it was. The temporality of the statement is foregrounded through the question of its locality; to write of a world that no longer physically exists, but a world whose memory is contested, is to raise the question of whom one is writing *for*. The narrator is positioned neither certainly inside nor outside the Mecca; the audience's position, and the speech act itself, are likewise unsettled by the question of what defines insider knowledge. What is eventually "wise" about "the way of the Mecca" is the narrator's empathetic understanding and judgment, but the limitations of such outsider "wisdom" are also evident. If the narrator of "In the Mecca" is distanced from insider wisdom about the social world she recollects, distanced even by the "wise" tone by which an insider's account may be conveyed, her retrospective representation of the Mecca positions readers similarly. Rejecting the condescendingly moralistic or impressionistically spectacular visions of mass media representations of urban decline, Brooks instead makes her readers aware of their complicity in constructing a narrative that can contain the heterogeneous voices of the Mecca.

Like the initial sentence of the poem, which is both authoritative in its tone and disorienting in its ambiguity, the subsequent introductory passages evoke linguistic tensions that exist throughout the poem. The poem proceeds with a statement directly addressed to the reader, establishing a more explicit context for the subsequent narrative of counter-memory:

> Sit where the light corrupts your face.
> Mies Van der Rohe retires from grace.
> And the fair fables fall.
>
> (407)

"Truth is the significance of fact," wrote Mies van der Rohe (qtd. in Harvey 31), but the language of Brooks's opening explodes the rationalist foundations of such a modernist urban vision. Technological efficiency does not in itself produce improved social conditions, nor can "truth" be ascertained apart from the power relations in which it is embedded, especially when the "truth" in question exists only in contested memory, memory of a community displaced by a project designed by Mies van der Rohe himself. This paradoxical opening introduces a narrative that continually challenges readers' expectations with its dense wordplay. If the corrupt light evokes the contrast of hope and despair in prior representations of the Mecca, Brooks's post-modernist fables refuse to rest with simple oppositions of corrupt and fair. The poem accentuates, and denaturalizes, the racial associations of metaphors of light and darkness introduced in this opening. The "light" which "corrupts your face" draws attention to the lightness or darkness of "your face." And the "fall" of "the fair fables" raises the question of how narratives representing such dystopian worlds as the Mecca are "fair," suggesting that fairness is a matter of hegemony rather than of truth or accuracy. Brooks's characters live in a world of economic restriction, but their narratives represent an unpredictable array of responses, personal and political, to this world that defy totalizing "fables."

The introduction to the narrative's protagonist demonstrates the blend of demoralizing poverty and idiosyncratic vision that characterizes the residents of Brooks's Mecca:

S. Smith is Mrs. Sallie. Mrs. Sallie
hies home to Mecca, hies to marvelous rest;
ascends the sick and influential stair.
The eye unrinsed, the mouth absurd
with the last sourings of the master's Feast.
She plans
to set severity apart,
to unclench the heavy folly of the fist.

(407)

The story of Mrs. Sallie, who is first designated by the more public, official name one might see on her mailbox ("S. Smith"), is immediately situated in the context of racial and class inequality. In contrast to the humiliation of her job as a domestic worker, of preparing "the master's Feast," Mrs. Sallie's Mecca apartment is a "marvelous" refuge. But this refuge is also defined by the "sick and influential stair" she must climb, with "influential" suggesting how the physiological and psychological effects of poverty are interwoven. The densely charged language that follows in the description of Mrs. Sallie likewise blends the physiological with the psychological, but not to suggest that she is absolutely determined by the limitations of her social class and impoverished surroundings. Mrs. Sallie's response to her social position, and to the racism that defines this position, is deliberate: she "*plans*/ to set severity apart,/ to unclench the heavy folly of the fist" (emphasis added).

As empathetic as the narrator's understanding of Mrs. Sallie's mode of coping with her world is, the description of her that follows does not "set severity apart" in indicating the psychological cost of her resignation:

Infirm booms
and suns that have not spoken die behind this
low-brown butterball. Our prudent partridge.
A fragmentary attar and armed coma.
A fugitive attar and a district hymn.

(407)

The jarringly disconnected images suggest a character who is herself "fragmentary," tormented by "fugitive" repressed emotions. The dissociated sensual imagery is interspersed with language referring to those moral codes that define her mode of perseverance. Mrs. Sallie's "prudence," here mocked in the narrator's playfully familiar description of "our prudent partridge," is revealed more fully when she is inside her apartment:

Now Mrs. Sallie
confers her bird-hat to her kitchen table,
and sees her kitchen. It is bad, is bad,
her eyes say . . .
. . . .
Her denunciation
slaps savagely not only this sick kitchen but
her Lord's annulment of the main event.
"I want to decorate!" But what is that? A
pomade atop a sewage. An offense.
First comes correctness, then embellishment!
And music, mode, and mixed philosophy
may follow fitly on propriety
to tame the whiskey of our discontent!

(410)

The simple description of her kitchen as "bad" sparks a chain of associations that reveal Mrs. Sallie's "prudence" as part of a moral code that is based in Christian faith, but which is more properly defined by class and gender codes of "propriety." This emphasis on propriety, on "correctness" first, and *"then* embellishment," defines Mrs. Sallie's strength as a frugal mother who makes the most of her limited means, but it also unveils the limitations of a moral code based on the bourgeois appearance of goodness rather than on actual social and economic justice. It suggests, that is, how social codes of "propriety" relate to the possession (or lack) of property.

The first section of the poem, which traces Mrs. Sallie's ascent to her fourth-floor flat, concentrates on the dreams of the neighbors she passes, even if these dreams are as modest, as transitory, as contingent as her initial desire for a moment of rest. Neither the characters that Mrs. Sallie encounters on her way home nor her nine children can be understood in stereotypical terms; they are conveyed with psychological complexity, often paradoxically. Their public personae are belied by the often contradictory motivations that underlie their self-presentation. The description of Hyena, a "striking debutante," most blatantly reveals a contrast between public appearance and private motivation: "a fancier of firsts./ One of the first, and to the tune of hate,/ in all the Mecca to paint her hair sun-gold" (408). Her self-fashioning as a "striking debutante" with "sun-gold" hair concisely accentuates how racism structures codes of feminine beauty, yet her "tune of hate" suggests her complicity with the mode by which she distinguishes herself from other black women.

Not all of the characters who appear in the beginning of the poem are so obviously self-centered as Hyena is. However, those who seek to authorize their identities in narratives of transcendence, whether religious or secular, are also ironically undermined. Prophet Williams, for example, "rich with Bible . . . reeks/ with lust for his disciple," and even more strikingly, is responsible for his wife's violent death, a responsibility that the narrator extends to her "kinswomen":

Ida died in self-defense.
(Kinswomen!
Kinswomen!)
Ida died alone.

(408)

Finally, the young poet Alfred, a school teacher who believes in the religion of art, who "reads Shakespeare in the evenings or reads Joyce,"
later

. . . goes to bed with Telly Bell
in 309, or with that golden girl,
or thinks, or drinks until the Everything
is vaguely a part of One thing and the One thing
delightfully anonymous
and undiscoverable.

(409)

Immediately following such metaphysical speculations, such questions as "what was their one Belief?/ what was their joining thing?"
(409), is an arrestingly different sound: "A boy breaks glass and Mrs.
Sallie/ rises to the final and fourth floor" (410). This break between the
poet's meditations and Sallie's preparation of her family's dinner—
ham hocks, greens, yams, and cornbread—sets the tone for the quest
that sustains the rest of the narrative. Counting her children at dinner, she notices her daughter's absence and asks, "WHERE PEPITA
BE?" (415).

The child's disappearance changes the poem's mood from tentative
calm to impending violence. The narrative proceeds more rapidly,
more unpredictably, from dialogue to monologue, from spoken monologue to interior monologue. The characters respond to the news of the
child's disappearance with separately internalized visions of violence,
but their narratives are linked by their shared emphasis on racial op-

pression. The transformation of Mrs. Sallie's other children is, not surprisingly, most striking. Their characters are idiosyncratically differentiated at first. For example, there is Yvonne, who dreams of love, and whose defiant reason for chewing Doublemint gum parodies her mother's code of propriety:

> It is very bad,
> but in its badness it is nearly grand,
> and is a crown that tops bald innocence
> and gentle fright.
>
> (411)

Then there is Melodie Mary, who "likes roaches,/ and pities the gray rat" (412), whose sympathy for such unacknowledged everyday victims identifies her vision quite closely with the narrator's. In contrast, her brother Briggs, "adult as a stone/ (who if he cries cries alone)" (412), is consumed by anger. For him,

> Immunity is forfeit, love
> is luggage, hope is heresy.
> Gang
> is health and mange.
>
> (413)

As distinct as each of their characters are, Mrs. Sallie's children are united in their hatred of what their poverty denies them:

> [they] hate sewn suburbs;
> hate everything combed and strong; hate people who
> have balls, dolls, mittens and dimity frocks and trains
> and boxing gloves, picture books, bonnets for Easter.
> Lace handkerchief owners are enemies of Smithkind.
>
> (412)

When they are summoned to look for their sister, the children likewise react to her disappearance with visions distinctive to their characters, but they share a sense of deprivation, of feeling

> . . . constrained. All are constrained.
> And there is no thinking of grapes or gold
> or of any wicked sweetness and they ride
> upon fright and remorse and their stomachs
> are rags or grit.
>
> (416)

The neighbors that Mrs. Sallie and her children ask for help likewise are instantly transformed by the news of the child's disappearance. Their descriptions of Pepita, their speculations of what happened, and their evasions of questions tell us more about their characteristic modes of dealing with fear than they tell us about the lost child. As Gayl Jones states, the question "'Where is Pepita?' often becomes 'Where am I'?" (200). The first tale significantly is a great great-grandmother's recollection of slavery, while the second is a religious man's meditation on the Nazi death camps, linking the loss of the black child with "all old unkindnesses and harms" (417) in a parody of the Twenty-third Psalm. Each subsequent tale—whether of incidental violence, sensational crime, religious passion, isolation, retribution, or drunken delusion— evokes the fears, desires, and dreams of its teller. And each stands out in sharp relief from the more abstract, unresponsive "Law," which arrives, but "does not quickly go/ to fetch a Female of the Negro Race," and instead asks "a lariat of questions" (420-21).

Most notably contrasted with the Law are the young poets whose angry voices resonate among the more disparate, more desperate outbursts of their older neighbors. There is, again, the introspective Alfred,

> . . . (who might have been an architect)
> [who] can speak of Mecca: firm arms surround
> disorders, bruising ruses and small hells,
> small semiheavens: hug barbarous rhetoric
> built of buzz, coma and petite pell-mells.
>
> (422)

The initial portrait of the "untalented" artist of "decent enough no-goodness" (409) is modified considerably by the more detailed presentation of his later vision as the resident poet of the Mecca. Alfred not only intimately knows the architecture, history, and everyday social life of the Mecca, he also understands the need for a vision that can integrate this local knowledge with a broader understanding of the African diaspora. His admiration for Léopold Senghor is conveyed in a meditative vision that is romantic, at times escapist, but nonetheless resonant in its affirmation of negritude:

> Believes in beauty
> But believes that blackness is among the fit filters.
> Old cobra
> coughs and curdles in his lungs,
> spits spite, spits exquisite spite, and cries,
>   "Ignoble!"
> . . . .
> Senghor sighs and, "negritude" needing,
> speaks for others, for brothers.
>
> (422)

Alfred's affirmation of "negritude" does not match the revolutionary directness of the poet Don Lee (who is now Haki Madhubuti), however, whose uncompromising black nationalist stance is introduced immediately after:

Don Lee wants
not a various America.
Don Lee wants
a new nation
under nothing;
. . . .
wants
new art and anthem; will
want a new music screaming in the sun.

(423-24)

The introduction of the known black nationalist poet to the mix of fictional characters, especially following the intrusion of the Law, reminds readers that Brooks's reconstruction of the fallen Mecca is no poetic exercise in nostalgia. There are a number of characters in the Mecca who call for retributive violence, but the inclusion of Lee's black nationalist stance among the apocalyptic calls for bloody upheaval situates the conflicts of "In the Mecca" within the racial politics of the 1960s, as Brooks connects the remembered past to the more defiant present. As R. Baxter Miller writes, "the Lee in the poem lives at the midpoint between mimesis and reality" (164), but he occupies a space in the poem that differs from the other Mecca tenants. His apocalyptic, but utopian vision reaffirms how the struggles defining Brooks's characters are confined neither temporally nor spatially to their lives in the Mecca. The incipient violence that constantly threatens their existence is likewise not confined to the urban slum; it is instead endemic to a nation structured by racial oppression.

The apocalyptic vision of "In the Mecca" is ultimately tempered with the innocent voice of the murdered child Pepita, who is finally discovered beneath a cot "in dust with roaches" (433), the victim of hateful, purposeless violence. Her murderer is a man who too "looks at the Law unlovably," but whose hatred is murderous and suicidal. As in "Boy Breaking Glass," in which the child's "broken window is a cry of art" (438), or even "The Blackstone Rangers," the notorious South Side gang members who "exulting, monstrous hand on monstrous hand,/ construct, strangely, a monstrous pearl or grace" (448), the conclusion of "In the Mecca" looks to an unlikely source of poetic expression, the poignant voice of the murdered child, to convey the urgent need to listen closely to the dispossessed. While sounding the alarm for action, Brooks ultimately speaks for the voiceless, the child who

> . . . never went to kindergarten.
> She never learned that black is not beloved.
> Was royalty when poised,
> sly, at the A and P's fly-open door.
> Will be royalty no more.
> "I touch"—she said once—"petals of a rose.
> A silky feeling through me goes!"
> Her mother will try for roses.
>
> (433)

The conclusion of "In the Mecca" subtly affirms the need for active transformation, both of self and society, even if it seems too late, even if it is provoked by tragic loss. Mrs. Sallie may not be able to save her daughter's life, but her "try for roses" is an act that validates her own life as it commemorates her daughter's (Jones 203).

Brooks writes in *Report from Part One* how the experience of celebrating black self-determination in the late 1960s changed her understanding of poetry's social role:

My aim, in my next future, is to write poems that will somehow successfully "call" (see Imamu Baraka's "SOS") all black people: black people in taverns, black people in alleys, black people in gutters, schools, offices, factories, prisons, the consulate; I wish to reach black people in pulpits, black people in mines, on farms, on thrones, not always to "teach"—I shall wish often to entertain, to illumine. My newish voice will not be an imitation of the contemporary young black voice, which I so admire, but an adaptation of today's G.B. voice. (183)

If the linguistic and rhetorical complexity of "In the Mecca" is often imposing, the poem nonetheless registers Brooks's transformed social vision for poetry, a vision that celebrates those performative acts that meet the urgent needs of the historical moment, that are necessarily destructive as they are creative. "In the Mecca" accentuates the fragmentary, ephemeral aspects of Mecca life, stressing the sense of disconnection which paradoxically links its characters—disconnection from place, from community, and from the past. Such local, specific experiences that are nonetheless linked by shared patterns of oppression and failed hopes also evince the bitter ironies of rational urban planning, from Burnham to Mies van der Rohe. By foregrounding the narratives of those displaced by "urban renewal," Brooks underscores the need for not only reconstructing urban communities, but also the collective memory of these communities. Rather than the authoritatively detached rendering of the Mecca as "one of the most remarkable Negro slum exhibits in the world," Brooks dialogically represents this world in the imagined voices of the Mecca residents. The complexity of this vision is nowhere more evident than in the characterization of the Mecca's resident poet, Alfred. His transformation from the sensualist we first encounter on "the sick and influential stair" is ultimately as instructive as it is entertaining and illuminating. Like Brooks's poetic (re)vision of the Mecca, his concluding vision synthesizes a local knowledge of his community, in all of its dystopian despair, with a more comprehensive understanding of the historical need for the poet's utopian social role:

I hate it.
Yet, murmurs Alfred—
who is lean at the balcony, leaning—
something, something in Mecca
continues to call! . . .

. . . .

an essential sanity, black and electric,
builds to a reportage and redemption.
 A hot estrangement.
 A material collapse
that is Construction.

(433)

From *MELUS* 23, no. 3 (Fall 1998): 3-20. Copyright © 1998 by *MELUS*. Reprinted by permission of *MELUS*.

Notes

1. See Kenny J. Williams, "The World of Satin-Legs, Mrs. Sallie, and the Black-stone Rangers: The Restricted World of Gwendolyn Brooks," for a concise explanation of the now obscure history of the Mecca Building, which is omitted even from official documents such as the major biographies of D. H. Burnham.

2. Brooks, "Work Proposed for 'In the Mecca,'" *Report from Part One* 189. All citations from *Report from Part One* will hereafter be cited parenthetically as *Report*.

3. The black population of Chicago grew extraordinarily rapidly between the 1910s and 1960s. As an early migrant from Mississippi explained, wherever "one stopped on the way . . . the mecca was Chicago" (qtd. in James R. Grossman, *Land of Hope: Chicago, Black Southerners, and the Great Migration* 4). According to Nicholas Lemann, "During the 1940s, the black population of Chicago increased by 77 per cent, from 278,000 to 492,000. In the 1950s, it grew by another 65 per cent, to 813,000; at one point 2,200 black people were moving to Chicago every week" (qtd. in Charles Scruggs, *Sweet Home: Invisible Cities in the Afro-American Novel* 14). See Scruggs 13-37 on the significance of urban migration for African American literature.

4. Brooks's readers have generally followed her account of her turn toward black cultural nationalism. She cites the 1967 Fisk University Writers Conference as the event that drew her toward the Black Arts Movement. The division of Brooks's career into an early period of poetry characterized by stylized formalism and a later period of poetry informed by her commitment to black nationalism tends to underestimate the po-

litical import of her pre-1967 writings. Brooks's dedication to black self-determination is more explicit after 1968, however, as she, for example, committed herself to black-owned publishing projects. On the impact of the Fisk Conference on Brooks's political consciousness, see *Report from Part One* 84-86 and George E. Kent, *A Life of Gwendolyn Brooks* 195-202. For a cogent essay that typifies critical accounts of Brooks's "conversion" to the Black Arts Movement, see Addison Gayle, Jr., "Gwendolyn Brooks: Poet of the Whirlwind."

  5. The best known example of such criticism would be Jane Jacobs's *The Death and Life of Great American Cities*. See David Harvey, *The Condition of Postmodernity* 66-98 for an incisive overview of postmodernist critiques of "the modernist idea that planning and development should focus on large-scale, metropolitan-wide, technologically rational and efficient urban *plans*, backed by absolutely no-frills architecture . . ." (66). Beauregard surveys the role that racial politics increasingly played in the post-World War II discourse of urban decline. See especially 160-216.

  6. See also Kent, *A Life of Gwendolyn Brooks* 42 on Brooks's experience of working in the Mecca.

  7. On the various drafts of "In the Mecca," see Kent, *A Life of Gwendolyn Brooks* 130-31, 211-22.

Works Cited

Beauregard, Robert A. *Voices of Decline: The Postwar Fate of US Cities*. Cambridge: Blackwell, 1993.

Brooks, Gwendolyn. *In the Mecca*. 1968. *Blacks*. Chicago: Third World, 1987. 401-56.

_____. Interview by George Stavros. *Contemporary Literature* 11.1 (Winter 1970): 1-20. Rpt. Brooks, *Report*, 147-66.

_____. *Report from Part One*. Detroit: Broadside, 1972.

Gayle, Addison, Jr. "Gwendolyn Brooks: Poet of the Whirlwind." *Black Women Writers (1950-1980): A Critical Evaluation*. Ed. Mari Evans. Garden City, NY: Anchor-Doubleday, 1984. 79-87.

Grossman, James R. *Land of Hope: Chicago, Black Southerners, and the Great Migration*. Chicago: U of Chicago P, 1989.

Harvey, David. *The Condition of Postmodernity*. Cambridge, MA: Blackwell, 1989.

Jacobs, Jane. *The Death and Life of Great American Cities*. New York: Random House, 1961.

Jones, Gayl. "Community and Voice: Gwendolyn Brooks's 'In the Mecca.'" Mootry and Smith 193-204.

Kent, George E. *A Life of Gwendolyn Brooks*. Lexington: UP of Kentucky, 1990.

Lipsitz, George. "History, Myth, and Counter-Memory: Narrative and Desire in Popular Novels." *Time Passages: Collective Memory and American Popular Culture*. Minneapolis: U of Minnesota P, 1990. 211-31.

Martin, John Bartlow. "The Strangest Place in Chicago." *Harper's* (December 1950): 86-97.

"The Mecca: Chicago's showiest apartment has given up all but the ghost." *Life* 31.21 (19 Nov 1951):133-39.

Miller, R. Baxter. "'Define ... the Whirlwind': Gwendolyn Brooks's Epic Sign for a Generation." *Black American Poets Between Worlds, 1940-1960*. Ed. R. Baxter Miller. Knoxville: U of Tennessee P, 1986. 160-73.

Mootry, Maria K., and Gary Smith, eds. *A Life Distilled: Gwendolyn Brooks, Her Poetry and Fiction*. Urbana: U of Illinois P, 1987.

Scruggs, Charles. *Sweet Home: Invisible Cities in the Afro-American Novel*. Baltimore: Johns Hopkins UP, 1993.

Williams, Kenny J. "The World of Satin-Legs, Mrs. Sallie, and the Blackstone Rangers: The Restricted Chicago of Gwendolyn Brooks." Mootry and Smith 47-70.

A Prophet Overheard:
A Juxtapositional Reading of
Gwendolyn Brooks's "In the Mecca" _____

Sheila Hassell Hughes

Sheila Hassell Hughes interprets Brooks's "In the Mecca," arguing that the poem appeals to both white and black audiences because it addresses themes and issues important to both. Further, she argues, the poem is designed to represent several perspectives because the Mecca apartment complex is a microcosm of the larger racial and gender problems plaguing the United States and American history. Hughes briefly discusses the ambivalence of both white and black and male and female audiences toward Brooks's adoption of the Black Arts movement's political aesthetic. Hughes's primary objective is to investigate how "In the Mecca" operates on multiple local, national, gendered, and temporal levels. It is this richness of perspective that gives the poem depth and unsettles readers who feel compelled to identify Brooks as a writer exclusively addressing a black audience or exclusively addressing a white audience. Additionally, Hughes analyzes the layers of polarities that the poem engages—black/white, male/female, adult/child, North/South, and rich/poor—to predict an American decline into further instability if people of all persuasions do not learn to communicate more effectively and honestly.   — M.R.M.

As Gwendolyn Brooks's last collection of poetry to be published by a mainstream press (Harper, 1968), and the first to come out of her conversion to the Black Arts Movement, *In the Mecca* marks the end of one age for the poet, and the beginning of another. Situated in the cramped confines of a slum tenement on Chicago's South Side, the title poem is local—even narrow—in focus. But the work continues to speak beyond both its particular subject and its point of articulation; indeed, it is in part because "In the Mecca" is such an intense "reportage"

(31) that it also functions as a prophecy of "time/ crack[ing] into furious flower" ("The Second Sermon on the Warpland," *Mecca* 54).

Much of the critical debate surrounding Brooks's work has focused on the tension between the particular and the universal, the localized and the transcendent. White critics (feminist and otherwise) have tended to fault her later work, especially, for too narrow a focus and affiliation. The work is not deemed to offer non-Black readers an enticing—or, in Charles Bernstein's terms, "absorptive"—experience. Brooks's attention to the particulars of Black life, it would seem, renders her poetry less accessible to whites and therefore falls short of a "universal" appeal and a "transcendent" value.[1] A number of Black (mostly male) critics, in contrast, heralded Brooks's political shift of the late 1960s as a necessary turn both inward, to her own community, and outward, beyond the confines of the feminine psyche explored in her earlier epic "The Anniad." These critics valued the strong sense of place and position in Brooks's work and saw no merit in striving to appeal to a broader—i.e., white—readership. They charged her earlier poetry, in fact, with too pleading a tone and with a high aestheticism that actually excluded most Black readers. "Universal" and "transcendent" were understandably read as code-words for white appeal. After all, both terms assume a certain relationship to place and space—a geographic, economic, and/or psychic mobility—at odds with the experience of Blacks living in cramped kitchenettes in Jim-Crow Chicago.

Despite what either these latter critics or the 1950 Pulitzer Prize might suggest, however, Brooks never wrote directly or explicitly for a white audience. She was always concerned to represent, to speak to, and to sanctify Black life as she knew it—most especially in the Bronzeville section of Chicago. But clearly, when she adopted the Black Arts credo that "true Black writers speak *as* blacks, *about* blacks, and *to* blacks" (*Report* 195), she heightened awareness of her social location and political position, rhetorically situating herself and her readers in a new way.

Part of what I, as a white feminist critic, want to argue here is that this newly visible political alignment reduces neither the aesthetic merit of Brooks's later poetry nor its social value beyond the Black community. Indeed, the poet's word remains richly multivalent, in part because she recognizes that the social location from which she speaks is as complex and shifting as it is precise. Although her other rhetoric might seem to favor one line of identification over another (racial rather than gender solidarity, for instance), her poetic practice exemplifies an indissoluble tension and multiplicity. In her poetry, she simultaneously speaks from the margins and centers of *both* Black culture *and* the dominant white society, unsettling the opposition between various kinds of insiders and outsiders in the process.

She exhibits, in fact, the very kind of "both/and conceptual orientation" that Patricia Hill Collins identifies as essential to Black feminist thought. Black women have developed this mode of consciousness, Collins argues, to "negotiate [the] contradictions" inherent in "being simultaneously a member of a group and yet standing apart from it" (207). In contrast to standard Western "either/or dichotomous thinking"— an approach that relies on binary oppositions, which inevitably revert to hierarchies—Black feminist thought examines a "matrix of domination . . . structured along [multiple] axes" (230). Brooks's poetry speaks from the matrix, and her voice reverberates in both directions along the axes of race, class, and gender.

The first part of this essay will attempt to sketch the matrix, surveying the conditions of Brooks's literary production and reception, in an attempt to establish how a "politics of location" is intrinsic to her spatial poetics. But my rhetorical concerns also extend to the border between the sociopolitical and the spiritual realms—to ways the poetry exceeds history and geography, speaking *beyond* its location even as it speaks *out of* and *for* it. Through the poet's figuration of space, both excess and absence function not as a strictly spiritual transcendence of time and place, but rather as the reverse image of a necessary liberation. This kind of freedom begins in a particular time and place but potentially extends beyond it. The "ex-static"[2] call for liberation is what I consider the prophetic element of "In the Mecca."

The second half of the essay then offers a "juxtapositional" reading of the prophetic word in Brooks's poem. With this epic, in particular, the poet destabilizes a whole series of sociopolitical dichotomies—inside/outside, center/margin, here/there, and us/them—in two ways: first, by revealing a complex layering of social, historical, and even geographical forces at play in one seemingly monolithic site (the Mecca building) and, second, by relocating the poem's ultimate "conclusion" beyond the borders of her text. She both maps the matrix and points the way out. Read as an ironic and inverted parable, the poem issues a prophetic call for radical reader-response and responsibility—even across the very lines of race and culture, time and place that Brooks herself delineates so powerfully. All three aspects of the poet's work—the political, the poetic, and the prophetic—are tied to her location, and this is precisely why she continues to speak so powerfully beyond a particular place. Her poetry may not be universal or transcendent in the traditional sense of the words (i.e., timelessly open to identification and appropriation by a privileged white audience), but it continues to speak a liberatory word with implications for both Black and white readers. In contrast to an "integrationist" approach that seeks to salve wounds and consciences, and to reduce tension for the sake of inclusion, a juxtapositional reading aims to expose, even amplify, tensions as a means to transformation. My goal is not to redeem Brooks's more "militant" poetry for a white audience so much, perhaps, as to work out my own redemption as a reader in response to a prophetic word overheard—to formulate an ethical response to a call not meant for me.

Brooks's Social Location as Interpenetrated Space

In the most obvious sense of "location," Gwendolyn Brooks is a Chicago poet. She was Poet Laureate of Illinois for more than three decades, in fact, and the constancy of her geographic identification lends a continuity to her long and varied poetic career. Brooks's parents moved to the South Side of Chicago when she was an infant, and she lived there until her death in 2000, at age eighty-three. For many years, she lived in a series of cramped and damp apartments—basements, garages, and kitchenettes (*Report* 52)—and struggled to make ends meet with Henry Blakely, whom she married in 1939. As Blacks, they faced both a severe housing crisis in the urban migration "mecca" of Jim-Crow Chicago[3] and a job ceiling that prevented economic advancement. Brooks lived in the same quarter, frequented the same neighborhoods, and described the same streets, for a lifetime, and, from her earliest published collection, her poetry addressed the realities of poor and working-class African Americans in that urban environment.

From the first, the constraining effects of this location on the young poet were countered by the practices of an older generation that had learned how to "make a way out of no way" and a nurturing space out of a confining place. Brooks's parents were the first encouragement to her writing. Her mother had faith that her daughter was to become "the lady Paul Laurence Dunbar" (*Report* 56), and her father, who dropped out of college to support his family, "revered books and education" (52) and gave his daughter her first writing desk (56). Given the spatial limits of the family home, there was obviously no paternal "library" in which to read and write. The girl's bedroom—small, childish, feminine—thus served as the site of her poetic production for many years. Having written poetry regularly since the age of seven (55), Brooks achieved some degree of recognition early and garnered additional support from the larger Black literary community. As an adolescent, for example, she was mentored by both James Weldon Johnson and Langston Hughes (173-74). By the time she graduated from high school, she was publishing poems almost weekly in the *Chicago Defender* and had started an amateur literary magazine (Kent, *A Life* 25). Remarkably, from an age when most writers are still exploring the most intensely private and purely expressive modes, Brooks was writing with a sense of both a public audience and her place in a larger tradition. It is equally remarkable, perhaps, that for the next half-century her geographic, social, and rhetorical locations never dramatically changed.

So it was also on the South Side of Chicago, in a time of financial crisis but growing racial awareness and solidarity for Brooks, that she received her first formal training as a poet. In 1941, Inez Cunningham—editor of *Poetry Magazine* and a bold liberal for her day (*Report* 174)—crossed town from the posh white neighborhood known as the "Gold Coast" to offer a writing workshop in the Negro district of "Bronzeville." The intense scrutiny Brooks encountered in the workshop was the first truly critical response she had received, and it served to spark her poetic impulse. This led to a series of writing prizes and publications in literary magazines, and eventually to a book contract. The enthusiastic response from family, friends, and neighbors was to "thank heaven and Harper's" (72). There was no sense from Brooks's Black supporters that she should be anything but thrilled with her prestigious white publisher. This was the late 1940s, after all, and she was seen as paving new inroads for Black writers—Black women writers especially (Erkkila 192).

The critical response to her first collection of poetry, *A Street in Bronzeville* (1945), was quite positive. The poetry was populist in theme, yet modernist in technique (Gary Smith 129). Black readers appreciated seeing in print the particular urban rhythms and characters they knew so well, while the larger audience of whites enjoyed the opportunity to see into this other world—and both recognized the power of her imagistic verse and balladry. The volume was hailed by the dominant white press as written by an evidently "solidly Chicago person," which nonetheless "would be superb . . . in any year by any person of any color" (Engle 3). It was considered fresh "city-folk poetry" ("Review" 5).

There were also patronism and warning discernible in the tone of such reviews, however, as in all those of her early work. Inevitably, it was both notable and negligible that Brooks was a "Negro poet," and while she was widely praised for having "universal" appeal, the category was most often a white construction. She was commended for her strongly focused, or localized, powers of observation, for her direct treatment of things, yet chastised when this focus or location was too far beyond the dominant field of view. A review of *Annie Allen* (1949), which praises its "Cellini-like lyrics," for example, worries that, when the poetic talent "devotes itself to setting forth an experience even more special and particularized than the usual poetic experience, then it puts itself under unnecessary strain." When the poem deals with colorist discrimination against dark women within the Black community, for example, the critic asks, "Who but another negro can get the intimate feeling, the racially particular . . . the oblique bitterness . . . ?" (Redding 6-7). The poet was expected to "stand in" as a singular representative of her people and mediator to white readers. Exploring differences and exposing divisions within the Black community could only frustrate white expectations of a monolithic racial identity and experience. While racial solidarity is certainly one of the poet's goals from the first, she always both celebrates diversity and recognizes the ways internalized oppression can work to make "outsiders within."

In a review for *Poetry*, William Stafford alternatingly situates Brooks as a definitive *insider* and as marginal. "Sometimes," he claims, "the poems are confusingly local in reference." It would thus seem that being a non-white racial "insider" can be disorienting: It distracts the poet from the bearings of the surrounding white culture, and confuses her (white) readers with an obscure locality. On the other hand, Stafford also sets *In the Mecca* within the context of Brooks's earlier publications by defining these as "books that look in." Gwendolyn Brooks is a "spokesman" for her race, he explains, and she "'looks in' to a group more avowedly than any of the earlier writers" (Stafford 26). This seems to imply that Brooks somehow stands outside or on the margin of her people, looking *in at* them, gaining "insight" (26) and then speaking *out for* them. This rhetoric relies on a geographic schema of containment that puts the poet in her place (as a Negro) even as it accords her some token of privilege and exceptional power of transcendence (as a poet). She is like other Blacks by virtue of her race, and different by virtue of her relation to a white tradition and audience. Stafford's model cannot account for diversity within the racialized "Other." In a similar vein, Norris Clark argues that Brooks exhibits her "dual heritage" as an African American and that, while her unique expression of a Black aesthetic marks her among "black cultural nationalists," she ought not to worry about reaching a large, popular Black audience: "As a spokesperson for the black masses, Brooks is literally different from those for whom she writes; consequently she is the 'seer and sayer,' the Emersonian poet, who articulates the needs, ideas, aspirations of others" (94-95). In this framework, the Black poet speaks *for* Blacks, but not necessarily *to* them. Indeed, this description of her people suggests a singularly inarticulate, even illiterate, "mass" trapped inside the limits of their race.

Alternatively, of course, to "look in" from the inside is also to look within the self, to glimpse one's psychic interior with "insight." Indeed, when claiming the universality of Brooks's poetry, her early reviewers tend to argue from the uniqueness of the individual creative mind. The poet speaks *as*, *about*, and *to* all of humanity precisely because she speaks as an utterly free individual. If her race were to serve as more than accident, it would necessarily become a limiting factor, determining her vision and voice as less than transcendent. Blackness, then, would be both an interior space discrete and closed off from the white "universe" and a bodily exterior cloaking a racially unmarked (i.e., white) mind. Brooks's social location might give her a way *in* to the world she depicts, but her poetic imagination must provide a way *out*.

Writing four decades later, Sisi Donald Mosby's reflections on the time offer an interesting inversion of this segregated and dualistic spatialization:

Upon deciding I was a writer I devoured the artsy literary review magazines. There was very little in them about black writers. After reading *A
Street in Bronzeville* I understood the sense of apartness I felt when I read
the reviews. I realized I was an outsider peeping through the window.

In *A Street in Bronzeville* everything was in sharp focus. It was about
me. I lived there, I walked those streets, and I knew the people. . . . It was
like being born again! (in Madhubuti 23)

In this schema, by contrast, the white literary machine and the dominant culture it represents are an edifice into which Black writers and
citizens, as outsiders, can only peer. Although *Bronzeville* addresses
Black life in "kitchenettes" and other enclosed spaces, poems such as
"The Sundays of Satin-Legs Smith" and the title-poem of the collection itself also locate Black life in the street. Implied is the sense that
this world not only borders, but also surrounds and impinges upon, the
privileged containment of white life. What Brooks's book does for
Mosby is focus his gaze on the exterior space he inhabits—the streets
he walks, the other outsiders he knows there—and transform that exterior into a privileged site of self-knowledge and a different kind of "insight." And what his response to this call reveals is that the poet is not
merely a spokesperson addressing whites on his behalf, but that she is
in an important way speaking *to* him, *to Blacks*.

Brooks's relationship to the street and its Black occupants changes,
of course, over the course of her career. Initially, her complicated status
as insider/outsider to the Black community was shaped by her youthful
experience in Chicago's "Black Belt." She was, in her own terms, a
"DARK" girl (*Report* 57) and felt colorist discrimination from other
Blacks. She explains that she fell easily into no group, fit nowhere. Her
"welcoming, enveloping" (39) home and the writing retreat it provided
compensated for the cold reception she sometimes received in her
community, but it alone could not alleviate the misfit's sense of restriction. Her autobiography begins with the following revelation, phrased
in significantly spatial terms: "When I was a child, it did not occur to

me, even once, that the black in which I was encased (I called it brown in those days) would be considered one day, beautiful" (37). Coupled with the protective embrace of her strongly religious mother, this sense of alienation—figured as a kind of bodily enclosure—must have intensified her natural inclination toward isolation.

So while she drew her material from the larger world of Bronzeville—"I wrote about what I saw and heard in the street," she claims (*Report* 133)—she often did so from a safe window above it. And while poems such as "a song in the front yard" express a secret desire to explore "down the alley,/ To where the charity children play" (*Selected Poems* 6), the poet clearly always relished privacy for writing. From a young age Brooks is both inside and outside the world she portrays, writing "above" it in a literal sense but also both caught and embedded in it. What privileges she has enjoyed—a loving home, an education, extraordinary mentors—remove her from the typical Bronzeville experience even as they enable her to see it with a poetic eye. But Brooks never really "transcends" that space as so many of her white critics suggest, if only because it remains her primary site of identification. It is not until later in her career, however, when she makes that identification more overtly political, that she starts reading and writing poetry with young gang members and earns what Mari Evans has called her "PhD in the street" (84).

Unlike the typical laureate, Brooks's urban vision has always had a certain "bleakness" (Gary Smith 129), and the spaces of her city have most often appeared in her poetry as constraining to Black inhabitants. Indeed, her work has sometimes been considered "naturalistic" for its emphasis on "entrapment and the desire to escape" (130-31). Brooks was certainly sympathetic toward this trait in Richard Wright's fiction, and argued for the necessity of a narrow focus (*Report* 160). She accepts the view that "some people when oppressed, when walled in, when unable to reach The Enemy, will turn upon themselves" and destroy the seeds of their own future (74). While the poet herself exposes racism and poverty as very real constraints, she refuses to portray the trap as inevitable or ultimate, and so her work is not strictly naturalistic. But escape by individual transcendence (moral, spiritual, or otherwise) is not the alternative outcome Brooks is interested in exploring, either. Rather, from her earliest work, she issues a hopeful call for a communal effort toward resistance and survival—to "civilize a space" for future growth.[4]

Certainly one factor in this cultural optimism is Brooks's sense of her place in and indebtedness to a generally inclusive and nurturing community. Of Hughes, who was a special inspiration to Brooks, she observes, "Mightily did he use the street." Interestingly, she describes his encouragement in spatial terms: "Langston Hughes . . . considered literature not his private inch, but great acreage. The plantings of others he not only welcomed but busily enriched. . . . The young manuscript-bearing applicant never felt himself an intruder . . ." (*Report* 71). Brooks thus admires how Hughes makes of the urban street a vast and peopled garden, and, in her roles as writer, mentor, and teacher, she emulates this throughout her life. Fostering several generations of new Black writers is one of the great accomplishments of her career.

Perhaps because the boundaries of any community are somewhat permeable, Brooks both finds and makes a place for herself at the center of Black cultural life, even as she struggles with being a misfit and outsider at times. Her place in American letters, by contrast, changed dramatically with the publication of *Annie Allen* (1949), which seemed to cement her "universal" status with the Pulitzer Prize. This collection showed the same focus on Bronzevillean life as her previous book, with even more attention given to the lives of girls and women. It includes, notably, "The Anniad," a mock epic about a girl's coming of age. It also contains poems with a wry critique of white racist indifference, voyeurism, and charity. Its form evinces a more extreme high modernism, however, which drew both appreciation and suspicion from white reviewers and Black readers alike. While those like Redding feared seeing her formal talents "dribble away in the obscure and too oblique" (7), most members of her Black audience may well have been dismayed for opposite reasons, finding the vision of Black life eclipsed by a high formality. Both reactions suggest a dichotomy between content and form (a Black inside and a white outside) that would become more intense during the Black Arts Movement.

Some Black critics also saw the book as obscuring Black life and cutting short Black communication by the direction of its appeal. It was heard, in many ways, as a call to whites. Don L. Lee (later Haki Madhubuti), addresses this conflict in his preface to her 1972 autobiography *Report From Part One*:

> *Annie Allen* (1949), important? Yes. Read by blacks? No. *Annie Allen* more so than *A Street in Bronzeville* seems to have been written for whites. For instance, "The Anniad" requires unusual concentrated study . . . [and] the book has . . . a pleading tone. . . . there is too much "Grant me that I am human, that I hurt, that I can cry." (17-18)[5]

Although she would defend her early work, in general, as being "political" and full of "rage,"[6] Brooks seems to have accepted Lee's critical retrospective on the tone of *Annie Allen*. Describing the state of Black poetry at that time, she wrote in 1975: "The Forties and Fifties were years of high poet-incense; the language-flowers were thickly sweet. Those flowers whined and begged white folks to pick them, to find them lovable" ("Flowers" 1).

The authorization by the white literary establishment that the Pulitzer represented nonetheless gave Brooks a kind of "footing" that Lee acknowledges. The praise from white quarters, which Lee points out "*all* quarters" encouraged her to accept gratefully—expanded Brooks's cultural access and accessibility across racial lines. It brought both international recognition and a new following among "those 'negro' blacks who didn't believe that one is legitimate unless one is sanctioned by whites first." It also enabled her to get more work writing reviews and such, which was good experience and provided necessary funds (Lee 16-19).

The Bean Eaters (1960), a less extensively experimental book, seemed to amplify the societal critique voiced in Brooks's earlier volumes. White and Black readers and critics considered it more "social," and while the latter may have welcomed this, the former often found it too much so. One reviewer for *Poetry*, Brooks recalls, chastised her for a "bitter" tone and "revolutionary" tendency (Tate 43). Brooks acknowledges that in those years "it was whites who were reading and listening to us, salving their consciences—our accusations didn't hurt too much. But I was repeatedly called bitter" (*Report* 176). Even the more positive reviews would be cast in a suspicious light a decade later, with the poet's heightened awareness of the power behind white patronage: "They thought I was lovely," she says. "I was a sort of pet" (177).

So there is this tension in the poet's own appraisal of her early work: On the one hand it was written with a conscious appeal to human goodness and white sympathy, from an integrationist perspective (*Report* 175); on the other hand, it echoed a pre-conscious identification *as*, *about*, and *to* Blacks (Tate 40). Both the poet's self-positioning and her vision of audience was multiple, inviting variant appropriations and critiques of her work, so that no singular critical evaluation seems to do justice to its rhetorical complexity.

Brooks's fourth major collection of poetry, *In the Mecca* (1968), is generally considered a transitional work. Indeed, Betsy Erkkila describes the epic title poem thus: "Begun in the fifties as a novel for juveniles, 'In the Mecca' is a kind of palimpsest that inscribes Brooks's changing and conflicting designs."[7] Erkkila reads the shift as a move "from the female-centered vision of her earlier poems toward the increasingly male-centered vision of her work after 1967" (218). The white feminist critic suggests that Brooks had been moving toward a concept of "female bonding" (219) and "interracial sisterhood" (208) that her identification with Black nationalism short-circuited. While I would question any singular "centering" of Brooks's complexly spatial poetics, there is probably at least some truth to Erkkila's observation. Given that many of the poet's most ardent supporters had, from the first, been Black men—her father, Langston Hughes, and her husband, who sacrificed his own writing career to foster hers (Kent, *A Life* 53)—it is not surprising that she might have experienced the cultural and social bonds of race as strong lines of identification, and might thus have been resistant to any white feminist efforts to disrupt those ties in the social upheaval of the late 1960s and '70s (Tate 47).[8]

Of course, Black feminist critics like Gloria Hull and Claudia Tate have noted a similar change in gender emphasis, but they have been more sympathetic toward Brooks's goals and strategies. Their main interest is in seeing more of the Bronzeville women in her poetry, rather than in restoring or achieving a feminist-integrationist vision. Not surprisingly, Black male critics represent Brooks's transition—and thus "In the Mecca"—quite differently. Lee and Clark, for example, both stress the shift from an integrationist to a liberationist or revolutionary vision. To do justice to the interplay of these factors in the construction of place and space of the poem, I do not want to reduce the poem to a simple expression of Brooks's consciousness, or to a single perspective on it, but rather to read it as a shifting space of complex processes, with multiple points of identification.

Analyzing the poem in spatial terms might seem to undermine my concern with social processes and political movement. Indeed, the modern Western philosophical trend has been to oppose both place and space to time.[9] Geographer Doreen Massey outlines this dominant schema in *Space, Place, and Gender*, explaining that the spatial would be marked by stasis, by the absence of time, and therefore by the impossibility of movement or change. In Foucauldian terms, space signifies "the dead, the fixed, the undialectical, the immobile" (149). Place and space, in this framework, are mutually opposed to history and progress, so any local claims, any political action based on a sense of place could only be variations on "reactionary nationalisms." Clearly, this implies a judgment of "the politics of location" as anti-progressive and ahistorical.[10]

Recent postcolonial, feminist, and postmodern approaches, however, suggest alternative senses of place—of geographic, social, and subjective locations—that are not simply reactionary. Sites of identification, these theories suggest, are both contested and contestatory territory: Even as particular places are fought over, they provide space for critique of other, more apparently stable or central places. Similarly, in the work of Black feminist critics bell hooks and Barbara Smith, "home" (as in "home girl") operates as a figurative space that can accommodate retreat as well as resistance.[11] All such particular locations, hooks and Smith imply, are in some sense multiple.

In approaching a politics of location more explicitly, hooks, Carol Boyce Davies, and others exhibit this double-edged sense of place. In her argument for "choosing the margin as a place of radical openness" (*Yearning* 145-53), for example, hooks refuses the temporal and geographic closure that would claim to define a place once and for all, and so resists the labels "anti-progressive" and "ahistorical." hooks's work, among others', demonstrates what Michael Keith and Steve Pile assert in *Place and the Politics of Identity*: A different sense of place is being theorized, no longer passive, no longer fixed, no longer undialectical—because disruptive features interrupt any tendency to see once more open space as the passive receptacle for any social process that cares to fill it—but, still, in a very real sense, about location and locatedness (5). In Massey's terms, this is an "extraverted" sense of place, which means seeing in terms of "open and porous networks of social relations" (121) rather than borders or boundaries. It means acknowledging that "localities can be present in one another, both inside and outside at the same time" (6), and that "the fortunes of individual places cannot be explained by looking only within them." Larger economic relations, for example, play a role in constructing particular social spaces (20). Place, which exists as "a particular articulation" of social relations, thus also "includes relations which stretch beyond—the global as part of what constitutes the local, the outside as part of the inside" (5).

With these theories in mind, I read Brooks's location—geographic, social, and rhetorical—as more complex, fluctuating, and open than her classifications as a "Chicago poet," "Black woman," or "cultural nationalist" might suggest. The multiplicity at play in each of these designations, and the recombinant potential of all three, makes for sites of potentially progressive politicization—of political "movement" as well as "alignment"[12]—opening the possibility for localized perspectives to function in liberatory ways. An "extraverted" sense of place helps to explain how the Mecca building serves as such a multivalent signifier in Brooks's poem, and suggests why the particular poetic word so powerfully "stretch[es] beyond" the sphere of its articulation.

However much Brooks stays in one place all her career, there is certainly a mid-life shift or turn in her social posture. The event which precipitated this was her attendance at a Black Writers' Conference at Fisk University in the spring of 1967. Whereas the by-then renowned poet had been "loved" at the white colleges where she had been speaking, she was only "coldly respected" among the "New Blacks" at Fisk. What she had unwittingly walked into was a hotbed of Black nationalism and a new Black aesthetic, and it was a "blood-boiling surprise" to the fifty-year-old poet (*Report* 84). A generational divide opened, and she found herself an outsider once more.

Although Brooks was at first amazed and confused by the Black community she met at Fisk, her own experience was ultimately confirmed and validated by their expressions. Messages like "Black is beautiful" (*Report* 172-73) drew the darker sister "in" in a new way and rang prophetic in her ears. This, and the accompanying "Up against the wall white man!" (85), would necessarily hold a different import for those more clearly "outside," of course. Thus, it is with some amusement that Brooks recalls the self-immolating response of one young white man, who jumped up to shout ecstatically, "Yeah, yeah, kill 'em. . . . Kill 'em all!" (168). She herself emphasizes the inside/outside distinction of race, but suggests it is a social effect rather than an essential feature: "Your *least* prerequisite toward understanding of the new black is an exceptional Doctorate which can be conferred only upon those with the proper properties of bitter birth and intrinsic sorrow. I know this is infuriating, especially to those professional Negro-understanders" (85). The poet's goal thus becomes to reach all Blacks everywhere with her call to identification as Black, and to convert those who do not as yet understand the "new Black." But this appeal does not extend across racial lines. Brooks appears to have foregone any hope or sense of responsibility toward a white audience, and was resistant, at least in the seventies, toward a broader "third world" identification (204-05). Group solidarity among Blacks—in Africa and the diaspora—was the first and necessary step toward liberation.

Brooks clearly identifies her own teachers and students as the primary audience to whom she devotes her work in *Mecca*. The book itself is dedicated "*To the memory of Langston Hughes;/ and to James Baldwin, LeRoi Jones,/ and Mike Alexandroff,/ educators extraordinaire*" (vi). These Black men—literary, cultural, and social heroes—form the line in which she seeks to follow. It is they, rather than an identifiable set of literary foremothers, who have mentored the poet and provided models of teaching. In her second dedication—of the title-poem—she redirects this line of influence into the future, and in doing so broadens it to include other women writers. The poem is dedicated ("*IN TRIBUTE*—") to thirteen of her students from the late 1960s (Melhem 162), almost half of whom are female. She may not be interested in recovering and reconstructing lost Black female "influences,"[13] but she does seem committed to fostering a more inclusive future.

Brooks's shift toward a Black audience is also exemplified by her move to a Black publisher. *In the Mecca* was Brooks's last book to come out with Harper, and although she left on amicable terms, her change marked a definite shift in allegiance. The poet claimed in 1967 that she had been able, from the first, to have everything she would want published, but she also recognized that others had not been so fortunate (*Report* 136), and eventually she saw it as her duty and responsibility to support Black publishing efforts. She moved to Detroit's Broadside Press in 1969 and, later, to Third World Press, based in Chicago. Brooks thus took pains to relocate both the production and the reception of her work within a Black space.

We might expect white critics to be somewhat nonplussed by this move. How does one respond to a work so deliberately directed away from oneself? One strategy would be denial—pretending that nothing had changed—and another, chastisement. In "Gwendolyn Brooks: An Appreciation from the White Suburbs" (1969), Dan Jaffe actually employs both. He praises the recently published *Mecca* as "a major attempt at synthesis" (58) and emphasizes that "there have been no drastic changes in the tactics and subjects she has dealt with over the years." He also stresses the individuality of her poetic voice, which he rightly observes is multiple, and implies that this is what makes at least some of her poems universal—"some that will undoubtably be read so long as man cares about language and his fellows" (53). Jaffe also assumes a very intimate tone for a critical essay. He frequently refers to the poet as "Gwen Brooks"—something her Black colleagues do only in their personal essays of tribute.[14] He appears to be forcing a certain closeness—between his position in the white suburbs and hers in the Black inner-city—that the poet herself resists.

It is, in fact, the inside/outside dichotomy that presents the problem for Jaffe. "The label 'Black poetry,'" he argues, cannot do justice to her varied abilities, to her breadth. While he accepts the identification "*as* Black" to some degree, he argues that this must be sacrificed to achieve the universal: "The paradox is that poets are committed to step outside of themselves in order to find the special within themselves" (52). The white critic thus privileges a broad, exterior space, which aligns nicely with the white suburbs from which he speaks, over the constraints of a close, Black, urban perspective. Going beyond, transcending, necessarily means speaking to whites. In what sounds today like a shocking demand on the oppressed to humanize her oppressor, Jaffe asserts that

> . . . the real question is not what Gwen Brooks has to say to those who have shared her experiences, who already know some of what she has to say. The real question is whether or not she can make the alien feel. The purpose of art is always to communicate to the uninitiated, to make contact across seemingly insurmountable barriers. Can the poet make the white feel black. . . . can [she] make a comfortable white . . . respond? (54-55)

Here, the dominant white becomes the "alien," the pitiable outsider, who must be reconciled through the emotional labor of the privileged Black poet. She must build the bridge to justify herself and redeem whites by making them identify with her. This expectation—which women writers of color have so well critiqued in books like *This Bridge Called My Back* (Moraga and Anzaldúa), *Black Feminist Thought* (Collins), and *Changing Our Own Words* (Wall)[15]—is precisely the one Brooks rejects in the late sixties. When Tate asks her whether there is "a liability in promoting the practice of segregated literary criticism?" the poet asks in reply, "How are you going to force white critics to learn enough about us? . . . whites are going to say what they choose to say about us, whether it's right or wrong, or just say nothing. . . . We should ignore them" (Tate 45). If transcendence and universality mean appealing to white readers and critics, Brooks rejects these as goals for her work.

Clearly, Brooks's position on this complicates my own project. How can I, a white woman, engage her work and urge others to do so, with the knowledge that the poet is not writing to us, that she is, in some sense, determined to ignore us? I have no easy answer to offer, but I start with the belief that her posture grants me no excuse likewise to ignore her. Indeed, she states that when white critics "just say *nothing* . . . [this] is another very effective way of dealing with us" (Tate 45). The political and ethical implications of calls for segregation have always been very different when issued by Blacks than by whites, after all. One group practices it as a strategy for survival and liberation, the other as a means of domination. Whatever my response to Brooks's work, it is my responsibility; I am accountable for my dealings with the text. I thus seek to negotiate a response different from Jaffe's demand for a personal white address, from the anonymous white man's shout for his own execution, and from Erkkila's lament for the lost vision of women's common oppression. Each of these articulations lacks sufficient awareness of the speaker's own position in relation to the Black-identified woman poet. What else is there, then, besides hegemony, segregation, or silent guilt and martyrdom?

A Juxtapositional Reading of "In the Mecca"

What I propose here is a "juxtapositional" reading of Gwendolyn Brooks's poetry. This means acknowledging that the prophetic voice one hears may not be meant for oneself. Nonetheless, one overhears it from a different but nearby ("juxta") location, and desires to heed its call. One might even draw closer to the site of its utterance, in hope of coming alongside, but not displacing, its original audience. This kind of identification with others—an ex-static extension of the self that comes "next to" (both beside and secondary to) the intended community of reception—may be able to find prophetic meaning for itself in relation. What then, I ask, do I overhear the prophet saying to her people? And how can I and other "outsiders" heed that call alongside them and for us all?

The idea of "juxtaposition" is actually helpful for approaching Brooks's poetry in a number of ways. At the most literal level, a juxtapositional diction and syntax are primary to her poetics. Hortense Spillers explains:

> By displacing the familiar with the unfamiliar word, Brooks employs a vocabulary that redefines what we know already in a way we have not known it before. The heightened awareness that results brings to our consciousness an *interpenetration* of events which lends them a new significance. (234; emphasis mine)

Such juxtaposition is evident in "In the Mecca" when, for example, Loam Norton observes: "Anointings were of lice. Blood was the spillage of cups." The only non-Black character in the piece, Norton "considers Belsen and Dachau" when faced with any danger.[16] In a parody of the Twenty-third Psalm, he juxtaposes modern concentration camps to biblical pastures and "the House of the Lord." Because he does so in response to the tragic disappearance of a little Black girl, this "redefines" both sites of suffering (the death-camp and the urban slum) as well as the religious pastoral ideal[17] and faith in divine rescue.

The way in which positive and negative images are "yoked and co-ordinated" (Kent, "Poetry" 78) here is an expression of what Theophus Smith identifies as a distinctly Black aesthetic and cultural practice.[18] In this example, the immediate realities provide the more powerful images (lice and blood), tarnishing the traditional spiritual ones (anointings, overflowing cups), rather than being sacramentalized by them. "... jungles or pasture" and "the house of the Lord" therefore become suspect as sites of refuge for either persecuted Jews or poor Black children, whose "gaunt/ souls were not restored, their souls were banished" (16).

Clark concludes that such descriptive passages—"devoid of racial polemic or black rhetoric" (87) but nonetheless gut-wrenching—are the most vivid examples of a genuinely Black aesthetic. He explains that Brooks "does not tell us that there is evil. . . . rather, she shows us . . . that we may learn a moral insight from the juxtaposition." Further, he argues that "the true aesthetic significance, thematically, is that the black lives [in the Mecca] . . . are meaningful and reflect an 'ultimate reality' in formal juxtaposition to expectations" (89). Black life itself, by its very existence in America, is lodged against dominant visions of reality and poses alongside them (or juxtaposes) an alternative view. In the city, these contrasts are all the more notable for being crammed into a limited space. The oddities of Brooks's diction, then, reflect the frictions of urban living,[19] and the poet's representation of the space of inner-city Black life implies an "interpenetration" of events or processes which lends places both "inside" and "outside" a new significance.

In terms of the actual places juxtaposed in her work, Brooks ranges broadly. Most notably, though, she imports the image and idea of Africa to signify on the experience of Blacks in America. Brooks's post-1967 identification with Africa was a kind of journey home for the woman who had, as a second-class citizen, struggled to be "at home" in America, yet it was no idyllic haven. In her descriptions of her travels to the continent, she emphasizes the great gulf between the two places and her own inability to bridge it. In fact, the poet finds her most powerful tool to be one of the clearest markers of the irrevocability of the loss (*Report* 88). English itself becomes, for her, both a space of exploration and a place of confinement. When Africa then appears as a home to which she can never return,[20] the poet turns to the construction of "Afrika" as a sphere of memory and imagination, a sacred space with the potential to sacralize Black life in the diaspora of the modern social "whirlwind." She does this by envisioning Afrika as a shared and shifting space of identity. In her later poem "To the Diaspora," she writes,

> When you set out for Afrika
> you did not know you were going.
> Because
> you did not know you were Afrika.
> You did not know the Black continent
> that had to be reached
> was you.
>
> (*To Disembark* 41)

Erkkila reads this, along with Brooks's claim to be "essentially an essential African" (*Report* 1), as a "celebration of the sameness and universality of black nature across personal, historical, and national bounds" that effaces the very particularity and multiplicity that had always funded her poetic vision (Erkkila 224). "Nature" is not the only

way to talk about identity, nationhood, and racial consciousness, however, and the unique and different are still prominent in Brooks's poetry. Indeed, her use of "the Black continent" is an imaginative and political construct meant to produce certain effects—pride, solidarity,
survival, and liberation—in the midst of overwhelming opposition.
Because the site of ultimate reference is not literal, it avoids a reactionary naturalization and dehistoricization of place. Indeed, Brooks's
project is profoundly concerned with history and its irrevocability.
Writing *as* an Afrikan, or *as* Black, Brooks relocates herself with a politicized identity that exceeds this (or any) place. She resists the role of
victim to racist social forces not by a transcendent escape of history
and geography, but by insisting upon a liberatory deconstruction of the
site of oppression itself. Her goal is a radical reconstruction from
within.

With "In the Mecca," Brooks uses Africa to sacramentalize Black
struggle in the United States by a kind of "interpenetration" or super-
imposition, importing its image to Chicago's South Side. The result is a
powerfully ironic juxtaposition of places. The towering Mecca building signals the Saudi holy city of Islam: the center to which Malcolm X
had made his pilgrimage in 1964.[21] Built as a monument to modern
American progress, the complex would seem to claim a mystical and
holy power, issuing from elsewhere, to reward, guide, soothe, and sub-
due its inhabitants. At the same time, by taking its name from Africa,
the new-world construct seeks to absorb and nullify the other world's
mythic power, along with its people. Making claims to other places can
be a colonizing move, rather than a liberating one, depending on the
agent and motives.

The actual Mecca building is a palimpsest, marking the processes of
American history. It was built as a modern apartment building in 1891,
"a splendid palace, a showplace of Chicago. . . ."[22] R. Baxter Miller takes
this date to be significant because "it designates a post-Darwinian
world. In American history, industrialization had ended the dream of
an agrarian world," and urban progress and technology were replacing

communal and spiritual ideals (147). But by 1912, whites had abandoned the South Side of Chicago to the Black Belt, and the Mecca building had become a residence for "the black elite" (Melhem 165). Its name thus stands for Chicago itself as a Black urban "mecca." The building's decline was precipitated during the Great Depression, and it rapidly deteriorated to a slum. At this point, the ironic progression of its name is completed: from ancient spiritual home, to modern urban palace and symbol of material progress, to the pathetic endpoint of Black urban migration. Lerone Bennett, Jr., describes this last reality as "Black boys and girls who came North looking for the Promised Land and found concrete deserts" (Madhubuti 14).

In 1941, the Mecca location was purchased by the Illinois Institute of Technology, which was housed (in juxtaposition) across the street. This other building, designed by Mies van der Rohe, stood as a monument not only to modern technology, but also to modern art. The plan was for the technical school to tear down the Mecca slum and expand its own magnificent facilities onto that site (Melhem, "Mecca" 166). ITT's campaign to have the building condemned and demolished as a "fire-trap" came with no real offer of "escape," however. The threat of forceful eviction—to "be placed" somewhere[23]—is no rescue from the slum.

It is significant, then, that the body of Brooks's poem begins with these lines: "Sit where the light corrupts your face./ Mies Van der Rohe retires from grace./ And the fair fables fall" (5). Melhem summarizes the import of these lines as "the failure of religion, art, and politics in confronting American life." White, Western fables of triumph or redemption have not extended to the Black urban slum. Modern art, in particular, is powerless to save the Mecca: "Indeed," Melhem concludes, "modern art turns away" (167) while state institutions bulldoze and appropriate the spaces of Black life and history for their own advancement. As an abandoned project of modernity, the Mecca stood as a crumbling tower of Babel—a failed attempt at transcendence. As Mecca, it marked the ruin of faith in postmodern times. It stood as a blight, corrupting the view and preventing the expansion of the state's technological enterprises. After a decade of protest and threatened riots, the Mecca building was finally razed in 1952.

The slum tenement resurrected in Brooks's poem raises questions of faith and politics through yet more specific invocations of Africa. The first is in the querying imagination of the frustrated poet Alfred. He reads "Joyce/ or James or Horace, Huxley, Hemingway" and "thinks, or drinks until the Everything/ is vaguely part of One thing and the One thing/ delightfully anonymous/ and undiscoverable" (7). Steeped in white Western tradition, he has learned to look for a unifying and universal principle—something vague and anonymous, surely something disconnected from the "smear" of poverty he faces daily. This is not his only source of knowledge, though. He questions:

> When there were all those gods
> administering to panthers,
> jumping over mountains,
> and lighting stars and comets and a moon,
> what was their one Belief?
> what was their joining thing?
>
> (7-8)

This question raises two issues: imposing external white, Western frames (monotheism or monolithism) on other cultures (Alfred can only read Africa through Emersonian eyes); and the resistance strategy of finding or forging a "joining thing" (such as Blackness) as a means of coming together in the face of racism, isolation, and poverty.

Alfred also recalls Africa more specifically in his identification with Léopold Senghor, the poet elected first president of independent Senegal in 1960. Alfred, the would-be poet, "can speak superbly of the line of Leopold." Senghor stands for him as a symbol of both a Black aesthetic—he "Believes in beauty./ But believes that blackness is among the fit filters"—and a politics of location—he "listens/ to the rich pound in and beneath the black feet of Africa." This other place to which Alfred aspires exists as power, potential, and openness, as opposed to the over-wrought spaces of Europe and America. Senghor, he imagines, is "rootless and lonely" in Europe and rejects Western standards of beauty and construction: "gargantuan gardens careful in the sun,/ fairy story gold, thrones, feasts, the three princesses,/ summer sailboats/ like cartoon ghosts or Klansmen, pointing up/ white questions, in blue air. . . ./ No." The African does not surround himself with protective, opulent, and sinister materials; instead, he "loves sun" (20-21).

And "sun" is precisely what is missing from the Mecca building. Alfred's perception of place and space is especially acute. Just as he, too, "might have been a poet-king" (20), envisioning and shaping a new nation, so he also "might have been an architect" (19). He "can speak of Mecca" in poetic terms, showing real insight into its architecture. He describes the U-shaped structure: "firm arms surround/ disorders, bruising ruses and small hells,/ small semiheavens: hug barbarous rhetoric/ built of buzz, coma and petite pell-mells." Individual apartments are "small hells" or "small semiheavens" squeezed together by the firmness of the overall structure (20). The dirt courtyard, littered with trash and broken glass,[24] is the central site of noise, violence, and confusion. Trapped in the arms of this building, this small world, Alfred imagines Africa as an alternative source of poetry and politics. His vision is ultimately powerless to transform the Mecca, however, since for all his insight, "Alfred has not seen Pepita Smith" (19). He has not yet found a way to connect "the line of Leopold" with the lives of Blacks lost in America.

"Don Lee," the only historical figure residing in the Mecca, suggests the possibility of such a connection. Unlike Alfred, he has deliberately extricated himself from white philosophical influences, and his Black nationalist message "stands out in the auspices of fire/ and rock and jungle-flail" (21). Whereas Alfred can only speak of what he sees and knows, Don Lee "wants." His desire, his demands, are clear, and they make him a charismatic leader. The nation he imagines and proposes is a wholly new construction—"a new nation/ under nothing"—and he wants for it "new art and anthem; will/ want a new music screaming in the sun" (22). So the sun appears in his vision of the Black nation, also, but with more violent imagery.

In addition to Pepita, other Meccan figures are lost to varying degrees, and Lee would be the one to call them out into the sun, if they could hear him. Hyena, the "striking debutante" or prostitute (Greasley 14), is lost in a white-identified aesthetic and internalized racism. "A fancier of firsts," she is "One of the first, and to the tune of hate,/ in all of the Mecca to paint her hair sun-gold" (6). The sun—emblem of Africa elsewhere—ironically images Hyena's bleached-blonde hair, symbol of black self-hate. Philip Greasley argues that since Hyena's name refers to one of the "ignoble African animals," she serves a deromanticizing function in the poem (14). But Hyena does not know she is Afrika. When she leaves the Mecca, oiled and perfumed, she is "off to the Ball"—a euphemism laden with white fantasy. Her imagination does not stretch far, and it does not enable her to see or value Pepita: "'a puny and a putrid little child'" (21).[25]

Just as Hyena's hopes are pinned on "the Ball," so a multitude of characters in the building seek identification with alternative spaces: St. Julia has prayer pastures (5), Melodie Mary compares her home to China (9), Loam Norton recalls Belsen and Dachau (15), Great Gram recalls the slave cabin, and Mrs. Sallie imagines trading places with the white mother in whose home she labors (15). Each struggles to remember or envision an alternative space, but none ultimately succeeds in escaping or transcending the tragedy of the Mecca (16). We see them, finally, in its dim doorways and hallways. Even Pepita, who liked to play in the "fly-open door" of the A&P, and who might have gone to kindergarten, is confined in death to lie "in the dust with roaches" under Jamaican Edward's cot (31).

But it is Alfred and Don Lee, in particular, whose external identifications serve the struggle to speak from the Mecca "as Blacks." In order to damn the architecture that constrains them, they must expose the reality of the Mecca as a ruin, but they—or the poet—must also question its inevitability. Simultaneously to portray the construct as a prison or trap and also to suggest the possibility of dismantling it from the inside, is the challenge. The Meccans, all, must be shown as constrained but not dehumanized, oppressed but not obliterated, or the call for their liberation would be hopeless and meaningless. Don Lee is an image of Black power. Alfred shows potential for growth. That some others have fashioned "small semiheavens" in the midst of infernal architecture is a sign of hope.

But if the name "Mecca" symbolizes an African-identified paradise, then the poem is an ironically inverted parable about the nature of such a place—perhaps a negative imprint of it—rather than a map for how to reach it. And if the poet invites readers on a pilgrimage, she does so only obliquely. Instead of identifying the road or way to Mecca, the poet begins, "Now the way *of* the Mecca was on this wise" (4; emphasis mine). D. H. Melhem identifies this as a parabolic introduction with a biblical tone (167), and, indeed, it does echo the gospel pattern "the Kingdom of Heaven is like . . . ." The images of "black unity and harmony," which Greasley explains are Brooks's attempt to "provide positive imaging by which blacks can move toward" self and communal liberation (15), are largely missing from this poem. There is little here to fund an image of either "the Kingdom" or "the spirit of the united black community to come."[26] The prophetic tone is thus primarily critical rather than visionary, although the critique itself can be taken as an inside-out kind of vision.

The poem is mythical and biblical not only in its style but also in its sources. It draws together remnants of Dante's descent into hell, the pastoral ideal of the Twenty-third Psalm and the American-Johnny-Appleseed-Dream, and the parables of the lost coin and sheep, for example, to fashion a loosely narrative quest. A little girl has gone missing, and the entire massive project must be searched to find her. Apartment by apartment, floor by floor, the Mecca is combed, and its inhabitants questioned. What emerges in the poem is not only the loss and containment of the little girl—who has been murdered and stuffed under a bed—but the multitudinous losses that comprise the lives of those who are trapped in the building. The Mecca, despite its expansiveness, provides little space for the exercise of freedom, and so is experienced primarily as a place of confinement. The walls of the building itself might be seen as constructed from the cramped lives and constricted voices of its inhabitants. They have become immobile bricks in their own prison-house.

The construction of Brooks's poem mirrors the monumental architecture of its setting. "In the Mecca" appears on the page in thick, long columns of irregular verse. Individual characters and their unique "places" are crowded in. Juxtaposed, they jostle against each other and press out against a jagged margin. This jumble of voices and places is punctuated with stark expressions that struggle to emerge from the depth of confusion—the most notable being Mrs. Sallie's cry in the Black vernacular, "WHERE PEPITA BE?" Offset by uppercase letters, this singular and panicked call is soon resubmerged in crowded multiplicity:

> . . . Cap, where Pepita? Casey, where Pepita?
> Emmett and Melodie Mary, where Pepita?
> Briggs, Tennessee, Yvonne, and Thomas Earl,
> where may our Pepita be?
>
> (13)

The mother thus questions her older children by name, striving to preserve each one's unique place. But they reply in an anonymous chant of ignorance: "Ain seen er I ain seen er I ain seen er/ Ain seen er I ain seen er I ain seen er" (14). The plosive sounds of the girl's name and BEing are diffused into dull anonymity and absence. Word slides into word, voice blends into voice, face blurs into face in the Mecca's cramped quarters, against a mother's cry and vision that insist on the particularity of a singular loss.

Like her initial recognition—"SUDDENLY, COUNTING NOSES, MRS. SALLIE/ SEES NO PEPITA. 'WHERE PEPITA BE?'"—the mother's question to her neighbors comes in a longer line, standing out slightly but insistently from the cluttered stanzas: "One of my children is missing. One of my children is gone" (15). Each neighbor then replies, in ignorance of Pepita's whereabouts, with his or her own story of space, place, and loss.

Against inhuman pressures from without, characters strive to construct points of connection or shrines of meaning in their ever-narrowing spaces. What they reject or cling to may not appear sensical to those outside the Mecca building or poem, but it is part of a larger survival strategy. Melodie Mary's mind, for instance, cannot encompass any grief too large. Her world is too small and too full of pain already. So, for Pepita's older sister,

> headlines are secondary.
> It is interesting that in China
> the children blanch and scream,
> and that blood runs like a ragged wound
> through the flesh of the land.
> It matters mildly. . . .

But, she wonders, "Where are the frantic bulletins/ when other importances die?" and she identifies with something smaller and closer to her own compact existence:

> Trapped in his privacy of pain
> the worried rat expires,
> and smashed in the grind of a rapid heel
> last night's roaches lie.

The young girl "likes roaches,/ and pities the gray rat" (10), substitute images for her missing sister.

She shares something of her brother Briggs's need for self-containment. In the vice-grip of external pressures, he determines to maintain his own rigid boundaries. He selects an armor more rigid than the roach's, though: "Briggs is adult as a stone/ (who if he cries cries alone)." This fossilized existence protects him from loss, but it also precludes the sense of growth, hope, empathy, or community that might breed change. Thus, when he must go out among the gangs, "across the intemperate range," he perceives that "Gang/ is health and mange./ Gang/ is a bunch of ones and a singlicity." For a boy for whom "Immunity is forfeit, love/ is luggage, hope is heresy," and the risk of annihilation mounts daily, the violent price of joining a gang seems reasonable. The poet urges her readers to feel the pain of this dilemma—"Please pity Briggs" (11)—but cautions against objectifying the Meccans as wholly "other" and thus further solidifying the walls of their containment. ". . . there is a central height in pity," she writes, highlighting the self-elevation that would disguise itself as depth, "past which man's hand and sympathy cannot go";

> past which the little hurt dog
> descends to mass—no longer Joe,
> not Bucky, not Cap'n, not Rex,
> not Briggs—and is all self-employed,
> concerned with Other,
> not with Us.

(11)

With this line, the poem invites its readers in—to see its inhabitants as "Us," and to struggle alongside, in the dim and cramped quarters, to make meaning and to search for points of outlet and transformation in the Mecca walls.

Of course, any attempts by "outsiders" to make sense and safety out of such a site of oppression risk ethical compromise. When whites finally do arrive to track down Pepita—in the form of "The Law" with a "lariat of questions" (18-19)—they do so primarily to contain black crime within the color line and to pronounce sentence upon it. They show no interest in the distraught black mother or show any ability to follow her lead. Their form of rescue merely effects another trespass.

As Brooks's determination to write "*to* Blacks" suggests, there is no easy entrance here for the white reader. Resolved to ignore her white readers, she leaves us to knock at the door. In Charles Bernstein's terms, I am frequently caught between the absorptive pull (imaginatively identifying as an insider) and the opposing push (against white—and white feminist—incursion). In recognizing the latter force as a necessary resistance from those more thoroughly "inside," I can neither oppose it nor harness it for myself. I can only enter a necessary dance, in and out of the push-and-pull, to remain engaged, to keep moving, and to keep pressing toward the kind of action the poem might be calling for. It is my contention that readers with racial privilege need not simply turn away in grief from the prophet's hard word, like the rich young man in the gospel story. But if our entrance into discipleship begins with an act of identification, it ultimately requires, like camels through the eyes of needles, a more radical transformation of spatial relations than can be achieved by mere good will.[27]

Brooks's poem is thus much more than a depiction of a particular place. With "In the Mecca," she begins to issue a call for liberation, represented as a communal construction out of that ruined space. Rooted in the particularities of poor Black Meccans, this liberation appears only in negative representation, or in the "negative space" cut by the Mecca's architecture. Freedom, in this case, is what is excluded or crowded out of the urban tenement. It figures in this palace-come-prison as absence, excess, and loss. Because it is viewed as a crumbling ruin, the Mecca building is seen to "open" to other possibilities. When the Mecca finally ruptures, what crosses its prison-like threshold is the transgressed and murdered body of a little girl. It is, then, her victimization that ultimately signals the necessity of freedom, her loss that points to the meaning of her life, and her silence that signals the necessity of speech and of poetry.

Brooks's poem concludes with the discovery of Pepita's body in Jamaican Edward's apartment. That he, St. Peter like, "denies and thrice denies a dealing/ of any dimension" with her confirms that this act of violence upon another Meccan is not only a crime but also a betrayal—of communal, political, and spiritual proportions. What exactly Edward has done to his little neighbor is not clear, but there are ample clues to suggest sexual violation, thus complicating any easy identification of the Mecca, or of a male-identified cultural nationalism, as a singularly "safe space."

After death, Pepita is to be carried out and away from the Mecca. Her departure is a tragic, anti-transcendent escape of the constraints of racism and poverty; the budding poet (whose name means 'little seed') will, after all, never bloom, but neither will she learn "that black is not beloved." Nor will she grow into the apathy of adults like Queenie King who "little care, Pepita, what befalls a/ nullified saint or forfeiture/ a child" (27).

Reading a transcendent sense of "rapture" (as ecstasy, spiritual transport, or apocalyptic rescue) into Pepita's departure from the Mecca is severely complicated by the reality of rapture as sexual conquest. Rape is prevalent in the poem itself, and it is primarily Black female bodies that are in real danger of objectification and exploitation. If, as Betsy Erkkila summarizes, the Black woman appears in African American women's literature as "the site of social rupture, the place where the contradictions of American culture are located and exposed" (199), then we must read the transgression of Pepita's body as double: She is ruptured, broken, and violated, and she is also raptured, removed, and carried across the Mecca's borders. She is a ruptured site, and her rapture ruptures the communal site. The hole she leaves behind is also a hole in the Mecca's architecture—the first brick removed from the prison walls. Her loss is thus both a radical dismemberment of the Meccan "community" and the sign of a needed re-membering and re-imagining of a more powerfully self-identified Black community.

Alfred, another poet, finally begins to hear his prophetic calling only with the uncovering of Pepita's body:

> I hate it.
> Yet, murmurs Alfred—
> who is lean at the balcony, leaning—
> something, something in Mecca
> continues to call! Substanceless; yet like mountains,
> like rivers and oceans too; and like trees
> with the wind whistling through them.
>   And steadily
> an essential sanity, black and electric,
> builds to a reportage and redemption.
>   A hot estrangement.
>   A material collapse
>   that is Construction.
>
>   (31)

What Alfred sensed before only as a "rending" (27), he perceives now as a potential space for transformation. The collapse and construction that he envisions depend upon his ability to bear witness to what is substanceless—to Pepita's death and absence. The prophet's task, like the poet's, is a sane "reportage" of what exceeds articulation. In a reversal of traditionally gendered roles, then, Alfred finally becomes a bit of fertile ground for the sowing and growth of Pepita's seed. Without this possibility, the meaning of her name is wholly ironic: Pepita would fall only as the parabolic seed upon rock or among thorns, a tragic remainder in a concrete desert.

But Alfred, leaning toward another Meccan voice for the first time, figures a hopeful future growth. This hope emerges more clearly in the poems which follow the epic, in the volume's "After Mecca" section.

In "Sermon on the Warpland," for example, the poet preaches: "Say that our Something in doublepod contains/ seeds for the coming hell and health together" (49). Brooks never separates her vision of health from her social critique, or call for justice. She asserts that healing for some will surely mean "hell" for others—the ultimate juxtaposition. In this way, "In the Mecca" reads as a parable of inversion: one in which the coming "kingdom" is signaled by a reversal of social status.[28]

Brooks's message was in fact heard as a prophetic call by those "inside" her community of racial "outsiders." In her aptly titled poem "Our MZ Brooks: Clearing Space at the LOC," Eleanor Traylor represents the response to "In the Mecca" from those within the movement:

> Querying her glance calls loudly, yet unperturbed,
> "Pepita, Pepita, where is Pepita?
> "Pepita, Pepita, where is Pepita?
> "Pepita, Pepita, where is Pepita?"
> . . . Answers "hoodo holler" through
> the white washed room
> gathering like some gentle
> cloud
> raining on the memory
> of our dreams:
> Pepita here! Pepita here! Pepita, here is Pepita!
> Pepita here! Pepita here! Pepita, hear Pepita.
> We are all, Pepita, here.
>
> (59-60)

Brooks's young Black audience—women and men alike—are identified with and as Pepita, drawing together and re-membering the dispersed Black family under their mother-prophet's wing.

How other readers experience this calling and coming "Something," this apocalyptic birth-in-death, surely depends on how we relate to the Mecca as an historical, mythical, and social space, and how our reading of the poem receives the "seedpod" of the prophet's word. The meaning of a parable resides, after all, in its reception.

We should note, of course, that Brooks resists the title "prophet." George Stavros, in a 1969 interview with the poet, calls her series of "Sermon[s] on the Warpland" (in *Mecca* and *Riot*) "apocalyptic and prophetic," to which Brooks replies, "They're little addresses to black people, that's all," and changes the subject (*Report* 152). Stavros pushes her again, asking if she doesn't speak in "the voice of the prophet, speaker to the people . . . ?" and Brooks responds, "I don't want to be 'a prophet.' . . . I am not writing poems with the *idea* that they are to become 'social forces.' . . . I don't care to proceed from that intention" (153). Nonetheless, Brooks began writing in the late sixties with a new awareness that, if "shrieking into the steady and organized deafness of the white ear was frivolous," there were, in contrast, "things to be said to black brothers and sisters, and these things, annunciatory, curative, inspiriting, were to be said forthwith, without frill and without fear of white presence" ("Flowers" 1). This is how she characterizes Black poetry of that time in general, resisting any of the special status that "prophet" might imply.

If the prophetic is understood as a social construction—a category of speech determined by those "inside" a community which is "outside" the dominant order, a speech coming out of the inner being ("exousia"), a speech which nonetheless takes one beyond the borders of the self, in radical, "ex-static" identification with the Other (e.g., Black brothers or Africans)—then Gwendolyn Brooks's poetry is prophetic.[29] Reading between the lines of her own denial, after all, we can conclude that she does not reject this role altogether; she merely resists claiming it as her intention or goal. What true prophet, after all, desires to be a prophet? Isn't resistance to the title necessary to deserving it?

Taken as a prophetic text, "In the Mecca" requires a double-edged reading that attends to difference as well as similarity, anti-absorption as well as absorption, and criticism as well as affirmation. If white feminist critics are to enter the text in imaginative identification with Black women, for example, we must recognize the Mecca's marginal location not only as a site of shared pain, but also as a "space of refusal" (hooks 150) that resists the class and race privileges we would unwittingly bring with us. As parable, the poem may speak secrets we as "outsiders" are yet unable to hear. It also necessarily remains open and unfinished—anticipating a liberation fulfilled only in the actual response of its hearers/readers "outside" or "beyond" the textual realm.

Gwendolyn Brooks's work resists any simple "integration." Her work is based instead on a model of juxtaposition that highlights the need for liberation, and the potential necessity for radical reversals. She exposes the dangers of colonizing another's place and the strategic need for segregated spaces. She depicts ruined enclosures as prisons whose remaking from within has yet to begin.

Brooks's epic poem does have a transcendent aspect in that it draws meaning and power from another location—a realm beyond the text and beyond its own sociohistorical time and place. The representation of this space, however, emerges primarily in its negative image. Brooks's poem clearly demonstrates how the absence of freedom, community, and divine presence can be felt and figured as a radical call for their historical construction.

Whereas womanist theologian Katie Cannon characterizes Black women's literature as a "living space carved out of the intricate web of racism, sexism, and poverty" (7), I read "In the Mecca" as an exposition of deathly places—ruin, prison, tomb, hell—with a concomitant challenge to reclaim and transform them from within. This carries redemptive potential. As Miller argues, in Brooks's epic, "revealing the paradox of the American Dream suffices, for to show one's reader paradise is not the only way to save his soul" (158).[30] For those of us reading juxtapositionally, it remains up to us to "work out our own salvation" in response to Brooks's parable of infernal architecture. And to do so means recognizing not only that we are equally embedded in the "matrix of domination," but also that a shift in posture is possible. Indeed, we might need to undergo some radical "dislocation" to squeeze through the eye of the needle.

Two Poems for Gwendolyn Brooks

A Prophet Imagined

I want to say that you are an angel
and from you, Jacob-like, I'll wrestle
a blessing in the dark

or I'd say you were a master
from whose table I'd beg crumbs
like a dog, like a gentile woman

won't you cast out the unclean spirits
from my children?

but then I'd have my lines crossed
wouldn't I?
my history inside-out

for white has been so long so loved
and black, a belated chosenness

A Prophet Overheard

you were not calling me but
I heard you calling

calling the sisters,
brothers, children
in your house, in Chicago,
in Afrika

the house was burning and
you were calling them
OUT

calling out to them
but I heard you from
over here
in my back yard

I wanted to run down the alley crying
but it was your alley and
your fire and your voice and

so I stood at the gate and whispered
yes
yes

I say *amen*
to your *No*

the flames licked my face
a love, angry
and not meant for me

some hear your voice as a brook
bubbling, a river
turning, a sister
singing

but it singes me
a hot call
guiding, gilding, still
                    —Sheila Hassell Hughes

From *African American Review* 38, no. 2 (Summer 2004): 257-280. Copyright © 2004 by Sheila Hassell Hughes. Reprinted by permission of Sheila Hassell Hughes.

Notes

1. In a particularly interesting reinterpretation of these terms, George Kent defends the "legitimate universalism" of Brooks's work: "Her poems tend not to represent a reach for some preexisting Western universal to be arrived at by reducing the tensions inherent in the Black experience," he explains. Rather, "their universalism derives . . . from complete projection of a situation of experience's space and *vibrations* (going down deep, not transcending)" ("Poetry" 73-74).

2. I employ this term to identify the locational aspect of the ecstatic speech here: The poet speaks out of (ex) her own station and status, and in so doing exceeds the stasis of utter confinement.

3. Kent summarizes how the mass migration of blacks to Chicago during the Depression and Second World War (totaling 100,000) was condensed into an area that expanded by only one square mile (*A Life* 52).

4. This phrase appears in the sonnet "First Fight, Then Fiddle," in *Annie Allen* (*Selected Poems* 54).

5. Brooks herself has also judged *Annie Allen* as a studious collection in the years following her 1967 political and aesthetic "conversion." "The Anniad" she labels as "an exercise, just an exercise" (in Hull and Gallagher 32). Of course, I see no need to reduce the significance of the poem to the poet's own intent or appraisal. It is important to note, for instance, that black women critics have valued the work for the way it, more than any other, gives sustained attention to black female experience (Hull and Gallagher; Tate; Guy-Sheftall).

6. In an interview with Claudia Tate, Brooks upbraids the interviewer for not using the word political in a broad enough sense, and says, "I'm fighting for myself a little bit here because I believe it takes a little patience to sit down and find out that in 1945 I was saying what many of the young folks said in the sixties. . . . The poets of the sixties were direct. There's no doubt about it . . . [but] my works express rage and focus on rage" (Tate 42-43).

7. See Melhem's (161) and Miller's (146) essays on the poem for more detailed explanations of the work's evolution over a decade.

8. If her racial politics are radical or separatist, rather than integrationist, her gender politics are the opposite. Like many womanists, Brooks, acting from a concern for community cohesion in the face of overwhelming pressures from the "outside," would reject white feminist liberationist ideals. She explains to Tate: "There's a lot going on in this man-woman thing that bothers me . . . but these are family matters. They must be worked out within the family. At no time must we allow whites, males or females, to convince us that we should split. I know there's a lot of splitting going on now. . . . It's another divisive tactic dragging us from each other, and it's going to lead to a lot more racial grief. The women are not going to be winners on account of leaving their black men and going to white men, to themselves, or to nobody" (47). The image of "dragging us from each other" is a powerful one, given the legacy of slaves forcibly separated from their natural families (in Africa and in the United States).

9. Borrowing from psychoanalytic and semiotic theories, I take "place" to refer to one's location, situatedness, or the position from which one perceives and speaks to

others. One's place, in this sense, determines and is determined by a relation to others that is often oppositional. In relation to place, "space" signals something more fluid. Space implies freedom of movement, or expansiveness. If place is the point, space is the continuum. In this schema, place signals the particular and immanent, and space the universal and transcendent. The former is not simply contained within the latter, however, for the border is permeable and inside and outside can shift. Space can also imply something that is created in, or hollowed out of, some place or mass.

10. D. Harvey, *The Conditions of Postmodernity* (Oxford: Blackwell, 1989), summarized in Massey 139-40.

11. hooks remembers the historical role of African American women in creating "homeplaces"—sites of resistance and healing—for family and community. hooks stresses her appreciation of this as a chosen, rather than essential, role. Barbara Smith discusses her choice of a title in the introduction to *Home Girls: A Black Feminist Anthology.* "Home girls" refers to girls from "the neighborhood" (a term that encompasses and connects multiple literal black neighborhoods in the U.S.), but it also articulates the need for a home, a "place to be ourselves," to be at home with each other and escape the role of the social outsider. Smith outlines a number of ways that "home" is complicated for black women: the ambivalent role of women in the family, and also the broader black community, in transmitting "fear and shame . . . as well as hope" (xxii); the problem of conformity within a group pressed to define itself in opposition to oppression (xxxix); the "psychic violence" of incorporating that oppression as self-hatred; and the need for a concept of the "simultaneity of oppression" for "coalition building" across different social locations.

12. I borrow these terms from Diana Fuss's introduction to *Inside/Out: Lesbian Theories, Gay Theories,* in which she maps the space of "the closet."

13. When Hull presses Brooks about the absence of heroic female figures in her poetry from the sixties and seventies, Brooks explains, "These people who influenced me so much in the late sixties tended to be men. . . . The women—what can I say about them? . . . Well what were the women doing . . . aside from amening what the others did. . . . I didn't say 'Okay, women are supposed to take the back seat and I won't write about them.' . . . there was this tendency on the part of the women—announced too—to lift the men up, to heroize them" (Hull and Gallagher 36-37).

14. Two tribute anthologies have been published: *To Gwen With Love,* ed. Brown, et al. (1971); and *Say That the River Turns: The Impact of Gwendolyn Brooks,* ed. Madhubuti (1987).

15. In Wall, for example, Valerie Smith describes the appropriation of black women's intellectual labors: "Black women are employed, if not sacrificed, to humanize their white superordinates, to teach them something about the content of their own subject position" ("Black Feminist Theory" 46). As Collins and Delores Williams both suggest (in *Sisters in the Wilderness*), the surrogate maternity and emotional labor required of black women within the institution of the mammy-hood (in slavery and in decades of domestic service) comprised one expression of this "employment" or "sacrifice."

16. As a Jew living among Blacks, of course, Norton is both a fellow outsider to the majority culture and an outsider to (or "within") the Black community.

17. Brooks's ironic punning on names comes into play here as well: "Loam" refers to a friable (or fragile) soil mixture. Loam Norton, however, is trapped like the other Meccans in a concrete desert.

18. In *Conjuring Culture*, Theophus Smith argues that the maintenance of opposites in tension is an important part of black cultural and sacred practices. The idea of "pharmakon"—or that which functions as both poison and cure—is significant to his discussion.

19. Madhubuti may have something like this in mind when he states that "she has created form to fit an urban content" (xi). One critic of "In the Mecca" sees this "layering" method as a weakness, arguing that the poem "ought to have . . . unrelenting directness . . . but is overwrought with effects—alliterations, internal rhymes, whimsical and arch observations—that distract from its horror almost as if to conceal the wound at its center" (Rosenthal [1969], in Wright 27). This, it seems to me, is a deliberate strategy to mimic the effects of tenement living—too much life, too much detail (beautiful and horrible) crowded into a space too small to contain it, all of it cluttering and obscuring the deepest tragedies and potentialities.

20. While some of her friends and colleagues were emigrating from the States to countries in Africa, she appears not to have considered this seriously.

21. One of the poems in "After Mecca," the latter part of the collection *In the Mecca*, is called "Malcolm X." In it, Brooks writes, "And in a soft and fundamental hour/ a sorcery devout and vertical/ beguiled the world./ He opened us—/ who was a key,/ who was a man" (39). Malcolm's life and vision—both political and spiritual— are pictured as opening and releasing black people from internal and external means of confinement.

22. This description concludes John Bartlow Martin's commentary, which introduces Brooks's poem (2).

23. In his piece on the building for *Harper's Magazine*, Martin quotes one Mecca resident as follows: "They say they gonna place us somewhere. Place us! I don't wanta be placed anywhere myself. They might place me in some mudhole somewhere and I never did live like that" (97).

24. According to Martin's description (2).

25. Certainly this image of the female prostitute—as vain, self-absorbed devourer—appears to lack a certain critical feminist edge. Insofar as it portrays the destructive effects of white standards of beauty upon black women, in particular, it actually challenges traditional misogynistic representations, however. I should also point out that Hyena is just one of many female figures in the poem (including Pepita and Mrs. Sallie), and that Jamaican Edward provides a male counterpoint. He, in fact, is the more violent "hyena"—preying on the small and helpless wanderer in the Mecca-desert.

26. Greasley cites Brooks (*Report* 81) quoting Lerone Bennett.

27. Matthew 19:16-25. In this episode, a rich young man turns away from discipleship because Jesus tells him he must sell all that he has and give the money to the poor. When he turns away in grief, the teacher explains to his followers that it is easier for a camel to pass through the eye of a needle than for the rich to enter the Kingdom of Heaven.

---

28. See Crossan's *In Parables*, 53ff, for an explanation of parables of inversion. The gospel story of the rich young man, discussed above, also hinges on social reversals. Indeed, Jesus comments to his disciples on the coming kingdom: "But many who are first will be last, and the last will be first" (Matthew 19:30).

29. In *Say That the River Turns*, a compilation edited by Madhubuti in tribute to Brooks, images such as mother, prophet, priestess, and goddess recur in younger writers' tributes to the poet. For example, Ginger Mance, in the poem "She," writes: "She/ wakes spirits within us/ old and young calls forth/ the yet to come" (25).

30. Miller has a particularly religious focus in his reading of the poem, highlighting biblical, sermonic, and prophetic elements. The tie between spiritual and literary emphases comes, for example, in his analysis of Melodie Mary's identification with roaches and rats. He concludes that the point is "not that life is crushed inevitably, it is, rather, that even the most lowly insect is sacred. . . . Although the imagery indicates naturalism, the statement suggests transcendentalism" (149).

Works Cited

Bernstein, Charles. *A Poetics*. Cambridge: Harvard UP, 1992.

Brooks, Gwendolyn. *Annie Allen*. New York: Harper, 1949.

_____. *The Bean Eaters*. New York: Harper, 1960

_____. *In the Mecca*. New York: Harper, 1968.

_____. "Of Flowers and Fire and Flowers." Madhubuti 1-2.

_____. *Report from Part One*. Detroit: Broadside, 1972.

_____. *Riot*. Detroit: Broadside, 1969.

_____. *Selected Poems*. New York: Harper, 1963.

_____. *A Street in Bronzeville*. New York: Harper, 1945.

_____. *To Disembark*. Chicago: Third World P, 1981.

Brown, Patricia L., et al., eds. *To Gwen With Love*. Chicago: Johnson, 1971.

Cannon, Katie Geneva. *Black Womanist Ethics*. Atlanta: Scholars, 1988.

Clark, Norris B. "Gwendolyn Brooks and a Black Aesthetic." Mootry and Smith 81-99.

Collins, Patricia Hill. *Black Feminist Thought*. New York: Routledge, 1990.

Crossan, John Dominic. *In Parables*. New York: Harper, 1973.

Engle, Paul. "Chicago Can Take Pride in New, Young Voice in Poetry." 1945. Wright 3-4.

Erkkila, Betsy. *The Wicked Sisters: Women Poets, Literary History, and Discord*. New York: Oxford UP, 1992.

Evans, Mari. "Afterword." Madhubuti 84.

Fuss, Diana, ed. *Inside/Out: Lesbian Theories, Gay Theories*. New York: Routledge, 1991.

Greasley, Philip A. "Gwendolyn Brooks's 'Afrika.'" *Midamerica* 13 (1986): 9-18.

Guy-Sheftall, Beverly. "The Women of Bronzeville." Wright 153-64.

hooks, bell. *Yearning*. Toronto: Between the Lines, 1990.

Hull, Gloria T., and Posey Gallagher. "Update on *Part One*: An Interview with Gwendolyn Brooks." *CLA Journal* 21.1 (1977): 19-40.

Jaffe, Dan. "Gwendolyn Brooks: An Appreciation from the White Suburbs." 1969. Wright 50-59.

Keith, Michael, and Steve Pile. *Place and the Politics of Identity*. New York: Routledge, 1993.

Kent, George E. *A Life of Gwendolyn Brooks*. Lexington: UP of Kentucky, 1990.

_____. "The Poetry of Gwendolyn Brooks." 1971. Wright 66-80.

Lee, Don L. (Haki R. Madhubuti). "Gwendolyn Brooks: Beyond the Wordmaker—The Making of an African Poet." Preface to Brooks, *Report from Part One* 13-30.

Madhubuti, Haki R. (Don L. Lee), ed. *Say That the River Turns: The Impact of Gwendolyn Brooks*. Chicago: Third World P, 1987.

Martin, John Bartlow. "The Strangest Place in Chicago." *Harper's Magazine* Dec. 1950: 86-97.

Massey, Doreen. *Space, Place, and Gender*. Minneapolis: U of Minnesota P, 1994.

Melhem, D. H. "In the Mecca." Wright 161-81.

Miller, R. Baxter. "'Define . . . the Whirlwind': Gwendolyn Brooks's Epic Sign for a Generation." 1986. Wright 146-60.

Mootry, Maria K., and Gary Smith, eds. *A Life Distilled: Gwendolyn Brooks, Her Poetry and Fiction*. Urbana: U of Illinois P, 1987.

Moraga, Cherrie, and Gloria Anzaldúa, eds. *This Bridge Called My Back: Writings by Radical Women of Color*. New York: Kitchen Table, 1981.

Redding, J. Saunders. "Cellini-Like Lyrics: A Review of *Annie Allen*." 1949. Wright 6-7.

"Review of *A Street in Bronzeville*." 1945. Wright 5.

Smith, Barbara. "Black Feminist Theory and the Representation of the 'Other.'" Wall 38-57.

_____, ed. *Home Girls*. New York: Kitchen Table, 1983.

Smith, Gary. "Paradise Regained: The Children of Gwendolyn Brooks's *Bronzeville*." Mootry and Smith 128-39.

Smith, Theophus. *Conjuring Culture*. New York: Oxford UP, 1994.

Stafford, William. "Books that Look Out, Books that Look In." 1969. Wright 26.

Tate, Claudia, ed. *Black Women Writers at Work*. New York: Continuum, 1983.

Traylor, Eleanor. "Our MZ Brooks: Clearing Space at the LOC." Madhubuti 59-60.

Wall, Cheryl, ed. *Changing Our Own Words*. New Brunswick: Rutgers UP, 1989.

Williams, Delores. *Sisters in the Wilderness*. Maryknoll: Orbis P, 1993.

Wright, Stephen Caldwell, ed. *On Gwendolyn Brooks: Reliant Contemplation*. Ann Arbor: U of Michigan P, 1996.

"My Newish Voice":
Rethinking Black Power in
Gwendolyn Brooks's Whirlwind_____

Raymond Malewitz

Raymond Malewitz outlines the historical and cultural context of Brooks's engagement with the Black Arts movement. Ironically, Brooks, whose poetry carved a place for black, female voices to be heard in modernist realms, was dismissed by many in that movement. The dismissal indicates a flaw in the approach of the Black Arts movement writers: they wanted to use art as a means to expedite sociopolitical change toward patriarchal African ideologies, and this approach was reductive and hurtful to black female artists who were struggling to gain equality. However, Malewitz maintains that Brooks's "Sermon on the Warpland" adds a feminist critique to the masculine voices that dominated the Black Arts movement. Brooks's poems provide an experienced voice of reason that reflects a revitalized agenda to gain equality for all. Malewitz centers his analysis on the historical events of 1968, the year Brooks published *In the Mecca*. — M.R.M.

In his influential essay "Nationalism and Social Division in Black Arts Poetry of the 1960s," Phillip Brian Harper defines late sixties' black epistemology through opposing structures of unity and discord. Using Amiri Baraka's "SOS" and "Black Art" as models, he argues that the latter, divisive poem trumps its predecessor's general call for racial solidarity, and that this act of superseding necessitates a reexamination of the common conceptions of Black Nationalism within the Black Aesthetic. "[S]ocial division within the black community," he contends, "is fundamentally constitutive of Black Arts nationalism"; Baraka's work, serving as a synecdoche for all subsequent Black Arts poetry, performs these divisions with manifold ferocity (248).

Harper modifies this claim with an eye towards sexual and epistemological concerns in his revision of the essay within the collection *Are We Not Men?* Following a long line of previous critics,[1] Harper defines Black Nationalism as an essentially male project, and writes that "insofar as black identity [. . .] depends upon identification specifically *as man* [. . .] blackness will partake of the very uncertainty, tentativeness, and burden of proof that [. . .] characterize conventional masculinity" (40). Within this patriarchal orientation, Harper establishes two female archetypes: older poets such as Gwendolyn Brooks who make "Baraka's [initial unifying] enterprise [their] own," and younger counterparts such as Sonia Sanchez and Nikki Giovanni who "[wrote] beyond the 'call' manifested in [. . .] 'SOS,'" and espoused the later, polemical Barakan ideals (46). Thus, he divides the movement along sexually encoded ideological lines, with those who simply repeat Baraka's "call" and therefore "succumb to the rhetoric" on one side, and those who incorporate a "phallic standard of political engagement" to actively challenge such rhetoric on the other (43, 52). Harper's comments leave little doubt as to where his aesthetic interests lie, and he dismisses Brooks from the remainder of the essay after providing an oft-quoted passage from her 1972 autobiography, *Report from Part One*:

My aim, in my next future, is to write poems that will somehow successfully "call" (See Imamu Baraka's "SOS") all black people, black people in taverns, black people in alleys, black people in gutters, schools, offices, factories, prisons, the consulate; I wish to reach black people in pulpits, black people in mines, on farms, on thrones[.][2]

Curiously, Harper's quotation omits the final sentence of Brooks's statement: "My newish voice will not be an imitation of the contemporary young black voice, which I so admire, but an extending adaptation of today's G.B. voice" (RPO 183). This omission and other comparable lacunae are problems endemic to the scholarship concerning both Brooks's relationship to the Black Arts movement and, more generally, the position of black women within the patriarchal organizations of

Black Power. Houston Baker, for example, uses the same elided quotation to argue that Brooks "cast[s] her lot with the new generation" (108), while Arthur Davis insists that "like many young and middle-aged writers, she [came] under the influence of the Black Aesthetics Movement" (100). In each of these cases, Brooks is figured as a passive agent with respect to Black Arts; she "submits" to its rhetoric, where alternative figures such as Baraka and Giovanni construct and reconstruct its epistemology.

The purpose of this essay is to interrogate (and finally to challenge) such suppositions and to recover what "newish voice" Brooks brings to her poetry upon exposure to the younger poets. Examining her three "Sermons on the Warpland," I argue that Brooks actively resists both the simplistic unitary rhetoric of Black nationalism and the ideologically polemical stance that Harper describes. Shifting her poetry away from the performative (and ultimately coercive) aspects of both positions, Brooks instead employs a rhetoric of ambivalence in her representation of the nascent Black Aesthetic. In so doing, she situates the Black Nationalist movement, and, concomitantly, the black community from which it sprung, as highly contested hermeneutical spaces of inquiry, locations where previously irreconcilable social divisions can be negotiated and redefined. By examining this alternative response to the question of Black Nationalism, we can begin to see Brooks not only as a figure influenced *by* the Black Arts movement, but, more importantly, as a poet whose work challenges and reconsiders the grounds upon which the movement rests. This study therefore offers a critical alternative to the previous ideological understanding of the Black Arts movement by uncovering a feminine (if not feminist) counterpart to Baraka's masculine aesthetic program.

"Define and/ medicate the whirlwind"

Critics such as Angela Jackson and Norris B. Clark consider the events of 1967 to be the transformative impetus behind Brooks's interest in the new Black Aesthetic. During the spring of 1967, Brooks attended the Second Writers' Conference at Fisk University, where she met the fiery Baraka and witnessed his galvanizing effect upon the primarily black audience. Shortly thereafter, Brooks befriended Walter Bradford, the man who would introduce her to the Blackstone Rangers and to whom the "Second Sermon" would be dedicated. Late in the year, Brooks facilitated the Rangers' poetry workshops in Chicago, while contemplating the transfer of her own publications from the white-owned Harper and Row to Dudley Randall's new Broadside Press. These decisions illustrate the changes that were taking place in her catholic mind, and, as Brooks's autobiography makes clear, the decisions resulted in a radical shift in her poetic program. Writing just three years later, she would categorize 1967 as the fulcrum about which her poetry turned: "Until 1967 I had sturdy ideas about writing and about writers which I enunciated sturdily. [. . .] Until 1967 my own blackness did not confront me with a shrill spelling of itself" (RPO 73, 84).

Published the following year, *In the Mecca* marks Brooks's first poetic engagement with the "shrill spelling" of blackness.[3] In a shrewd analysis of the work, Norris Clark describes the ways in which Brooks's political transformations reproduce themselves in her poetic explorations, offering a sense of the changes in Brooks's epistemological landscape:

> Her emphasis has shifted from a private, internal, and exclusive assessment of the identity crises of twentieth-century persons to a communal, external, and inclusive assessment of the black cultural experience. That change not only corresponds to the fluctuating social, political, and ideological positions of the national black American communities during the sixties and seventies, but it also correlates with the evolution of aesthetic humanism's fundamental concerns about the nature of reality, our relationship to it and its vast variety. (84)

Although Clark separates the sociopolitical/black and aesthetic/ humanist components of Brooks's project, when examining the two poems that close the collection—"The Sermon on the Warpland" and the "Second Sermon"—I find the two projects to be inextricably linked. In both poems, Brooks casts "the nature of reality" and "our relationship to it" as necessarily political questions that pertain directly to the diverse meanings ascribed to Black Nationalism. As her epigram to "The Sermon on the Warpland" makes clear, "The fact that we are black/ is our ultimate reality," and it is from *this* reality and its manifold implications that Brooks tests her "newish voice." It is upon this reality that Brooks builds her own conception of the Black Aesthetic.

Brooks begins "The Sermon on the Warpland" with a series of structural paradoxes: "And several strengths from drowsiness campaigned/ but spoke in Single Sermon on the warpland./ And went about the warpland saying No" (451). Beginning in medias res, Brooks jars the reader into the lyric present of her poem while alluding to a preceding, though absent, structure. This hypotactic entry and its repetition in the third line join with the explicit binaries in the stanza—"strengths"/ "drowsiness," "saying" (proclaiming)/ "no" (negating), and "several"/ "Single"—to destabilize causation and offer a hermeneutical key to the poem. To understand the "warpland," the reader must confront the elaborate ways in which accumulation of meaning, with paradox and juxtaposition, is a necessary component of the black "reality."

What is the warpland? Lesley Wheeler maps the polyvalency of the term to the Sermon on the Mount, the "warped land" of an America torn by racial strife, the "'war planned' by black nationalists against white America, and even a 'warplane,' a carrier for this militant message" (231). Embedded within these possibilities lie both paradox and consonance. Just as Brooks claims to speak a "Single Sermon" from "several strengths" (note the genderless designation here), her polysemous subject—"warpland"—challenges her readers through a language of what could be called motivated ambiguity or, more polemically, a feminine semiotics of black empowerment.

This language contrasts greatly with that of Baraka, whose thematically analogous "Sermon for Our Maturity" illuminates the divide between the masculine and feminine lexicons of Black Power. In the poem, he outlines his Black Nationalist project in terms both singular and direct:

> We want to see you again as ruler of your own space
> Big Negro
> Big ol Negro
> > growin
> > wind storm flyin thru
> > your huge blue lung
> > Lung filled with hurricanes
> > of transparent fingerpops
> > and need to be changed to moans
> Stretch out negro
> > Grow "Gro
> > Gwan "Gro Grow
> Stretch out Expand . . .
>
> > > > > > > > (15)

While his language can stray from the literal ("transparent fingerpops"), the bulk of Baraka's message is a clear appropriation of Manifest Destiny rhetoric: the male Negro must rule his own space. Indeed, as Harper suggests, "Ambivalence can have no place [. . .] in the prosecution of such a revolutionary political program as the Black Aesthetic was supposed to represent" (52). Sandra Hollin Flowers takes this sentiment one step further, claiming, "When the masses become confused about ideology, the entire philosophy loses credibility" (12).[4] But whereas Baraka's plain style presents little room for political ambivalence, Brooks's poem embraces and indeed requires a reader who actively interrogates the precepts upon which Black Power rests. As such, when Brooks finally employs imperatives in her "Second Sermon," she couches them in opacity:

Salve salvage in the spin,
Endorse the splendor splashes;
Stylize the flawed utility;
Prop a malign or failing light . . .

(454)

Through the elaborate, sonic word play of "salve salvage" and "splendor splashes," Brooks casts poetic language as a genderless, abstract, and therefore unstable political mechanism that must be negotiated and transformed by the reader.

In so doing, Brooks's poem challenges the implicitly hierarchical relationship between speaker and reader of the Black Aesthetic. As Harper argues, poets such as Baraka engender divisions within the black community through a binary system of "I" (or "we")/ "you" wherein the poet achieves a position of cultural authority. Conversely, "any 'you' that these Black Arts poets invoke can function as a negative foil against which the implicit I who speaks the poem can be distinguished as a politically aware, racially conscious, black nationalist subject" (48). In the "Sermon for Our Maturity," this binary arises in Baraka's assumption of "we" and subsequent diminution of the reader to "you" or "Negro." Brooks's poetry makes no such claims—in fact, she announces the opposite by assuming a voice of "several strengths." Her voice thereby enacts a process of the black community speaking to itself and explores the diverse implications of its "ultimate reality" from a position within, rather than external to, its audience. Lesley Wheeler disparages such a move, writing that in so doing, the poem "minimiz[es] Brooks's literary authority" (231). But this seems to be exactly Brooks's point; by minimizing her own authority, she maximizes her black audience's political efficacy: a perfect inversion of the Barakan program.

Thus, Brooks's poetry moves away from prescriptive imperatives towards a program comparable to the consciousness-raising efforts of the women's liberation movement of the late sixties. Both manifestations of the broader "Movement" redefine their audience demographics, speaking directly to their oppressed compatriots rather than white patriarchal figures of power. Moreover, the efforts foreground the incomplete applicability of any holistic ideology and champion the complexity of any social or cultural epistemology. As Alice Echols writes,

> [F]or some women's liberationists consciousness-raising was a way to avoid the tendency of some members of the movement to try to fit women within existing [. . .] paradigms. By circumventing the "experts" on women and going to women themselves, they would be able to not only construct a theory of women's oppression but formulate strategy as well. (166)

Lisa Maria Hogeland classifies these strategies as "fundamentally heteroglossic process[es]"; individual personal narratives are brought into dialogue with "public and political discourses [in ways that] [. . .] yield new feminist meanings" (33-34). In an analogous manner, Brooks critiques those who would advance simplistically optimistic conceptions of the future black nation state, arguing that the seed of Black nationalism contains the possibility of triumph and failure: "Say that our Something in doublepod contains/ seeds for the coming hell and health together" (451). The phonic echo of "hell" and "health" within the "doublepod" emphasize the ineluctable paradoxes at the very core of the movement's push towards collectivity. These paradoxes grow stronger as Brooks speculates on the future of the movement, moving from its manifest pains to its ambiguous pleasures:

> Prepare to meet
> (sisters, brothers) the brash and terrible weather;
> the pains;
> the bruising; the collapse of bestials, idols,
> But then oh then!—the stuffing of the hulls!
> the seasoning of the perilously sweet!
> the health! the heralding of the clear obscure!
>   (451)

Rethinking Black Power in Brooks's Whirlwind   **261**

Harper would classify the "heralding of the clear obscure" as the necessary result of "writing beyond Baraka's 'SOS,'" a fumbling towards what a unified black nation state would resemble.[5] But within this oxymoron and the equally vague "seasoning of the perilously sweet," Brooks (rather playfully) dramatizes the inevitable problems that surface when taking up the mantle of an oracular sermonizer. Instead of focusing upon the end of Black Nationalism, and instead of describing what this end will be, she foregrounds the process that will ultimately make the obscure future clear and lays bare the limits of her own ideological position.

To this end, Brooks couches her one prescription, her great prophetic power, in a tautology, calling for the black community to "Build now your Church [. . .]/ with lithe love":

> With love like black, our black—
> luminously indiscreet;
> complete; continuous.
>
> (452)

Like the punning of "warpland"/war-planned, Brooks's "indiscreet" love is also in-discrete, blending social and ideological positions with one another until all are "complete; continuous." If her poem has a message, it invests this message in its readers rather than upon the page. Only they can decide how to love "like black" or determine what "our black" means. Her recapitulation of the call for unity is therefore not a repetition. Whereas Carmichael would situate Black power as a "clos[ing] of ranks" or a call for "group solidarity [for] social and political viability," (44) for Brooks it is the development of a broad spectrum from which her people, "black and black," can embrace their differences while uniting under the general principle of black love.[6]

To loosely appropriate Roland Barthes's famous distinction, what Brooks has done in "The Sermon on the Warpland" is to create a "writerly" text rather than the "readerly" texts of her younger, radical

Black Arts contemporaries. Barthes's definition of the former seems quite applicable to both Brooks's poem and her political program:

> The writerly text is a perpetual present, upon which no consequent language (which would inevitably make it past) can be superimposed; the writerly text is ourselves writing, before the infinite play of the world [. . .] is traversed, intersected, stopped, plasticized by some singular system (Ideology, Genus, Criticism) which reduces the plurality of entrances, the opening of networks, the infinity of languages. (5)

Brooks writes her Black Arts poetry in a mode that firmly resists calcification, and even when she is programmatic, her work radiates with interpretive possibilities. For example, "The Second Sermon" contains a series of imperatives that offer a "plurality of entrances" into the Black aesthetic. Beginning with the proclamation "This is the urgency: Live!/ and have your blooming in the noise of the whirlwind," Brooks certainly seems to incite the black community to action, but does so in such a way as to shroud her objective in ambiguity (453). What, after all, does it mean to "[bloom] [. . .] in the noise of the whirlwind?" Later, when describing the landscape of the "whirlwind," she uses an equally ambiguous lexicon:

> All about are the cold places,
> all about are the pushmen and jeopardy, theft—
> all about are the stormers and scramblers, but
> what must our Season be, which starts from Fear?
>
> (455)

These are far from rhetorical questions for Brooks's audience, whom she insists must "Define and/ medicate the whirlwind," for "the whirlwind is our commonwealth" (455, 454). Suggesting both the commonwealth of a racially divided America and the commonwealth-to-be of a black nation state, Brooks's whirlwind contains and combines both possibilities and then delivers them through her sermonic prosody. As R. Baxter Miller writes, this puzzle intuits an "Imaginative Mind that resolves disparities," but one who is defined by negation:

> Not the easy man, who rides above them all,
> not the jumbo brigand,
> not the pet bird of poets, that sweetest sonnet,
> shall straddle the whirlwind.
> Nevertheless, live.
>
> (454)

Whereas Miller interprets these lines as a clear indication of "a speaker possessed [of] some intuitive truth which neither the characters in the poem nor the readers outside fully understand," I contend that this negative definition actually projects outside of the text to Brooks's imagined conception of a black readership (157). The semantic disjunction between the imperative sentence "Nevertheless, live" and its preceding, descriptive list seems to invest the reader with at least the hope of understanding, and therefore "medicating" the whirlwind through an intense encounter with the "writerly" text. That Brooks calls attention to the limitations of poetic form ("not the pet bird of poets") only emphasizes the semantic shift she requires. Like the first Sermon's call for black love, her adjuration to "live" relocates the site of meaning from the written page to the projected, material space of the unified black community.

As a political statement, this projection necessarily occurs in time as well as space, for as Brooks makes clear, the polysemy that her poems strive to maintain cannot, and indeed should not, persist through time. Projecting her program of "living" into an apocalyptic future, she hypothesizes a moment when "time/ cracks into furious flower," when "A garbageman is dignified/ as any diplomat," when "Big Bessie [. . .] stands in the/ wild weed," and implicitly, when her poem's goal has been completed (456). In this "moment of highest quality," when the hierarchical stratification of society collapses, her poem shifts from the collective considerations of "several strengths" to become a celebration of the independent black individual, as evinced by "Big Bessie." "She is a citizen," Brooks writes, signifying her ascent to a position of empowered efficacy. This is the ultimate transference that Brooks asks her readers to imagine: to look upon her poetry as a signifier of the yet-to-be, and as a path from which to reach the halcyon future of a "medicated" whirlwind or the "wild weed"—and not as a statement unto itself. As Brooks's repetitive final line suggests, this future draws near: "Conduct your blooming in the noise and whip of the whirlwind" (456). Calling upon both the black community and time itself (recall "time /cracks into furious flower"), her conclusion points dramatically towards the interpretive possibilities for and of the future.

"Watermirrors and things to be reflected"

Historical events that followed Brooks's publication of *In the Mecca* severely tested the optimistic resolve of Brooks's first two Sermons. The violent summer of 1968, which saw devastating race riots sweep through urban America and the assassination of Martin Luther King, heralded a new militancy in Brooks's prosody, evinced by her subsequent collection *Riot* (1970). An inescapable trace of aesthetic nihilism pervades the polyvalency of the first two Sermons, as if Brooks's political program had inadvertently led the "writerly text" to its logical extremes—the death of the author and the birth of a new, rewriting reader. In the midst of conflict, she alters her method of representation. Whereas her first two Sermons adopt an aesthetic of motivated ambiguity to project interpretive possibility out of the text, in her "Third Sermon," she inscribes these possibilities within her very prosody. Taking the Chicago riots following Martin Luther King's assassination as the dominant leitmotif of the collection, Brooks willingly records the divisions of racial conflict between whites and blacks, proponents of violent and nonviolent direct action, and men and women.

Brooks arranges *Riot* such that "The Third Sermon on the Warpland" occupies a central position in the collection—in the very midst of both a metaphorical and a real race riot. The poem's cacophony of voices, perspectives, genres, and ideologies reproduce the chaotic and often contradictory contexts of this violent age. Because of their singular perspectives, these combating structural principles cannot capture the complexity of racial conflict. Through their juxtaposition, however, a dialogic superstructure begins to materialize, which offers new interpretive possibilities through the reflection or inversion of individual positions with respect to one another. This heteroglossic superstructure is the culmination of Brooks's evasive ideological perspective, for within the poem, Brooks modifies her program of semantic transfer and offers her own, reserved definition of the "warpland."

Brooks establishes both the dominant theme of her poem and its complications within the first stanza: "The earth is a beautiful place./ Watermirrors and things to be reflected./ Goldenrod across the little lagoon" (472). Borrowing the common mimetic trope—art being a mirror held up to the world[7]—Brooks foregrounds the issue of representation and consequently prepares the reader for an unmediated glimpse into "Warpland." Her choice of subjects immediately subverts this expectation, however, as "watermirrors" suggests that there will be many reflective media within her poem, each serving to illuminate certain elements of the landscape. Through an incredible shift between this stolid, emotionally evacuated stanza and the remaining, hyperkinetic passages, Brooks builds this dialogic tension into the very form of her poem. The idea of earth as a "beautiful place" contrasts with the subsequent stanza's theme of residual slave oppression, forcing the reader to reinterpret the former passage with ironic skepticism. Brooks therefore casts her "watermirrors" as distortions as much as reflections, and in so doing, suggests that any accurate depiction of the "Warpland" must be a collage of alternative velocities and ideologies, a concept that flickers into being only through the rapid juxtaposition of its component parts.

Even before this first stanza, Brooks's epigraph introduces the first of the poem's many paradigmatic voices that vie for the reader's confidence:

Phoenix:
"In Egyptian mythology,
a bird which lived for five hundred
years and then consumed itself in fire,
rising renewed from the ashes."
—Webster (472)

Set apart from the poem by italics and its position on the page, the definition seems to serve its common function as an objective perspective upon the poem's subject; it establishes the metaphoric parallels between the Phoenix, rising out of Africa, and the black community, who will also be "consumed" and "renewed" by the "fire[s]" of violence. This epigraphic mirror thereby offers a positive interpretation of the violence, suggesting, as many have argued, that black culture and society will somehow be regenerated through conflict.[8]

Such an interpretation leads Arthur Davis to describe her collection as a "journey into blackness," where "blackness" is equated with violent resistance. Comparable to Baraka's celebration of "the military aspects of national liberation" in a poem published that same year, Brooks's third Sermon positions the poet on the more militant side of black resistance (10). Two problems complicate this reading, however. Firstly, Brooks attributes the definition to Webster himself, the acclaimed American patriarch, rather than to his dictionary. This curious choice subverts the supposed objectiveness of the dictionary definition, raising the troubling question of ideological subjectivity: what currency can a dead white American claim in the representation of contemporary black revolution, let alone that of African myth? Brooks's use of Webster, a man who founded his dictionary to separate the American language from the oppressiveness of the Queen's English, only emphasizes the black community's need for a language of its own to defend itself from white, patriarchal oversimplification. Leading theoretician of the Black Arts movement Larry Neal argues that cultural aphasia is the very basis the movement: "The cultural values inherent in Western history must either be radicalized or destroyed, and we will probably find that even radicalization is impossible" (63). Thus Webster's "found poetry" proves difficult to simply appropriate without its residual, Western encoding. Secondly, and as an illustration of this process of linguistic transformation, Brooks transcribes Webster's definition in poetic form (a loose tetrameter), blurring the visual and auditory distinctions between its external position above the poem and the poem's first line (also a tetrameter).[9] This hybridization of form and content further destabilizes the ostensibly objective and external value of the epigraph and calls into question its efficacy as an appropriate, conceptually unifying principle for the riot.

The poem's closing remarks enforce this destabilization through a juxtaposition of voices. Just as the poem's speaker intones "Lies are told and legends made./ Phoenix rises unafraid," both the metaphor and its concomitant metrical scheme break down as another voice interrupts:

> The Black Philosopher will remember:
> "There they came to life and exulted,
> the hurt mute.
> Then it was over.
>
> The dust, as they say, settled."
>   (478)

This cryptic conclusion inverts the trope of the Phoenix rising, with the final lines moving from life to death, rather than a rebirth from the ashes. Like its historical counterpart, Martin Luther King, "the hurt mute" passes away, leaving chaos in its wake. While the lines do not necessitate a pessimistic reading of the riot, they do reinforce the incomplete applicability of such overarching myths to Brooks's subject. Caught within an uncertain historical moment, Brooks finds it literally impossible to determine whether the Phoenix is a "lie" or a "legend," and as such, within her poem, it functions as both.

The balancing of opposites within "Warpland" is not always so reconcilable, nor are the opposites always so clearly defined. For example, in a later passage Brooks introduces a white counterpart to the Black Philosopher, setting up an implicit binary, but immediately reconstitutes this opposition by locally displacing the Black Philosopher with the poem's speaker:

> Fire.
>
> That is their way of lighting candles in the darkness.
> A White Philosopher said
> "It is better to light one candle than curse the darkness."
>   These candles curse—
> Inverting the deeps of the darkness.
>
> (475)

By surrounding the White Philosopher's thoughts with those of the speaker instead of the Black Philosopher, Brooks shifts the focus of her critique. Opposing the former's aphoristic rhetoric (a rhetoric that the Black Philosopher also employs), the speaker establishes a different binary on her own terms, this time between white/light/philosophy and black/darkness/narration. The speaker inverts the power relations within this binary both semantically and syntactically ("candles curse"), and in so doing transforms a conceptual metaphor of Enlightenment thinking into a partial explanation for the horrors of the riot. Casting fire not as illumination or a promise of renewal, but rather as an eradicator of darkness, she implies that white culture's arrogant theorizing poorly masks its insidious but tangible role in the violence.

Darkness serves a secondary function as not only a symbol of the black community, but also that of an unrealizable absence, "the deeps of darkness." Brooks often incorporates absence into her juxtaposed structures, setting one idea against its underdeveloped opposite, only to champion this latter nonentity. Just as the people "went about the warpland saying No" in the first Sermon, Brooks frequently incorporates "do not" and "will not" constructions into her third Sermon's prosody. The aforementioned Black Philosopher maintains that his projected white audience "do[es] not hear" the rattle of slavery's chains, and as such, they "do not hear the remarkable music" of the "blackblues" (472). Later, the poem's speaker insists that

> A clean riot is not one in which little rioters
> long-stomped, long-straddled, BEANLESS
> but knowing no Why
> go steal in hell
> a radio . . .
>
> (474)

In both cases, the speaker clearly champions the alternative to the "not" clauses, whether that be the "blackblues" or a "clean riot," but does so in ways that refuse to define such alternatives. In the latter case, another speaker (or another train of thought) interrupts the original voice just as she begins to suggest what a "clean riot" would look like, leaving the concept veiled in darkness.

It may be tempting to cast such sudden interruptions and ephemeral alternatives as examples of the influence of jazz upon Brooks's form. "Mingus, Young-Holt, Coleman [and] John," certainly appear both explicitly and implicitly within the work, and the sudden shifts between speakers suggest the interplay of various instrumental voices within modern jazz compositions (474). But to attribute these absences wholly to structural considerations would be to miss a crucial point. Brooks's reluctance to define alternatives reflects her own difficulties with her chosen task of depicting the violence. Brooks cannot define a "clean riot," because her people *are* "long-stomped, long-straddled, BEANLESS," and also because the term itself defines an irreconcilable paradox. A "clean riot," like "the heralding of the clear obscure," suggests a level of logical causation that Brooks resolutely refuses to impart upon her depiction of the events. As her speaker baldly states, "what/ is going on/ is going on," independent of causal analysis or interpretation (474). All attempts to theorize what should or could have happened, she suggests, are irrelevant in the face of what *has* happened.

Just as Brooks finds it difficult to define what a riot should look like, she also resists assuming the unitary voice of the first two Sermons, for such a perspective would belie the ideological and cultural divisions within the late sixties' black community. She foregrounds these divisions by introducing many different black characters within her poem, each with his or her own characteristic speech patterns and viewpoints. When the Black Philosopher ominously blares, "I tell you, exhaustive black integrity/ would assure a blackless America," the poem shifts to Richard "Peanut" Washington, a young Blackstone Ranger whom Brooks had befriended in her poetry workshops, and his compatriots:

> "Coooooooll" purrs Peanut. Peanut is
> Richard—a Ranger and a gentleman.
> A Signature. A Herald. And a Span.
> This Peanut will not let his men explode.
> And Rico will not.
> Neither will Sengali.
> Nor Bop nor Jeff, Geronimo nor Lover.
> These merely peer and purr,
> And pass the Passion over.
>
> (427)

Using the same technique of negation that she employs earlier, Brooks describes the Rangers' refusal to passively accept or submit to ("explode") the tenets of the "Warpland": "Yeah!—/ this AIN'T all upinheah!" (427). While these voices send contradictory messages in contradictory lexicons, Brooks's presentation of the opposition makes it impossible to determine an external position with respect to either. Written at a time when black political organizations were increasingly divided between the late Martin Luther King's nonviolent program and Black power groups' calls for self-defense, the poem seems to identify with and celebrate both. In fact, Brooks's presentation suggests that the poem must set the two ideologies of black empowerment in a dialogue that makes no hierarchical distinction.

This is not to say that Brooks abandons all attempts to interpret the riot. She certainly divides her sympathy along racial lines, mocking the white-encoded "Law," and the reductive arguments of the white liberal: "'But WHY do These People offend themselves?' say they/ who say also 'It's time./ It's time to help/ These People.'" Elsewhere, in a moment comparable to her appropriation of Webster, another speaker recasts Hemingway's *Death in the Afternoon* to champion the bull over the (white) bullfighter: "We'll do an us!" yells Yancey, a twittering twelve./ "Instead of your deathintheafternoon,/ kill 'em bull!/ kill 'em bull!" (476).[10]

Nonetheless, to cast her poem simply as racially oppositional—a blind adherent to Baraka's vehemently antiwhite program—is also to miss the point. Through her ambitious project, she strives to capture the diversity and complexity of her race's relationship to the "Warpland." At times, her poem displays an audaciously playful humor, as in her description of young men's taste in stolen records: "They will not steal Bing Crosby but will steal/ Melvin Van Peebles." At other moments, her prosody reflects the poignancy and horror of the violence: "A woman is dead./ Motherwoman./ She lies among the boxes." For Brooks, any accurate portrayal of the riot must include all of these stories. She considers the riot, in other words, not only an historical event, but also a mosaic of black life. Her poetic negotiations of the community's diverse "watermirrors" therefore offer a more complete means by which to capture the late sixties' black experience.

Conclusions

What Brooks has done in all three poems, then, is to collapse Harper's masculine binary of unity and division. Her first and second "Sermons on the Warpland" present hermeneutical challenges to her newly defined audience, challenges that empower her readers to interrogate Black nationalism on their own terms. The third Sermon inscribes the polyvalency of black response through dialogic juxtaposition of one ideology upon another. Brooks positions herself in both cases as an interpretive medium through which the internal divisions within the black community can be reconciled or at least negotiated.

Brooks therefore offers an implicit alternative to our current conception of the Black Arts poet as a speaker of singular cultural authority. Although each poem employs the rhetorical devices of a sermon—exhortation, prophecy, and apocalypse—her approach is far from coercive or divisive. Brooks perceives a heteroglossic world that is filled with both uncertainty and possibility; instead of offering easy (and in hindsight inadequate) prescriptions for a black future, she carefully documents the black community's pluralities to outline what meanings can be gleaned through their confrontations.

Through this program, Brooks's poetry presents a challenge to those critics who would see the Black Arts movement as a calcified artifact of history. For the poet, her movement was always defined by the uncertainty of the historical present, and she was not alone in this judgment. In a letter to Brooks in late 1970, Larry Neal writes:

> Sister, Please, Please, Please, don't let some of us so-called 'young' writers intimidate you. [. . .] Try to understand that we are searching ourselves. We don't really know all there is to know, and you will have to help us. Therefore, don't be easy on us. We need the strictness of a mature hand to guide us.[11]

Neal's ambivalent evaluation of Brooks's abilities proves a useful starting point for new investigations of Black Arts epistemology. Just as Neal describes the "young" poets "searching for themselves," he identifies Brooks as an influential figure who likewise explores the regions of a plastic, inchoate black identity. That Neal (to my mind) misinterprets Brooks's approach as an expression of timidity, however, only emphasizes our need as critics to take up her "mature hand" and form new conceptualizations of her uncertain sociocultural moment. When we reimagine her poetry apart from the patriarchal standards of singularity, we will discover a "newish" and empowered female consciousness within the ideolog*ies* of Black Power.

From *Callaloo* 29, no. 2 (Spring 2006): 531-544. Copyright © 2006 by Charles H. Rowell. Reprinted with permission of The Johns Hopkins University Press.

Notes

1. See, for example, Komozi Woodard's *A Nation within a Nation: Amiri Baraka (LeRoi Jones) and Black Power Politics* (Chapel Hill: U of North Carolina P, 1999).

2. Quoted in Harper's essay, p. 224.

3. As B. J. Bolden writes in her study *Urban Rage in Bronzeville*, this claim can be overstated. "Brooks is indeed 'awake' during [the] years prior to her formal 'awakening' at the 1967 Fisk Black Writer's Conference" (162). Nonetheless, what concerns me most is not what her early poetry performs, so much as what changes she thinks her later work enacts.

4. In keeping with much other general scholarship on the movement, Flowers's study makes no mention of Gwendolyn Brooks.

5. Alternatively, Wheeler interprets the phrase as a declaration of "the difficult, or even irrational, in any poetry, including the poetry of the pulpit."

6. Quoted in Rod Bush's *We Are Not What We Seem: Black Nationalism and Class Struggle in the American Century* (New York: New York UP, 1999) 10.

7. See, for example, M. H. Abrams's extensive study *The Mirror and the Lamp* (New York: Oxford UP, 1953).

8. See, for example, Gertrude Reif Hughes, "Making It *Really* New: Hilda Doolittle, Gwendolyn Brooks, and the Feminist Potential of Modern Poetry," *On Gwendolyn Brooks: Reliant Contemplation*, ed. Stephen Wright (Ann Arbor: U of Michigan P, 2001) 206.

9. Adrienne Rich chooses this same device in her poem, "Integrity," beginning the piece with a definition by Webster that she sets in an ironically broken form. The parallels between Brooks's and Rich's projects suggest a richer relationship between the Black Arts movement and the second-wave feminist projects.

10. D. H. Melhem makes a comparable point in her *Gwendolyn Brooks: Poetry and the Heroic Voice* (Lexington: UP of Kentucky, 1987) 198.

11. Quoted in George Kent's *A Life of Gwendolyn Brooks* (Lexington: UP of Kentucky, 1990) 227.

Works Cited

Baker, Houston A., Jr. *The Journey Back: Issues in Black Literature and Criticism.* Chicago: U of Chicago Press, 1980.

Baraka, Imamu Amiri. *It's Nation Time.* Chicago: Third World Press, 1970.

Barthes, Roland. *S/Z.* Trans. Richard Miller. New York: Hill and Wang, 1974.

Brooks, Gwendolyn. *Blacks.* Chicago: Third World Press, 1992.

_____. *Report from Part One: An Autobiography.* Detroit: Broadside Press, 1972.

Bush, Rod. *We Are Not What We Seem: Black Nationalism and Class Struggle in the American Century.* New York: New York UP, 1999.

Carmichael, Stokely, and Charles V. Hamilton. *Black Power: The Politics of Liberation in America.* New York: Random House, 1992.

Clark, Norris B. "Gwendolyn Brooks and a Black Aesthetic." *A Life Distilled: Gwendolyn Brooks, Her Poetry and Fiction.* Ed. Maria K. Mootry and Gary Smith. Chicago: U of Illinois Press, 1987: 81-99.

Davis, Arthur P. "Gwendolyn Brooks." *On Gwendolyn Brooks: Reliant Contemplation.* Ed. Stephen C. Wright. Ann Arbor: U of Michigan Press, 2001: 97-105.

Echols, Alice. "Nothing Distant about It: Women's Liberation and Sixties Radicalism." *The Sixties: From Memory to History.* Ed. David Farber. Chapel Hill: U of North Carolina Press, 1994: 149-174.

Flowers, Sandra Hollin. *African American Nationalist Literature of the 1960s: Pens of Fire.* New York: Garland, 1996.

Harper, Phillip Brian. "Nationalism and Social Division in Black Arts Poetry of the 1960s." *Identities.* Ed. Kwame Anthony Appiah and Henry Louis Gates, Jr. Chicago: U of Chicago Press, 1995: 220-241.

_____. "Nationalism and Social Division in Black Arts Poetry of the 1960s." *Are We Not Men? Masculine Anxiety and the Problem of African-American Identity.* New York: Oxford UP, 1996: 39-53.

Hogeland, Lisa Maria. *Feminism and Its Fictions: The Consciousness-Raising Novel and the Women's Liberation Movement.* Philadelphia: U of Pennsylvania Press, 1998.

Hughes, Gertrude Reif. "Making It *Really* New: Hilda Doolittle, Gwendolyn Brooks, and the Feminist Potential of Modern Poetry." *On Gwendolyn Brooks: Reliant Contemplation.* Ed. Stephen C. Wright. Ann Arbor: U of Michigan Press, 2001: 186-212.

Jackson, Angela. "In Memoriam: Gwendolyn Brooks." *On Gwendolyn Brooks: Reliant Contemplation.* Ed. Stephen C. Wright. Ann Arbor: U of Michigan Press, 2001: 277-284.

Kent, George E. *A Life of Gwendolyn Brooks*. Lexington: UP of Kentucky, 1990.

Melhem, D. H. *Gwendolyn Brooks: Poetry and the Heroic Voice*. Lexington: UP of Kentucky, 1987.

Miller, R. Baxter. "'Define . . . the Whirlwind': Gwendolyn Brooks's Epic Sign for a Generation." *On Gwendolyn Brooks: Reliant Contemplation*. Ed. Stephen Wright. Ann Arbor: U of Michigan Press, 2001: 146-160.

Neal, Larry. "The Black Arts Movement." *Visions of a Liberated Future: Black Arts Movement Writings*. Ed. Michael Schwartz. New York: Thunder's Mouth, 1989: 62-78.

Wheeler, Lesley. "Heralding the Clear Obscure: Gwendolyn Brooks and Apostrophe." *Callaloo* 24 (2001): 227-235.

Woodard, Komozi. *A Nation within a Nation: Amiri Baraka (LeRoi Jones) and Black Power Politics*. Chapel Hill: U of North Carolina Press, 1999.

Signifying *Afrika*:
Gwendolyn Brooks's Later Poetry_____
Annette Debo

Annette Debo gives a historical and cultural context for pan-Africanism, a goal that W. E. B. Du Bois spent the majority of his life pursuing. Debo also explains why Brooks uses the variant spelling "Afrika" in her work. Outreach to Africa was a central tenet of the Black Arts movement, and Brooks, who continually challenged herself to grow as an artist, rose to the challenge. Debo discusses how Brooks wrote about her experience of Africa in her prose and poetry, arguing that she captures how blacks throughout the diaspora of Caribbean and African countries colonized by Europeans struggled for independence from their colonizers and comparing this struggle with the American Civil Rights movement. When European countries began to abandon their colonies, many blacks felt a common bond not only to rediscover their precolonial African cultures but also to reach out to other blacks who had suffered under European colonization. A point of particular contention was South Africa, which upheld its racist system of apartheid. Brooks was drawn to South Africans' stories of their struggles to be free. Debo fits Brooks's personal and artistic progression into the frame of colonial and postcolonial Africa.   — M.R.M.

"I know now that I am essentially an essential African," declared Gwendolyn Brooks in her 1972 autobiography *Report from Part One* (45). Her phrasing, which jars the twenty-first-century ear—for how could one of the most acclaimed African-American poets be an "essential African"?—reflects the cultural milieu of the Black Power Movement, which peaked in influence during the mid-1960s and early 1970s. The Black Power Movement was a Black nationalist movement which, along with its armed revolutionary groups like the Black Panthers, encompassed cultural nationalism.[1] Cultural nationalism, according to the critic Scot Brown, "has been broadly defined as the view that African Americans possess a distinct aesthetic, sense of values, and communal ethos emerging from either, or both, their contemporary folkways and continental African heritage" (6). Brooks became influenced by cultural nationalism through her experience with the Black Arts Movement, the artistic arm of the Black Power Movement, an experience that began during an explosive 1967 conference at Fisk University, a well-known story (Brooks, *Report from Part One* 84-86). Upon arriving at Fisk to read her work, Brooks immediately recognized that the tenor of this gathering was different: "I was in some inscrutable and uncomfortable wonderland. I didn't know what to make of what surrounded me, of what with hot sureness began almost immediately to invade me. *I* had never been, before, in the general presence of such insouciance, such live firmness, such confident vigor, such determination to mold or carve something DEFINITE" (85). Immersing herself in the energetic politics of the young writers, Brooks gleaned a number of sentiments from Black nationalism, the most significant of which, for the purposes of this article, was the intense focus on African roots for Black Americans. Because of the Black Arts Movement's influence, Brooks twice traveled to Africa to experience physically the land of her ancestors; she embraced the African hairstyle of the natural, vehemently repudiating straightened hair; she was inspired by the African independence wars; and she developed a self-identity as "an essential African." Brooks's poetry reflects her new convictions, and the presence of Africa in her poetry increased dramatically in the 1970s and 1980s.

In this article I explore how Africa signifies in Brooks's later poetry in an effort to tease out the meaning of being essentially African.[2] First, beginning in 1969 in *Riot*, Brooks chooses to spell "Afrika" with a "k," which is the Kiswahili spelling (*Blacks* 479).[3] Adopting this spelling allows Afrika to become a linguistic tie between Brooks's own writing and the African language then touted as the best option for diasporic peoples. Second, Afrika provides a center in which Blackness can be located. Brooks wants to connect her audience to the physical continent and people of Africa because, as Brooks has said, "The *essential* black ideal vitally acknowledged African roots" (Brooks, "Interview" 407). Third, Brooks wrote a number of poems specifically about the struggles against apartheid in South Africa. Primarily published in the 1980s, these poems strive to reinvigorate the American civil rights movement during the Reagan years. This Afrika is inspirational through its hard-fought battles, heroes, and martyrs. Lastly, in several poems, the signifier Afrika has little to do with the physical continent. Afrikan becomes an appellation for all Blacks involved in fighting racism and imperialism. Afrika also designates the mass of the diaspora, signifying the size and breadth of their numbers and power as they themselves become a continent.

I

Selecting the Kiswahili spelling of Afrika allows Brooks to gesture toward the African languages that should have been hers, if not for slavery. In reflecting upon her visit to East Africa in 1971, when she visited Nairobi, Kenya, and Dar es Salaam in Tanzania, Brooks laments her loss of African languages as a New World person in the African diaspora: "In the New Land, my languages were taken away, the accents and nuances of my languages were taken away. I know nothing of Swahili nor or any other African language." Having invested her literary life in English, Brooks considers "'how long it has taken me to secure for myself the accents, nuances, subtleties of the *English* language!' 'I do not have . . . another fifty-four years to learn the languages that are rightfully mine!'" (*Report from Part One* 88). Also sharing her lament for the loss of African languages in literature are African writers trained to write in English, most notably Ngugi wa Thiong'o who, in *Decolonizing the Mind*, vehemently argues for a return to African languages. Ngugi himself chooses to write in the Kenyan language Gikuyu as "part and parcel of the anti-imperialist struggles of Kenyan and African people" (28). Unifying the Black American struggle against racism with the African struggle against imperialism is one of Brooks's goals in these later poems, and so, logically, Brooks joins her own language with an African one.

Although Brooks lost the opportunity to master an African language the way that she mastered English, she did learn some basic Kiswahili during her travels in East Africa, and choosing Afrika provides her with a linguistic connection. She did not have, as Ngugi does, African languages to which she can return, but Brooks built a literary tie with the continent by provocatively selecting Afrika, even if her poetry was written in English, a colonizing language. In discussing her linguistic strategies, Brooks said, "I just feel that Blacks should be trying to develop some Black styles for themselves and I think that there is a way to do it in English. We are not all going to start writing in Swahili. But we can go farther along the road of Blackening English than we have gone already" (Martha H. Brown 55). The almost minute substitution of "k" for "c" actually changes the tenor of the word, introducing an African tone into an almost American word in much the same way that Brooks tweaks the sonnet form in her 1945 sequence *Gay Chaps at the Bar*, in which she uses near-rhyme and inconsistent iambic pentameter (*Blacks* 64-75). Brooks explained the change in spelling to the critic D. H. Melhem: "There is no sibilant *c* before vowels in African languages; the alternate spelling seems 'more authentic'" (*Gwendolyn* 227). *Africa* is a linguistic joining, mirroring the unification Brooks urgently seeks in Blackness.

In her adoption of Kiswahili, Brooks followed both Black Nationalist organizations and African writers. Maulana Karenga of the organization US explains why his organization chose Kiswahili as its representative language:

(1) Swahili is a pan-African language, that is, it is non-tribal, it is the only language in Africa that is non-tribal; (2) we cannot claim any tribe, we can only claim Africa itself, so we are the first Pan-Africans, of a sort. If we

choose Hausa, there's a Hausa tribe. If we choose Zulu, there's a Zulu tribe. So, then, where should we go but to Swahili, which has no tribe? (54)[4]

His arguments for Kiswahili as a nonaligned African language may have appealed to Brooks, who was certainly pursuing an identity as a Pan-African. Furthermore, at the 1966 Second Congress of African Writers, arguments were made for a common literary language in Africa, and Kiswahili was considered "the optimum choice by many advocates of Pan-Africanism" (Scot Brown 10). Following the lead of African writers would also have appealed to Brooks as she increased her allegiance to the continent of her ancestors.

II

In addition to a linguistic connection, Afrika provides a locus for Blacks all over the world; it offers a location for racial unity, another value prevalent during the Black Power period. As Brooks said upon arrival in East Africa, "This is BLACKland—and I am *black*" (*Report from Part One* 87). On this first trip to Africa, Brooks reveled in Blackness. While out walking among African people, Brooks comments: "Once off the pavement decline of the hotel, I begin to scream inside myself. I notify myself, 'The earth of *Africa* is under my feet!' Above me, white clouds! Blue, blue sky!" (*Report from Part One* 88). Besides the corporeal earth, Brooks notices the cut of the men's hair, and the women's vivid headwraps; in short, everything dazzles in her first rush of impressions. Brooks writes, "I gasp at what I see along the road. Colors and erectnesses and grace and amazing physical markings and *blackness* that I have seen in paintings, in movies, on television" (*Report from Part One* 123). For the first time Brooks's complexion, features, and hair allow her to blend with the majority of the people; in appearance, at least, she is an insider in Africa. In contrast, Africa is a place Whites cannot easily claim for their own, and Brooks enjoys their "affected heartiness" and "nervous bluster" as they travel into a land of people where their complexion, features, and hair cause them to stand out (87). Brooks even flirts with separatism, eyeing people of Indian descent living in Africa as "tourists in this land that belongs to *blacks*," and rejects condoning a multiracial Africa (90, 125). Enthusiastic and jubilant, Brooks presents an Africa of light, laughter, and color that could well serve as a "mother-home" to the newly awakening black consciousness in American Blacks (92).

Her poetry seeks to inculcate this same sense of unification with Africa in her intended audience, who by the 1970s were "all black people: black people in taverns, black people in alleys, black people in gutters, schools, offices, factories, prisons, the consulate; I wish to reach black people in pulpits, black people in mines, on farms, on thrones" (*Report from Part One* 183). In "Another Preachment to Blacks," Brooks expounds on the significance of Africa to American Blacks in what is not a tiresome sermon, in other words a typical preachment, but in what became a constant refrain in her work—a continual encouragement for Black Americans to look to Africa for inspiration.[5] Brooks opens the poem by addressing American Blacks because "you know/ so little of that long leaplanguid land" that is Africa (*to disembark* 59). Brooks names the rhythm, the "booming" of American Blacks, a poem, and she designates the poem itself "AFRIKA." The unification of Blacks is represented by two condensed Brooksian oxymorons— "dwarfmagnificent" and "busysimple"—that represent peoples of divergent temperaments, of different continents, who yet belong together (59). Their joining is predicated on a shared history on the continent Africa, and this tie to the continent is pivotal because it allows a history and physical location for Blackness, which Don L. Lee, now known as Haki Madhubuti, reinforces with his claim that "people find a sense of *being*, a sense of worth and substance with being associated with *land*" (28). Brooks again traveled to Africa in 1974, on this trip visiting Accra and Kumasi in Ghana, and she considered travel to Africa so critical to the development of Black American writers that she personally paid $4,000 for two students to accompany her. George E. Kent's biography documents her many monetary gifts to young writers and claims that for this particular expense, Brooks "felt that the trip changed their lives and was therefore quite happy about it" (221).

Nevertheless, the "African Fragment" of *Report from Part One*, whose title echoes Langston Hughes's poem "Afro-American Fragment" (*The Collected* 127) and whose sentiment echoes his disappointment in finding that Africans regard him as a "white man" in *The Big Sea* (103), is tension-filled because while Brooks needs Africa, she piercingly sees that the Africans do not need her and give "it seems—scarcely a thought [to] their stolen brothers and sisters over the way there, *far* over the way" (*Report from Part One* 89). While monumentally impressed with the African people and their definitive place in the world, she does not find the Black unity for which she hoped: "THE AFRICANS! They insist on calling themselves Africans and their little traveling brothers and sisters 'Afro-Americans' no matter *how* much we want them to recognize our kinship" (130). She is repeatedly identified as an "Afro-American" by Africans and thus situated as an outsider in their country, despite her appearance and heritage. As Black Americans emigrate to Africa, Africans are filled with doubts about what Black Americans can now offer to Africa, and Africans worry about keeping their own culture intact: "'Well, Afro-AMERICANS,' they likely mutter, '*you're* not going to come over here and take over *our own* country!'" (*Report from Part One* 129). In contrast, *Report from Part Two*, Brooks's second autobiographical volume, comments on her second trip to Africa, but by the time she had published this book in 1996, she had reconciled her earlier tension between desiring acceptance as an African and the impossibility of that happening in Africa. Brooks describes a conversation between her husband, Henry Blakely, and an African woman, in which Blakely laments, "'We Blacks in the United States envy you. You ARE AFRIKANS. You KNOW this country is YOURS—that you

BELONG here. We Blacks in the United States don't know *what we are*'" (*Report from Part Two* 51). Brooks documents how his confusion is incomprehensible to the African woman who replies, "with impatient semi-contempt, '*YOU* Ameri*CAINE!*'" (*Report from Part Two* 51). Gone is Brooks's dismay with that opinion—and the accompanying stress in the text—because now she knows the African opinion. In this second volume the suggestions of a migration back to Africa are gone, and while Africa remains a powerful symbol of Blackness, of sister- and brotherhood, and of unity, its usefulness is circumscribed.

III

While the symbol of Africa as a homeland assumed a lesser role for Brooks as she moved past the heyday of the Black Power Movement, Afrika continued to signify through the battles against apartheid in South Africa about which Brooks wrote a number of poems, many in the 1980s. By that time, the time of the conservative Reagan years, the American civil rights struggle had cooled, and in hopes of renewing it, Brooks offered the inspirational model of South Africa. These poems inform and instigate, none more so than "Winnie" and "Song of Winnie," which Brooks credits with "mark[ing] a very significant change in [her] writing" (Brooks and Hawkins 275).

"Winnie" is a dramatic monologue voiced by Nelson Mandela, the South African icon of resistance during apartheid, president of South Africa from 1994 to 1999, and the husband of Winnie Mandela in 1988, when this poem was published. In this poem Nelson is validating Winnie, using his voice to authenticate her and to explain who she is to Black Americans, "all ye/ that dance on the brink of Blackness" (Brooks, *Winnie* 2). Because Nelson was incarcerated as a political prisoner from 1962 to 1990, Winnie was the visual representation of him for the nation, and she took up his fight against apartheid. Brooks's poem draws a portrait of Winnie as, alternately, a "sumptuous sun/ for our warming" or "ointment at the gap of our wounding" (1). She is left little individuality, a sacrifice that the poem acknowledges, but it, like the antiapartheid movement, has to ignore the person in favor of showcasing a dynamic symbol of resistance. She is now "the founding mother" (1). Nelson announces: "your vision your Code your Winnie is woman grown./ I Nelson the Mandela tell you so" (2). By his words and reputation, Winnie is positioned to incite and inspire Black Americans. However, the irony of using, in 1988, a male voice to validate a female persona is not lost on Brooks, who commented in an interview with Melhem,

> Mischievously, the poet wants you to understand that Nelson (like many *another* man) wants you to understand that HE guarantees Winnie's Quality! (The very fact that he feels obliged to *make* that statement indicates his understanding that Winnie's strength, courage, and influence are independent! She is devoted to and admiring of her husband, but she is capable of standing firmly on her own feet.) (*Heroism* 28)

In a second dramatic monologue entitled "Song of Winnie," one of Brooks's longer poems at 358 lines, Brooks turns to Winnie's voice to sound the call to arms.[6] Winnie opens her song with

> Hey Shabaka.
> Donald and Dorothy and William and Mary.
> Angela, Juan, Zimunya, Kimosha.
> Soleiman, Onyango and Aku and Omar.
> Rebecca.
> Black Americans, you
> wear all the names of the world!
>
> Not a one of you ex-Afrika Blacks out there
> has his or her Real Name.
>   (3)

With these lines Brooks reinforces the displacement of American Blacks by implying that their real home, despite the impossibility, is Africa, and thus all American Blacks are lacking their "Real Name[s]." Reaching across to the diaspora, Winnie informs her audience who, although they are "crisp and resolute and maximum," are not "disorder[ing] the décor/ by looking at it too hard" (3, 4). In other words, Black Americans, despite their heritage and abilities, are not challenging the status quo in their own country. But perhaps if Winnie tells her own story, which in many ways is the story of her people, Black Americans will begin to understand the worldwide struggle against European imperialism and to reevaluate their own political situation.

While this Winnie also represents ideal womanhood and the radical poet, her most significant role in this poem is as a symbol of determination and combativeness. Brooks flattens her persona into a symbol somewhat in imitation of the real Winnie Mandela, for Winnie herself conceded, "I have ceased a long time ago to exist as an individual. The ideals, the political goals that I stand for, those are the ideals and goals of the people in this country" (Mandela 26). However, Brooks's Winnie is a poetic construction, built upon what she knew of the actual Winnie and what she hoped for her: "I have always considered her very strong and properly called heroic," Brooks told Sheldon Hackney (162). Brooks commented on her portrayal of Winnie to Melhem:

I have tried to paint a picture of what the Woman must be like. The picture is "built" out of nuance and supposition and empathy. I figure she is composed of womanly beauty, of strengths female and male, of whimsy, willfulness, arrogance and humility, tenderness, rawness, power, fallibility, finesse, a "sweet" semi-coarseness which is the heavy fruit of daily oppression/ fury/pain. And gloriousness!—glory. She is a glory. (Heroism 34)

While Brooks had seen documentaries about Winnie, she had not met Winnie and claimed, "I feel that I came so close to nailing her down in that little book, that I feel I don't want to meet her. I want to believe that

Critical Insights

she is everything that I've put in that long poem" (Hackney 163).[7] Her portrait is both accurate and wishful, real and constructed. Brooks's Winnie is pure essence; she is presented as the role model to which all Blacks should aspire.

However, after serving as a national symbol, the real Winnie Mandela's reputation tarnished, which happened after Brooks's poem was published. Unable to hold their marriage together after three painful decades of separation, Winnie and Nelson separated in 1992 and divorced in 1996. Additionally, Winnie was convicted on charges linked to the kidnapping and murder of Seipei Moketsi in 1991, but on appeal her six-year sentence was reduced to a fine. In 2003 she was convicted on charges related to a bank loan scandal and received a five-year sentence plus one year suspended. Both of these cases were controversial, and Winnie continues to proclaim her innocence. While the truth behind these legal cases is not yet clear, Winnie's immense sufferings, her own imprisonment, her banning, her constant harassment, and her internal exile in Brandfort during apartheid are well known. She is no longer the pristine national symbol she was when Brooks wrote her poem, but her full story, set in the horrific years of apartheid and its aftermath, has not yet been told.

Brooks's specific construction of Winnie emphasizes her most potent influences: "I learned to bond the faith-steam of my mother/ and the retrieval-passion of my father/ and the thriving the bloodfire of the Pondoland people" (Brooks, *Winnie* 5). Winnie's mother was excessively religious, and while Winnie rejected the ineffective Christian god to whom her mother prayed, she inherited her mother's passion and single-minded determination. From her father, a history teacher, Winnie inherited an accurate vision of South African history that their school textbooks failed to cover:

He would put the textbook aside and say: "Now, this is what the book says, but the truth is: these white people invaded our country and stole the land from our grandfathers. The clashes between white and black were originally the result of cattle thefts. The whites took the cattle and the blacks would go and fetch them back." That's how he taught us our history. (Mandela 48)

The Pondoland people, when Winnie was growing up, were still "totally tribal," passing along their rituals, their traditional beliefs, their value as a people, and their love of their land. Winnie remembers after learning the history of her people that "you tell yourself: 'If they failed in those nine Xhosa wars, I am one of them and I will start from where those Xhosas left off and get my land back'" (Mandela 48). Winnie's final significant influence came when she moved to Johannesburg in 1953 and became politicized by her urban friends and her marriage to Nelson. These influences translate into an emphasis on her people and their history, a drive to reclaim her land, and a political fight demanding simple justice for South Africa:

> It Is Ridiculous For These Many Millions Of Blacks,
> In Their Land, In Their Land,
> To Waltz To The Tune Of The Limited White Music,
> And This Cannot Go On.
>
> (Brooks, *Winnie* 9-10)

This just, determined, and combative Winnie is the essence of Blackness that this poem hopes to transfer to Black Americans.

In her role as a catalyst for Black America, Brooks's Winnie tells the story of the tragedies caused by apartheid and the continuing battles against apartheid. In her widespread critique of the whites who invaded "the Land of the Black People," Winnie accounts for the many dead who were "dear persons" and for whom she and her people are not allowed to have funerals, unless the government itself so dictates (Brooks, *Winnie* 10, 6). She mentions, albeit somewhat cryptically—Brooks demands that her audience inform itself about South African politics—the secret police, the murder of children, the government "beasts" who believe that "humanitarianism is for other countries" (6), the absurdly restrictive laws that dole out death as the penalty for singing, the 1976 Soweto student uprising and subsequent massacre, the corrupt Black leaders, and her own mistreatment. Nonetheless, Winnie speaks for resistance; she promises "a daylight/ out of the Tilt and Jangle of this hour," which we now know was only a scant two years away in 1990 when the dismantling of apartheid began (17).

Brooks wrote more poems about the struggle against apartheid, which are also meant to inculcate revolution against racial injustice in the United States "The Near-Johannesburg Boy" uses a persona much like Hector Pieterson, a 13-year-old boy shot in the back during the Student Uprising in Soweto on June 16, 1976. Brooks commented on her inspiration for this poem in an interview with Susan Howe and Jay Fox:

I have a poem called "The Near-Johannesburg Boy" . . . that I wrote because I was listening to the news one evening and the anchor said that little black children in South Africa were meeting each other in the road and asking the equivalent of: "Have you been *detained* yet? How many times have you been *detained*?" I thought that was perfectly appalling. And I wanted to empathize with one of those children, so in the poem I impersonate a boy of about fourteen who begins, "My way is from woe to wonder." (2)

The poem's persona is ready to fight "like a clean spear of fire" (Brook, *The Near-Johannesburg Boy* 4), phrasing reminiscent of *umkhonto we sizwe*, which translates as "spear of the nation" and refers to the military wing of the African National Congress (ANC). The Soweto uprising was in response to the governmental decree that black secondary schools must teach in Afrikaans. Twenty thousand students marched in protest, and the government troops shot hundreds of children, including Hector Pieterson. These deaths led to riots and more deaths; government-owned buildings were burned; police officers were attacked. The death toll is unclear: "The SA Institute of Race Relations estimated 618 killed and 1,500 injured—most of them school students; to judge from Press reports the figures were much higher. By June 1977, of 21,534 prosecuted for such alleged offences as public violence, rioting, sabotage, incitement and arson, 13,553 had been convicted, nearly 5,000 of them under eighteen" (Benjamin 113). Winnie Mandela herself bears witness:

> I was there among them, I saw what happened. The children picked up stones, they used dustbin lids as shields and marched towards machine guns. It's not that they don't know that the white man is heavily armed; they marched against heavy machine gun fire. You could smell gunfire everywhere. Children were dying in the street, and as they were dying, the others marched forward, facing guns. No one has ever underestimated the power of the enemy. We know that he is armed to the teeth. But the determination, the thirst for freedom in children's hearts, was such that they were prepared to face those machine guns with stones. That is what happens when you hunger for freedom, when you want to break those chains of oppression. Nothing else seems to matter.
>
> We couldn't stop our children. We couldn't keep them off the streets. (Mandela 114)

Brooks expertly captures the pulse of these children longing for freedom in her poem, which builds from simple information about the situation in South Africa to the crescendo of the battle. The persona, "with hundred of playmates," walks to the "forbidden" place, where they are the ones forbidden because of the color of their skin (4). Using heavy repetition and alliteration—techniques with a long tradition in the poetry of war—Brooks takes her readers to the battle:

There, in the dark that is our dark, there,
a-pulse across earth that is our earth, there,
there exulting, there Exactly, there redeeming,
    there Roaring Up
(oh my Father)
we shall forge with the Fist-and-the-Fury:
we shall flail in the Hot Time:
we shall
we shall.
    (Brooks, *The Near-Johannesburg Boy* 4)

There is the battle, the final stance, the mere students who dare fight a government "armed to the teeth." Hector and his "playmates" represent another radical Afrikan model for invigorating American Blacks.[8]

IV

The final way in which Afrika signifies for Brooks is that, in several poems, it moves beyond marking anything physically connected to the continent of Africa. In "Young Afrikans," "Afrikan" is a distinctive title of approbation, bestowed upon all Blacks involved in the just struggle for civil rights and identity. These Afrikans are "of the *furious*," a phrase that echoes Brooks's oft-quoted "The Second Sermon on the Warpland" where "the time/ cracks into furious flower. Lifts its face/ all unashamed. And sways in wicked grace" (Brooks, *to disembark* 34; Brooks, *Blacks* 456). Published only two years apart, 1970 and 1968, respectively, these poems are set within the heat of the civil rights movement; this is the hot time that Brooks's 1980s poems seek to restore. This poem applauds the revolutionaries "Who take Today and jerk it out of joint" (Brooks, *to disembark* 34). The battle is ongoing; the flowers, which symbolize the Afrikans, are "rowdy" and need to be well informed. They must know "where whips and screams are,/ [know] where deaths are, where the kind kills are" (34). As always,

Brooks's exquisite wordplay can be seen in these lines, particularly in "where the kind kills are" which can become the kind that kills, probably indicating white people opposed to the civil rights gains in this context, but the elimination of "that" provides hard-edged alliteration as well as ambiguity because "kind" could be an adjective. Similarly, now is not a time for "the milkofhumankindness" but for fury (34). The Afrikans are willing to use violence, reflecting the later years of the civil rights movement when many participants moved beyond the nonviolent approach espoused by Martin Luther King, Jr. In other poems, notably *Riot*, Brooks expresses a sensibility that violence is acceptable in such a dire fight and when one's people have been attacked with violence for so long and on such a large scale.[9] The Afrikans also reject the status quo; they refuse to entertain any longer "the/ leechlike-as-usual who use,/ adhere to, carp, and harm" (34). This "hot" time—a phrase used also in "The Near-Johannesburg Boy" and echoed by Toni Morrison in *Beloved*'s stream-of-consciousness monologue, where she is reliving the loss of Sethe and the Middle Passage as "a hot thing" (213)—promises concrete change that white Americans can only "await"; their power slips and they can only witness events. The poems end powerfully with a promise of rebirth, like the phoenix image Brooks uses elsewhere: "across the Changes and the spiraling dead,/ our Black revival, our Black vinegar,/ our hands, and our hot blood" (34). These Afrikans are revolutionaries; they fight a just battle; they use violence when necessary; they offer a "Black revival" (34).

Afrika also signifies the African diaspora, a body millions strong, itself a continent. In "To the Diaspora," Brooks describes a circular journey of diasporic Blacks, a journey that she knows will lead them to Afrika, which in this case is themselves: they are "the Black continent/ that had to be reached" (*to disembark* 41). Their journey will lead them to that realization, a realization of solidarity, size, and power. In this poem Brooks speaks as a much older observer watching a journey that she has seen before, has perhaps taken herself. The people who have "set out" are younger, and while they enjoy her support and "loyalty," they "would not have believed [her] mouth" (41). However, they have made the journey, one in which they began to shine as "the diamonds/ of you, the Black continent" (41). They themselves are the wealth and splendor of Afrika; they have also been stolen by imperialist traders, but unlike the mere gems, they are finding themselves, and on that journey, finding Afrika. At the end the sun spills illumination on them so that they can see the truth, can see the battles yet to be fought that are now more pitched, more acute than in the 1960s when there was more energy available. They must venture into "the dissonant and dangerous crescendo" because more work is "to be done to be done to be done" (41). However, because they are themselves the size and solidity of a continent, the battle against racism and imperialism is possible.[10]

The size and power of this continent makes a difference—as Brooks told Melhem in 1988, numbers matter to white power brokers, and Blacks have strength and power in numbers:

The "Black Situation" of this time resembles that of the early Fifties, with the Fifties' head-pats and spankings of what were then called "Negroes." With this difference: white power's nervous, irritable wariness. Because white power figures remember what a lot of Blacks don't: the late Sixties, which showed (mirabile dictu) that Blacks working together—or even, in *some* circumstances, just being together—are themselves powerful. Secret acknowledgment of that reality is one of the reasons that the phrase "the Sixties" has been shadowed of late, ridiculed, sometimes spat on: there is a jumpy desire for oblivion of that awareness of Black strength and potential resourcefulness. (Melhem, *Heroism* 34)

However, Blacks were not using their numbers to their advantage in the 1980s, and Brooks addresses the lagging civil rights movement in "Another Preachment to Blacks." The push for rights has become "a nightmare all contrary" with "eyeless Leaders" and faltering "follow- ers" (*to disembark* 60-61). In an interesting rejection of the move- ment's traditional reliance on Christianity, God's reliability is also in question as Brooks describes him as "a mad child . . . mashing/ whatwhen he wills" (61). Brooks calls on Blacks to "force through the sludge" whether they feel that God is with them or not (61). Published in 1981 this poem laments the loss of the energy of the late 1960s. Brooks insists that "my nourishment of nourishments was in the years 1967 to 1972. As I've said of those years, the 'new' black ideal italicized black identity, solidarity, self-possession, self-address." She continues, "the air was hot, heavy with logic, illogic, zeal, construction. What years those were—years of hot-breathing hope, clean planning, and sizable black cross-reference and reliance" (Brooks, "Interview" 407). Even with the well-documented problems like sexism that Brooks concedes, the energy at that time forced monumental changes that have now, she is afraid, been turned into "imitation coronations" (*to disembark* 62). Instead of finding Afrika—a language of power, a centering place, a revolutionary inspiration, a term of solidarity—the term "Afrika" has become a false cry, a useless concept when the very people who invoke it go home to "thy 'Gunsmoke', to/ thy 'Gilligan's island' and the NFL," to a thin and corrupting American culture (63). Moreover, this audience does not understand the Afrika that matters to Brooks. Instead of participating in sit-ins at lunch counters or riding in the front of buses or writing incendiary poetry or traveling to Africa, Black Americans are now tranquilized by an American culture epitomized by television, whose effect is to deaden rebellion. The inanity of *Gilligan's Island*, the falseness of *Gunsmoke*, and the foolish violence of the NFL represent an American culture that is corrupting the "'new' black ideal" by quietly sedating its followers. The fire has been lost, but it can still be regained, and it is located in Afrika.

In the end Afrika is an expansive signifier—a linguistic tie to African languages, a center of Blackness, an inspiration, and an appellation—and it is of the utmost importance to Brooks. Brooks felt that finding her own Afrikanness, even if she could never be African, was a way to complete herself. Being an "essential African" rescued her from remaining "a 'Negro' fraction," a thin imitation of European culture (*Report from Part One* 45). Brooks used that personal identity in her poetry, and she sought to share that centering with all American Blacks. With the South African poet Keorapetse Kgositsile, Brooks shouts, "MY NAME IS AFRIKA!" (*to disembark* 31).

From *Callaloo* 29, no. 1 (Winter 2006): 168-181. Copyright © 2006 by Charles H. Rowell. Reprinted with permission of The Johns Hopkins University Press.

Notes

1. In an interview with Melhem, Brooks delineates her reasons for preferring the name *Black* over *African American*. In deference, I am following Brooks's lead:

> The current motion to make the phrase "African American" an official identification is cold and excluding. What of our Family members in Ghana?—in Tanzania?—in Kenya?—in Nigeria?—in South Africa?—in Brazil? Why are we pushing *them* out of our consideration?
> The capitalized names *Black* and *Blacks* were appointed to compromise an open, wide-stretching, unifying, empowering umbrella. (*Heroism* 32)

In the same interview Brooks reiterates this point: "I share *Family*hood with Blacks wherever they may be. I am a *Black*. And I capitalize my name" (33).

2. A number of critics have begun addressing the role of Africa in Brooks's poetry. In *Gwendolyn Brooks* and *Heroism in the New Black Poetry*, Melhem comments on Brooks's personal sense of African identity. Harry B. Shaw notes Brooks's lament for Black Americans' loss of their African heritage, and William H. Hansell more pointedly connects the violence in Brooks's poetry to Africa's "testimony to a warlike heritage" ("The Poet-Militant" 75). In a particularly provocative argument, John F. Callahan looks at African influences on Brooks through the oral nature of her later poetry, and he claims that "her sense of oneness with the continuum of African culture leads her to a spirit of generosity and an expansiveness of language" (69). Philip A. Greasley also analyzes Brooks's use of Africa: "Her mature usage of African imagery makes clear the lifelong tensions experienced by blacks in white America, embodies Brooks's activist program for black poetic, political, and spiritual action, and provides a symbolic center linking much of her post-1967 poetry" (9). Greasley's analysis is conceptually disappointing and poorly written; among other inconsistencies, Greasley assigns a quotation from Don L. Lee's preface in *Report from Part One* to Brooks herself (14). However, our ideas share some similarities. Greasley also comments on Brooks's romanticization of Africa, although he accuses her of primitivism (12), and he notes that Brooks's trip to East Africa forced a recognition of the reality of contem-

porary Africa (13). Lastly, Joyce Ann Joyce adopts the useful tactic of looking not at Africa in Brooks's work but at the related issue of how her poetry meets the criteria of Afrocentrism.

3. Melhem erroneously claims that Brooks's initial use of "Afrika" with a "k" is in "Horses Graze," published in *Beckonings* in 1975 (*Gwendolyn* 227).

4. The name of Karenga's organization stands for "us" Black people, as compared to "them," the white people (Scot Brown 2).

5. In his analysis of the earlier form of this poem titled "Boys. Black." Hansell also emphasizes that "'Afrika'—always spelled with a 'k'—is held out as an essential inspirational source, even if to the young men, Afrika had been little more than a name on a map." He further comments that "Brooks believes that even if the connection between Afrika and Afro-Americans seems insignificant . . . it is real and important" ("Essences" 65, 65-66).

6. For *Winnie* I count 389 lines in the 1988 edition published by Third World Press with 358 lines in "Song of Winnie"; Melhem quotes Brooks as tallying 377 lines (*Heroism* 35). The printing format may have been slightly altered between editions. Melhem calls "Song of Winnie" a "metapoem" through which "Brooks is making a didactic, political, and finally a philosophical statement" (*Heroism* 27-29). *Winnie* is also briefly glossed by Brenda R. Simmons.

7. When answering interviewer Alice Fulton's question as to whether the poetic philosophy she attributes to Winnie is really her own, Brooks replies, "Yes, here I do have her considering herself as poet, which she really is, essentially. If you've seen the documentaries, you would understand what I mean" (Brooks, *Poets in Person*). While Brooks does not specify exactly which documentaries she was referring to, she certainly used information presented in the documentary *Winnie & Nelson Mandela*.

8. "The Near-Johannesburg Boy" is more fully explicated by Melhem (*Heroism* 21-23).

9. See Hansell ("Essences" 65) and Annette Debo.

10. See Callahan 69-70.

Works Cited

Benjamin, Anne. Introduction and chapter introductions to *Part of My Soul Went with Him*, by Winnie Mandela. Edited by Anne Benjamin and adapted by Mary Benson. New York: Norton, 1984.

Brooks, Gwendolyn. *Blacks*. Chicago: Third World, 1994.

_____. "Interview." *TriQuarterly* 60 (Spring/Summer 1984): 405-10.

_____. *The Near-Johannesburg Boy and Other Poems*. Chicago: Third World Press, 1986.

_____. *Poets in Person: Gwendolyn Brooks with Alice Fulton*. Audiocassette. Chicago: Modern Poetry Association, 1991.

_____. *Report from Part One*. Detroit: Broadside Press, 1972.

_____. *Report from Part Two*. Chicago: Third World, 1996.

_____. *to disembark.* Chicago: Third World, 1981.

_____. *Winnie.* Chicago: Third World, 1988.

Brooks, Gwendolyn, and B. Denise Hawkins. "Conversation." In *The Furious Flowering of African American Poetry,* edited by Joanne V. Gabbin, 274-80. Charlottesville: UP of Virginia, 1999.

Brown, Martha H. "GLR Interview: Gwendolyn Brooks." *The Great Lakes Review* 6.1 (1979): 48-55.

Brown, Scot. *Fighting for US: Maulana Karenga, the US Organization, and Black Cultural Nationalism.* New York: New York UP, 2003.

Callahan, John F. "'Essentially an Essential African': Gwendolyn Brooks and the Awakening to Audience." *North Dakota Quarterly* 55.4 (Fall 1987): 59-73.

Debo, Annette. "Reflecting Violence in the Warpland: Gwendolyn Brooks's *Riot.*" *African American Review* 39, nos. 1-2 (Spring/Summer 2005): 143-52.

Greasley, Philip A. "Gwendolyn Brooks's 'Afrika.'" *Midamerica: The Yearbook of the Society for the Study of Midwestern Literature* 8 (1986): 9-18.

Hackney, Sheldon. "A Conversation with Gwendolyn Brooks." *Conversations with Gwendolyn Brooks,* edited by Gloria Wade Gayles, 155-64. Jackson: U of Mississippi P, 2003.

Hansell, William H. "Essences, Unifyings, and Black Militancy: Major Themes in Gwendolyn Brooks's Family Pictures and Beckonings." *Black American Literature Forum* 11.2 (Summer 1977): 63-66.

_____. "The Poet-Militant and Foreshadowings of a Black Mystique: Poems in the Second Period of Gwendolyn Brooks." In *A Life Distilled: Gwendolyn Brooks, Her Poetry and Fiction,* edited by Maria K. Mootry and Gary Smith, 71-80. Urbana: U of Illinois P, 1987.

Howe, Susan Elizabeth, and Jay Fox. "A Conversation with Gwendolyn Brooks." *Literature and Belief* 12 (1992): 1-12.

Hughes, Langston. *The Big Sea.* 1940. New York: Hill and Wang, 1993.

_____. *The Collected Poems of Langston Hughes.* Edited by Arnold Rampersad and David Roessel. New York: Vintage, 1994.

Joyce, Joyce Ann. "The Poetry of Gwendolyn Brooks: An Afrocentric Exploration." In *On Gwendolyn Brooks: Reliant Contemplation,* edited by Stephen Caldwell Wright, 246-53. Ann Arbor: U of Michigan P, 1996.

Karenga, Maulana Ron. "The Black Community and the U: A Community Organizer's Perspective." In *Black Studies in the University,* edited by Armstead L. Robinson, Craig C. Foster, and Donald H. Ogilvie, 37-54. New Haven: Yale UP, 1969.

Kent, George E. *A Life of Gwendolyn Brooks.* Lexington: UP of Kentucky, 1990.

Lee, Don L. Preface, "Gwendolyn Brooks: Beyond the Wordmaker—The Making of an African Poet." In *Report from Part One,* by Gwendolyn Brooks, 13-30. Detroit: Broadside, 1972.

Mandela, Winnie. *Part of My Soul Went with Him.* Edited by Anne Benjamin and adapted by Mary Benson. New York: Norton, 1984.

Melhem, D. H. *Gwendolyn Brooks: Poetry and the Heroic Voice.* Lexington: UP of Kentucky, 1987.

_____. *Heroism in the New Black Poetry: Introductions and Interviews.* Lexington: UP of Kentucky, 1990.

Morrison, Toni. *Beloved.* New York: Knopf, 1988.

Ngugi wa Thiong'o. *Decolonizing the Mind: The Politics of Language in African Literature.* Portsmouth, NH: Heinemann, 1986.

Shaw, Harry B. *Gwendolyn Brooks.* Boston: Twayne Publishers, 1980.

Simmons, Brenda R. "Gottschalk and the Grande Tarantelle." In *On Gwendolyn Brooks: Reliant Contemplation,* edited by Stephen Caldwell Wright, 224-29. Ann Arbor: U of Michigan P, 1996.

Winnie & Nelson Mandela. Directed By Peter Davis. Produced by National Black Programming Consortium and Villon Films. California Newsreel, 1986.

Reflecting Violence in the Warpland:
Gwendolyn Brooks's *Riot*_____

Annette Debo

Annette Debo examines *Riot*, a poem in which Brooks expresses sympathy for the anger blacks felt after Martin Luther King, Jr., was assassinated. This black unrest resulted in riots that left homes, businesses, and some lives destroyed. Brooks is sympathetic to the violence because it reflects blacks' anger at the injustice of lynching and other types of violence they were forced to endure during the nineteenth and twentieth centuries. Brooks's objective is to get her audience to acknowledge the history of violence perpetrated against blacks by whites in America. In the essay, Debo provides historical details about John Cabot, a white character in the poem who is killed in the riots, noting Brooks's strategy in centering her poem on him. Cabot becomes an unfortunate representative of all the whites who in the past have hurt or destroyed blacks with impunity, but, ironically, he does not understand the history of violence he represents and therefore does not understand why blacks are enraged. Debo also discusses Brooks's use of the phoenix as a metaphor for the repetition of history as the police, representatives of a justice system that favors whites, revisit violence on blacks. In *Riot*, Brooks argues that, unless something changes, Americans will be doomed to repeat the cycles of violence that keep the country from finding peace.   — M.R.M.

Gwendolyn Brooks opens the second part of *Riot* with the following lines:

> The earth is a beautiful place.
> Watermirrors and things to be reflected.
> Goldenrod across the little lagoon.
>
> (lines 1-3)

Besides affirming the unorthodox beauty of the urban setting, in these lines Brooks provides the metaphor of mirroring for the events chronicled in *Riot*, a series of three poems about the 1968 Chicago riots, which directly followed the assassination of Dr. Martin Luther King, Jr.[1] These poems refuse the restrictive poetic forms for which Brooks's early poetry is well known and critically rewarded—they are post-1967, that is, after Brooks attended the Second Black Writers' Conference at Fisk University[2]—and in their sweeping verse, they encompass the white John Cabot who is killed in the riots, the young African Americans who are consumed in the energy and fire of the riot (but who like the phoenix will rise again), the outside white viewers who cannot understand, the "Black Philosopher" who analyzes the events, and the African American lovers who rise like the phoenix. The violence and apparent chaos of this riot are, significantly, caused by African Americans; it is, as Dr. King wrote and Brooks herself quoted in her epigraph, "the language of the unheard." However, if riots are indeed a language, to return to Brooks's metaphor of mirroring, then it is a language learned from white lynchers.

This language of violence and Brooks's implicit condoning of violence in *Riot* provide a probable explanation for the scant attention this poem has received from literary critics outside of three thorough and insightful readings from D. H. Melhem, William H. Hansell, and James D. Sullivan.[3] Alternatively, *Riot* has received little critical attention perhaps because it falls in the post-1967 section of Brooks's career. Too often Brooks's poetry is divided into discrete sections rather than considered a continually developing, cohesive body of work. Most frequently, her early poetry, with its intense experimentation in traditional poetic forms, is the material anthologized and critically explored, and her poetry written after 1967, a line Brooks herself drew and critics reinforced, is neglected. However, there are also critics who prefer her later poetry and who call the early poetry "traditional," "accommodationist," or "white" (Clark 85). In contrast, as I read Brooks's early poetry, I find that it, like her later poetry, responds to what she sees happening in the arts and in politics—it is all politically informed.[4] Like the poems of Langston Hughes, Brooks's work evolves, and her interest in the connection between race and violence is clear both before and after 1967, as is her continual experimentation with form. Her poetry develops; it does not suddenly become "black" after the Fisk Conference, nor does the latter half of her work lack integrity by becoming too simplistic in its form.

In this article, I extend the discussion of violence in *Riot* through a sociohistorical analysis that allows the 1960's violence inscribed in this poem and advocated by the Black Aesthetic its proper position in the long history of American violence. My argument opens with the contention that Brooks's metaphor of mirroring is pivotal in *Riot* because it connects the 1968 riots to the violence aimed at African Americans since their arrival in the Americas in the sixteenth century. The 1960's riots were caused by white racism, and mirror the white-initiated violence. Following that point, I place the 1968 riots in the continuum of violent protest in American history. For many oppressed groups, riots have been a way of achieving political power. The 1968 riots were part of an American protest tradition that began when English settlers refused to pay their taxes to an oppressive power. Instead of constituting un-Americanness, African Americans were also rejecting political powerlessness in a particularly American way. Brooks is not validating anarchy by representing the riots positively; rather, she is presenting the riot as a valid method for achieving political reform. After historically positioning the riots, I use the research of sociologists to argue that because the 1968 riots were politically successful, they had positive effects on the African American community, which translates in *Riot* into the creation of a new type of people and strong intimate relationships. Brooks's long poem ends with celebration because the riots were empowering; they offered confidence and engendered love. *Riot*, a scandalous poem in 1968, was in part neglected by critics because it advocates (black) violence as an avenue for social change in US race relations, but contextualizing the poem's events in

American history defuses that perspective and allows *Riot* a fairer hearing.

* * *

In *Riot*, Brooks connects the violent image of African Americans lashing out in a riot to the violence historically inflicted upon them in the "warpland" (which in Brooksian poetic technique can read as "warp land," "war land," or even "warped land") through the "water-mirrors" that reflect—sometimes clearly, sometimes distorted by ripples—the truth of nature and the truth of violence ("The Third" 2).[5] The "things to be reflected" through the violence of riots are the moments of white mob violence, generally lynchings, inflicted upon the African American community. Even in her first book of poetry, *A Street in Bronzeville* published in 1945, Brooks inscribes in "Ballad of Pearl May Lee" the satiric voice of a woman whose lover is lynched for consensual sex with a white woman who afterward cries rape (*Blacks* 60-63). In an interview, even though she is directly commenting on colorism, Brooks stipulates that this poem is about "*rage*," "woman rage" (Tate 43). Her critique of white lynch violence strengthens over time, and in 1960 her volume *The Bean Eaters* covers the lynching of Emmett Till in "A Bronzeville Mother Loiters in Mississippi. Meanwhile, a Mississippi Mother Burns Bacon" and "The Last Quatrain of the Ballad of Emmett Till"; the would-be lynchers during the 1957 Arkansas school integration in "The *Chicago Defender* Sends a Man to Little Rock"; and a lynch mob during neighborhood integration in "The Ballad of Rudolph Reed" (*Blacks* 333-39, 340, 346-48, 376-78).

However, the 1968 riots were not viewed as a reflection of white mob violence but rather as an outrageous explosion. In Brooks's poem, the riot's outside (white) watchers say, "But WHY do These People offend *themselves*?" rejecting the fact that riots form in response to past and continuing white violence, and refusing to acknowledge their own culpability ("The Third" 99). The 1968 report of the Kerner Commission—

a presidential commission convened to explain the 1960's riots—flatly states that "the events of the summer of 1967 are in large part the culmination of 300 years of racial prejudice" (95), and the more liberal sociologists immediately studying the riots connected them to the larger patterns of white-initiated violence beginning with slavery.[6] Louis H. Masotti, for example, traces American racial violence through six phases: suppression of African American slavery and slave revolts; lynching of African Americans; white-dominated riots aimed at African American persons; white-dominated riots in which African Americans fought back; and African American-dominated riots aimed at white property (99-127). Clearly, five of the six patterns identify the violence as initiated and controlled by white Americans.

In the light of this past and continuing abuse, the 1960's riots should have come as no surprise. The real oddity is that they were aimed at property and not explicitly at white persons. Furthermore, the Kerner Report blames white Americans for developing and sustaining black ghettos, where the riots occurred, and the insightful question, "What white 'interests' came into play in the ghetto during and after the great migration which had not been significant theretofore?" was asked by Richard E. Rubenstein to try to account for the existence and proliferation of ghettos (122). His answers are disquieting. "First," he claims, "ghetto land, which had not been considered valuable before 1945, rose in value dramatically in the 1950s," creating incentive for white Americans with real estate connections ("suppliers, builders, bankers, construction workers, speculators, brokers, landlords") to sustain the overcrowded, poorly maintained housing (122). Second, the new and growing population created new consumers, most of whom had to pay exorbitant credit rates since their income was limited and unstable. Third, African Americans largely supported the Democratic political party, "whose principal interest, as far as Negroes were concerned, was to provide just enough direct benefits to keep ghetto votes in line" (122-25). In sum, Rubenstein compellingly argues that many white Americans economically preyed upon the surging population of northern African Americans, providing substantial evidence of white culpability in creating the economic inequities that caused the 1960's riots. Again, the Kerner Report corroborates: "White racism is essentially responsible for the explosive mixture which has been accumulating in our cities since the end of World War II" (91).

In the first part of *Riot*, also entitled "Riot," Brooks unerringly pins the blame for the riots on privileged white Americans through their representative John Cabot. Cabot's very name connects him to the Italian explorer John Cabot, whose "discovery" of North America supported English claims to the continent, as well as to the Christian heretic John Wycliffe, a chief forerunner of the Protestant Reformation.[7] Brooks describes Cabot through his physical whiteness, his ostentatious possessions, his extravagant habits, and his panic at finding himself in the riot's path:

> all whitebluerose below his golden hair,
> wrapped richly in right linen and right wool,
> almost forgot his Jaguar and Lake Bluff;
> almost forgot Grandtully (which is The
> Best Thing That Ever Happened To Scotch), almost
> forgot the sculpture at the Richard Gray
> and Distelheim; the kidney pie at Maxim's,
> the Grenadine de Boeuf at Maison Henri.
>
> Because the Negroes were coming
>   down the
> street.
>   (lines 2-12)

Cabot sees "blackness" in definitive opposition to himself—in color, in class, in sophistication, in taste—and chooses not to recognize his own guilt in the economic and racial inequities of his country; he drives his Jaguar to his elite suburban home; and he dies "expensively" in the riot (31). Thoroughly a European American with his response of "*Que tu es grossier!*" (How gross you are!) to the rioters, Cabot, in his own mind innocent of any wrongdoing, calls to "any handy angel" to deliver him (lines 18, 23).[8] However, as the mob reaches him, an "old/ averted doubt jerked forward decently"; Cabot is aware, as the civil rights organizers claimed, that his lifestyle is made possible through denying basic material and spiritual needs to others, particularly African Americans (lines 28-29). In their oppression lies the wealth of the US as well as that of Cabot. In exquisite parody, his dying line is "Lord!/ Forgive these nigguhs that know not what/ they do," a rendition of Jesus's dying words laced with racism and no sense of repentance, or even acceptance, for his own sins (33-35).

* * *

As white Americans cracked down on the 1960's rioters with increasing police force and decried the riots as un-American, they overlooked how collective violence has consistently been a way of achieving political change throughout the history of the United States. Masotti even asserts that "violence is an integral part of the American way of life. Major social changes in this country, including the assimilation of many minority groups, have, almost without exception, been accompanied by violence" (138). Americans' first violent act, according to Howard Zinn, was waging war against the British. He testifies that "this was accomplished by seven years of warfare, in which 25,000 in the Continental Army were killed, about one out of every eight men who served. To judge the extent of this violence one would have to consider that the same ratio of dead in our present population [in 1967] would amount to a death list of one and a half-million" (qtd. in Masotti et al. 138). Like Zinn and Masotti, Rubenstein proclaims violence to be very American, and debunks what he terms "the myth of peaceful progress." Claiming that this myth developed during the Cold War when the US fabricated a peaceful past to help justify its political model, Rubenstein describes the United States as a nation of radically disparate peoples living "their differences peaceably." He argues that "either because the land was fertile or the people hard-working, or because no true aristocracy or proletariat ever developed on American soil, or because the two-party system worked so well," the extensive US middle class is composed of groups that have achieved "power, prosperity and respectability merely by playing the game according to the rules. . . . The result, it was said, was something unique in world history—real progress without violent group conflict. In such an America there was no need—there never had been a need—for political violence" (5-6).

Then, using copious evidence, Rubenstein debunks "the myth of peaceful progress," demonstrating instead that collective violence is "neither un-American nor, in every case, unnecessary and useless" (9). He designates as collective violence the American Indian resistance against European settlers stealing their land; the 18th-century "debtor farmer" revolts that included the Shays Rebellion and the Whiskey Rebellion; violence between Americans during the Revolution; the Civil War and the subsequent guerrilla warfare; 19th-century labor rebellions; 19th-century nativist violence against the Irish, Italians, and Jews; and, finally, the 1960's violence (24-33)—rebellions that had varying degrees of success but that were all thoroughly American.

Therefore, if the riot constitutes an authentically American act, rather than an aberration in American history, what was the civil rights era riot, and who was its perpetrator? The 1960's riots were, according to Robert M. Fogelson, "articulate protests against genuine grievances in the black ghettos" rather than "meaningless outbursts," as many city officials interpreted them (22, 14). They were a legitimate rebellion against "economic deprivation, consumer exploitation, inferior education, racial discrimination, and so forth" from a desperate people who had exhausted other avenues of protest (Fogelson 22). Particularly testifying to their purposeful nature is their target; the rioters attacked real property, the symbol of prosperity that they had been denied. Also sig-

nificant is who participated in the riots. Rioters were not, as initially assumed, from a criminal underclass, nor were the riots planned and exe-
cuted by political militants—sociologists have conclusively disproved
those theories. Instead, "the picture that emerged was that the rioters
were not drawn from one particular social class. Every stratum of the
ghetto contributed its share of rioters" (Sears and McConahay 25). Additionally, many of the people who did not participate, while decrying
the devastation, still sympathized with the rioters, as Brooks apparently did. The "dream deferred," in Langston Hughes's words, did explode in the 1960s ("Harlem [2]" 1).

In a 1970 interview, Brooks spoke about *Riot*, revealing her own
feelings of sympathy for the rioters, anger against white Americans,
and empathy for the young African Americans protesting entrenched
and pervasive racism. She reported that she had in mind King's proclamation that "A riot is the language of the unheard." One riot photograph in particular drew her attention: consuming fully one-half of a
news sheet, it depicted "a throng of young men in their teens coming
down the street . . . and they looked so alive and so annunciatory. It occurred to me to wonder how a certain kind of young white man faced
with such a throng and faced with his own confrontation with his own
innards would react" (Drotning 174). The space where these allegedly
threatening young black men emerge with their message of the new
black power, then, is the warpland of the riots, a battleground where
African Americans finally fought back with collective violence.
Brooks supports, arguably even celebrates, that recuperation of power,
asserting, "Nobody gets excited about white power, and black power
merely means that black people who have been weak and helpless for
so long will no longer be so. I'm all for that" (Drotning 174).

The collective violence itself is covered in "The Third Sermon on
the Warpland," the second part of *Riot*, which establishes the controlling metaphor of the phoenix: "in Egyptian mythology, a bird which
lived for five hundred years and then consumed itself in fire, rising
renewed from the ashes" (epigraph). Under this metaphor, African

Americans were brought to the land that is now the US almost 500 years ago and are now ready for a phoenix-like birth process. The community is consumed by fire during the riots, but Brooks emphasizes the fire's constructive possibilities: if the community burns, then it will be re-born whole and beautiful afterward. The lines "Lies are told and legends made./ Phoenix rises unafraid" (lines 104-05) contain the essence of the riot: it is a moment of fire and explosion that will lead to wholeness.[9]

The riot itself is recreated in a montage of images. It begins with the peaceful image of "goldenrod across the little lagoon" (line 3), recalling Brooks's deployment of the common daisy as a metaphor for beauty in her novel *Maud Martha* (rpt. in *Blacks*). But on West Madison Street is Jessie's Kitchen, where customers are now watching the "crazy flowers" "spreading/ and hissing *This is/ it*" (lines 20, 21-23). A sudden pause strikes the neighborhood as the riot begins. Then "the young men run" (line 24). They loot stores but steal selectively, choosing the African American Melvin Van Peebles over the white Bing Crosby. Young people, "BEANLESS," "long-stomped, long-straddled"—in other words, desperately poor, beaten down, and "straddled" by white Americans for nearly 500 years, with no sophisticated analysis of their situation, simply join in, stealing a radio with which to listen to artists like James Brown (33). Brooks's choice of James Brown is notable; she continually emphasizes African American artists and cultures in the rioters' decision, signifying that their choices are not haphazard. Fires are set, candles "curse—/ inverting the deeps of the darkness" (lines 49-50). Then arrives "The Law," and the rioters scatter (line 56). After the National Guard and the guns arrive, an African American woman, a mother, a lover, "a gut gal" dies (line 71). Who has killed her is unexplained, but she dies directly after the Guard arrives, and the newspaper reports that "Nine die" in all (line 80). The *Sun-Times* also offers to check out rumors, an indication of the shadowy nature of riots; few facts exist beyond the death toll. Refusing to participate are the Rangers, a well-known Chicago gang with the savvy not to join the explosion; they refuse to be crucified again. They "merely peer and purr,/ and pass the Passion over" (lines 92-93). In short, not gangs, not criminals, not even militant activists, but ordinary people protest their poverty and political powerlessness through the riot.

Interspersed with the riot's participants is the Black Philosopher who interprets the events as they happen. Initially, the Black Philosopher provides a rationale for the riot: "Our chains are in the keep of the Keeper/ in a labeled cabinet/ on the second shelf by the cookies" (lines 5-7). The gluttonous white Americans, whose only interest is in gorging on the sweet parts of life, refuse to hear the rattling of the chains and instead "crunch" their cookies (11). Militantly, the Philosopher suggests that they should listen better because the music is named "'A/ Death Song For You Before You Die,'" as has just happened to Cabot (lines 12-13). At the poem's end, the Philosopher offers additional insights. She describes the riot's participants:

> "There they came to life and exulted,
> the hurt mute.
> Then it was over.
>
> The dust, as they say, settled."
> (lines 107-10)

In these lines, Brooks captures the nature of a riot: the participants roar to life, speaking when before they were unheard, and then, in a matter of days, it is over. What remains is the phoenix's re-birth, which happens in the final part of *Riot*.

* * *

A suggestive result of the 1960s riots was a surge in self-esteem among African Americans. Over the twentieth century, according to sociologists, African American identity changed from "the racial self-hatred characteristic of the predominantly southern black population of 1900 to the more positive black identity of today's [1973] black militants" (Sears and McConahay 188). After studying the 1965 riot in Watts, California, David O. Sears and John B. McConahay argue that a major legacy of the riot was "increased pride in blackness": "Blacks' image of blackness became notably more positive over time, following the riot. Black pride was particularly strong among the New Urban Blacks. It appeared to have become a core mainstream value in the contemporary northern urban ghetto, where the best educated and best informed blacks showed the highest levels of black pride" (195).

Brooks taps into this new formulation of black identity and pride in the last part of *Riot*, "An Aspect of Love, Alive in the Ice and Fire," a celebratory poem of human intimacy made possible by the riots. Brooks's title alludes to Robert Frost's poem "Fire and Ice," which considers whether the world will end through fire (passion, desire) or ice (ire, hate). Brooks borrows Frost's meditation on the world's end to insert her pair of lovers into the apocryphal scene created by the riot. After the violence and chaos, what is to be celebrated and valorized is the connection between people, especially between heterosexual lovers. She opens the poem with "It is the morning of our love," not the evening; the world and the day are just beginning (line 1).[10] Like the phoenix that rises from ashes, this couple thrives in a new world, on a street that is now "imperturbable," unrocked by violence (line 25). They are concerned with themselves, with their own love. The chaos of the outside world makes possible this relationship because besides living in a new world, these are new people. Both are strong in confidence—confidence produced by fighting back, by standing up against oppression. The male partner, for example, is "a lion/ in African velvet . . . level, lean,/ remote" (lines 14-16). The pair embodies the fight that has taken place in the street; they are created by the ice and fire, but they live within it and beyond it: "This is the shining joy;/ the time of not-to-end" (lines 20-21). It is in allowing these final lines of tranquility, strength, and love that the battle has made the difference.

* * *

The remaining question is why *Riot*, as well as the entire post-1967 partition of Brooks's career, has not received more critical attention. The violence discussed here is certainly a factor. To accept this poem is perhaps a tacit acceptance of violence as a necessary part of the Civil Rights movement when the national holiday belongs to Dr. King, who rejected riots as a profitable vehicle for social change. In *Riot*, Brooks joins a throng of militant voices demanding immediate social change. Sounding outrageous, her voice reads the riots as positive and does not call for a cessation of violence; instead, violence creates tangible political and personal gains. She sounds much like Malcolm X, who said about the language of the white man, "Let's learn his language. If his language is with a shotgun, get a shotgun. Yes, I said if he only understands the language of a rifle, get a rifle. If he only understands the language of a rope, get a rope" (108).[11] She sounds much like Amiri Baraka, who demands "'poems that kill.'/ Assassin poems, Poems that shoot/ guns" (lines 19-21). She sounds much like Stokely Carmichael with his call for "black power," like H. Rap Brown, like Medgar Evers, like Bobby Seale, like many militant black voices who terrified white America, as illustrated by a 1967 advertisement from a large manufacturing concern, an advertisement echoed by others published in police journals:

The New Bauer Ordinance Armored Police Car will stop 30-06 rifle bullets at point blank range. It has a 360° turret that will mount a machine gun, riot gun, water cannon, flamethrower and grenade launcher. The body is protected by high voltage electricity. The body is designed to protect against Molotov Cocktails and the vehicle carries sufficient water and foaming agents to put out gasoline fires. Can be used to control riots or just to patrol the tough districts. Plenty of room in the back for stretchers or to take in those unruly prisoners. This vehicle was designed by the same people who designed the XM706 (tank) now being used in Viet Nam. (qtd. in Masotti et al. 1)

Similarly frightened by the riots and the militant voices, the FBI reacted with intense surveillance and persecution of contentious individuals. Likewise, literary critics may have found this material intimidating. Even Brooks later softened positions she had taken during the late 1960s and early 1970s.

Besides the threatening content, one of the most pervasive criticisms of Brooks's later poetry is that she overly simplified its form. However, that criticism cannot easily be made of *Riot*, the complex structure of which, particularly in "The Third Sermon on the Warpland," has meant its critical neglect or assessment as ineffective.[12] In contrast, I believe it to be at least as successful as the other two sections, if not more, because its form mirrors the chaotic form of a riot, becoming an exquisite manipulation of form, like Brooks's earlier poetry but without the conventional European poetic types. This section is disjointed, much is left unexplained, and Brooks uses many obscure local references. *Riot* is precisely what and how a riot is—local, chaotic, explosive, fragmentary. The imagery jumps from the Black Philosopher predicting the action to a local restaurant where people watch the riot, to the young men looting stores, to the fires being lit, to the police's arrival, to the death of a mother, to a newspaper ad promising rumor confirmation, to the restrained Rangers, to the clueless white observers, and, finally, back to the Black Philosopher. Refusing to synthesize the material for her readers, Brooks offers glimpses of the riot, simultaneous events that are only later sorted into a linear story for retelling even by the historians. Readers are inundated by the disparate images, piling upon each other fast and furious, with no transitions, no warnings, and no explanations. Our confusion is akin to the country's confusion in 1968 as it watched its urban centers explode.

By 1977 Brooks herself was disappointed in *Riot*. "*Riot* was really an effort at communication with a lot of people. I didn't succeed except in patches," Brooks said (Hull and Gallagher 33). But perhaps she could not have succeeded because of its timing, too close to the very real conflagrations of the 1960's riots. Perhaps as we look back from the twenty-first century, our view is clearer. The riots no longer pose such a frightening vision and can instead be viewed more fairly in the American tradition of violence that appears sometimes necessary for social change. Living on the south side of Chicago, Brooks knew the conditions that caused the uprisings as well as the wellspring of grief and explosion of frustration that followed the assassination of Dr. King. More than any other figure, King stood for nonviolence, and when white Americans responded even to him with bullets, the "unheard," as he phrased it, suddenly and loudly were heard.

Just as the riots were not an anomaly in American history but instead part of a disquieting US tradition of violence, *Riot* is not an anomaly in Brooks's body of work or even notably different from her pre-1967 poetry. As she said, "No, I have not abandoned beauty, or lyricism, and I don't consider myself a polemical poet. I'm a black poet, and I write about what I see, what interests me, and I'm seeing new things. Many things that I'm seeing now I was blind to before, but I don't sit down at the table and say, 'Lyricism is out.' No, I just continue to write about what confronts me" (*Report* 151). However, the riots were controversial, escaping reasonable assessments, as the police reacted ever more strongly. The literary response imitated the prevailing political winds, and *Riot* was not anthologized; it was read by few and dismissed by most.

In 1971, Addison Gayle, Jr., wrote in *The Black Aesthetic* that "the serious black artist of today is at war with the American society as few have been through American history" (1872), a statement that calls for the same revolution that Maulana Karenga advocates in his prevailing definition of the Black Aesthetic. Brooks must be allowed, by critics, to evolve into the space defined by Gayle and Karenga.[13] At the same time, however, the violence that she chronicles in *Riot* and her other later poetry should not be seen as extraordinary, even if critics like Gayle and Karenga saw themselves as involved in a uniquely violent revolution. On the contrary, the violence was reasonable, given the perpetual threat of overwhelming white racist violence, and it was particularly American, following the models of many oppressed groups who gained political power through the last resort of violent action. In the end, for Brooks, the violence produces confident, loving people who exist in "the shining joy;/ the time of not-to-end" ("An Aspect" lines 20-21); they embody the phoenix risen from the ashes.

From *African American Review* 39, nos. 1/2 (Spring 2005): 143-152. Copyright © 2005 by Annette Debo. Reprinted by permission of Annette Debo.

Notes

1. *Riot*'s table of contents describes the work as "a poem in three parts." These three are listed as "Riot," "The Third Sermon on the Warpland," and "An Aspect of Love, Alive in the Ice and Fire." For documentation, line numbers begin again in each part because they are reprinted individually.

2. See Brooks, *Report* 84-86, for a description of her experience at the Fisk conference.

3. For brief treatments of *Riot*, see Kent and Shaw. Also see Furman, who, I argue, misreads the poem in her claims that for Brooks, "the most tragic aspect of riots is that black people are the victims" and that Brooks's "people do not rise again" (6, 7).

4. See Bolden for a persuasive reading of the political nature of Brooks's early poetry.

5. Miller interprets "the warpland," also named in Brooks's "The Sermon on the Warpland" and "The Second Sermon on the Warpland," as "not geographical place but military design—a 'war planned'—and the problem of distortion, the 'warp land'" (156).

6. The report of the Kerner Commission and the Kerner Report both refer to the Report of the National Advisory Commission on Civil Disorders.

7. See Melhem for an intricate gloss of Brooks's allusions to John Cabot and John Wycliffe.

8. Hansell makes the interesting point that "the rioters and John Cabot literally speak different languages" ("The Role" 22).

9. See Shaw for more analysis of the poem's re-birth theme.

10. Brooks removed this line from later reprints of the poem. She explains: "I had to remove the first line—'It is the morning of our love'—when Carolyn Rodgers called to tell me she had found it opening a Rod McKuen poem in *Listen to the Warm*. Even though I wrote mine first!—as can be seen in the hard-cover edition of *Riot*, which includes a dated script-version of the poem. Such a horror is every writer's nightmare. Poets, doubt any 'inevitability'" (*Report* 187).

11. Hansell noted the similarities between Brooks and Malcolm X ("The Role" 22).

Critical Insights

12. See Kent 237.

13. See Hansell's "The Poet-Militant and Foreshadowings of a Black Mystique: Poems in the Second Period of Gwendolyn Brooks" for a delineation of three periods in Brooks's poetry. See Taylor for one of the few more evolutionary readings of the development of her poetry.

Works Cited

Baraka, Amiri. (LeRoi Jones). "Black Art." *Black Magic*. Indianapolis: Bobbs-Merrill, 1969.

Bolden, B. J. *Urban Rage in Bronzeville: Social Commentary in the Poetry of Gwendolyn Brooks, 1945-1960*. Chicago: Third World, 1999.

Brooks, Gwendolyn. *Blacks*. Chicago: Third World, 1994.

_____. *Report from Part One*. Detroit: Broadside, 1972.

_____. *Riot*. Detroit: Broadside, 1969.

Clark, Norris B. "Gwendolyn Brooks and a Black Aesthetic." Mootry and Smith 81-99.

Drotning, Phillip T., and Wesley W. South. *Up from the Ghetto*. New York: Cowles, 1970.

Fogelson, Robert M. *Violence as Protest: A Study of Riots and Ghettos*. New York: Doubleday, 1971.

Frost, Robert. *The Poetry of Robert Frost*. New York: Holt, 1969.

Furman, Marva Riley. "Gwendolyn Brooks: The 'Unconditioned' Poet." *CLA Journal* 17.1 (1973): 1-10.

Gates, Henry Louis, Jr., and Nellie Y. McKay, eds. *The Norton Anthology of African American Literature*. New York: Norton, 1997.

Gayle, Addison, Jr. "The Black Aesthetic: Introduction." Gates and McKay 1870-77.

Hansell, William H. "The Poet-Militant and Foreshadowings of a Black Mystique: Poems in the Second Period of Gwendolyn Brooks." Mootry and Smith 71-80.

_____. "The Role of Violence in Recent Poems of Gwendolyn Brooks." *Studies in Black Literature* 5 (1974): 21-27.

Hughes, Langston. *Collected Poems*. Ed. Arnold Rampersad. New York: Vintage, 1994.

Hull, Gloria T., and Posey Gallagher. "Update on *Part One*: An Interview with Gwendolyn Brooks." *CLA Journal* 21.1 (1977): 19-40.

Karenga, Maulana. "Black Art: Mute Matter Given Force and Function." Gates and McKay 1973-77.

Kent, George E. *A Life of Gwendolyn Brooks*. Lexington: UP of Kentucky, 1990.

Malcolm X. *Malcolm X Speaks: Selected Speeches and Statements*. Ed. George Breitman. New York: Pathfinder P, 1965.

Masotti, Louis H., et al. *A Time to Burn? An Evaluation of the Present Crisis in Race Relations*. Chicago: Rand McNally, 1970.

Melhem, D. H. *Gwendolyn Brooks: Poetry and the Heroic Voice*. Lexington: UP of Kentucky, 1987.

Miller, R. Baxter. "'Define . . . the Whirlwind': Gwendolyn Brooks's Epic Sign for a Generation." *On Gwendolyn Brooks: Reliant Contemplation*. Ed. Stephen Caldwell Wright. Ann Arbor: U of Michigan P, 2001. 146-60.

Mootry, Maria K., and Gary Smith, eds. *A Life Distilled: Gwendolyn Brooks, Her Poetry and Fiction*. Urbana: U of Illinois P, 1989.

Report of the National Advisory Commission on Civil Disorders (Kerner Report). Washington: GPO, 1968.

Rubenstein, Richard E. *Rebels in Eden: Mass Political Violence in the United States*. Boston: Little, Brown, 1970.

Sears, David O., and John B. McConahay. *The Politics of Violence: The New Urban Blacks and the Watts Riot*. Boston: Houghton Mifflin, 1973.

Shaw, Harry B. *Gwendolyn Brooks*. Boston: Twayne, 1980.

Sullivan, James D. "Killing John Cabot and Publishing Black: Gwendolyn Brooks's *Riot*." *African American Review* 36 (2002): 557-69.

Tate, Claudia, ed. *Black Women Writers at Work*. New York: Continuum, 1983.

Taylor, Henry. "Gwendolyn Brooks: An Essential Sanity." Mootry and Smith 254-75.

Killing John Cabot and Publishing Black:
Gwendolyn Brooks's *Riot*_____

James D. Sullivan

James D. Sullivan argues that Brooks's *Riot* reflects her own revolt against American mainstream literary patronage. Brooks's decision to publish *Riot* with Broadside Press, a black-owned publisher, marks her own aesthetic contribution to the struggle for positive black self-expression and self-definition that was the focus of the late-1960s Black Arts movement. Brooks made this physical and artistic move at a cost, but, for her, it was an investment in a future that would see an end to racism and violence. That *Riot* was published with Broadside Press simultaneously nuanced both black audiences' and white audiences' perceptions of the work and raised questions about the role of black-owned presses in countering negative perceptions of blackness. Brooks wanted to get black and white audiences to think critically about the sociopolitical climate of revolution that informed America in the late 1960s, and she wanted people to act to change America for the better. Sullivan analyzes the figurative language in the poem and centers his discussion on Brooks's narrative strategy in employing John Cabot as the focal character. He argues that Cabot operates on two levels: as a representative of the condescending attitudes of whites who did not interact with or make an effort to understand the injustices blacks had experienced and as a representative of the differences between the agendas of black publishers and white publishers.   — M.R.M.

In the late 1960s, at the height of her career, Gwendolyn Brooks changed publishers, switching from Harper & Row, a major press that could give her widespread distribution and publicity, to small, new, African American-run Broadside Press. Harper & Row had just published arguably her most accomplished book, *In the Mecca*, in 1968. Sloughing off, the very next year, great stretches of her mainstream-poetry-buying public was a profoundly anti-economic move. Many who had bought her work in the past would now have significant difficulty finding it—indeed, even learning it existed—given the considerably smaller resources of poet Dudley Randall's then-recently founded press. *Riot* would be among the first books (granted, a small one—a chapbook, really) published by, essentially, a one-man operation that had, until that year, 1969, published only broadsides.

This move has usually been interpreted as a sign of Brooks's commitment to African American cultural nationalism. In fact, she said so herself: "I've been telling everyone who's black, 'You ought to have a black publisher,' and of course that was easy for me to say. I have left Harper not because of any difficulty therewith, but simply because my first duty is to the estimable, developing black publishing companies" (qtd. in Israel 104). And after she started publishing with Haki R. Madhubuti's Third World Press, she told an interviewer:

I couldn't possibly think of going back to any white publisher. I'll always be with a black publisher and if Third World Press discontinues its operations, though it doesn't seem to have any prospects of that, I shall publish my own work. I will never go back to a white press. But I left them, as you probably know, because I wanted to encourage the Black publishers who at that time needed clients. (Brown and Zorn 54)

Not only, in fact, did Brooks forgo the greater royalties she might have received through Harper & Row, but she donated her royalties from *Riot* back to Broadside Press, thus extending Randall's small resources so that he could afford to publish other African American poets (Melhem 190).

An admirable commitment—the poet withdraws her considerable cultural capital from one institution and deposits it in another otherwise undercapitalized venture, shoring up its finances and thus encouraging it to flourish. All this cultural finance and politics, however, has seemed to some commentators external to the poetry. Kenny J. Williams, for one, regarding Brooks's overt identification with all things cultural nationalist, charges, "Changing one's hairstyle and refusing certain amenities from a white reading public, while perhaps significant political statements, are ultimately far more cosmetic than substantive" (63). That is, such moves do not much affect the poetry or the way we read it.

But *Riot*, Brooks's first Broadside Press book, just like any other literary text, depends on a specific material form to reach its audience. Poems reach their audiences not as abstract linguistic constructs that are pretty much the same whatever their material published form, but either as performance or as printed artifacts. As performance, the venue and occasion of the recitation, as well as the delivery and gestures of the reciter, inflect the poem for the audience. As for *Riot*, the material qualities and the provenance of the artifact—as Jerome McGann has argued in his call for a "materialist hermeneutics" (11)— emphasize and create, inflect and deflect the text's meanings. Since Brooks chose to publish *Riot* with Broadside, readers had to approach the book through a specifically African American context. That context was tied to the artifact that bore the text. Readers of her earlier Harper & Row books had, famously, not always considered it necessary to allow significance to the racial context of the poems' composition. But with *Riot*, not only the poet, but also the publisher, the retailers (primarily African American-run businesses), and crucially the target market of presumed readers were black. The domination of the whole communicative process by African Americans greatly decreased the likelihood of anyone's reading the poem through a lens of universal white humanism.

Up through the late 1960s, white critics had made statements about Brooks and her work that, in retrospect, look foolish, but at the time seemed reasonable to them. They had not yet, after all, learned to think of their own whiteness as a racial category, so they had difficulty appreciating experiences specifically marked as non-white as applicable to or even as a part of a universal human experience as they understood it. In fact, as Henry Taylor has pointed out, since the publication of her first book, *A Street in Bronzeville*, in 1945, white critics had often praised Brooks as "a fine poet, not regardless of her color, but despite it" (267). The publication of her work within a predominantly white context and for a predominantly white audience allowed and perhaps encouraged such judgments. The first major review of her work, the one she has said "initiated My Reputation" (Brooks, *Report from Part One* 72), took this approach. Paul Engle, reviewing the book for the *Chicago Tribune*, praised the sonnet sequence "Gay Chaps at the Bar" thus:

> And finest of all, they can be read for what they are and not, as the publishers want us to believe, as Negro poems. For they should no more be called Negro poems than the poems of Robert Frost should be called white poetry. . . . The finest praise that can be given the book is that it would be a superb volume of poetry in any year by any person of any color. (4)

To praise the book in that forum at that time perhaps required stripping away the specifically black elements, praising it as though a white poet might have produced it.[1]

J. Saunders Redding, in an equally positive review of Brooks's 1949 *Annie Allen* for the *Saturday Review of Literature*, also felt a need to strip away specifically black references in order to praise the book as a whole. He deplores the tendency of modern poetry to address a limited audience and regrets Brooks's tendency, in some poems, to address a black "coterie." He refers specifically to "Stand off, daughter of the dusk" (Brooks, *Blacks* 137), with its reference to color distinctions within the black community:

> But when [Brooks's] talent devotes itself to setting forth an experience even more special and particularized than the usual poetic experience then it puts itself under unnecessary strain. . . . Who but another Negro can get the intimate feeling, the racially particular acceptance and rejection, and the oblique bitterness of this?

The question is whether Miss Brooks or any other poet (now when so many people find modern poetry obscure and unrewarding) can afford to be a coterie poet. (6-7)

What speaks to experiences particular to an African American readership must be discounted in order to praise the book as an otherwise universal achievement. In ironic retrospect, "Stand off . . ." looks fairly accessible when compared to the clotted rhetoric of the book's centerpiece, "The Anniad," an intimidating performance clearly addressed primarily to the high modernist coterie of the 1940s—certainly not to any wide public.

Most notoriously and explicitly, Louis Simpson, in reviewing Brooks's 1963 *Selected Poems*, wrote, "I am not sure it is possible for a Negro to write well without making us aware he is a Negro. On the other hand, if being a Negro is the only subject, the writing is not important" (25).[2] This outright dismissal of African American experience as a fitting subject matter for poetry, predictably enough, provoked a response. Hoyt W. Fuller used it as Exhibit A at the beginning of his essay "Toward a Black Aesthetic" to show the indifference and racism of white audiences when it comes to African American art (4-5). Placing Fuller's essay at the beginning of his landmark critical anthology *The Black Aesthetic*, Addison Gayle, Jr., positioned Simpson's remark as the provocation against which the book's whole theoretical and critical structure was built: a turning away from a white audience indifferent or even hostile to African American art in order to construct works addressed to a specifically black audience.

By the late 1960s, when Brooks was turning away from a white audience for her work anyway, Dan Jaffe acknowledged the value of African American experience as a topic for poetry, but he located its value in a white audience's reception:

There may be some who will maintain that only a black can judge the validity of Gwen Brooks's poems, or those of any other black poet. The real judgment they may insist is not to be made by white readers and critics. . . . But the real question is not what Gwen Brooks has to say to those who have shared her experiences, who have already known what she has to say. The real question is whether she can make the alien feel. The purpose of art is always to communicate to the uninitiated, to make contact across seemingly incontrovertible barriers. Can the poet make the white feel black; the healthy, sick; the defeated, hopeful? One of the measures of a black poet's work is whether he can make a comfortable white (who has not had his sense of language and humanity thoroughly shattered) respond. (54-55)

To be fair to Jaffe, he does not insist that white readers are the only proper judges for African American poetry: "This is not to say that Gwen Brooks's poetry will have no value for black readers. They may well find their own surprises" (55). And, in fact, he takes the step of acknowledging the racial and cultural standpoint from which he makes his judgment, titling his essay "Gwendolyn Brooks: An Appreciation from the White Suburbs"—certainly an advance from earlier critics who conflated whiteness with universal humanism, from which they then excluded whatever was specifically non-white.

By the late 1960s, when Brooks had begun to identify herself with the cultural nationalist Black Arts Movement, she began making public statements, in forums addressed primarily to a black audience, about the limitations of white critics. For a 1968 profile in *Ebony*:

I am absolutely free of any fear of what any white critic might say because I feel that it's going to be most amazing if any of them really understand the true significance of the struggle that's going on. . . . They will probably look at the blacker products and disapprove of them because, naturally, they have to disapprove of disapproval of themselves. (Garland 56)

For a 1971 interview in *Essence*: "Whites are not going to understand what is happening in black literature today. Even those who want to sympathize with it still are not equipped to be proper critics" (Brooks,

Report from Part One 176-77). She included this interview in her 1972 autobiography, which she also published through Broadside Press. In fact, the book emphasizes this rejection of white criticism by restating it in two other prominent places. At the end of the book's central autobiographical essay, a "Report from Part One," she writes:

> There is indeed a new black today. He is different from any the world has known. He's a tall-walker. Almost firm. By many of his *brothers* he's not understood. And he is understood by *no* white. Not the wise white; not the Schooled white; not the Kind white. Your *least* pre-requisite toward an understanding of the new black is an exceptional Doctorate which can be conferred only upon those with the proper properties of bitter birth and intrinsic sorrow. I know this is infuriating, especially to those professional Negro-understanders, some of them so *very* kind, with special portfolio, special savvy. But I cannot say anything other, because nothing other is the truth. (85-86)

Don L. Lee (Haki R. Madhubuti) opens his preface to the book by quoting this very paragraph (13). So the whole book begins—as does *The Black Aesthetic*, with Gayle placing Fuller's quotation of Simpson right at the start—with an explicit rejection of a white context and a white readership.

By publishing *Riot* with Broadside Press, Brooks materially removed her work from a white context and placed it into a black context. The Harper & Row imprint, the imprint of the large commercial publisher, carried with it the business interests of that publisher—to reach as wide a market as possible, an implicitly universal address to all potential purchasers of poetry books. This implicitly universal address, of course, issued from a predominantly white business that saw the most money to be made in a white reading public, one numerically larger and typically with more disposable income to spend on books than an African American readership. The address may have been universal, but the context of its utterance, the publication of the book, was white. The criticisms and reviews of Brooks's work quoted above (other, perhaps, than Jaffe's somewhat more self-conscious one) were similarly made on behalf of a presumably universal audience, but uttered from within a "white" context.[3] Publishing with Broadside placed *Riot* in a specifically African American context. This was not a white publisher's presentation of a black poet's work (black art, white artifact), but a work written, published, and distributed all in a black context. It had to be read as culturally specific rather than as universal.

At the beginning of "The Sermon on the Warpland" in *In the Mecca*, Brooks quotes Ron Karenga: "The fact that we are black/ is our ultimate reality" (*Blacks* 451). This statement explicitly rejects earlier white critics' calls for a universal humanism in her work and directs the audience to read what follows as specifically addressing African American experience. Rather than affix this statement to the start of everything she wrote from then on, Brooks made sure that the artifact bearing her text always emerged out of an African American material context. The route by which one arrived at *Riot* and all her subsequent books would be through African American institutions.

* * *

The artifact Broadside Press produced for Brooks was designed to fit this work of poetry into everyday life: a title that told the African American audience this book would address recent events in the community's experience, a page count (twenty-two, many with only a few lines) small enough for practically anyone to wedge a complete reading into the most hectic day's schedule, a price of one dollar that would fit nearly anyone's budget. As she said in a 1969 interview, she wanted to reach "black people who would never go to a bookstore and buy a $4.95 volume of poetry written by anyone" (Brooks, *Report from Part One* 149). The price welcomed readers. It was a price for anyone with a pocket of spare change. The higher prices of her earlier books, on the other hand, immediately divided those who encountered the artifact between, on one hand, people for whom poetry is a priority on which they are willing to spend their money and, on the other hand, that majority for whom it is a low priority if any at all and who would not ordinarily lay out their scarce cash for it. In her favorite story of reaching a popular audience, Brooks reports on a group of young poets walking into a tavern with her and reading their work to some appreciative patrons who never would have gone to a poetry reading, no matter how well advertised or conveniently scheduled.[4] This incident, which she refers to again and again in interviews and in her autobiographical writing, became a touchstone for her, evidence of a popular constituency for poetry that, given the current status of the genre, remains, usually, just outside the poet's reach. The low price for *Riot* was an attempt to lower the barrier between her art and that popular audience so that anyone might step over it.

On the back cover, the author's photo shows her in a natural hairstyle. Her gaze is direct, the composition more that of a snapshot than a portrait. The photographic style and the plain cotton shirt she wears indicate together that the hairstyle is not a fashion statement but a political statement. The photo indicates that the artifact emerges from a black nationalist cultural context, and the back cover blurb specifies the historical and political context for reading the poem: "It arises from the disturbances in Chicago after the assassination of Martin Luther King in 1968."

The front cover is black: The names of the poet and the press as well as the price are small white spaces in a black field. That is, the field of discourse here, rather than the typical white (i.e., white page interrupted by black ink; the space of public discourse intruded upon by a black voice) is here black. The intrusion upon the black space is, here, white.[5] A roughly torn white circle, a wound in the blackness, holds the jumbled red capitals of the title *RIOT* in contrast with the stately typography of the poet's name. Open the cover, and the book further emphasizes the establishment of a black context by, paradoxically, quoting a white writer (Henry Miller, writing in the 1940s) in the epigraph. Here, too, the design is white on black. Typographically, the design once again emphasizes that these are little white words in a big black space:

It would be a terrible thing for Chicago if this black fountain of life should suddenly erupt. My friend assures me there's no danger of that. I don't feel so sure about it.

Maybe he's right. Maybe the Negro will always be our friend, no matter what we do to him. (3)

The quotation emphasizes three points: white misunderstanding of black attitudes, white fear of black power, and a dawning awareness in this one white writer that blacks may have interests and desires contrary to those of the white majority.

Turn the page again, and one sees, overleaf from the Miller quotation and opposite the title-page, a reproduction of a painting, *Allah Shango*, by Chicago artist Jeff Donaldson: two young men behind a sheet of glass, stenciled "GLASS," "SHEET," and, most pointedly though smaller, "Made in USA." Each touches the glass with one hand; one holds a long African statuette by its base. He holds it low, like a club next to the glass—not threatening, just ready. Miller could be describing these young men. One cannot say what they are thinking, though they clearly feel self-assured, but one knows that the club-like artifact of African culture can smash the invisible barrier. Any moment now, a pane may shatter. The Miller quotation and the Donaldson painting represent the liminal moment before all changes violently. A terrible beauty is about to be born. The book is therefore designed so as to complicate and unsettle any white presence (Miller feels uneasy; the perspective in Donaldson's painting is from the vulnerable side of the glass) while it suggests a context of black cultural authority. Even the dedication—"For Dudley Randall,/ a giant in our time" (7)—makes perfect sense within the small world of black publishing, where he was enormously influential, but not within the larger, white-controlled world of commercial publishing. The material qualities of the artifact, therefore, are designed to establish an African American context for both interpreting and judging the poem. A reading that presumes a white universal perspective must appear irrelevant or absurd.

The first of the poem's three parts, "Riot," makes explicit the irrelevance of trying to understand the April 1968 disturbances in Chicago from an external perspective. One must understand it from inside, from the point of view of the community that exploded. The choice of epigraph alludes to the historical irony that the death of the American prophet of nonviolence unleashed a storm of violence. Brooks quotes Martin Luther King, Jr.: "A riot is the language of the unheard" (9). The proper response to violence is not to condemn it, but to inquire into its causes. What has led people to this extreme? What have they been trying to say? King used the line in a speech at Ohio Northern University a few months before his murder. In the midst of explaining his theory of nonviolence, he said:

> But in condemning violence it would be an act of irresponsibility not to be as strong in condemning the conditions in our society that cause people to feel so angry that they have no alternative but to engage in riots. What we must see is that a riot is the language of the unheard. (King)

What they have to say had not been adequately addressed in public discourse, just as specifically African American experience had been excluded as a legitimate literary focus in prior criticism of Brooks's work. In *Riot*, especially in the second part, she lets the rioters speak. She writes what earlier critics would specifically exclude as an acceptable topic. This book expresses explicitly what the critics quoted above had not heard or had not wanted to hear in her work.

"Riot" introduces us to the white, prosperous, highly cultured (in European tastes), and liberal John Cabot. The riot is described from his point of view, but by a speaker who mocks him throughout the poem. She does not accept his well-educated perspective as authoritative, but rather as contemptible. Brooks had used this technique before—white point of view, black speaker unsympathetic with it—in, for example, "The Lovers of the Poor" and "Bronzeville Woman in a Red Hat," both in her 1960 *The Bean Eaters*. Cabot would apparently see himself as more liberal than the bigoted suburban matron in "Bronzeville Woman in a Red Hat." After all, he socializes with those "Two Dainty Negroes in Winnetka" (9), and even as the rioters take him down, he imagines himself a Christly sacrifice, blessing his executioners: "Lord!/ Forgive these nigguhs that know not what they do" (10)—a virtuoso of condescension—"nigguhs" expressing the contempt his forgiveness only implies. Like the lovers of the poor from "the Ladies' Betterment League" who, visiting from suburban Lake Forest and Glencoe, gag at "the urine, cabbage, and dead beans,/ Dead porridge of assorted dusty grains,/ The old smoke, *heavy* diapers, and, they're told,/ Something called chitterlings" (*Blacks* 350), Cabot too takes olfactory offense at "the fume of pig foot, chitterlings, and cheap chili" (10). He resembles also the addressee of the 1945 poem "The Sundays of Satin-Legs Smith," who would object to Smith's bad taste. But in "Riot," Brooks does not chide gently as she does in those other three poems. Satin-Legs Smith turns and makes the prosperous white liberal who would prefer geraniums and Grieg to Smith's own choices into the object of his own scathing scrutiny. In this historical moment, Cabot, not Smith, is the one with the distorted values, limited social perceptions, and narcissistic world view.

Here, Brooks does not restrain anger elsewhere sublimated. In the 1945 "Negro Hero," Dorie Miller sublimates his anger at whites by killing Japanese. For "Riot," on the other hand, Brooks lets her characters express such anger directly. In "In the Mecca," Way-Out Morgan may "consider Ruin" (*Blacks* 431), and Amos may call for the "long blood bath" (*Blacks* 424), but in "Riot" Brooks lets such characters act out the violence that has heretofore festered and fed upon itself in their imaginations. She seems to let Way-Out Morgan, with his slogan "Death-to-the-Hordes-of-the-White-Men!" (*Blacks* 430), out from his tiny apartment and into the street, where he shares his hoarded guns with Satin-Legs Smith. This is Way-Out Morgan's long-awaited "Day of Debt-pay" (*Blacks* 431) for, among Brooks's other martyrs, Emmett Till, Rudolph Reed, and Medgar Evers. When Cabot looks up and sees that "the Negroes were coming down the street" (9), one may see the great host of Brooks's characters from her earlier work on the march.

Even those like Cabot who consider themselves good liberals are not exempt. In a 1971 interview, Brooks spoke caustically about the white literary friends she had made in earlier phases of her career. She had come to realize that, to them, she was a social token, a signifier of their liberalism, just like Cabot's "Two Dainty Negroes in Winnetka."

> They thought I was lovely. I was a sort of pet. They thought I was nice. I believed in integration, and so did they. Almost every time they'd have a gathering, I'd be one of them. But now, I rarely see these people, though a couple still call themselves my friends. (*Report from Part One* 177)

In Cabot, she is, of course, killing a fictional character, but he seems to represent the white Chicago literati with whom she used to socialize. While "The Lovers of the Poor" gently satirizes self-regarding and condescending philanthropy, a white reader could easily enough see the critique as directed at someone else, someone less sensitive, and laugh along with the speaker at those silly ladies. In "Riot," however, a sympathetic white reader's self-perception as "the wise white . . . the Schooled white . . . the Kind white" is irrelevant to the rioters "coming toward him in rough ranks./ In seas. In windsweep" (9).

The poem destroys "whitebluerose" John Cabot and, by implication, all the European-derived aesthetic assumptions with which he is associated. We are, after all, introduced to him in the first stanza through his tastes, the touchstones he cannot lay aside and by which he judges all else. As the rioters approach, he

---

almost [but never quite, of course] forgot his Jaguar and Lake Bluff;
almost forgot Grandtully (which is The
Best Thing That Ever Happened To Scotch); almost
forgot the sculpture at the Richard Gray
and Distelheim; the kidney pie at Maxim's,
the Grenadine de Boeuf at Maison Henri.

(9)

As these cultural references are irrelevant in understanding the riot, their literary equivalents would be irrelevant to judging *Riot*. Brooks, furthermore, presents Cabot's destruction through one of the most prestigious poetic forms in the English tradition: blank verse, the form most famously wielded by Shakespeare, Milton, and Wordsworth. Though we are not told Cabot's literary tastes, no doubt he would profess to admire such work. Within these regular, formal lines, Cabot perceives the rioters, in contrast, "coming toward him in rough ranks" (9). The blank verse expresses the myopic white point of view, but it will not contain—in fact, it celebrates—the black rage that bursts out in splinters in the next section.

In the second section, "The Third Sermon on the Warpland," the unheard find their language. Actually, Brooks rejects generalized views of the riot as a single experience or the rioters as a unified mass of the sort Cabot perceives bearing down on him. The riot is full of individualized experiences, so she presents it as a collage. Some of the vignettes appear on pages of their own, some juxtaposed with another vignette, isolating the fragments from one another so that it is materially impossible for a reader of the chapbook to see the riot whole, but only through glimpses.

One vignette presents the news media, specifically the *Chicago Sun-Times*, not so much as a source of information as a clearinghouse for rumors. Brooks quotes the tag that peppered the news section of that paper throughout the days of the riot: *"Rumor? check it/ at 744-4111"* (17). Nor does the Black Philosopher, a character who appears intermittently throughout the poem, offer much in the way of an over-all interpretation. His final comment is:

"There they came to life and exulted, the hurt mute.
Then it was over.

The dust, as they say, settled."

(20)

He focuses on the element of joy, but he does not presume to suggest where it all leads. The gangbangers do not know how to respond either: "'Cooooooool!' purrs Peanut [a leader in the Blackstone Rangers gang] ./ . . ./ This Peanut will not let his men explode./ . . ./ These merely peer and purr,/ and pass the Passion over" (18). This ambivalent exclamation may be either admiration for what he sees around him or an admonition to "his men" to stay cool, to remain aloof from this disorganized passion, to maintain their discipline. They go so far as to confer with their enemies, the Disciples, with whom they are "mutual in their 'Yeah!—/ this AIN'T all upinheah!'" (18). According to D. H. Melhem, *upinheah* is "a Black English expression of the sixties [that] means 'hip,' 'with it,' smart or clever. The language stresses the young men's communality" (198-99). Yes, their communality, but in an ambivalent way. Their use and Brooks's use of the argot reinforces the sense of a coherent community by forming a linguistic boundary that excludes outsiders and expresses their alienation from what is happening to their community. They do not participate in and are not a part of this watershed event. Facing the Rangers, across the page gutter, the white liberals—Cabot's political cousins—are visually paired up with the gangbangers in their alienation from the riot. Their language too expresses simultaneously a solidarity with and an alienation from the community that was exploding. Like the Rangers, they disapprove; they season their disapproval, however, not with admiration, but with condescension:

"But WHY do These People offend
themselves?"
say they
who say also "It's time.
It's time to help
These People."

(19)

They interpret the riot as signifying the African American community's incapacity to organize and govern itself, requiring the intervention of "the wise white . . . the Schooled white . . . the Kind white." The
excessive satire, indeed the caricature, of white liberals in this vignette,
imbedded, once again, within an artifact that establishes a specifically
African American context, stresses all the more the rejection of an external perspective on these events. Even if people inside the community do not fully understand it, outsiders who try to interpret it will only
sound ridiculous.

Brooks excludes also points of view that might express sympathy
with the rioters yet condemn their violence, as though "A clean riot"
were possible:

A clean riot is not one in which little rioters
long-stomped, long-straddled, BEANLESS
but knowing no Why
go steal in hell
a radio, sit to hear James Brown
and Mingus, Young-Holt, Coleman, John, on V.O.N.
and sun themselves in Sin.

(14)

They have no theory or understanding of their hunger such as the Black
Philosopher might provide. They only know their transgression is ex-
hilarating. Their hunger is more spiritual than material, yet its expres-

sion, of course, has material consequences: arson, looting, vandalism, death. Though beanless, rather than plunder a West Side restaurant, they burn it so as to watch "Crazy flowers/ cry up across the sky" (12). And they loot radios and records, not food—black pop music such as that by Melvin Van Peebles to feed their souls rather than "Jessie's Perfect Food" to feed their bellies. King's "unheard," though perhaps "not knowing Why" themselves, express their strongest needs through their choice of what to steal.

Having so meticulously crafted a context of moral sympathy with the rioters, Brooks does not flinch at the most tragic fact of the riot: People died. No one of the likes of John Cabot died in the Chicago riot, but nine African American men did. To mourn them, however, would implicitly condemn the event that killed them. So she takes another route. She imagines one who might be, in more sentimental hands, a particularly pathetic victim, a "Motherwoman" and then, rather than mourn the death, she celebrates the life. "She lies among the boxes/ (that held the haughty hats, the Polish sausages)," her body but a container, like the boxes, hardly relevant after use. Nor is she corpse-like, but looking now rather "in newish, thorough, firm virginity/ as rich as fudge is if you've had five pieces." The closest the vignette approaches to mourning is the line that begins the list of some of her life's pleasures—"Not again shall she"—but any hint of regret gets lost then, after the "shall," in a tenseless list of friends, lovers, and hints of a full life (16). As in some of Brooks's other poems about dead women, particularly "southeast corner" and "the rites for Cousin Vit," this one describes the woman's passing as an expression of her abundant liveliness.

Immediately below the "Motherwoman" vignette, Brooks offers a rejection of mainstream tragic sensibility. A twelve-year-old boy (probably no reader of Hemingway's book on bullfighting, but capable as any of us of plucking a phrase out of the cultural atmosphere) shouts, "Instead of your deathintheafternoon/ kill 'em bull!/ kill 'em bull!" (16). Immature? Yes, but without comment, an expression of the spiritual release some of the rioters felt.

The third vignette on that page becomes, by juxtaposition, linked to the others: "The Black Philosopher blares/ 'I tell you, exhaustive black integrity/ would assure a blackless America . . .'" (16). Whatever that means, Brooks's ellipsis suggests he has been cut off in the middle of explaining it. He "blares" so as to be heard amid the chaos of the riot. No one is listening to him. Back on the first page of this "The Third Sermon on the Warpland," he could offer Marxist comments on the relationship between European-derived culture and the African labor that made it economically possible:

> Our chains are in the keep of the Keeper
> in a labeled cabinet
> on the second shelf by the cookies,
> sonatas, the arabesques . . . .
>
> (11)

And he suggests that the "remarkable music" the white listener does not hear, "The *black*blues," both derives from that condition of enslavement and oppression and also expresses an impulse for vengeance. It is, addressing the white who does not listen, "A/ Death Song For You Before You Die" (11). Before the riot starts, the Black Philosopher has ample space in which to theorize, but in the midst of the riot, people act without thought. Twelve-year-old Yancey, the anti-Hemingway, doesn't care about the cultural theory, but in the excitement of the moment blurts out with exuberant anger. Brooks exhorts her readers in the last line of "The Second Sermon on the Warpland" at the end of *In the Mecca*, "Conduct your blooming in the noise and whip of the whirlwind" (*Blacks* 456). When the tornado arrives, the cultural materialist philosopher may keep shouting and explaining all he likes, but nobody will or even can listen to him as they are engaged, all around him, in authentic expression. Like theorizing, mourning becomes possible only at some remove from the "the noise and whip of the whirlwind." In the midst of what Brooks saw as an historical turning point for her community, to pause for mourning would be a sentimental abdication of the responsibility to see clearly and to act upon "what/ is going on" (14).

Previous experience with white critics had taught Brooks that such material would be judged harshly if published in a mainstream context. Within this painstakingly crafted alternative context, the voice of the white liberal, as we have seen above, must seem irrelevant. So when that voice deplores the violence—"But WHY do These People offend *themselves?*"—to deplore it is made, within this context, to seem a wrong response. Brooks offers the Phoenix myth as a framework for a more positive response. She uses a dictionary definition of the word as epigraph for "The Third Sermon": "In Egyptian mythology, a bird which lived for five hundred years and then consumed itself in fire, rising renewed from the ashes.—Webster" (11). She reminds her readers that fiery destruction and death are a prelude to renewal and that this mythic framework has an African provenance. That is, having rejected a white cultural context likely to deplore the violence, she provides an African framework within which to see it more positively. And rather than the white liberal approach of declaring from outside the community, "It's time to help/ These People" (19), she offers, directly overleaf from that parody of condescension, an image of self-renewal. Furthermore, memory will no doubt distort and transform these events into legend. Whatever actually happened in the riot matters less than what people do with the opportunities it presents: "Lies are told and legends made./ Phoenix rises unafraid." Perhaps most important is what happens next, when "The dust, as they say, settled" (20).

Rather than offer a realistic description of the sort of social renewal Brooks hoped for in the aftermath of the riot, the third part, "An Aspect of Love, Alive in the Ice and Fire," suggests instead Brooks's utopian hopes. In this love poem, this free-verse aubade, one lover addresses another as they rise to part in the morning. In a book of wildly shifting tones—between Cabot and the speaker in "Riot," from one vignette to another in "The Third Sermon"—the last poem uses the most surprising tone of all: tenderness. Whereas "The Third Sermon" has blasted the experience of the riot apart into a dozen often irreconcilable perspectives, the book ends with a moment of intimacy. The title suggests that this couple has indeed found a way to "Conduct [their] blooming in the noise and whip of the whirlwind." This is the rebirth Brooks hopes for, the closeness of these two lovers writ large, a unity made possible now by the riot's destruction of an unhealthy social structure.

The first line reads, "It is the morning of our love." The second stanza refers to their union "In a package of minutes" and calls the two lovers "Merry foreigners in our morning" (21). At the start of their new relationship after, apparently, their first night of making love, they feel giddy still with the novel excitement of one another's bodies. This moment of falling in love, in all its intensity of pleasure, holds promise of rich delight stretching onward through the foreseeable time to come. Such a morning is no time to objectively consider how such love sometimes sours or how, even if it lasts a lifetime, it cannot maintain that hilarious intensity forever. This is, rather, the moment to feel the greatest awareness of their unity:

> There is a moment in Camaraderie
> when interruption is not to be understood.
> I cannot bear an interruption.
> This is the shining joy;
> the time of not-to-end.
>
> (22)

When "The dust [has] settled" from the riot, Brooks hopes for and encourages this response: an intense feeling of community. As the now-lovers may have known one another before, may even have felt some connection before this night, African Americans of Chicago would certainly have felt a shared identity before the incidents described here, but the poem offers a hope that this powerful shared experience would lead to a richer sense of communion than ever before. The Phoenix rises in all hopefulness for five hundred richly fulfilling years.

Yet "Because the world is at the window/ we cannot wonder very long" (21). They have their varying responsibilities within the community they are creating. Though the speaker hates any interruption in their new intimacy, "We go/ in different directions/ down the imperturbable street" (22). The chapbook ends, in fact, with the acknowledgment—exhortation, perhaps—to responsibility within the new situation.

* * *

Looking back on *Riot*, Brooks did not feel entirely satisfied with her achievement. In an interview, she stressed the new direction her career took with its publication, along with her judgment that she had not quite succeeded: "*Riot* was really an effort at communication with a lot of people. I didn't succeed except in patches. It too [like *In the Mecca*] is meditative" (Hull and Gallagher 33). In 1969, she was torn between her high modernist ambitions, most fully achieved in *Annie Allen*, and her desire ever since the tavern reading to reach a popular audience. Thus, Arthur P. Davis, for one, considers the first part, "Riot," "Gwendolyn Brooks at her best," while the tessellated "Third Sermon," "is written in the poet's obscure style" (102). Brooks herself cringed when she learned that the first line of "An Aspect of Love"—"It is the morning of our love"—had appeared in a Rod McKuen poem, and so she removed the line from all subsequent reprintings (Brooks, *Report from Part One* 187). To echo a poet of such mass appeal was, as yet, too low-culture for her.

The late sixties do not, of course, mark a clean break in Brooks's poetry. The literary sophistication of her earlier work persists in the later work, and the political thrust of her later work pervades her earlier work as well.[6] After all, she considered the 1959 "We Real Cool" her greatest success by her new popular standards; of her later work only

"The Boy Died in My Alley," from the 1975 *Beckonings*, in her judgment, came close (Hull and Gallagher 20).

Riot, however, makes a decisive break in the material contextualization of Brooks's poetry. Before that chapbook, her books arrived in one's hands through the ostensibly transparent medium of a major publishing house. One was not to notice the institutional mediation, but read transparently through it to the poet's work. A publication is not, however, an utterance of only the writer, but an utterance also of the publisher and of the other institutions—such as retailers, schools, and libraries—through which the artifact passes. Each institution, in conveying the text, places its own quotation marks around it, offering it—even when expressing full approval—within the context of its own values and interests, which are, of course, not always the values and interests of the writer. The reception of Brooks's work through 1968 clearly demonstrates the extent to which a publisher's imprint inflects both the way a work is valued and the way it is understood. When contrasted with Broadside, it becomes clear that Harper's imprint is racially marked as white and that it carries a set of assumptions and values with which Brooks wished, by the late 1960s, to dissociate herself. Literary publishers specifically identified as African American, such as Broadside Press and Third World Press, on the other hand, quote the text (Brooks's or anybody else's) within a context of values and interests specifically marked as black, in the process placing more emphasis and value than do publishers marked as white upon the depiction of and comment on African American cultural and social experience, and they thus encourage readings that particularly value these aspects of the texts.

In the 1960s, Brooks was coming to understand poetry not simply as a set of texts, but as a cultural practice that implicated a broad range of people who produce, distribute, and consume poetry in a variety of contexts and settings—from the editorial offices of Harper & Row and the armchairs of her reviewers to the workshops she conducted in her living room for local college students and the tavern they wandered into for their impromptu reading—each of which inflects the text's meanings. Who publishes a literary work is, therefore, not just a commercial accident, a note upon the spine or title-page irrelevant to the meat of the book. The founding of small African American presses such as Broadside and Third World made it possible to publish work identified with African American cultural nationalism without that level of irony added to the text by reliance on white cultural institutions. The challenge here for the criticism of African American literature is to recognize that literature always appears under the name not only of an author, but also of a racially marked publishing institution whose mission always inflects the work.

From *African American Review* 36, no. 4 (Winter 2002): 557-569. Copyright © 2002 by James D. Sullivan. Reprinted by permission of James D. Sullivan.

Notes

1. Ann Folwell Stanford, however, reads "Gay Chaps at the Bar"—as well as "Negro Hero," also included in *A Street in Bronzeville*—as searing racial critique. Stanford's reading suggests that Engle picked a series of poems with some of the greatest engagement in racial politics in order to deny the relevance of a racially specific interpretation.

2. Upon the 1993 reissue of Brooks's *Selected Poems*, Simpson wrote that, after his notorious 1963 review, Brooks had thanked him for it, and he insisted that his remark had subsequently been misinterpreted (Wright 23). In the second volume of her autobiography, Brooks reprints her teasing introduction to Simpson's reading at a Poetry Society of America event, alluding playfully to that infamous remark (*Report from Part Two* 114-15).

3. Ironically, this includes the remarks of African American reviewer J. Saunders Redding.

4. The fullest account of this incident appears in Kent 210-11, though Brooks comments in an interview on Kent's lack of "sympathy with my constant announced concern for the taverneers" (Hull and Gallagher 22).

5. The cover was designed by Cledie Taylor, who also used a white-on-black design for the 1966 Broadside Press broadside edition of Brooks's poem "We Real Cool." On the ways that particular design choice can alter readings of this poem, see Sullivan 33-38.

6. Other critics have commented on the continuities before and after 1967, the year Brooks has claimed to have made the decisive break in her career. See, for example, Baker 50, Bolden xiv, Lindberg 284-85, and Lowney 19.

Works Cited

Baker, Houston A., Jr. *Singers of Daybreak: Studies in Black American Literature.* 1974. Washington, DC: Howard UP, 1982.

Bolden, B. J. *Urban Rage in Bronzeville: Social Commentary in the Poetry of Gwendolyn Brooks.* Chicago: Third World P, 1999.

Brooks, Gwendolyn. *Blacks.* Chicago: David, 1987.

_____. *Report from Part One.* Detroit: Broadside P, 1972.

_____. *Report from Part Two.* Chicago: Third World P, 1996.

_____. *Riot.* Detroit: Broadside P, 1969.

Brown, Martha H., and Marilyn Zorn. "GLR Interview: Gwendolyn Brooks." *Great Lakes Review* 6.1 (1979): 48-55.

Davis, Arthur P. "Gwendolyn Brooks." Wright 97-105.

Engle, Paul. "Chicago Can Take Pride in New, Young Voice in Poetry." Wright 3-4.

Fuller, Hoyt W. "Toward a Black Aesthetic." *The Black Aesthetic.* Ed. Addison Gayle, Jr. Garden City: Anchor, 1972. 3-11.

Garland, Phyl. "Gwendolyn Brooks: Poet Laureate." *Ebony* July 1968: 48-56.

Hull, Gloria T., and Posey Gallagher. "Update on *Part One*: An Interview with Gwendolyn Brooks." *CLA Journal* 21.1 (1977): 19-40.

Israel, Charles. "Gwendolyn Brooks." *American Poets Since World War II: Part 1: A-K.* Ed. Donald J. Greiner. Dictionary of Literary Biography 5. Detroit: Gale, 1980. 100-06.

Jaffe, Dan. "Gwendolyn Brooks: An Appreciation from the White Suburbs." Wright 50-59.

Kent, George E. *A Life of Gwendolyn Brooks.* Lexington: UP of Kentucky, 1990.

King, Martin Luther, Jr. Address. Ohio Northern U, Ada, OH. 11 Jan. 1968. Heterick Memorial Library, Ohio Northern U. 21 Mar. 2000.

Lindberg, Kathryne V. "Whose Canon? Gwendolyn Brooks: Founder at the Center of the 'Margins.'" *Gendered Modernisms: American Women Poets and Their Readers.* Ed. Margaret Dickie and Thomas Travisano. Philadelphia: U of Pennsylvania P, 1996. 283-311.

Lowney, John. "'A material collapse that is construction': History and Counter-Memory in Gwendolyn Brooks's 'In the Mecca.'" *MELUS* 22.3 (1998): 3-20.

McGann, Jerome. *The Textual Condition.* Princeton: Princeton UP, 1991.

Melhem, D. H. *Gwendolyn Brooks: Poetry and the Heroic Voice.* Lexington: UP of Kentucky, 1987.

Redding, J. Saunders. "Cellini-Like Lyrics." Wright 6-7.

Simpson, Louis. "Don't Take a Poem by the Horns." *Book Week* 27 Oct. 1963: 6, 25.

Stanford, Ann Folwell. "Dialectics of Desire: War and the Resistive Voice in Gwendolyn Brooks's 'Negro Hero' and 'Gay Chaps at the Bar.'" *African American Review* 26 (1992): 197-211.

Sullivan, James D. *On the Walls and in the Streets: American Poetry Broadsides from the 1960s.* Urbana: U of Illinois P, 1997.

Taylor, Henry. "Gwendolyn Brooks: An Essential Sanity." Wright 254-75.

Williams, Kenny J. "The World of Satin-Legs, Mrs. Sallie, and the Blackstone Rangers: The Restricted Chicago of Gwendolyn Brooks." *A Life Distilled: Gwendolyn Brooks, Her Poetry and Fiction.* Ed. Maria K. Mootry and Gary Smith. Urbana: U of Illinois P, 1987. 47-70.

Wright, Stephen Caldwell, ed. *On Gwendolyn Brooks: Reliant Contemplation.* Ann Arbor: U of Michigan P, 1996.

"The Kindergarten of New Consciousness": Gwendolyn Brooks and the Social Construction of Childhood_____

Richard Flynn

Richard Flynn looks at how Brooks's early and later poetry and prose shows how children navigate the rocky terrain of poverty and racial oppression. She celebrates their courage in an effort to encourage future generations. Particularly in Brooks's later poetry, a focus on children is a logical and necessary strategy. Her poetry consistently creates a forum for critiquing racism, sexism, history, social injustice, and the corrosive nature of unchecked power. One of Brooks's goals is to teach her readers to think critically about how the past informs the present and future so that they do not repeat past mistakes. A significant part of Brooks's poetry and prose incorporates children as subject matter or characters, Flynn writes, because Brooks wants to reach out to black and white youth and teach them to move beyond destructive and negative biases that can impede their growth into self-actualized individuals and productive citizens.   — M.R.M.

We watch strange moods fill our children, and our hearts swell with pain. The streets, with their noise and flaring lights, the taverns, the automobiles, and the poolrooms claim them, and no voice of ours can call them back. . . . We cannot keep them in school; more than 1,000,000 of our black boys and girls of high school age are not in school. . . . It is not their eagerness to fight that makes us afraid, but that they go to death on city pavements faster than even disease and starvation can take them. As the courts and the morgues become crowded with our lost children, the hearts of the officials of the city grow cold toward us.

(Wright 136)

I GIVE YOU MY GALLERY.

So many boys. Boys. Lincoln West. Merle. Ulysses. Shabaka. Martin D. The Near-Johannesburg Boy. Diego. Kojo. Seven boys in a poolroom during schooltime. The Pool Players, Seven at The Golden Shovel—

> We real cool. We
> Left school. We
>
> Lurk late. We
> Strike straight. We
>
> Sing sin. We
> Thin gin. We
>
> Jazz June. We
> Die soon.

Die soon. Today, many such boys—their girl friends, too—EXPECT to "die soon." In Chicago. In New York. In Springfield, in Philadelphia. In Whatalotago, Alabama. In Detroit. (In Washington D.C.?) They do not expect to become twenty-one. They are designing their funerals. Their caskets will be lined with Kente cloth. They choose their music: they want rap, they want Queen Latifah.

(Brooks, *Report from Part Two* 123-24)

In *Report from Part One*, Gwendolyn Brooks gives an account of her "conversion" to Black[1] militancy at the 1967 Fisk Writers' Conference. Impressed by the energy and anger in the work of Amiri Baraka (then LeRoi Jones) and others, Brooks recognized that "there is indeed a new black today." Acknowledging that for most of her life "almost secretly [she] had felt that to be black was good," she writes that she had "'gone the gamut' from an almost angry rejection of my dark skin by some of my brainwashed brothers and sisters to a surprised queen-hood in the new black sun." "I . . . am qualified," Brooks proclaims, "to enter at least the kindergarten of new consciousness now" (84). Since *In the Mecca* (1968), Brooks has published her work exclusively with Black presses such as Broadside, Third World Press, and her own David Company, work characterized by a turn toward free verse as well as increasingly direct political content. Although the "kindergarten of new consciousness" fostered in Brooks a new Black identity and a new sense of Black people as her primary audience, her poetry, as she insisted in an interview with Claudia Tate, has always been "'politically aware'" (42).

Part of her political project has been a clear-eyed, tough, and compassionate look at the plight of children. From *A Street in Bronzeville* (1945) to the present, Brooks's work has used the image and voice of the child to negotiate a complex poetic strategy that explores "childhood" as a position from which to critique prevailing constructs of class and race. For Brooks, the subject of childhood represents a means through which she can interrogate and unmask dominant notions of domesticity and child-rearing as part of her own radical social and poetic agenda.

Childhood as a subject would gain force in the '40s and '50s for other American poets, including Robert Lowell, Elizabeth Bishop, and Randall Jarrell. But for most poets the subject of childhood was steeped in nostalgia, indicative of the growing trend toward introspection among White intellectuals occasioned by the rise of a newly psychologized self. By contrast, Brooks chose to write about "the children of the poor," to borrow the title of her sonnet sequence from *Annie Allen*. Critic Gary Smith argues that, "if Brooks's poetry about adults is bleak, her poetry about children is even more so" (130): "Her children do not exist in a pastoral world apart from the socioeconomic and psychological problems that beset her adult characters." Despite this bleakness, Smith argues, children represent "hopeful possibilities" and the transformative potential of "imagination or a radical innocence"

(139). Nevertheless, as Brooks's work makes increasingly clear, the imaginative potential and radical innocence of the Romantic child had to be revised or translated for an age in which innocence was reified, radicalism suspect, and color consciousness discouraged, and in which dissent itself became the subject of Congressional investigations.

Prior to the McCarthy-era backlash, Chicago had become an intellectual and artistic mecca; according to Robert Bone, "the flowering of Negro letters that took place in Chicago from 1935 to 1950 was in all respects comparable to the more familiar Harlem Renaissance" (448). Brooks's career began in those years, during the same cultural moment as the newly prominent Black social scientists trained by Robert Park's Chicago School of Sociology at the University of Chicago. Years before cultural critics would routinely discuss the social construction of race, gender, and sexuality, works written in part or in whole by these social scientists attest to how profoundly the material and emotional circumstances of children are affected by "color-caste" and class distinctions. Drake and Cayton's *Black Metropolis* (1945), a sociological study of Brooks's South Side neighborhood,[2] Dollard and Davis's *Children of Bondage* (1940), and Davis and Gardner's *Deep South* (1941) demonstrate clearly that childhood is a social construct. Many of these same scholars contributed to *An American Dilemma*, Gunnar Myrdal's 1944 study of race relations in the United States which would prove controversial when the Supreme Court relied on its findings in deciding *Brown v. Board of Education* (1954).[3] Although the opportunities and working conditions for Black scholars in the U.S. were still "shaped by racism," as William Banks notes (130-31), the emergence of the new Black scholarship coupled with the promise of integration made the '40s a hopeful time. But this hope proved to be short-lived. By the 1950s, anti-communist hysteria fueled a resurgence of White supremacist racism as virulent as that during the early decades of the twentieth century. After the '40s, the redefinition of childhood was subsumed under the prevailing cold war family values ideology.

* * *

Brooks's poetry explores even more fully the view shared by Black scholars that no single definition of "childhood" could accurately describe the lives of Black children. When *A Street in Bronzeville* was published on August 15, 1945, World War II was coming to an end and the Cold War was still on the horizon. Despite segregationist policies in the armed forces, the war years and immediate postwar years promised expanded opportunity for Black males in the urban North. In her "public" war poems in the volume, Brooks confronts the complicated intersection of race and masculinity. But while the war poems are the most overtly political poems in the volume, *A Street in Bronzeville* is no less engaged with homefront politics. The complexity of Brooks's depiction of masculinity in the volume both complements the more "domestic" poems in the book and foreshadows Brooks's *Annie Allen* (1949) and *The Bean Eaters* (1960), later poetry which, Susan Schweik observes, "more and more confront[s] political conflicts and violence *within* U.S. culture" (326).[4] Brooks's politics are deliberately subtle, a strategy that enables her to assume a highly effective, if understated, role as an advocate for Blacks in America.

Among the models for social protest that Brooks had likely read was Richard Wright's documentary book *12 Million Black Voices* (1941), an eloquent and searing indictment of the plight of urban Blacks after the Northern migration, lavishly illustrated with photographs chosen by Edwin Rosskam from the files of the Farm Security Administration. Long a fan of Wright's work, Brooks was delighted to receive Wright's complimentary reader's report for Harper which concluded, "Miss Brooks is real and so are her poems." Writing to thank him, Brooks confessed to Wright that he "had been a literary hero of hers for years" (Kent 63). Among the poems Wright had singled out for praise was Brooks's now-famous poem "kitchenette building": "Only one who has actually lived and suffered in a kitchenette could render the feeling of lonely frustration as well as she does" (qtd. in Kent 62). Wright's indictment of the kitchenette in *12 Million Black Voices* paints kitchenette life as hopeless in a way that Brooks's poem does not:

The kitchenette is the author of the glad tidings that new suckers are in town, ready to be cheated, plundered, and put in their places.

The kitchenette is our prison, our death sentence, without a trial, the new form of mob violence that assaults not only the lone individual, but all of us, in its ceaseless attacks.

The kitchenette with its filth and foul air, with its one toilet for thirty or more tenants, kills our black babies so fast that in many cities twice as many of them die as white babies. . . .

The kitchenette creates thousands of one-room homes where our black mothers sit, deserted, with their children about their knees.

The kitchenette blights the personalities of our growing children, disorganizes them, blinds them to hope, creates problems whose effects can be traced in the characters of its child victims for years afterwards. (105-10)

Though Brooks depicts unflinchingly the "blights" on the personalities of children and adults in Bronzeville, her kitchenette is not merely the site of victimization. Brooks's "things of dry hours and the involuntary plan,/ Grayed in and gray," feel the "giddy sound" of dreams, unable to compete with the "strong" demands of "'rent,' 'feeding a wife,' 'satisfying a man.'" A place of "crowding darkness" with its share of "child victims," the street of the title sequence is populated by specific human beings. If in other circumstances Brooks's kitchenette dwellers might "Flutter, or sing an aria down these rooms," they have more pressing and practical concerns:

We wonder. But not well! not for a minute!
Since Number Five is out of the bathroom now,
We think of lukewarm water, hope to get in it.
(*Blacks* 20)[5]

Hortense Spillers has noted Brooks's "commitment to life in its unextraordinary aspects," which shows us that "common life is not as common as we suspect" (234). Brooks's kitchenette dwellers are potential artists whom necessity has reduced to numbers waiting in line for the kitchenette's overcrowded bathrooms, but the ironic diminishment of their "hope" nevertheless points to that hope's tenacity. Without obscuring the material circumstances of her characters, Brooks nevertheless insists on their value beyond their status as victims. And Spillers (echoing an earlier essay by Houston Baker) describes this dynamic in terms of a dialectic that offers the reader "a model of power, control, and subtlety" that "transcends ideology."[6]

If by "transcending ideology," Spillers means that Brooks's poetry refuses to approach the political in programmatic ways, then perhaps she is accurate in her assessment. Brooks writes poetry, after all, not the kind of documentary realism so effective in the Wright/Rosskam volume. But Brooks's poetry is ever attentive to the dominant ideologies of the postwar era, when liberal historians and critics were to proclaim "the end of ideology" altogether.[7] An age of so-called "consensus history," the '50s saw the invention of the White suburban family as a cultural norm and media icon. Exaggerated fears of the Red Menace coexisted uneasily with a vision of the nation as a consumer paradise. At the end of the decade, Daniel Bell would tell the affluent readers of *The End of Ideology* (1960) that there was an "actual decline of crime in the United States," and point out that most crimes were now committed by "youths and . . . minority groups, principally the Negroes. . . . The greatest number of crimes in Chicago," continues Bell, "is committed in 'Bronzeville,' the narrow, choked Negro ghetto which runs like a dagger down the south side" (141). But Bell goes on to reassure his White audience that, "however fierce the juvenile gang wars in East Harlem, the intermittent slashings in Bronzeville, or the rumbles in North Beach, it is clear that the score of violence today in no way approaches the open, naked brawling of even thirty or forty years ago" (157).

Dismissing the "assertion that modern life is more violent" as "largely a literary creation," Bell describes the "myth of crime waves" as a result of "the blurring, culturally and ecologically, of class lines. . . . With the rise of movies and other media," he concludes, came a "widening" of "'windows' into the full range of life, from which the old middle class had largely been excluded" (157). Bell's "dagger down the south side," viewed through middle-class television windows, was willfully blind to the vibrant life so apparent in Brooks's *Bronzeville*. Most telling is Bell's equation of "youths" and "minority groups, principally the Negroes." A culture that reduces the man "of De Witt Williams on his way to Lincoln Cemetery" to "nothing but a/ Plain black boy" is one that both dismisses the value of childhood and denies adults their maturity. For the "Negro Hero" (suggested by Dorie Miller, whose heroism at Pearl Harbor necessitated his defiance of segregationist military rules), the maturity it takes to "kick their law into their teeth in order to save them" is predicated on a rejection of received notions of both childhood and adulthood:

> . . . the delicate rehearsal shots of my childhood massed in mirage before me.
> Of course I was a child
> And my first swallow of the liquor of battle bleeding black air dying and demon noise
> Made me wild.

> It was kinder than that, though, and I showed like a banner my kindness.
> (*Blacks* 48-49)

The equation of child and Black man as (in this instance, noble) primitive is successfully interrogated in the poem. The speaker rejects the notion that his heroic act is occasioned by the mere "boy itch to get at the gun." The image of the wild child is rejected in favor of the image of a man: "I loved. And a man will guard when he loves." This is not to say that the "Negro Hero" has rejected his child-self; rather, he rejects a naïve version of childhood, and by showing "like a banner" his kindness, he also rejects a stereotypical version of Black male adulthood. Brooks recognizes that Black men's and women's attempts to construct their subjectivities are impeded by the "constant back-question" of a culture that insists on their inferiority (49). That her heroes are often able to negotiate successfully the intra-subjective relationship between their adult and child selves is remarkable in that they must not only bridge the temporal and experiential gap between maturity and childhood, but they must do so in opposition to a law that circumscribes their material and emotional existence. The White middle-class view that equates childishness with blackness per se negates full participation in citizenship, both for Black American soldiers and for growing Black children.

Instead, Brooks's heroes, like Maud Martha, "reckon" with "annoyances," a gray existence of "roaches, and having to be satisfied with the place as it was":

> The sobbings, the frustrations, the small hates, the large and ugly hates, the little pushing-through love, the boredom, that came to her from behind those walls (some of them beaver-board) via speech and scream and sigh—all these were gray. And the smells of various types of sweat, and of bathing and bodily functions (the bathroom was always in use, someone was always in the bathroom) and of fresh or stale love-making, which rushed in thick fumes to your nostrils as you walked down the hall, or down the stairs—these were gray.
>
> There was a whole lot of grayness here. (*Blacks* 205-06)

Had Bell attended to "literary creations" like *Maud Martha* (1953), he would have seen Bronzeville heroes and heroines deprived of a widening of windows, who nevertheless have a clear-eyed perception of the world outside through "a half-inch crack" (*Blacks* 319). These "literary creations" struggled to make sense of the maimed bodies of men home from the war and the dissonant images in "the Negro press (on whose front pages beamed the usual representations of womanly Beauty, pale and pompadoured)" which "carried the stories of the latest Georgia and Mississippi lynchings" (*Blacks* 319-21). If the "kitchenette folks" of Maud Martha's (and Brooks's) Bronzeville "would be grand, would be glorious and brave, would have nimble hearts that would beat and beat" (321), they would do it in the face of a relentless racist ideology. Bell's stereotypes, in fact, find their antithesis in Brooks's poetry, which works to undermine the ways in which even liberal ideology interpellates its victims.

Such pervasive misconceptions of Black life in America were wide-ranging and historically sedimented in intellectual circles, and so the Black scholars in the '30s and '40s relied on the strategic erasure of race. Though among what Du Bois termed "the talented tenth," they knew firsthand the effects of racial discrimination. Allison Davis, the first Black professor hired by the University of Chicago and the first to receive tenure (in 1948), had spent most of his life earning intellectual distinction in segregated institutions.[8] His research during the forty years he was at Chicago focused on the personality and development of children and adolescents, particularly the influence of social class on learning, which led to pioneering work on cultural bias in intelligence testing. He was the co-author of two major studies of social anthropology—*Children of Bondage: The Personality Development of Negro Youth in the Urban South* (1940), with John Dollard, and *Deep South* (1941), with Burleigh and Mary Gardner.

Under the influence of White mentors like W. Lloyd Warner, author of *Social Class in America* (1949), scholars like Davis recognized the rigidity of "color-caste" distinctions and chose to focus on economic and social class as a strategy for a more effective remediation of inequities. In addition, recognizing the growing influence of psychoanalysis and social psychology, they enlisted the new prestige of those disciplines in order to make their case. In his preface to *Children of Bondage* (1940), Davis thanks his collaborator John Dollard for helping him achieve "a genuine integration of psychoanalytical and sociological understanding" (xvii). Employing a Freudian-inflected behaviorism as an interpretive schema, Davis and Dollard present case histories of "eight Negro adolescents in the Deep South [New Orleans, Louisiana, and Natchez, Mississippi] selected to represent all class positions in Negro society [whose] experiences illustrate the fundamental controls which each class exercises over the socialization of its members" (xxiii-xxvii). Firm in their insistence that social-Darwinist theories of race are unscientific, they argue that differences between groups are cultural and social, and that the effects of invidious discrimination are psychologically damaging to children.

In 1947, with his colleague, psychologist Robert J. Havighurst, Davis published a child-rearing manual with the commercial publisher Houghton Mifflin. Titled *Father of the Man: How Your Child Gets His Personality*, the book is a curious amalgam of self-help and scholarship. Addressed to middle-class mothers (10), and concerned mostly with private behavior and psychological concerns, *Father of the Man* nevertheless draws on the authors' scholarly study "Social Class and Color Differences in Child-Rearing," published in the December 1946 issue of *American Sociological Review*. This research, based on 200 "guided interviews" with "fifty mothers [of young children] in each of four groups, white middle class, white lower class, Negro middle class, and Negro lower class"—most of them residents of Chicago's South Side ("Social Class" 700)—is also presented as Appendix I in *Father of the Man* (215-19).

Though the Wordsworthian title of the latter study might suggest a Romantic faith in divine childhood, more accurately, it reflects Davis's background as a poet and literary critic.[9] In addition to chapter epigraphs by Shakespeare, Auden, William Saroyan, Steinbeck, and Lewis Carroll, Davis includes epigraphs from Sterling Brown's *Southern Road* and Brooks's *A Street in Bronzeville*, published two years earlier. His use of Brooks's work in the context of a child-rearing manual from a major trade publisher for an audience of middle-class (presumably White) mothers illustrates the cultural and ideological dissonance between his claims for childhood as a universal human stage and his concern about the specific effects of social-class and color-caste distinctions on actual children. Chapter III of *Father of the Man*, entitled "Silver Spoon or Sugar Teat?" bears two epigraphs, one from Brooks and one from Davis's mentor, W. Lloyd Warner:

> A class system also provides that children are born into the same status as their parents. A class society distributes rights and privileges, duties and obligations, unequally among its members.
>
> —W. Lloyd Warner

> I've stayed in the front yard all my life.
> I want a peek at the back. . . .
> And maybe down the alley,
> To where the charity children play,
> I want a good time today.
> They do some wonderful things.
> They have some wonderful fun.
> My mother sneers, but I say it's fine.
> How they don't have to go in at quarter to nine.
>
> —Gwendolyn Brooks (17)

Davis's omissions from Brooks's poem are telling. Aside from truncating the end of the third and all of the last verse paragraphs, the ellipsis omits the speaker's hunger and urgency to explore the unfamiliar, and most likely her sexuality: "Where it's rough and untended and the hungry weed grows./ A girl gets sick of a rose./ I want to go in the back yard now" (*Blacks* 28).[10] Abstracted from its context in the "Street in Bronzeville" sequence, "a song in the front yard," in Davis's edited version, is a far less threatening—and a far less complex—poem. The little girl who speaks "a song" expresses admiration for the "bad woman" Johnnie May because she intuits that her "bad" identity is largely a matter of masquerade:

But I say it's fine. Honest, I do.
And I'd like to be a bad woman, too.
And wear the brave stockings of night-black lace
And strut down the street with paint on my face.

(*Blacks* 28)

Davis intentionally obscures the issue of race in his study as part of a strategic insistence that class differences are far more important than color differences.[11] Brooks's front-yard singer, however, is far more rebellious and complicated: The emblems of her rebellion are both "brave" and "night-black." The painted face seems to the speaker to provide an identity that can be assumed at will, perhaps a form of racial as well as sexual masquerade, but the poet maintains an ironic distance from the speaker, knowing that such performances have limited transgressive potential. However, the child speaker's monologue as "a song" helps her to negotiate difficult questions of self in the context of a specific culture and community. As Brooks demonstrates in the volume as a whole, identity, like community and culture, cannot be satisfactorily reduced to "good" vs. "bad." The diversity of Bronzeville belies easy moral distinctions; populated by a wide variety of characters from the heroic to the hypocritical, *A Street* refuses to shy away from the neighborhood's pervasive tensions over class and color.[12] And Brooks as author generally refrains from easy judgment. One surmises, for instance, that the mother of the front-yard singer has acted out of love and concern for the child's well-being. But since, inevitably, "a girl gets sick of a rose," that protective restraint has left the girl ill-equipped to confront the realities of the world she longs to experience. The mother's too rigid morality is inadequate sustenance for the incipient adolescent, who begins to question the binaries of class—working poor vs. charity cases—of sexuality, and, arguably, of color—the purity of the rose vs. night-black lace stockings.

While she seems sympathetic to the girl's longings, as her biographer George Kent observes, Brooks "rejected the exotic vein of the

Harlem Renaissance," injecting "satire and realism" into her portraits of ordinary Bronzevillians (66-67). Reminiscent of Allison Davis's 1928 *Crisis* essay (see n9), Brooks's contribution to *Phylon*'s 1950 symposium on "The Negro Writer"—"Poets Who Are Negroes"—cautions Negro writers against getting carried away by the "ready-made subjects" of Black life: "No real artist is going to be content with offering raw materials. The Negro poet's most urgent duty, at present, is to polish his technique. . . . The mere fact of lofty subject, great drive, and high emotion," Brooks argues, is insufficient to make poetry, because these qualities lack "embellishment," "interpretation," and "subtlety" (312). Though often read as a product of "the strain that Brooks felt in attempting to negotiate a fruitful relationship between race and art . . . during a historical period that mingled racial pride with an integrationist ethos" (Mootry, "Down" 9), Brooks's essay assumes that the

> Negro . . . cannot escape having important things to say. His mere body, for that matter, is an eloquence. His quiet walk down the street is a speech to the people. Is a rebuke, is a plea, is a school. (312)

This is not the observation of a poet single-mindedly heralding art over political engagement. Her injunction to the Negro poet to "polish his technique" is directed at focusing "his way of presenting his truths and his beauties, that these may be more insinuating, and, therefore, more overwhelming" (312).

In May, 1950, Brooks received the unexpected news that she had won the 1950 Pulitzer Prize for Poetry for *Annie Allen*. As the first Black person to win the Pulitzer Prize, she was thrust into a public role as cultural observer and spokeswoman, particularly regarding race matters. Despite this newfound fame, she and her husband and son were still living in a two-room kitchenette at 623 East 63rd Street. In early 1951, the thirty-three-year-old Brooks was delighted to find herself pregnant with her second child, Nora. Hoping to raise enough money for a down payment on a house, she sought to supplement the meager $500 advance she had received for her novel *Maud Martha* (1953) and turned to writing feature stories for popular magazines. Among these stories was "How I Told My Child About Race," published in the June 1951 *Negro Digest*. Brooks recalls an incident of racist violence, when "six or seven young white men" threw "handfuls of rocks" and shouted "'Look at the nig-gers'" at Brooks and her then five-year-old son Henry, Jr., during their evening stroll by "the beautiful buildings of the [U]niversity" of Chicago. Brooks vowed with bitter irony "never again to take evening walks east of Cottage Grove with [her] son":

> Formerly I had felt that if any place at all was safe, the university district, mecca of basic enlightenment and progressive education would be safe. The buildings, with their delicate and inspiring spires, seemed now to leer, to crowd us with mutterings—"Oh no, you black bodies!—no sanctuary here. You have found no sanctuary, you will find no sanctuary anywhere. This beauty is not for you, the architects, the builders, did not have the elongations of your filthy shadows in mind as they worked, as they shaped. Get out, get out, get out. . . ." (30)

When Henry, Jr., asks "why—why—why—would 'those men' want to hurt us," his mother regains her composure, explaining that those with "light skins" feel that they are "better than us and that therefore they are entitled to rule others":

> When you are bigger you may be able to help them change the way they feel by teaching them. . . . you are a *person*, and good, wise, and helpful to the world. Even without *their* education in mind, you would want to be good, wise and helpful anyhow. While you are little and helpless, you can do nothing but try to see trouble before it hits you with stones, and get away from it as best you can. (10)

The richly contradictory symbol of the University of Chicago occasions an expression of rage, though tempered somewhat by her tone of equanimity as she speaks to her son. Though it was home to Allison Davis and, for its time, represented a progressive approach to race relations, the University was nonetheless a stately and visible symbol of White privilege in Brooks's Black neighborhood. Furthermore, as she contemplates the imminent birth of her daughter Nora, Brooks knows that a similar explanation of race will have to be repeated.

These concerns are further expressed in her early '50s journalism which appeared in Black journals like *Phylon* and *Negro Digest*, as well as in an essay Brooks wrote for the travel magazine *Holiday* titled "They Call it Bronzeville" (October 1951). Addressing the magazine's White audience using the conceit of a "white Stranger who enters Bronzeville for the first time" (61), Brooks demonstrates the intersection of class and race in the construction of childhood by contrasting the children of Woodlawn—"the elite area of Bronzeville"—with those of "Bronzeville proper." In the Woodlawn neighborhood of "brown-brick bungalows and attractive small apartment houses . . . the children"

> are very light, or maybe apricot, a sort of sunburst brown. If, unhappily, the children are dark, just plain out-and-out dark that nothing can be done about, that not even Golden Peacock or Black and White bleach can "help," then their parents have to spend money on clothes, have to force music or art through those black unfortunate fingers, have to maneuver those black bodies into the right social situations, have to "scheme." (62)

But eight-year-old Clement Lewy lives "an interesting life, a life perhaps like an unmixed batter—lumpy, vaguely disheveled." Clement, a latchkey child whose "mother has grown listless since her husband deserted her," nevertheless looks alert, almost too alert; he looks happy, he is always spirited. He is in second grade. He does his work and has been promoted at the proper times. At home he sings. He recites little poems. He tells his mother little stories wound out of the air. His mother glances at him once in a while. She would be proud of him if she had the time. (63)[13]

As with the children who populate Brooks's first two volumes of poems, the restrictions of color and class impinge on the promise of artistry. The very existence of a ghetto, "something that should not exist—an area set aside for the halting use of a single race," Brooks argues, has a profound effect on children's attempts to negotiate what is "essentially only what is ordinary: human struggle, human whimsicality, and human reach toward soul-settlement" (61).

The photographs accompanying the article (undoubtedly chosen by the editors rather than Brooks) contradict Brooks's portrayal of Bronzevillians as ordinary human beings. Rather, they are drawn as entertainers and exotics: a debutante ball at "an exclusive Bronzeville social club"; a gathering of artists and writers; Eldzier Cortor, nationally known Chicago artist, depicted with a nude man wearing a Haitian ritual mask; a light-skinned cover girl posing for "*Tan Confessions*, a racy sister magazine of *Ebony*, influential Negro monthly"; and "Sepia Show Girls" at the White-owned Club De Lisa. The lone remaining photograph depicts a boy of six or seven drinking from a glass by a window in an obviously shabby apartment. The caption reads: "HIS ARM BROKEN, his mother dead, his father vanished, this Bronzeville waif looks wistfully at life from the window of his foster home" (114). Brooks's effort to teach the White Stranger that Bronzeville is "a place where People live" (116), is undercut by the photo spread which suggests that Bronzeville is a place of dancing, singing, happy, exotic, oversexed adult Negroes who abuse and neglect their children.

When Ursula Nordstrom proposed a volume of children's verse in 1955, Brooks tackled the task with vigor, writing the poems in *Bronzeville Boys and Girls* (1956) at the rate of a poem a day (Kent 122). Like most first-time children's writers, she was given no choice of illustrators or any input regarding the illustrations themselves. And once again the disparity between her text and the accompanying illustrations is telling. Ronni Solbert's black-and-white line drawings portray the Bronzeville children, sometimes with stylized Black facial characteristics, but all with white faces. According to George Kent, Brooks found the illustrations disturbing. Granted, the poems themselves do not mention race, except obliquely, in keeping with the integrationist ethos then endorsed by Brooks. Perhaps recognizing that the poems would be judged according to the standards of what Nancy Larrick called "the all-white world of children's books," Brooks implies race only in the title of the volume and in the dramatic monologue by Gertrude, which begins "When I hear Marian Anderson sing,/ I am a STUFFless kind of thing" (*Bronzeville Boys and Girls* 31). Portending the negative criticism Brooks would receive for being too political in her adult volume *The Bean Eaters* (1960), Doris M. King, writing in the Black quarterly *Phylon*, gently chided the poet for introducing "a note of social comment" into her otherwise delightful poems about "those untranslatable people who 'come trailing clouds of glory.'" Replete with condescending and universalizing descriptions of children—"the stubborn but facile minds of children, the literal though wildly imaginative" (93)— King's review faults the poems depicting the material conditions of Bronzeville because their "social comment" "encumber[s] the universal wonder of childhood." Preferring the poems that "interpret life from the inside out," King argues that the best poems in the book "are not about Bronzeville boys and girls, but simply boys and girls" (94).

That King should prefer the poems that are "unfettered by social implications" confirms the difficulty Brooks faced in disrupting the idealizing and sentimental view of childhood endorsed by mainstream culture in the '50s. In the best poems in the volume, Brooks employs a surface sentimentality in order to undermine it, as in the pathos of "Otto":

It's Christmas Day. I did not get
The presents that I hoped for. Yet,
It is not nice to frown or fret.

To frown or fret would not be fair.
My Dad must never know I care
It's hard enough for him to bear.

(38)

D. H. Melhem has compared the poems of *Bronzeville Boys and Girls* to Robert Louis Stevenson's *A Child's Garden of Verses* (*Gwendolyn* 95-99), but although the comparison is sometimes apt, there is none of Stevenson's irony at the child's expense. The ironies of Brooks's volume explore the disparity between the sentimental conventions of a mid-'50s children's book (including the inapt and often inept illustrations) and the everyday lives of Bronzeville children, such as "John, Who Is Poor," a boy reminiscent of the Clement Lewy of the *Holiday* article and *Maud Martha*:

Oh, little children, be good to John!—
Who lives so lone and alone.
Whose Mama must hurry to toil all day.
Whose Papa is dead and done.

Give him a berry, boys, when you may,
And, girls, some mint when you can.
And do not ask when his hunger will end,
Nor yet when it began.

(38)

The last stanza's ironies seem doubly addressed to adult and child readers, as if Brooks anticipates that the child reader will inevitably ask the question the poet forbids. Doris King's preferred Wordsworthian childhood is confronted with the restricted urban spaces where nature is represented by a lone tree or a child's fantasy of escaping to the country, where it is unlikely that the boys and girls whom the speaker exhorts to be "kind" to John will find berries or mint to relieve his hunger. Thus poems like "Rudolph Is Tired of the City" or "Lyle" deliberately reject a poetic that would require children's poetry to be "as light and free and delightful as the child" (King 92). Rather than "arousing . . . nostalgia" in adult readers, these poems seem calculated to point out the dangers of a nostalgia that obscures the actual conditions of children. Given the relationship between Brooks and her editors at Harper, and the cultural climate of the mid-'50s, Brooks is quietly subversive in these poems, which prefigure the powerful children's monologues in *Children Coming Home* (1991).[14]

* * *

In the '50s, Brooks wrote as a young mother whose poetry was essential for the well-being of her own children in a racist society; today, she writes as a poet with decades of a political commitment to working closely with children and poetry. In her work of the '60s and '70s, Brooks's children are catalysts for change, both as symbols and through their own poetic voices: The remembered "infant softness" of Emmett Till becomes a symbol that awakens the conscience of the Mississippi mother for whose sake he has been lynched ("A Bronzeville Mother Loiters in Mississippi. Meanwhile, a Mississippi Mother Burns Bacon," *Blacks* 333-39), while the voice of the murdered Pepita S. in her couplet at the end of "In the Mecca" ("I touch"—she said once—"petals of a rose./ A silky feeling through me goes!" [*Blacks* 433]) "becomes the most vital voice of the community," as Gayl Jones (203) points out. By 1975, Brooks had become increasingly concerned with fostering children's vital voices, so that rather than being "offered in distorted images through the mirrors of others," as Jones says of Pepita, they may "speak for [themselves]" (203). In her *ars poetica*, published in *a capsule course in Black Poetry Writing* (1975), Brooks instructs novice writers to "Remember that ART is refining and evocative translation of the materials of the world!" (Brooks et al. 11) and calls for "a new black literature" that will "italicize black identity, black solidarity, black self-possession, and self-address" (3).

This commitment and hopefulness manifested itself in action throughout the '70s and '80s as Brooks conducted informal poetry workshops for children in her neighborhood, published several writing guides for young people, and tirelessly promoted poetry and literacy as ways of living meaningfully in an increasingly hostile world. As Poetry Consultant at the Library of Congress in 1985-86, Brooks gave generously to the Washington area community, visiting schools and paying for a series of readings by young poets out of her own pocket, as I and other members of the D.C. poetry community at the time observed firsthand. In *Very Young Poets* (1983) Brooks offers solid advice to child poets that poems can address both the fantasy worlds of "kings and princesses" and the actual world of "blue jeans, school and lessons and teachers and garbagemen, babies, old people, McDonald's hamburgers, gardens, jail and prisoners" (12). Rather than romanticize children's "stubborn but facile minds," Brooks exhorts her young poets to read not just the "many kinds of poetry," but "also the news, stories, biography, history, science books and news-magazines. These will help you THINK," she admonishes, "and your thoughts will inspire more poems" (15). "In all this willful world/ of thud and thump and thunder," she writes in one of the "Eight Poems for Children" concluding the volume,

> Books are meat and medicine
> and flame and flight and flower,
> steel, stitch, cloud and clout,
> and drumbeats on the air.
>
> (27)

By 1986, however, in *The Near-Johannesburg Boy*, dedicated "to the students of Gwendolyn Brooks Junior High School, Harvey, Illinois," it becomes clear that books alone may not provide enough "meat and medicine." For children who "flail in the Hot Time" (4) in South Africa, or who confront the possibility of "Early Death" in urban America with its proliferation of guns and the temptations of the "small seductive vial" of crack (18-19), poetry seems insufficient weaponry. In a world where Black children in South Africa "ask each other: 'Have you been detained yet? How many times have you been detained?'" (3) or where Black children in Chicago know that "Death is/ just down the street; is most obliging neighbor;/ can meet you any moment," only a communal expression of grief and anger provides a fitting memorial "Of the Young Dead":

> What is to cherish is the child
> who loved us, who loved science and the sunshine,
> who
> wished the world well.
> Keeping those gifts of self, beyond the changes,
> we keep the living light of our young dead.
>
> (18)

Faced with the erosion of Black empowerment in the '80s and '90s, even Brooks's optimism reaches its limits. In *Children Coming Home* (1991), a collection of twenty powerful dramatic monologues in children's voices, Brooks's children emerge as casualties of national policies which promote the fiction of a color-blind society while social and economic disparities between Black and White communities increase.

Deliberately abandoning the formal virtuosity that characterized her earlier work, Brooks represents children's voices through a seemingly simple, declarative method, which is underscored by the volume's design: an old-fashioned children's composition book, with a black-and-white mottled cover. The prefatory poem, "After School," delineates the odds against children's empowerment in a culture that devalues them:

> Not all of the children
> come home to cookies and cocoa.
> Some come home to crack cocaine.
> Some come to be used in various manners.
> One will be shot on his way home to warmth, wit and wisdom.
>
> One teacher mutters "My *God*, they are gone."
> One is ripe to report Ten People to the Principal.
> One muses "How have I served or disturbed them today?"
> One whispers "The little Black Bastards."
> One sees all children as clothing: the blue blouse—
> the green dress—the tight-fitting T-shirt.
>
> One will take home for homework each of the
> twenty, the thirty, the forty one.

Against a backdrop of over-crowded classrooms, domestic and street violence, and even the war in the Persian Gulf, the twenty children who speak in the volume live a social reality far removed from—and far more complex than—the children of *Bronzeville Boys and Girls*. Institutionalized violence against the family, which often breeds intra-family violence and abuse, is portrayed unflinchingly. Even attempts at Afrocentric education to foster self-esteem seem ineffective in the world of *Children Coming Home*. For Tinsel Marie, who has learned about "The Coora Flower" that "grows high in the mountains of Itty-go-luba Bésa,"

School is a tiny vacation. At least you can sleep. . . .
But now it's Real Business.
I am Coming Home.
My mother will be screaming in an almost dirty dress.
The crack is gone. So a Man will be in the house.

I must watch myself.
I must not dare to sleep.

(1)

Sala learns that in "East Afrika" her name "means gentleness," but
there is little gentleness in her life. Feeling herself "sucked into earth,"
"whipped through the wind," and "drowning, oddly, in an odd ocean,"
she anaesthetizes herself with alcohol:

Well, now I am coming home.
I shall be better
after the aspirin and wine.

(8)

Undoubtedly, D. H. Melhem notes, Brooks "sees today's children in
their context, and . . . proclaims an emergency" ("Afterword" 158), but
even in the midst of emergency the poems offer hope for children's potential to employ poetic language in order to make sense of their world.
Though the monologues are spare and often despairing, their poetry
emerges in the silences between declarative statements, in associative
leaps, and in metonymic resonances. Jamal's monologue, "Nineteen
Cows in a Slow Line Walking," is a telling illustration of Brooks's
craft. Jamal has seen the cows on a train "when [he] was five years old"
(though the reader surmises he is not much older when he speaks the
poem):

Each cow was behind a friend.
Except for the first cow,
who was God.

I smiled until
one cow near the end

jumped in front of a friend.

That reminded me of my mother and of my father.
It spelled what is their Together.

I was sorry for the spelling lesson.

I turned my face from the glass.

(2)

Jamal perceives the line of cows as an orderly procession led by a be-
nevolent God. Reading the line of cows from the moving train, he wit-
nesses a disruption of that order (which is also a breach of friendship)
that "spells" out for him the disruption in his family life. Jamal's "reading" is supplanted by the institutional forces of family and school in
such a way that he turns from the glass that is both his window on the
world and a mirror in which he can see his own image. The associative
seeing of the meaningful relationship among the cows is thus converted into a mere lesson in which getting it right produces an abdication of poetic ways of seeing. And yet the process of that loss is reproduced by the monologue itself, so that, in a very real way, Jamal has
achieved a saving grace by converting the loss into poetic utterance.

Jamal, like young Martin D., who finds in the books his father provides "fire" that is an antidote to "school," which "has made [him]
crispy-cold," must fight to be resilient in a society in which children's
empowerment through language has become an expendable luxury. As

Brooks learned in "the kindergarten of new consciousness" of the Black Power Movement, the institutions of the school and the family, which should foster children's well-being, too often perpetuate their pain. Like the inhabitants of the "kitchenette building" of the '40s, Brooks's children of the '90s must seek out their own strength and solace; Novelle takes comfort in the love of her "warm and wide and long" Grandmother with whom she eats "walnuts and apples/ in a one-room kitchenette above The/ Some Day Liquor Gardens" (4). As the poems in *Children Coming Home* attest, the "crowding darkness" of *A Street in Bronzeville* has intensified.

In the sonnet sequence "the children of the poor" (*Annie Allen* [1949]), Brooks questions the efficacy of art for embattled children; "First fight. Then fiddle" (118), she advises. Her poetry, at once advocacy and artistry, demonstrates that fighting and fiddling may be part of the same project. In the course of over fifty years of writing for and about children, Brooks's complex negotiation of childhood teaches us that the failure to see children in the specificity of their lived circumstances "makes a trap for us." Childhood, seen through the reifying lens of a romanticized nostalgia, naturalizes children's "little lifting helplessness, the queer/ Whimper-whine" (115). Rather than empowering children, we see them, at best, as representations of our own "lost softness." We look away from evidence of suffering, making "a sugar" in the face of their vulnerability. By posing uncomfortable social questions in the disarming voices of child speakers, Brooks subtly employs the image of the innocent child to expose not-so-innocent social practices, and offers a compelling critique of the ways in which these practices construct the child as "quasi, contraband" (116). In letting children speak, through her own poetic voice, and in helping them find their own voices, she provides both "arms and armor" for social change. In the '40s, Brooks first posed the question "What shall I give my children? who are poor,/ Who are adjudged the leastwise in the land" (*Blacks* 116). At the end of the century, her question has not yet received a sufficient answer.

From *African American Review* 34, no. 3 (Fall 2000): 483-499. Copyright © 2000 by Richard Flynn. Reprinted by permission of Richard Flynn.

Notes

1. In keeping with Brooks's practice, I use the term *Black* rather than *African American* throughout this essay. One reason Brooks prefers the term *Black* is that it promotes solidarity among people of color throughout the world; another is that she continues to see the usefulness of the term for promoting Black pride; her speaker Kojo in *Children Coming Home* says, "I am other than hyphenation." Brooks explains her unpopular "objection . . . to the designation African-American" in *Report from Part Two* (132-33).

2. Brooks's article "Why Negro Women Leave Home" in the March 1951 issue of *Negro Digest* engages in a public debate with St. Clair Drake's "Why Men Leave Home" (Apr. 1950) and Roi Ottley's "What's Wrong with Negro Women" (Dec. 1950). For an account of the debate in relation to Brooks's war poetry, see Schweik 115-22. *Black Metropolis* was based on the Cayton-Warner research in the '30s, research which also formed the basis for Wright's *12 Million Black Voices*. Wright contributed the introduction to the first edition.

3. Though the work of progressive Black scholars was published frequently during the 1940s, their names (including Dr. Davis's) are relegated to the acknowledgments in Myrdal's book. Nevertheless, in light of what Stuart Whitfield describes as the "right wing and racist attacks on his book as Communist [which] became common in the following decade" (23), it is evident that the intellectual climate before the Cold War was much more hospitable to the work of Black scholars than it would become under the specter of McCarthyism. The chilling effects on the social sciences of "the alliance between anti-Communists and white supremacists" after *Brown* is discussed in Schrecker 393, 404-11.

4. Schweik argues that poems such as "Negro Hero" and "Gay Chaps at the Bar" both transgress normative gender roles and serve as ironic protests against the segregationist policies of the armed forces. The passage of "Negro Hero" that Schweik finds most telling is the third and fourth stanzas, in which the speaker figures himself in the "image of the soldier-as-really-a-child . . . half-feral and half-spoon-fed" and in the "image of the soldier-as-Real-Man . . . with full self-awareness." That the two images exist simultaneously in the Negro Hero's "divided self," Schweik argues, "provide[s] a startlingly subversive representation of maleness" (119-20). Though I offer a somewhat different reading of the passage, my reading reinforces rather than negates Schweik's analysis. In another useful essay, Ann Folwell Stanford argues that Brooks's "battlefield exists simultaneously on foreign fronts, in the trenches, on Chicago streets, and even at home" (198).

5. For an interesting and provocative interpretation of Wright's and Brooks's depictions of kitchenette living, see Griffin, esp. 69-82 and 100-14.

6. Even as late as the '70s, *ideological* was a negative adjective in the literary

critic's lexicon. Baker, in his pioneering 1972 essay "The Achievement of Gwendolyn Brooks," concludes that "the critic (whether black or white) who comes to her work seeking only support for his ideology will be disappointed for, as Etheridge Knight has pointed out, she has ever spoken the truth. And truth, one likes to feel, always lies beyond the boundaries of any one ideology" (28). Spillers's essay, which first appeared in Gilbert and Gubar's anthology *Shakespeare's Sisters* in 1979, concludes, "No ideologue, Brooks does not have to be" (235). One recognizes, of course, the cultural moment in which Baker and Spillers write, but one must also recognize that Brooks's writing, editing, and teaching during the same cultural moment was explicitly and unashamedly "ideological."

7. The phrase *the end of ideology* is from Daniel Bell's 1960 book of the same title. Stuart Whitfield's comment on the orthodoxy of public school textbooks influenced by the "consensus history" is germane here: "Intellectuals who wrote obituaries for ideology in the 1950s either used the term in a restrictive sense (referring to the eclipse of socialism among themselves) or had not examined the American history texts that public schools adopted" (55). Drawing on Frances FitzGerald's description of how history textbooks underwent an "ideological freeze during the Cold War" (FitzGerald 44), Whitfield discusses how attacks by "business associations and right-wing citizens' groups" made textbooks bland in order to make them acceptable to a host of conservative ideologues. The Texas legislature, for instance, voted to require loyalty oaths of all textbook writers and passed a resolution requiring that textbooks emphasize "'our glowing and throbbing history of hearts and souls inspired by wonderful American principles and traditions'" (FitzGerald 37-38).

8. Davis, the first Black professor employed by the University of Chicago, was hired only because the liberal Julius Rosenwald Fund paid his salary; he was not permitted to buy a house in Hyde Park or even to use the faculty club (Hillis 117). The valedictorian of the class of 1924 at Williams College, Davis had not been permitted to live on that campus (Oleck 39). Hoping to become a poet, Davis then took the M.A. in literature from Harvard, taught for a few years and studied anthropology, earning a second M.A. from Harvard in 1932 and becoming co-director of field research in social anthropology until he took a teaching position at the historically Black Dillard University in 1935. Joining the University of Chicago in 1940 as a research associate, he earned the Ph.D. in 1942. Later in life, he served as a member of the President's Commission on Civil Rights under Lyndon Johnson, and was the recipient of a MacArthur Foundation "genius grant' shortly before his death in 1983.

9. A contributor of poetry and essays to W. E. B. Du Bois's *The Crisis* during the '20s, Davis was not only concerned with literature for its own sake, but was concerned with what he took to be stereotypical representations of Blacks in literature, by both Black and White authors. In a 1928 essay for *The Crisis*, Davis assailed the vogue of primitivism during the Harlem Renaissance: "Our 'intellectuals,' then," he states in his conclusion, "both those in literature and those in race criticism, have capitalized on the sensational aspects of Negro life, at the expense of general truth and sound judgment. Primitivism has carried the imagination of our poets and storytellers into the unhealthy and the abnormal. A sterile cynicism has driven our Menckenized critics into smart coarseness" (286).

10. Davis and Havighurst's chapter concerns two families, the Washingtons, who are poor and Black and live in a kitchenette, and the Bretts, who are comfortably middle-class, White, and live in a ten-room home (though the race of neither family is directly specified in the book). For Davis and other Black sociologists of his generation, the strategic erasure of race intended to appeal to their liberal audiences and mentors led them to think of class in social rather than economic terms. Such strategies were challenged by more radical thinkers such as Marxist sociologist O. C. Cox. In a series of articles and in his major study *Caste, Class, and Race* (1948), Cox took on the Black sociological establishment and the "Negro as caste" school for their failure to realize "the reality that capitalism requires the continuation of an exploitable class in order to preserve itself" (Jones 157-58). See Cox, esp. 489-508.

11. "a song in the front yard" can be fruitfully read alongside other poems in *A Street* that concern intra-racial color prejudice, including "patent leather," "southeast corner," "the ballad of chocolate Mabbie," "Ballad of Pearl May Lee," and, arguably, "Sadie and Maud." What Brooks later termed "the angry rejection of my dark skin by some of my brainwashed brothers and sisters" (*Report from Part One* 86) provides a significant inspiration for Brooks in many of the poems in *A Street in Bronzeville*. The earliest discussion of the theme of intra-racial color prejudice in Brooks's work is Arthur P. Davis's 1962 article "The Black-and-Tan Motif in the Poetry of Gwendolyn Brooks." The theme, which grew out of Brooks's own experience of prejudice as a dark-skinned Black, is present throughout her career—in *Annie Allen* and *Maud Martha*, as well as poems as recent as "The Life of Lincoln West" (1970) and Fleur's dramatic monologue "Our White Mother Says We Are Black But Not Very" from *Children Coming Home* (1991). For an excellent discussion of the theme of intra-racial prejudice in Brooks's work, see Erkkila 185-234.

12. Chapter 13 of *Father of the Man*, "The First Child Against the Second," concerns sibling rivalry and bears as one of its epigraphs the first stanza of Brooks's "the murder": "This is where poor Percy died,/ Short of the age of one./ His brother Brucie, with a grin,/ Burned him up for fun" (Davis and Havighurst, *Father* 119; Brooks, *Blacks* 38). Davis and Havighurst's point is that sibling rivalry is inevitable in the "restricted" nuclear family prevalent in Europe and America, and they point to "folk groups" where extended families alleviate such rivalry. In Brooks's poem, the "murder" is the result of the mother's leaving her children unsupervised (kitchenette living being unconducive to extended families). But she obscures the role that material conditions play in the children's being left alone by allowing the "murder" to take place while the mother "gossip[s] down the street" (38). In a March 1969 interview with George Stavros, Brooks corrects this false note in the poem: "'The Murder' [sic] really happened except for the fact that I said the boy's mother was gossiping down the street. She was working. (I guess I did her an injustice there.)" (*Report from Part One* 153-54).

13. The portrait of Clement Lewy is reproduced nearly verbatim in the "kitchenette folks" chapter of *Maud Martha* (*Blacks* 256-58), albeit with a more poetic beginning: "Then there was Clement Lewy, a little boy at the back, on the second floor./ Lewy life was not terrifically tossed. Saltless, rather. Or like an unmixed batter. Lumpy."

14. See George Kent's account of Brooks abandoning her novel-in-progress *The Life of Lincoln West* in order to write *Bronzeville Boys and Girls* (119-23). The first

chapter of the novel was eventually published as a short story in 1963, and as a poem in 1970. Lincoln, "the ugliest boy/ that everyone ever saw," is a victim of intra-racial prejudice, because of his pronounced Black features. When he is seven, a White man in a movie theater makes a racist remark to his friend about Lincoln: "'THERE! That's the kind I've been wanting/ to show you! One of the best/ examples of the species. Not like/ those diluted Negroes you see so much of on/ the streets these days, but the/ real thing./ Black, ugly and odd. You/ can see the savagery. The blunt/ blankness. That is the real thing'" (*Blacks* 487-88). Lincoln disregards the racist context, focusing on the phrase *the real thing*, which the narrator says "comforted him" (489). That a work of similar power didn't make its way into Brooks's 1956 children's book is understandable, but in her later poetry for and about children, such issues are raised in an effort to "speak the truth to the people," as she says, quoting Mari Evans, in the epigraph to *Children Coming Home.*

Works Cited

Baker, Houston A., Jr. "The Achievement of Gwendolyn Brooks." 1972. Mootry and Smith 21-29.

Banks, William M. *Black Intellectuals: Race and Responsibility in American Life.* New York: Norton, 1996.

Bell, Daniel. *The End of Ideology: On the Exhaustion of Political Ideas in the Fifties.* Glencoe: Free P, 1960.

Bone, Robert. "Richard Wright and the Chicago Renaissance." *Callaloo* 28 (Summer 1986): 447-68.

Brooks, Gwendolyn. *Blacks.* Chicago: Third World P, 1987.

―――――. *Bronzeville Boys and Girls.* Pictures by Ronni Solbert. New York: Harper, 1956.

―――――. *Children Coming Home.* Chicago: David, 1991.

―――――. "How I Told My Child About Race." *Negro Digest* June 1951: 29-31.

―――――. *The Near-Johannesburg Boy and Other Poems.* Chicago: Third World P, 1986.

―――――. "Poets Who Are Negroes." *Phylon* 11 (1950): 312.

―――――. *Report from Part One.* Prefaces by Don L. Lee and George Kent. Detroit: Broadside P, 1972.

―――――. *Report from Part Two.* Afterword by D. H. Melhem. Chicago: Third World P, 1996.

―――――. "They Call it Bronzeville." *Holiday* (Oct. 1951): 60-67, 112-16.

―――――. *Very Young Poets.* Chicago: Third World P, 1983.

―――――. "Why Negro Women Leave Home." *Negro Digest* Mar. 1951: 26-28.

Brooks, Gwendolyn, Keorapetse Kgositsile, Haki R. Madhubuti, and Dudley Randall. *a capsule course in Black Poetry Writing.* Detroit: Broadside P, 1975.

Cox, Oliver, Jr. *Caste, Class, and Race: A Study in Social Dynamics*. New York: Doubleday, 1948.

Davis, Allison. "Our Negro 'Intellectuals.'" *Crisis* 35 (Aug. 1928): 257, 268-69, 284-85.

_____. *Social-Class Influences upon Learning*. The Inglis Lecture, 1948. Cambridge: Harvard UP, 1948.

Davis, Allison, Burleigh B. Gardner, and Mary R. Gardner. *Deep South: A Social Anthropological Study of Caste and Class*. Chicago: U of Chicago P, 1941.

Davis, Allison, and John Dollard. *Children of Bondage: The Personality Development of Negro Youth in the Urban South*. Washington: American Council on Education, 1940.

Davis, Allison, and Robert J. Havighurst. *Father of the Man: How Your Child Gets His Personality*. Boston: Houghton, 1947.

_____. "Social Class and Color Differences in Child-Rearing." *American Sociological Review* 11 (1946): 698-710.

Davis, Arthur P. "The Black-and-Tan Motif in the Poetry of Gwendolyn Brooks." *CLA Journal* 6 (Dec. 1962): 90-97.

Drake, St. Clair. "Why Men Leave Home." *Negro Digest* Apr. 1950: 25-27.

Drake, St. Clair, and Horace R. Cayton. *Black Metropolis: A Study of Negro Life in a Northern City*. Rev. ed. Intro. by Richard Wright. New foreword by William Julius Wilson. Chicago: U of Chicago P, 1993.

Erkkila, Betsy. *The Wicked Sisters: Women Poets, Literary History, and Discord*. New York: Oxford UP, 1992.

FitzGerald, Frances. *America Revised: History Schoolbooks in the Twentieth Century*. Boston: Atlantic Monthly P, 1979.

Griffin, Farah Jasmine. *"Who Set You Flowin'?" The African-American Migration Narrative*. New York: Oxford UP, 1995.

Hillis, Michael R. "Allison Davis and the Study of Race, Social Class, and Schooling." *Multicultural Education, Transformative Knowledge, and Action: Historical and Contemporary Perspectives*. Ed. James A. Banks. New York: Teachers College P, 1996. 115-28.

Jones, Butler A. "The Tradition of Sociology Teaching in Black Colleges: The Unheralded Professionals." *Black Sociologists: Historical and Contemporary Perspectives*. Chicago: U of Chicago P, 1974. 121-63.

Jones, Gayl. "Community and Voice: Gwendolyn Brooks's 'In the Mecca.'" Mootry and Smith 193-204.

Kent, George E. *A Life of Gwendolyn Brooks*. Lexington: UP of Kentucky, 1990.

King, Doris M. "The Feeling and Texture of Childness." Rev. of *Bronzeville Boys and Girls*, by Gwendolyn Brooks. *Phylon* 18 (First Quarter 1957): 93-94.

Larrick, Nancy. "The All-White World of Children's Books." *Saturday Review* 48 (11 Sep. 1965): 63-65, 84-85.

Melhem, D. H. "Afterword." Brooks, *Report From Part Two* 146-60.

_____. *Gwendolyn Brooks: Poetry and the Heroic Voice*. Lexington: UP of Kentucky, 1987.

Mootry, Maria K. "'Down the Whirlwind of Good Rage': An Introduction to Gwendolyn Brooks." Mootry and Smith 1-17.

Mootry, Maria K., and Gary Smith, eds. *A Life Distilled: Gwendolyn Brooks, Her Poetry and Fiction*. Urbana: U of Illinois P, 1987.

Myrdal, Gunnar. *An American Dilemma*. New York: Harper, 1944.

Oleck, Joan. "Allison Davis: 1902-1983." *Contemporary Black Biography*. 12. Detroit: Gale, 1997. 38-41.

Ottley, Roi. "What's Wrong with Negro Women." *Negro Digest* Dec. 1950: 71-75.

Schrecker, Ellen. *Many Are the Crimes: McCarthyism in America*. Boston: Little, Brown, 1998.

Schweik, Susan. *A Gulf So Deeply Cut: American Women Poets and the Second World War*. Madison: U of Wisconsin P, 1991.

Smith, Gary. "Paradise Regained: The Children of Gwendolyn Brooks's *Bronzeville*." Mootry and Smith 128-39.

Spillers, Hortense. "Gwendolyn the Terrible: Propositions on Eleven Poems." 1979. Mootry and Smith 224-35.

Stanford, Ann Folwell. "Dialectics of Desire: War and the Resistive Voice in Gwendolyn Brooks's 'Negro Hero' and 'Gay Chaps at the Bar.'" *African American Review* 26 (1992): 197-211.

Tate, Claudia, ed. *Black Women Writers at Work*. New York: Continuum, 1983.

Warner, W. Lloyd, with Marchia Meeker and Kenneth Eells. *Social Class in America: A Manual of Procedure for the Measurement of Social Status*. New York: Harper, 1949.

Whitfield, Stuart. *The Culture of the Cold War*. 2nd ed. Baltimore: Johns Hopkins UP, 1996.

Wright, Richard. *12 Million Black Voices: A Folk History of the Negro in the United States*. Photo direction by Edwin Rosskam. New York: Viking, 1941.

RESOURCES

Chronology of Gwendolyn Brooks's Life_____

1917	Gwendolyn Brooks is born in Topeka, Kansas, to David and Keziah Brooks. Five weeks later, the family moves to Hyde Park, Chicago.
1918	Gwendolyn's brother Raymond is born.
1921	The family moves to the South Side of Chicago.
1930	Brooks's first published poem, "Eventide," appears in *American Childhood Magazine*.
1934	Brooks graduates from Englewood High School and begins regularly publishing her work in the *Chicago Defender*'s weekly poetry column.
1936	Brooks graduates from Wilson Junior College.
1938	Brooks joins the National Association for the Advancement of Colored People (NAACP) Youth Council and becomes its publicity director.
1939	Brooks marries Henry L. Blakely II, a writer whom she met through the Youth Council.
1940	Brooks gives birth to a son, Henry L. Blakely III.
1941	Brooks takes poetry workshops with Inez Cunningham Stark.
1943	Brooks receives the Poetry Workshop Award from the Midwestern Writers' Conference.
1945	*A Street in Bronzeville* is published.
1946-1947	Brooks is named a Fellow of the American Academy of Arts and Letters; she also receives two Guggenheim Fellowships.
1949	*Annie Allen* is published.

1950	*Annie Allen* is awarded the Pulitzer Prize, making Brooks the first African American poet to receive the award.
1951	Brooks gives birth to a daughter, Nora.
1953	*Maud Martha* is published.
1956	*Bronzeville Boys and Girls*, a children's poetry collection, is published.
1960	*The Bean Eaters* is published.
1962	At the invitation of President John F. Kennedy, Brooks reads at a Library of Congress poetry festival.
1963	*Selected Poems* is published. Brooks teaches a poetry workshop at Columbia College in Chicago.
1964	Columbia College awards Brooks her first honorary degree.
1967	Brooks attends the Second Black Writers' Conference at Fisk University in Nashville, Tennessee, and is inspired to become involved in the Black Arts movement, to write more overtly political poetry, and to publish with small, black-owned presses.
1968	Brooks is named poet laureate of Illinois. *In the Mecca* is published.
1969	Brooks separates from Blakely. *Riot* is published.
1970	*Family Pictures* is published.
1971	Brooks travels in Kenya and Tanzania. *Aloneness* is published.
1973	Brooks reunites with Blakely, and the couple travel to England.
1974	*The Tiger Who Wore White Gloves* is published
1975	*Beckonings* is published. Brooks and Blakely travel in Ghana, England, and France.

1981	*To Disembark* is published.
1983	*Very Young Poets* is published.
1986	*The Near-Johannesburg Boy* is published.
1987	*Blacks* is published.
1988	*Winnie* and *Gottschalk and the Grande Tarantelle* are published.
1991	*Children Coming Home* is published.
1994	Brooks is named Jefferson Lecturer by the National Endowment for the Humanities.
1995	Brooks is awarded the National Medal of Arts.
1996	*Report from Part Two* is published.
2000	Brooks dies on December 3.
2003	*In Montgomery* is published.
2005	*The Essential Gwendolyn Brooks*, edited by Elizabeth Alexander, is published.

Works by Gwendolyn Brooks

Poetry

A Street in Bronzeville, 1945
Annie Allen, 1949
"We Real Cool," 1959
The Bean Eaters, 1960
Selected Poems, 1963
"The Wall," 1967
In the Mecca, 1968
Riot, 1969
Family Pictures, 1970
Aloneness, 1971
Black Steel: Joe Frazier and Muhammad Ali, 1971
Aurora, 1972
Beckonings, 1975
Primer for Blacks, 1980
To Disembark, 1981
Black Love, 1982
The Near-Johannesburg Boy, 1986
Blacks, 1987
Gottschalk and the Grande Tarantelle, 1988
Winnie, 1988
Children Coming Home, 1991
In Montgomery, 2003
The Essential Gwendolyn Brooks, 2005

Long Fiction

Maud Martha, 1953

Nonfiction

The World of Gwendolyn Brooks, 1971
Report from Part One, 1972
Young Poet's Primer, 1980
Report from Part Two, 1996

Children's Literature

Bronzeville Boys and Girls, 1956
The Tiger Who Wore White Gloves, 1974
Very Young Poets, 1983

Edited Text

Jump Bad: A New Chicago Anthology, 1971

Bibliography

Bambara, Toni Cade. Review of *Report from Part One*, by Gwendolyn Brooks. *The New York Times Book Review* (January 7, 1973): 1.

Barksdale, Richard K. "Humanistic Protest in Recent Black Poetry." *Modern Black Poets: A Collection of Critical Essays*. Ed. Donald B. Gibson. Englewood Cliffs, NJ: Prentice-Hall, 1973. 157-64.

Bell, Roseann P., Bettye J. Parker, and Beverly Guy-Sheftall, eds. *Sturdy Black Bridges: Visions of Black Women in Literature*. Garden City, NY: Anchor/Doubleday, 1979.

Bloom, Harold, ed. *Gwendolyn Brooks*. Bloom's Biocritiques. Philadelphia: Chelsea House, 2005.

_____. *Gwendolyn Brooks*. Bloom's Modern Critical Views. Philadelphia: Chelsea House, 2000.

_____. *Gwendolyn Brooks: Comprehensive Research and Study Guide*. Bloom's Major Poets. Philadelphia: Chelsea House, 2003.

Bolden, B. J. *Urban Rage in Bronzeville: Social Commentary in the Poetry of Gwendolyn Brooks*. Chicago: Third World Press, 1999.

Brown, Patricia L., Don L. Lee, and Francis Ward, eds. *To Gwen with Love: An Anthology Dedicated to Gwendolyn Brooks*. Chicago: Johnson, 1971.

Bryant, Jacqueline, ed. *Gwendolyn Brooks' "Maud Martha": A Critical Collection*. Chicago: Third World Press, 2002.

Callahan, John F. "'Essentially an Essential African': Gwendolyn Brooks and the Awakening to Audience." *North Dakota Quarterly* 5.4 (Fall 1987): 59-73.

Christian, Barbara. *Black Feminist Criticism: Perspectives on Black Women Writers*. New York: Pergamon Press, 1985.

Creekmore, Hubert. "Daydreams in Flight." *The New York Times Book Review* 4 (October 1953): 4.

Davis, Arthur P. "The Black-and-Tan Motif in the Poetry of Gwendolyn Brooks." *College Language Association Journal* 6.2 (December 1962): 90-97.

Dawson, Emma Waters. "Vanishing Point: The Rejected Black Woman in the Poetry of Gwendolyn Brooks." *Obsidian II* 4.1 (Spring 1989): 1-11.

Furman, Marva Riley. "Gwendolyn Brooks: The 'Unconditioned' Poet." *College Language Association Journal* 17.1 (September 1973): 1-10.

Gayle, Addison, Jr. "Gwendolyn Brooks: Poet of the Whirlwind." *Black Women Writers (1950-1980): A Critical Evaluation*. Ed. Mari Evans. Garden City, NY : Anchor Doubleday, 1984.

_____. "The World of Gwendolyn Brooks." *The New York Times Book Review* (January 2, 1972): 4.

Gayles, Gloria Wade, ed. *Conversations with Gwendolyn Brooks*. Jackson: University Press of Mississippi, 2003.

Gery, John. "Subversive Parody in the Early Poems of Gwendolyn Brooks." *South Central Review: The Journal of the South Central Modern Language Association* 16.1 (1999): 44-56.

Hansell, William H. "Aestheticism Versus Political Militancy in Gwendolyn Brooks's 'The Chicago Picasso' and 'The Wall.'" *CLA Journal* 17.1 (September 1973): 11-15.

_____. "The Uncommon Commonplace in the Early Poems of Gwendolyn Brooks." *College Language Association Journal* 30.3 (March 1987): 261-77.

Hudson, Clenora F. "Racial Themes in the Poetry of Gwendolyn Brooks." *College Language Association Journal* 17.1 (September 1973): 16-20.

Hughes, Gertrude R. "Making It *Really* New: Hilda Doolittle, Gwendolyn Brooks, and the Feminist Potential of Modern Poetry." *American Quarterly* 42.3 (1990): 375-401.

Hughes, Langston. "Name, Race, and Gift in Common." *Voices* 140 (Winter 1950): 54-56.

Hull, Gloria T. "A Note on the Poetic Technique of Gwendolyn Brooks." *College Language Association Journal* 19, no. 2 (December 1975): 280-85.

Kent, George E. "Gwendolyn Brooks' Poetic Realism: A Developmental Survey." *Black Women Writers, 1950-1980: A Critical Evaluation.* Ed. Mari Evans. Garden City, NY: Anchor Books, 1984. 88-105.

_____. *A Life of Gwendolyn Brooks.* Lexington: University Press of Kentucky, 1990.

Kufrin Joan. "Gwendolyn Brooks." *Uncommon Women.* Piscataway, NJ: New Century, 1981.

Kunitz, Stanley. "Bronze by Gold." *Poetry* 76.1 (April 1950): 55-56.

Lattin, Patricia H., and Vernon E. Lattin. "Dual Vision in Gwendolyn Brooks's *Maud Martha.*" *Critique* 25.4 (1984): 180-89.

Lindberg, Kathryne V. "Whose Canon? Gwendolyn Brooks: Founder at the Center of the 'Margins.'" *Gendered Modernisms: American Women Poets and Their Readers.* Ed. Margaret Dickie and Thomas Travisano. Philadelphia: University of Pennsylvania Press, 1996.

Littlejohn, David. *Black on White: A Critical Survey of Writing by American Negroes.* New York: Viking, 1966.

Loff, Jon N. "Gwendolyn Brooks: A Bibliography." *College Language Association Journal* 17.1 (September 1973): 21-32.

Lupack, Alan C. "Brooks' 'Piano After War.'" *The Explicator* 36.4 (Summer 1978): 2-3.

Madhubuti, Haki R., ed. *Say That the River Turns: The Impact of Gwendolyn Brooks.* Chicago: Third World Press, 1987.

Melhem, D. H. "Gwendolyn Brooks: Humanism and Heroism." *Heroism in the New Black Poetry: Introductions and Interviews.* Lexington: University Press of Kentucky, 1990.

_____. *Gwendolyn Brooks: Poetry and the Heroic Voice.* Lexington: University Press of Kentucky, 1987.

Miller, Jeanne-Marie A. "Bronzeville, U.S.A." *Journal of Negro Education* (Winter 1970): 88-90.

_____. "Riot." *Journal of Negro Education* (Fall 1970): 368-69.

Miller, R. Baxter. "'Define . . . the Whirlwind': Gwendolyn Brooks's Epic Sign for a Generation." *Black American Poets Between Worlds, 1940-1960.* Ed. R. Baxter Miller. Knoxville: University of Tennessee Press, 1986.

_____. *Langston Hughes and Gwendolyn Brooks: A Reference Guide.* Boston: G. K. Hall, 1978.

Morse, Carl. "All Have Something to Say." *The New York Times Book Review* (October 6, 1963): 4, 28.

Park, Sue S. "A Study of Tension: Gwendolyn Brooks's 'The *Chicago Defender* Sends a Man to Little Rock.'" *Black American Literature Forum* 11.1 (Spring 1977): 32-34.

Ryan, William F. "Blackening the Language." *American Visions* 3.6 (December 1988): 32-37.

Satz, Martha. "Honest Reporting: An Interview with Gwendolyn Brooks." *Southwest Review* 74.1 (Winter 1989): 25-35.

Saunders, Judith P. "The Love Song of Satin-Legs Smith: Gwendolyn Brooks Revisits Prufrock's Hell." *Papers on Language and Literature* 36 (Winter 2000): 3-18.

Shands, Annette Oliver. "Gwendolyn Brooks as Novelist." *Black World* (June 1973): 22-30.

_____. "Report from Part One." *Black World* (March 1973): 70-71.

Shapiro, Harvey. "A Quartet of Younger Singers." *The New York Times Book Review* (October 23, 1960): 32.

Shaw, Harry B. *Gwendolyn Brooks.* Boston: Twayne, 1980.

Smith, Gary. "Gwendolyn Brooks' 'Children of the Poor': Metaphysical Poetry and the Inconditions of Love." *Obsidian II* 1.1 (Spring/Summer 1986): 39-51.

Spillers, Hortense J. "Gwendolyn the Terrible: Propositions on Eleven Poems." *Shakespeare's Sisters: Feminist Essays on Women Poets.* Ed. Sandra M. Gilbert and Susan Gubar. Bloomington: University of Indiana Press, 1979.

Stern, Frederick C. "The 'Populist' Politics of Gwendolyn Brooks's Poetry." *MidAmerica* 12 (1985): 111-19.

Stetson, Erlene. "*Songs After Sunset* (1935-1936): The Unpublished Poetry of Gwendolyn Elizabeth Brooks." *College Language Association Journal* 24.1 (September 1980): 87-96.

Tate, Claudia. "Gwendolyn Brooks." *Black Women Writers at Work.* Ed. Claudia Tate. New York: Continuum, 1983.

Taylor, Henry. "Gwendolyn Brooks: An Essential Sanity." *Kenyon Review* 13 (Fall 1991): 115-31.

Werner, Craig. "Gwendolyn Brooks: Tradition in Black and White." *Minority Voices* 1.2 (Fall 1977): 27-38.

Whitaker, Charles. "Gwendolyn Brooks: A Poet for All Ages." *Ebony* (June 1987): 154-62.

Wilder, Amos N. "Sketches from Life." *Poetry* (December 1945): 164-66.

Wright, Stephen Caldwell. *The Chicago Collective: Poems for and Inspired by Gwendolyn Brooks.* Sanford, FL: Christopher-Burghardt, 1990.

_____, ed. *On Gwendolyn Brooks: Reliant Contemplation.* Ann Arbor: University of Michigan Press, 1996.

CRITICAL INSIGHTS

About the Editor

Mildred R. Mickle is Assistant Professor of English and English Coordinator at Penn State Greater Allegheny. She has published essays on Octavia E. Butler's works in the *Xavier Review*; *The Oxford Companion to African American Literature*, edited by William L. Andrews, Frances Smith Foster, and Trudier Harris (1997); and *New Essays on the African American Novel*, edited by Lovalerie King and Linda Selzer (2008). She published an essay on award-winning poet Lillian Allen in *Beyond the Canebrakes: West Indian Women Writers in Canada*, edited by Emily Allen Williams (2008). She also published an interview with Jaki Shelton Green, winner of the 2003 North Carolina Award in Literature, in *Obsidian III: Literature in the African Diaspora*. She has essays on Octavia E. Butler's works forthcoming in *Contemporary African American Fiction (1970-present)*, edited by Dana A. Williams, and *Strange Matings: Remembering Octavia E. Butler and Her Impact on Science Fiction and Feminism*, edited by Rebecca Holden and Nisi Shawl. She is currently at work on an essay on Percival Everett's collection of poems *re: f(gesture)* and on two volumes of her own poetry.

About *The Paris Review*

The Paris Review is America's preeminent literary quarterly, dedicated to discovering and publishing the best new voices in fiction, nonfiction, and poetry. The magazine was founded in Paris in 1953 by the young American writers Peter Matthiessen and Doc Humes, and edited there and in New York for its first fifty years by George Plimpton. Over the decades, the *Review* has introduced readers to the earliest writings of Jack Kerouac, Philip Roth, T. C. Boyle, V. S. Naipaul, Ha Jin, Jay McInerney, and Mona Simpson, and published numerous now classic works, including Roth's *Goodbye, Columbus*, Donald Barthelme's *Alice*, Jim Carroll's *Basketball Diaries*, and selections from Samuel Beckett's *Molloy* (his first publication in English). The first chapter of Jeffrey Eugenides's *The Virgin Suicides* appeared in the *Review*'s pages, as well as stories by Edward P. Jones, Rick Moody, David Foster Wallace, Denis Johnson, Jim Shepard, Jim Crace, Lorrie Moore, Jeanette Winterson, and Ann Patchett.

The Paris Review's renowned Writers at Work series of interviews, whose early installments include legendary conversations with E. M. Forster, William Faulkner, and Ernest Hemingway, is one of the landmarks of world literature. The interviews received a George Polk Award and were nominated for a Pulitzer Prize. Among the more than three hundred interviewees are Robert Frost, Marianne Moore, W. H. Auden, Elizabeth Bishop, Susan Sontag, and Toni Morrison. Recent issues feature conversations with Salman Rushdie, Joan Didion, Stephen King, Norman Mailer, Kazuo Ishiguro, and Umberto Eco. (A complete list of the interviews is available at www.theparisreview.org.) In November 2008, Picador will publish the third of a four-volume series of anthologies of *Paris Review* interviews. The first two volumes have received acclaim. *The New York Times* called the Writers at Work series "the most remarkable and extensive interviewing project we possess."

The Paris Review is edited by Philip Gourevitch, who was named to the post in 2005, following the death of George Plimpton two years earlier. Under Gourevitch's leadership, the magazine's international distribution has expanded, paid subscriptions have risen 150 percent, and newsstand distribution has doubled. A new editorial team has published fiction by Andre Aciman, Damon Galgut, Mohsin Hamid, Gish Jen, Richard Price, Said Sayrafiezadeh, and Alistair Morgan. Poetry editors Charles Simic, Meghan O'Rourke, and Dan Chiasson have selected works by Billy Collins, Jesse Ball, Mary Jo Bang, Sharon Olds, and Mary Karr. Writing published in the magazine has been anthologized in *Best American Short Stories* (2006, 2007, and 2008), *Best American Poetry*, *Best Creative Non-Fiction*, the Pushcart Prize anthology, and *O. Henry Prize Stories*.

The magazine presents two annual awards. The Hadada Award for lifelong contribution to literature has recently been given to William Styron, Joan Didion, Norman Mailer, and Peter Matthiessen in 2008. The Plimpton Prize for Fiction, given to a new voice in fiction brought to national attention in the pages of *The Paris Review*, was presented in 2007 to Benjamin Percy and to Jesse Ball in 2008.

The Paris Review won the 2007 National Magazine Award in photojournalism, and the *Los Angeles Times* recently called *The Paris Review* "an American treasure with true international reach."

Since 1999 *The Paris Review* has been published by The Paris Review Foundation, Inc., a not-for-profit 501(c)(3) organization.

The Paris Review is available in digital form to libraries worldwide in selected academic databases exclusively from EBSCO Publishing. Libraries can contact EBSCO at 1-800-653-2726 for details. For more information on *The Paris Review* or to subscribe, please visit: www.theparisreview.org.

Contributors

Mildred R. Mickle is Assistant Professor of English and English Coordinator at Penn State Greater Allegheny. She is the author of several essays on Octavia E. Butler's works and has published essays on Lillian Allen and an interview with Jaki Shelton Green.

Charles M. Israel is Professor of English at Columbia College in Columbia, South Carolina. He has published several critical articles on American and southern literature.

William T. Lawlor is Professor of English and Writing Emphasis Coordinator at the University of Wisconsin-Stevens Point. He is the author of *The Beat Generation: A Bibliographical Teaching Guide* (1998) and editor of *Beat Culture: Lifestyles, Icons, and Impact* (2005).

Jascha Hoffman writes for *The New York Times* and *Nature*. He lives in Brooklyn, New York.

Kathy Rugoff is Associate Professor of English at the University of North Carolina at Wilmington. Her work has appeared in *A Companion to Whitman* (2006), *Walt Whitman and Modern Music* (2000), and *Multicultural Literatures Through Feminist/ Poststructuralist Lenses* (1993).

Martin Kich is Professor of English at Wright State University-Lake Campus. He is the author of *Western American Novelists* (1995), and his work has appeared in *American Dreams: Comparative Dialogues in U. S. Studies* (2007) and *Notes on Contemporary Literature*.

Matthew J. Bolton is an English teacher and the academic dean of Loyola School in New York City. He earned his Ph.D. in English literature in 2005 from the Graduate Center of the City University of New York, where he wrote his dissertation on Robert Browning and T. S. Eliot. He received the T. S. Eliot Society's Fathman Young Scholar Award for work related to his dissertation. In addition to his doctorate, Bolton holds master's degrees in teaching and in educational administration from Fordham University. His research and writing center on connections between Victorian and modernist literature.

Robert C. Evans earned his Ph.D. from Princeton University in 1984. In 1982 he began teaching at Auburn University Montgomery, where he has been named Distinguished Research Professor, Distinguished Teaching Professor, and University Alumni Professor. External awards include fellowships from the ACLS, the APS, the NEH, and the Folger, Huntington, and Newberry libraries. He is the author or editor of more than twenty books and of numerous essays, including recent work on twentieth-century American writers.

Danielle Chapman is a Chicago poet and critic. Her work has appeared in *Poetry* and *The Chicago Tribune* as well as in *The Atlantic* and *The New England Review*.

Brooke Kenton Horvath is Professor of English at Kent State University. He is the author of *Understanding Nelson Algren* (2005) and coeditor of *Pynchon and* Mason & Dixon (2000). His creative works include the poetry collection *At Ground Zero* (1995).

A. Yemisi Jimoh is Professor of Afro-American Studies at the University of Massachusetts Amherst. She is the author of *Spiritual, Blues, and Jazz People in African American Fiction* (2002), and her scholarly articles have appeared in *MELUS* and *African American Review*. She has served on the editorial board for *MELUS* and is a former visiting fellow at the W. E. B. Du Bois Institute for Research in Afro-American Studies at Harvard University.

Lesley Wheeler is Professor of English at Washington and Lee University. Her scholarly publications include *Voicing American Poetry* (2008) and *The Poetics of Enclosure: American Women Poets from Dickinson to Dove* (2002). Her articles have appeared in *Studies in American Culture, Twentieth Century Literature, Shenandoah, African American Review*, and *Callaloo*. She is also the author of two poetry collections: *Heathen* (2009) and *Scholarship Girl* (2007).

Ann Folwell Stanford is Professor of English at The New School for Learning, DePaul University. She is the author of *Bodies in a Broken World: Women Novelists of Color and the Politics of Medicine* (2006). She has published articles on Leslie Marmon Silko, Jean Stafford, and Gwendolyn Brooks in *Women's Studies, NWSA Journal*, and *African American Review*.

John Lowney is Associate Professor of English and the Director of Graduate Studies at St. John's University. His books include *History, Memory, and the Literary Left: Modern American Poetry, 1935-1968* (2006) and *The American Avant-Garde Tradition: William Carlos Williams, Postmodern Poetry, and the Politics of Cultural Memory* (1997).

Sheila Hassell Hughes is Associate Professor of English and Chair of the Department of English at the University of Dayton. Her work has appeared in *Christianity and Native Cultures* (2004) as well as in *African American Review, Literature and Theology: An International Journal of Religion, Theory, and Culture, SAIL: Studies in American Indian Literature*, and *Religion and Literature*.

Raymond Malewitz is a lecturer in English at Yale University. He earned his Ph.D. from the University of Virginia in 2007 and his work has appeared in *Callaloo* and *Techknowledgies: New Cultural Imaginaries in Humanities, Arts, & TechnoSciences* (2007).

Annette Debo is Associate Professor of English and Director of the Literature Program at Western Carolina University. She earned her Ph.D. from the University of Maryland at College Park. Her articles have appeared in *Quarterly Review of Film and Video, College Language Association Journal*, and *College Literature*.

James D. Sullivan is Assistant Professor of English at Illinois Central College. He is the author of *On the Walls and in the Streets: American Poetry Broadsides from the 1960s* (1997).

Richard Flynn is Professor of English at Georgia Southern University. He is the author of *Randall Jarrell and the Lost World of Childhood* (1990) and a coeditor of *Children's Literature Association Quarterly*. His work has also appeared in *Still Seeking an Attitude: Critical Reflections on the Work of June Jordan* (2004), *Jarrell, Bishop, Lowell, & Co.: Middle-Generation Poets in Context* (2003), *Literature and the Child: Romantic Continuations, Postmodern Contestations* (1999), and *Gendered Modernisms: American Women Poets and Their Readers* (1996).

Acknowledgments_____

"Gwendolyn Brooks" by Charles M. Israel and William T. Lawlor. From *Cyclopedia of World Authors, Fourth Revised Edition*. Copyright © 2004 by Salem Press, Inc. Reprinted with permission of Salem Press.

"The *Paris Review* Perspective" by Jascha Hoffman. Copyright © 2010 by Jascha Hoffman. Special appreciation goes to Christopher Cox and Nathaniel Rich, editors for *The Paris Review*.

"Sweet Bombs" by Danielle Chapman. From *Poetry* 189, no. 1 (October 2006). Copyright © 2006 by Danielle Chapman. Reprinted by permission of Danielle Chapman.

"The Satisfactions of What's Difficult in Gwendolyn Brooks's Poetry" by Brooke Kenton Horvath. From *American Literature* 62, no. 4 (December 1990). Copyright © 1990 by the Duke University Press. All rights reserved. Used by permission of the publisher.

"Double Consciousness, Modernism, and Womanist Themes in Gwendolyn Brooks's 'The Anniad'" by A. Yemisi Jimoh was first published in *MELUS: The Journal of the Society for the Study of the Multi-Ethnic Literature of the United States* and is reprinted here with the permission of *MELUS*.

Wheeler, Lesley. "Heralding the Clear Obscure: Gwendolyn Brooks and Apostrophe." *Callaloo* 24.1 (2002), 227-235. Copyright © 2006 by Charles H. Rowell. Reprinted with permission of The Johns Hopkins University Press.

"Dialectics of Desire: War and the Resistive Voice in Gwendolyn Brooks's 'Negro Hero' and 'Gay Chaps at the Bar'" by Ann Folwell Stanford. From *African American Review* 26, no. 2 (Summer 1992). Copyright © 1992 by Ann Folwell Stanford. Reprinted by permission of Ann Folwell Stanford.

"'A Material Collapse That Is Construction': History and Counter-Memory in Gwendolyn Brooks's *In the Mecca*" by John Lowney was first published in *MELUS: The Journal of the Society for the Study of the Multi-Ethnic Literature of the United States* and is reprinted here with the permission of *MELUS*.

"A Prophet Overheard: A Juxtapositional Reading of Gwendolyn Brooks's 'In the Mecca'" by Sheila Hassell Hughes. From *African American Review* 38, no. 2 (Summer 2004). Copyright © 2004 by Sheila Hassell Hughes. Reprinted by permission of Sheila Hassell Hughes.

"'My Newish Voice': Rethinking Black Power in Gwendolyn Brooks's Whirlwind" by Raymond Malewitz. *Callaloo* 29.2 (2006), 531-544. Copyright © 2006 by Charles H. Rowell. Reprinted with permission of The Johns Hopkins University Press.

"Signifying *Afrika*: Gwendolyn Brooks's Later Poetry" by Annette Debo. *Callaloo* 29.1 (2006), 168-181. Copyright © 2006 by Charles H. Rowell. Reprinted with permission of The Johns Hopkins University Press.

"Reflecting Violence in the Warpland: Gwendolyn Brooks's *Riot*" by Annette Debo. From *African American Review* 39, nos. 1/2 (Spring 2005). Copyright © 2005 by Annette Debo. Reprinted by permission of Annette Debo.

"Killing John Cabot and Publishing Black: Gwendolyn Brooks's *Riot*" by James D. Sullivan. From *African American Review* 36, no. 4 (Winter 2002). Copyright © 2002 by James D. Sullivan. Reprinted by permission of James D. Sullivan.

"'The Kindergarten of New Consciousness': Gwendolyn Brooks and the Social Construction of Childhood" by Richard Flynn. From *African American Review* 34, no. 3 (Fall 2000). Copyright © 2000 by Richard Flynn. Reprinted by permission of Richard Flynn.

Index

Adell, Sandra, 124
Aeneid (Virgil), 44, 58, 139
Africa, 226, 231, 234, 249; Brooks in, 278, 280; romanticization of, 295
African American consciousness, 122
African American cultural nationalism, 189, 207, 277, 318, 339
African American vernacular, 122, 194, 331
African American women, 117, 119, 129, 134, 138
African American writers, 119, 128-129. *See also* Black writers
African diaspora, 68, 203, 231, 279, 286, 292
"African Fragment" (Brooks), 283
African languages, 278, 280, 294
African writers, 279
Afrika (variant spelling), 34, 278, 281, 284, 291, 294, 296
"Afro-American Fragment" (Hughes), 283
"After Mecca" (Brooks), 32, 189, 243, 251
"After School" (Brooks), 363
Alexander, Elizabeth, 22, 35
Alfred ("In the Mecca"), 200, 203, 206, 234, 236, 243
Alienation, 120, 143, 148, 219, 331
Allah Shango (Donaldson), 326
Allen, Annie (*Annie Allen*), 96, 104, 106, 115, 119, 129, 131, 134, 147, 149
Alliteration, 27, 68, 70, 85, 151, 290
Allusion, 95, 97, 117, 133, 155
Ambiguity, 34, 258, 263, 265, 292
American Dilemma, An (Myrdal), 345
American Evasion of Philosophy, The (West), 139
American Smooth (Dove), 22
"Among the Hills" (Whittier), 123
Amos ("In the Mecca"), 328

Andrews, Larry R., 45
Anger, 23, 32, 328, 334
Anglo-Saxon poetry, 69
"Anniad, The" (Brooks), 29, 44, 58, 62, 96, 116, 120, 122, 126, 129, 133, 137, 147, 211, 220, 249, 321; color motif, 135; language, 127; themes, 131
Annie Allen (Brooks), 3, 15, 29, 43, 46, 58, 96-97, 104, 106, 115, 142, 147, 149, 153, 182, 184, 216, 220, 320, 337, 344, 355, 370
"Another Preachment to Blacks" (Brooks), 282, 293
Apartheid, 6, 35, 279, 284, 287, 289
Apostrophe, 142, 145, 148, 154, 156
"Apostrophe, Animation, and Abortion" (Johnson), 143
Art and Imagination of W. E. B. Du Bois, The (Rampersad), 124
"Aspect of Love, Alive in the Ice and Fire, An" (Brooks), 310, 314, 335

Baker, Houston A., Jr., 24, 47, 103, 120, 122, 128, 139, 144, 256, 348, 369
Balance of power, 165, 174
"ballad of chocolate Mabbie, the" (Brooks), 25, 370
"ballad of late Annie, the" (Brooks), 59
"Ballad of Pearl May Lee" (Brooks), 25, 36, 302, 370
"Ballad of Rudolph Reed, The" (Brooks), 31, 302
Ballads, 5, 23, 29, 43
Banks, William, 345
Baraka, Amiri, 33, 100, 254, 256, 259, 262, 267, 272, 311, 343
Barthes, Roland, 262
Bean Eaters, The (Brooks), 30, 99, 147, 149, 222, 302, 328, 346, 359

Beauregard, Robert, 188, 208
Beauty standards, 117, 120, 122, 131, 137, 139, 199, 235, 251
Beckonings (Brooks), 101, 156, 338
Belief, 162, 169, 178, 181-182
Bell, Daniel, 348, 351, 369
Beloved (Morrison), 292
Bennett, Lerone, Jr., 233, 251
Beowulf, 68
Bernstein, Charles, 211, 241
Biblical references, 34, 66, 82, 230, 237
"Big Bessie Throws Her Son into the Street" (Brooks), 105, 152, 264
Big Sea, The (Hughes), 283
Black aesthetic, 115, 145, 217, 225, 230, 234, 254, 256, 258, 263, 301, 313
Black Aesthetic, The (Gayle), 43, 313, 321, 323
"Black-and-Tan Motif in the Poetry of Gwendolyn Brooks, The" (Davis), 370
"Black Art" (Baraka), 254
Black Arts movement, 6, 14, 21, 33, 36, 40, 47, 100, 144, 151, 207, 221, 255, 268, 273-274, 278, 322
Black Arts poetry, 254, 260, 263, 273
Black Atlantic, The (Gilroy), 138
"Black Boys and Native Sons" (Howe), 138
Black empowerment, 363
Black feminism, 47, 212, 223, 250
Black identity, 255, 274, 294, 310
Black Interior, The (Brooks), 101
Black men, 26, 161, 349
Black Metropolis (Drake and Cayton), 345, 368
Black Nationalism, 145, 204, 207, 222, 225, 254, 256, 261, 273, 277, 280
Black Philosopher (*Riot*), 34, 153, 300, 309, 312, 330, 332
Black Power movement, 33, 153, 256, 262, 272, 277, 281, 284, 367

Black publishing companies, 8, 24, 145, 226, 257, 318
"Black Wedding Song, A" (Brooks), 156
Black women, 117, 119, 129, 134, 139
Black writers, 211, 215, 218. *See also* African American writers
Black Writers' Conference (Fisk University, 1967), 22, 100, 142, 207, 225, 274, 278
Blackness, 4, 255, 257, 267, 278, 281, 284, 288, 294, 304, 310
Blacks (Brooks), 7, 10, 58, 92, 102
"Blackstone Rangers, The" (Brooks), 32, 189, 205
Blackstone Rangers (gang), 5, 34, 144, 153, 257, 271, 308, 312, 331
Blakely, Henry, 214
Blank verse, 27, 330
Bolden, B. J., 25, 29, 50, 274
Bone, Robert, 345
"Boy Breaking Glass" (Brooks), 189, 204
"Boy Died in My Alley, The" (Brooks), 338
"Boys. Black" (Brooks), 156, 296
Bradford, Walter, 257
Bragg, Linda Brown, 48
Briggs ("In the Mecca"), 201
Broadside Press, 24, 33, 227, 257, 317, 323, 338
Bronzeville (Chicago), 25, 211, 215, 219, 223
Bronzeville Boys and Girls (Brooks), 358, 364, 370
"Bronzeville Mother Loiters in Mississippi, A" (Brooks), 30, 36, 302, 361
"Bronzeville Woman in a Red Hat" (Brooks), 328
Brooks, Gwendolyn; children's verse, 358; education, 9; honors and awards, 10; influences on, 47, 93, 138; later

poetry, 100, 146, 278, 295; linguistic strategies, 280; poetic styles, 6, 43; Pulitzer Prize, 10, 15, 220, 355; sonnets, 97, 280; support of other artists, 283, 362; travel to Africa, 278, 280, 282; and white audience, 211, 226, 319, 321, 335

Brown, James, 308

Brown, Martha H., 280

Brown, Scot, 278, 281

Bruce, Dickson, 122

Bryant, Marsha, 42

Cabot, John (*Riot*), 33, 300, 304, 309, 314, 327, 329, 335

Callahan, John F., 295

Cannon, Katie, 246

Capsule Course in Black Poetry Writing, A (Brooks), 142, 362

Carmichael, Stokely, 33, 262, 311

Caste, Class, and Race (Cox), 370

Chicago, 93, 99, 117, 186, 188, 190, 192, 194, 207

"*Chicago Defender* Sends a Man to Little Rock, The" (Brooks), 45, 77, 302

Childhood, 344, 349, 352, 357, 367

Children Coming Home (Brooks), 101, 361, 364, 368, 370

"children of the poor, the" (Brooks), 3, 15, 46, 97, 367

Child's Garden of Verses, A (Stevenson), 360

Christian, Barbara, 47, 49

Civil Rights movement, 71, 279, 291, 293, 311

Clark, Norris B., 217, 223, 230, 256

Class system, 345, 351, 353

Clausen, Christopher, 104

Close reading, 75

Clyde, Glenda E., 45

Collins, Patricia Hill, 212, 250

Color-caste distinctions, 345, 351

Color imagery, 31, 84

Community, 211, 214, 218, 225, 229, 237, 242, 245, 249, 320, 324, 331, 335-336

Compression, 42, 97, 127, 130, 151

Confessionalism, 96, 102, 107

Conjuring Culture (Smith), 251

Consciousness, 116, 119, 122, 124, 131, 137-138

Consonance, 112, 258

"Coora Flower, The" (Brooks), 364

Cortor, Eldzier, 358

Couch, William, 170, 183

Counter-memory, 187, 189, 196

Cox, O. C., 370

Crisis, The (Du Bois), 369

Cullen, Countee, 117, 138

Culler, Jonathan, 144

Cultural aphasia, 268

Cultural bias, 351

Cultural diversity, 216

Cultural imperialism, 179

Darkness, 174, 183, 191, 196, 269, 347

David Company, 24

Davies, Carol Boyce, 224

Davis, Allison, 345, 351, 357, 368-369

Davis, Arthur P., 40, 43, 46, 129, 139, 256, 267, 337

Daydreams, 60, 63

Death, 166, 169, 172, 308, 312, 327, 333, 335

Debo, Annette, 35, 42

Decolonising the Mind (Ngugi), 279

Deep South (Davis and Gardner), 345, 351

Deformation of mastery, 120, 122

Democracy, 133, 163, 165, 169, 183

Despair, 100, 181, 196, 206

Destruction, 330, 335

Diaspora (African), 68, 203, 231, 279, 286, 292
Dickinson, Emily, 118, 127, 138
Diction, 27, 29, 56, 69, 80, 96, 130, 152, 194, 229
Disconnection, 198, 206
Discrimination, 138; interracial, 351; intraracial, 216, 218, 370
Disillusionment, 32, 40, 136, 180
Disruption, 80, 127, 366
"Do Not Be Afraid of No" (Brooks), 104, 112, 114
Domination, 179, 228
Donaldson, Jeff, 326
Double consciousness, 5, 44, 116, 119-120, 122, 124-125, 137-138
Double-Consciousness/Double Bind (Adell), 124
"Double V" concept, 163
Double voice, 167
Dove, Rita, 22, 145
Doyle, Laura, 182
"Dream Boogie" (Hughes), 184
Dreams, 169, 174, 177, 180
Du Bois, W. E. B., 5, 116, 120, 122, 125, 138
"Du Boisian Dubiety and the American Dilemma, The" (Lincoln), 125
Dubrow, Heather, 74
Dunbar, Paul Laurence, 104, 107, 117, 127, 138
DuPlessis, Rachel Blau, 157
Dystopia, 188, 193, 196, 206

Eagleton, Terry, 76
Early, Gerald, 124
"East Afrika" (Brooks), 365
Echols, Alice, 261
"Eight Poems for Children" (Brooks), 362
Eliot, T. S., 24, 26, 47, 63, 91-92, 98, 102-103

Ellison, Ralph, 138, 166, 183
Elshtain, Jean Bethke, 160
Enclosure, 166, 175, 183
End of Ideology, The (Bell), 348
Engle, Paul, 320, 339
Enjambment, 61, 79, 86
Epic heroes, 63, 67
Epics, 5, 44, 58, 61, 65, 68, 70, 127, 130
Erkkila, Betsy, 47, 146, 149, 153, 215, 222, 229, 231, 242
Essential Gwendolyn Brooks, The (Alexander), 92
Evans, Mari, 219, 371
Evers, Medgar, 32, 100

Faith, 162, 165, 178
False self, 125
Family Pictures (Brooks), 34, 41, 43
Father of the Man (Davis and Havighurst), 352, 370
Faust (Goethe), 123
Feminism, 47, 49, 108, 212, 223, 250
Fiedler, Leslie, 109, 113
"Fire and Ice" (Frost), 310
Fire imagery, 269, 300, 307, 312
"First fight. Then fiddle" (Brooks), 113, 249, 367
FitzGerald, Frances, 369
Flowers, Sandra Hollin, 259
Flynn, Richard, 47
Fogelson, Robert M., 306
Ford, Karen Jackson, 46
Formalism, 14, 74, 207
Foucault, Michel, 179
Fox, Jay, 289
Freedom, 133, 135, 212, 238, 241, 246, 250
Freedom riders, 68, 72
Freire, Paulo, 183
Fuller, Hoyt W., 321
Fulton, Alice, 296

Furman, Marva Riley, 41
Fuss, Diana, 250
Fussell, Paul, 161

"Gang Girls" (Brooks), 105
"Gay Chaps at the Bar" (Brooks), 28,
    46, 97, 155, 159, 163, 166, 168,
    183, 280, 320, 339, 368
Gayle, Addison, Jr., 41, 208, 313, 321
Gender politics, 249
Gender roles, 118, 120, 131, 134, 136,
    175, 177
Ghettos, 14, 303, 306, 310, 348, 358
Giles, Ron, 46
Gilroy, Paul, 138
Giovanni, Nikki, 48, 114, 255
Greasley, Philip A., 236, 251, 295
Great Gram ("In the Mecca"), 236
Greene, Thomas M., 144
Gwendolyn Brooks (Melhem), 295

Hackney, Sheldon, 286
Hair imagery, 63, 80, 96, 117, 132, 139,
    199, 236
Hansell, William H., 41, 43, 144, 295,
    300, 314
Harlem Renaissance, 4, 23, 128, 138
Harper, Phillip Brian, 254, 259, 262, 273
Harper & Row, 24, 145, 257, 317, 323,
    338
Harvey, David, 196, 208
Hatred, 77, 84, 125, 167, 204
Healing, 163, 174, 180, 244, 250
Hegel, Georg, 122, 124-125, 139
"Heritage" (Cullen), 118
Heroism, 165, 167, 182, 349
Heroism in the New Black Poetry
    (Melhem), 295
High-epic mode, 66, 68
Hill, Christine M., 50
Hogeland, Lisa Maria, 261

Holt, Thomas, 126
Homeplaces, 250
Homer, 58, 62, 128, 139
hooks, bell, 224, 246, 250
Hope, 9, 39, 111, 196, 201, 220, 237,
    240, 243, 294, 335, 348, 362
Horvath, Brooke Kenton, 146
Housing, 31, 188, 192
"How I Told My Child About Race"
    (Brooks), 356
How to Read a Poem (Eagleton), 76
Howe, Irving, 138
Howe, Susan, 289
Hubbard, Stacy Carson, 29
Hudson, Clenora, 175
Hughes, Gertrude Reif, 24
Hughes, Langston, 40, 42, 184, 283, 301,
    307; influence on Brooks, 3, 23, 47,
    103, 117, 127, 214, 220, 223
Hughes, Sheila Hassell, 47
Hull, Gloria T., 44, 119, 128, 134, 223,
    250
Hunger imagery, 176
Hyena ("In the Mecca"), 199, 236, 251

"I felt a funeral, in my brain"
    (Dickinson), 118
"I Love Those Little Booths at
    Benvenuti's" (Brooks), 95
Idealism, 122, 125, 139
Identity, 169, 172, 231, 291; African,
    34, 295; and double consciousness,
    44, 116; racial, 216
Ideology, 345, 348, 351, 369
Iliad (Homer), 58
Imagery, 26, 28, 45, 82, 146, 153, 182;
    colors, 31, 84; darkness, 174, 183,
    191, 269, 347; female, 134, 177; hair,
    63, 80, 96, 117, 132, 139, 199, 236;
    light, 177, 180, 184, 196; religious,
    81, 178

Imperialism, 279, 286, 293
In Montgomery, and Other Poems
    (Brooks), 101
"In the Mecca" (Brooks), 32, 101, 113,
    115, 188-189, 193-195, 204, 206,
    210, 213, 223, 229, 238, 241, 244,
    251, 328, 361
In the Mecca (Brooks), 22, 31, 41, 43,
    46, 150, 153, 187-188, 210, 216, 222,
    226, 251, 257, 265, 317, 324, 334,
    344
Innocence, 122, 344, 367
"Integrity" (Rich), 274
Intentionality, 175, 184
Intimidation of color, 131, 134
Invisible Man (Ellison), 183
Irony, 28, 31, 33, 77, 81, 118, 120, 360
Isolation, 219, 234
Israel, Charles M., 104

Jackson, Angela, 256
Jacobs, Jane, 208
Jaffe, Dan, 114, 227, 321, 324
Jahasz, Suzanne, 48
Jamaican Edward ("In the Mecca"), 236,
    242, 251
James, William, 123-124
Janssen, Ronald R., 46
Jarrell, Randall, 162
Jazz, 6, 190, 270
Jimoh, A. Yemisi, 44
"John, Who Is Poor" (Brooks), 360
Johnson, Barbara, 143
Johnson, James Weldon, 126, 214
Johnson, Mark, 46
Jones, Gayl, 194, 202, 361
Jones, LeRoi. *See* Baraka, Amiri
Joyce, James, 46
Juxtaposition, 63, 229, 232, 238, 244,
    246, 334
Juxtapositional reading, 213, 229

Kalaidjian, Walter, 42
Karenga, Maulana, 280, 296, 313, 324
Kent, George E., 27, 36, 40-41, 47, 50,
    106, 115, 135, 139, 144, 154, 214,
    223, 230, 249, 283, 339
Kerner Commission Report, 302, 314
Kgositsile, Keorapetse, 34, 36
King, Doris M., 359
King, Martin Luther, Jr., 36, 265, 268,
    272, 325, 327
Kiswahili, 278, 280
"kitchenette building" (Brooks), 93, 346,
    367
Knight, Etheridge, 369
Kojo (*Children Coming Home*), 368
Kunitz, Stanley, 43

Language, 56, 68, 72, 82, 146, 150,
    166, 169, 176, 183, 263, 300, 311
Language of the unheard, 300, 307,
    327
"Last Quatrain of the Ballad of Emmett
    Till, The" (Brooks), 16, 30, 36,
    302
Lattin, Patricia H., 49
Lattin, Vernon E., 49
Lee, Don ("In the Mecca"), 235
Lee, Don L. *See* Madhubuti, Haki R.
Lemann, Nicholas, 207
Lewis, David Levering, 123
Lewy, Clement ("They Call it
    Bronzeville"), 357, 370
Liberals, 327, 331, 335
Liberation, 212, 226, 228, 232, 237, 241,
    246
"Life of Lincoln West, The" (Brooks), 370
"Lifted Veil, The" (Eliot), 123
Light imagery, 177, 180, 184, 196, 269
Lincoln, C. Eric, 125
Lindberg, Kathryne V., 146
Line lengths, 32, 80, 112

Linguistic strategies, 280
Lipsitz, George, 189
Littlejohn, David, 103, 114
Location, 211, 213, 216, 223, 229, 233, 246, 249
Looting, 312, 333
Love, 63, 66, 82, 84, 121, 129, 133, 135, 137, 148, 151
"love note I" (Brooks), 169, 183
"love note II" (Brooks), 169, 183
"Love Song of J. Alfred Prufrock, The" (Eliot), 26, 63, 94
"Lovers of the Poor, The" (Brooks), 99, 328-329
Lowell, Robert, 91, 102
Lowney, John, 42
Lupack, Alan C., 46
Lure and Loathing (Early), 124
"Lyle" (Brooks), 361
Lynchings, 25, 28, 36, 302

McConahay, John B., 307, 310
McGann, Jerome, 319
Madhubuti, Haki R., 21, 29, 40, 101, 114, 145, 203, 218, 221, 233, 251, 282, 295, 318, 323
Madhubuti, Safisha N., 43
Malcolm X, 15, 32, 36, 100, 189, 232, 251, 311, 314
Male-female relations, 118
Mance, Ginger, 252
Mandela, Nelson, 284
Mandela, Winnie, 284, 286-288, 290
Manifest Destiny rhetoric, 259
Martin, John Bartlow, 186, 191-193
Masculinity, 346
Masotti, Louis H., 303, 305, 311
Massey, Doreen, 223, 250
Mastery of form, 119-120, 128
Maud Martha (Brooks), 7, 23, 44, 48, 102, 308

Mecca Building, 186, 207, 213, 225, 232, 235, 239
"Medgar Evers" (Brooks), 189
Melhem, D. H., 26, 36, 50, 104, 129-130, 146, 226, 237, 275, 280, 285, 293, 296, 300, 314, 331, 360, 365
Melodie Mary ("In the Mecca"), 201, 236, 239, 252
Memory, 67, 70, 137, 167, 196, 231
"Mental Cases" (Owen), 162
"mentors" (Brooks), 169, 183
Metaphors, 29, 41, 80, 130, 152, 172, 177, 196, 267, 300, 307
Meter, 27, 61, 69, 93, 96
Miller, Dorie, 164, 182, 328, 349
Miller, Henry, 325
Miller, R. Baxter, 41, 44, 150, 157, 204, 232, 246, 252, 264
Milton, John, 60, 62, 66, 70
Mirroring, 266, 272, 300, 302
Mock epics, 44, 60, 62
Modernism, 96-97, 104, 120, 126, 128, 130, 138
Modernism and the Harlem Renaissance (Baker), 120
"Montage of a Dream Deferred" (Hughes), 184
Mootry, Maria K., 36, 46, 183
Morrison, Toni, 182, 292
Mosby, Sisi Donald, 217
"mother, the" (Brooks), 6, 143
Murder, 25, 30, 32, 36
"murder, the" (Brooks), 370
Myth of Americanism, 130, 133

"Nationalism and Social Division in Black Arts Poetry of the 1960s" (Harper), 254
Native Son (Wright), 183
Naturalism, 219, 252
Neal, Larry, 268, 273

"Near-Johannesburg Boy, The"
(Brooks), 35, 101, 289, 292, 363
"Negro Artist and the Racial Mountain,
The" (Hughes), 3
"Negro Hero" (Brooks), 159, 163, 165,
168, 172, 183, 328, 339, 349, 368
Ngugi wa Thiong'o, 279
"Nineteen Cows in a Slow Line
Walking" (Brooks), 365
Nordstrom, Ursula, 358
Norton, Loam ("In the Mecca"), 230,
236, 250
"Notes from the Childhood and the
Girlhood" (Brooks), 29, 97, 104, 147

Odyssey (Homer), 59, 67, 139
"Of the Young Dead" (Brooks), 363
Off-rhyme, 28
Oppression, 250; racial, 201, 204, 216,
232, 240, 305; of women, 229
Ostriker, Alicia, 161
"Otto" (Brooks), 359
"Our MZ Brooks" (Traylor), 244
"Our White Mother Says We Are Black
But Not Very" (Brooks), 370
Owen, Wilfred, 162
Oxymorons, 130, 133

Palimpsest, 222, 232
Paradise, 65-66, 70
Paradise Lost (Milton), 60, 66
Paradoxes, 194, 196, 199, 206, 258, 261,
271
Park, Clara Claiborne, 107, 113, 115
Parks, Sue S., 45
"patent leather" (Brooks), 370
Patriotism, 133, 181
Peanut (*Riot*), 271, 331
Pepita ("In the Mecca"). *See* Smith,
Pepita ("In the Mecca")
Phenomenology of Spirit (Hegel), 124

Phoenix (myth), 34, 335, 337
Phrasing, 80, 82, 84, 289
"piano after war" (Brooks), 46, 169,
183
Pieterson, Hector, 289
Playfulness, 93, 167, 198, 262, 272
*Poems on Various Subjects, Religious
and Moral* (Wheatley), 4
Poetic meter, 27, 93, 96
Poetic style, 29, 118
"Poets Who Are Negroes" (Brooks),
355
Political consciousness, 45
Political reform, 301
Politics of location, 212, 223, 234
Polysemy, 258, 264
Polyvalency, 258, 265, 273
"Pool Players, The" (Brooks), 13
Pope, Alexander, 61
Post-traumatic stress disorder, 65
Pound, Ezra, 47
Poverty, 9, 187-188, 191, 196, 201, 219,
234, 242, 246
Power, 165, 167, 171, 174, 179, 184
Powerlessness, 172, 176, 184, 301, 309
Primary epics, 70
Principles of Psychology, The (James),
123
Prophecy, 211, 213, 225, 229, 237, 243,
245, 252
"Prophet Imagined, A" (Hughes), 247
"Prophet Overheard, A" (Hughes), 247
Psalms, 178, 202, 230
Public housing projects, 188
Pulitzer Prize, 147
Punning, 251, 262

Queenie King ("In the Mecca"), 242

Race relations, 28, 116, 169
Racial politics, 160, 204, 208

Racial solidarity, 216, 254, 281

Racism, 9, 33, 36, 99, 107, 197, 199, 219, 234, 242, 246, 301, 304, 307, 345; war as, 160, 162, 168-169, 173, 176, 180

Rampersad, Arnold, 124

Randall, Dudley, 24, 33, 43, 48, 257, 318, 326

Rape of the Lock, The (Pope), 61

Ray, David, 48

Rebellion, 118, 121, 170, 188, 294, 306, 354

Rebirth, 292, 309, 336

Redding, J. Saunders, 144, 147, 320, 339

Redemption, 233, 243

"Rejoinder, A" (Ellison), 138

Religious imagery, 81, 178

Report from Part One (Brooks), 49, 144, 205, 255, 277, 283, 295, 323, 343

Report from Part Two (Brooks), 144, 343, 368

Resistance, 113, 168, 179, 182, 220, 224, 234, 241, 245, 250

Revolution, 170, 173, 176, 179, 182

Rhyme, 25, 27, 29-31, 78-79

Rhynes, Martha E., 50

Rhythm, 78, 87, 112, 176, 282

Rich, Adrienne, 274

"Riders to the Blood-Red Wrath" (Bolton), 58, 68

"Riot" (Brooks), 10, 33, 36, 327-328, 335

Riot (Brooks), 33, 41, 43, 265, 278, 292, 299, 302, 307, 310, 312, 314, 318, 323, 327, 330, 337

Riots, 265, 300-301, 304, 306, 309, 311, 314, 327, 333

"rites for Cousin Vit, the" (Brooks), 97, 333

Romance, 133

Rosenberger, Coleman, 48

Rubenstein, Richard E., 303, 306

"Rudolph Is Tired of the City" (Brooks), 361

"Sadie and Maud" (Brooks), 370

St. Julia ("In the Mecca"), 236

Sala ("East Afrika"), 365

Sanchez, Sonia, 101, 255

Satan, 66, 71

Satire, 27, 128, 302, 332, 355

Saunders, Judith P., 45

Say That the River Turns (Madhubuti), 250

Schweik, Susan, 160, 182, 346, 368

Scott, Heidi, 43

Sears, David O., 307, 310

Second Congress of African Writers (1966), 281

"Second Sermon on the Warpland, The" (Brooks), 100, 152, 257, 259, 291, 334

Secondary epics, 70

Segregation, 28, 68, 72, 164, 172, 228, 346, 349, 368

Selected Poems (Brooks), 321, 339

Self, 167, 172

Self-consciousness, 119, 124

Self-determination, 205

Self-esteem, 309, 364

Self-hatred, 125, 236, 250, 310

Self-renewal, 335

Selfhood, 125, 167

Senghor, Leopold, 203, 234

"Sermon for Our Maturity" (Baraka), 259-260

"Sermon on the Warpland, The" (Brooks), 150, 244

"Sermons on the Warpland" (Brooks), 143, 149, 256, 273

Sexism, 29, 49
Sexual struggle, 183
Shaw, Harry B., 50, 104, 295
"She" (Mance), 252
Shoptaw, John, 157
Sibling rivalry, 370
Sight, 178, 180, 182
Simmons, Brenda R., 296
Singers of Daybreak (Baker), 103
Slavery, 68, 72
Smith, Barbara, 224, 250
Smith, Gary, 45, 47, 107, 344
Smith, Pepita ("In the Mecca"), 154, 200, 204, 235, 239, 242, 244, 251, 361
Smith, Sallie ("In the Mecca"), 32, 197, 199, 201, 205, 236, 251
Smith, Theophus, 230, 251
Smith, Valerie, 250
Social change, 42-43, 301, 305, 311, 367
"Social Class and Color Differences in Child-Rearing" (Davis and Havighurst), 352
Social class distinctions, 345, 351, 353
Solbert, Ronni, 359
"song in the front yard, a" (Brooks), 219, 353, 370
"Song of Winnie" (Brooks), 35, 284, 296
"sonnet-ballad, the" (Brooks), 59
Sonnets, 3, 23, 28, 30, 43, 46, 97, 168, 174, 178, 183, 280, 344, 367
"SOS" (Baraka), 254-255, 262
Souls of Black Folk, The (Du Bois), 5, 116, 120, 139
South Africa; apartheid, 279, 284, 287-288; politics, 288
South Side (Chicago), 93, 96, 99, 186, 189, 205
"southeast corner" (Brooks), 333, 370
Soweto uprising, 289

Space, Place, and Gender (Massey), 223
Speech, 242, 245, 249
Spillers, Hortense J., 42, 49, 121, 139, 229, 348, 369
Sport of the Gods, The (Dunbar), 117
Stafford, William, 216
"Stand off, daughter of the dusk" (Brooks), 144, 320
Stanford, Ann Folwell, 44, 139, 339, 368
Stark, Inez Cunningham, 24, 127, 183, 215
Stavros, George, 245, 370
Stereotypes, 99, 351
"Strangest Place in Chicago, The" (Martin), 186, 191
Street in Bronzeville, A (Brooks), 9, 11, 14, 22, 24, 28, 39, 46, 142, 147, 153, 159, 164, 183, 215, 218, 221, 320, 339, 344, 352, 367, 370
Sullivan, James D., 300
"Sundays of Satin-Legs Smith, The" (Brooks), 26, 45, 94, 218, 328
Swahili, 279-280
Swift, Jonathan, 62
Synecdoche, 26, 190, 254
Syntax, 25, 85, 109, 229

tan man (*Annie Allen*), 118, 130, 132, 134-135, 138
Tate, Claudia, 121, 129, 139, 146, 223, 228, 249
Taylor, Cledie, 339
Taylor, Henry, 96, 149, 320
"They Call it Bronzeville" (Brooks), 357
Third Life of Grange Copeland, The (Walker), 184
"Third Sermon on the Warpland, The" (Brooks), 34, 153, 155, 265, 307, 312, 314, 330, 334, 337
Third World Press, 24, 227, 318, 338

Thomas and Beulah (Dove), 22
Till, Emmett, 16, 30-31, 302, 361
Tinsel Marie ("The Coora Flower"), 364
To Disembark (Brooks), 10
"To the Diaspora" (Brooks), 231, 292
Tolson, Melvin, 104
"Toward a Black Aesthetic" (Fuller), 321
Towns, Saundra, 46, 49
"Transcendentalist, The" (Emerson), 123
Transformation, 213, 240, 243
Traylor, Eleanor, 244
Triple jeopardy, 119
True self, 125
"Trumpet Player" (Hughes), 117
12 Million Black Voices (Wright), 346, 368

"Ulysses" (Tennyson), 72
Unhappy consciousness, 125
Up From Slavery (Washington), 120
Updike, John, 108
Urban decline, 187, 190, 195, 208

Vendler, Helen, 75
Verse journalism, 14
Very Young Poets (Brooks), 362
Violence, 30, 42, 82, 302, 313, 327-328, 332, 335, 346, 356, 364; collective, 305, 307
Virgil, 61, 70, 128
Vision, 178, 180, 182
Voices of Decline (Beauregard), 188

W. E. B Du Bois (Lewis), 123
Wade-Gayles, Gloria, 119, 134
Walker, Alice, 134, 184
"Wall, The" (Brooks), 189
Wall of Respect (mural), 189
Waniek, Marilyn Nelson, 145
War, 60, 65, 67, 169; as racism, 160, 162, 168-169, 173, 176, 180

War poetry, 160, 162, 182, 346, 368
Warner, W. Lloyd, 351
Warnings, 14, 170, 181
Warpland, 258, 266, 269, 302, 307, 314
Washington, Booker T., 120
Washington, Mary Helen, 23, 49, 131, 134
Watts riot, 310
"We Real Cool" (Brooks), 45, 57, 113, 115, 337, 339
Weary Blues, The (Hughes), 23
West, Cornel, 139
Wheatley, Phillis, 4, 104
Wheeler, Lesley, 258, 260, 274
"white troops had their orders but the Negroes looked like men, the" (Brooks), 28, 173
Whitfield, Stuart, 368
"Why Negro Women Leave Home" (Brooks), 368
Williams, Delores, 250
Williams, Gladys Margaret, 43
Williams, Kenny J., 319
"Winnie" (Brooks), 35, 284
"Womanhood, The" (Brooks), 3, 29, 147
Woolf, Virginia, 182
Woolley, Lisa, 36
Wordplay, 85, 103-104, 117, 147, 196, 251, 260
"World and the Jug, The" (Ellison), 138
World War II, 159, 162, 170, 176, 182
Wright, Richard, 183, 219, 342, 346, 368

Yancey (*Riot*), 153, 334
"Young Afrikans" (Brooks), 291
"Young Heroes" (Brooks), 34, 36
Young, John K., 24
Yvonne ("In the Mecca"), 201

Zinn, Howard, 305